Reflections on Christian Living

DR. THEODORE B. KALIVODA

ISBN: 1499126921
ISBN 13: 9781499126921

Table of Contents

Introduction

Differing from books that center on one single theme, this writing treats a variety of topics, not your general run-of-the-mill ones but rather those that deal with unique experiences that have been a part of my life. I've learned many lessons, ones that have helped me put aside selfish and disorderly living of the past. Instead I've turned to a forward-looking life of exuberance in Christ.

Hopefully, you will find <u>Reflections on Christian Living</u> a challenge as you identify with its thoughts in your own Christian journey. The experiences I cite may not be identical to yours, but they may in some way carry a message that you can apply to your life.

One thing I must make clear at the outset. I don't intend to make the mistake of so many writers who try to revitalize readers by showing God's past interaction with certain Bible personalities and then to apply those examples to us. We often cite Scripture in which God deals with different people and then put ourselves in a box by saying that the same message applies to us in identical fashion. I admit that I've mistakenly done that in the past. But enough of that nonsense. I won't do it again. Each person is unique and must be treated as such, just as God sees us as uniquely different.

God dealt with Abraham, Noah, and Moses, for example, in special ways. He actually spoke to them, and they didn't question the authenticity of his message. There was no guessing that what they had heard somehow might be something their minds had concocted. Then on top of it, knowing the weakness of the human mentality as to how we tend to entertain thoughts of our own, God reinforced his presence by speaking to those great Bible characters at various other times. He did it audibly, so they knew it was God speaking. Then on top of it He even performed miracles that they could see, should they have had the slightest doubt who was behind it all.

Today it's different. We don't actually hear God's voice, that is, not audibly. Except in extraordinary situations, neither do we see him always reinforcing his messages through miraculous events. What we do have today is the Holy Spirit who indwells every believer and who communicates silently.

So I'm not about to talk to you about the experiences of Bible personalities to whom God spoke, and then to try to carry those experiences over to you in identical fashion. I'm going to give you straight-forward talk about the unique provision God has made for communicating with us today, and I can tell you right now that it won't be in the form of audible communication.

By the way, even if it were aural, we might not submit to it, like Moses who heard God speaking at the burning bush but argued with him because he didn't like the way he was being told to do things, especially to return to Egypt (he was also probably scared to death to do that, where he had murdered a fellow Egyptian forty years earlier).

Arguing with God seems to be a peculiar and mystifying trait of humans. We have got to come to grips with the fact that although we may not like the message God gives us, we had better listen and start obeying. Otherwise, we are forgetting the incomparable difference between the created (us) and the Creator, a fact that throughout the ages has led to humanity's woes.

Let's face facts, that in spite of our knowledge we don't know everything and never will. Scripture cites an example of our limitations by saying, that we don't know where the wind comes from nor where it goes; that is to say, that we feel the wind but can't see it. I'm sure that scientists retort by saying, "but we *will* know, just give us time." They hate to acknowledge humanity's limitations, the enormous gulf between us and our Creator.

It's all a matter of divine communication. Of course, we have to admit there's an element of fuzziness in discerning God's voice today, because you see, we are not one-hundred percent sure it's actually God speaking or whether it's our own thoughts. Furthermore, stepping out as to what we think are his directions, we often err by imposing our own human desires. But the fact is that God does communicate with us, not in the same manner as in biblical times, but He speaks nevertheless in different ways. Our job is to listen, to smother ego and other interfering thoughts of personal aggrandizement, and then wait to see the results.

God is not in a hurry, we are, all to our despair and to the quick decisions we make. But He knows our predicament. You see, reflected in our ways is a sin problem, one that causes us to aggrandize ourselves and to create an awful lot of confusion. But as Christians we can counteract it by determining to heed the Spirit's leading that gives us peace in decision making.

So let's get down to business in applying it all to this writing. Hopefully, you will see in these pages a distinct theme in which God communicates to you personally, such that will make a real difference in your life. I'm hoping you see yourself in that capacity.

By the way, although this book treats a number of different themes, it does have one central thought running throughout, which tells us that we deal with any of the topics by leaning directly on the Holy Spirit's leading. The Spirit's indwelling in itself is a miracle from God, which tells us that God favors us as seen through his blessings. In fact, the Holy Spirit is God's means of communicating to us, starting with Spirit-inspired Scripture.

Starting, then, with the book's very first division, <u>Blessed by God</u> and its accompanying chapter "We Are Special People," we begin seeing the Spirit's availability. Unfortunately, I as well as many others at one time or another have left the benefit unused. Emphasized in the first chapter, its message runs throughout the book, one that declares that God actually communicates with us today. The trouble is that we don't listen, as we stubbornly go about thinking it's up to us to decide on how to function rather than to let the Spirit direct us. It's probably a matter of our insistence on getting immediate help. You see, God's not in a hurry as we are. He sees things that we are currently unaware of, things that later dawn on us of his benevolence.

I must relate a personal experience I recently had that corroborates the idea of God's communication. My car insurance was due, so tossing around in my head was whether I should continue my current coverage or simply change to a liability policy. The car was getting old, and by the way, so was I. Lying in bed one night, I was awash in thoughts about what to do about coverage. All of a sudden the idea hit me that it was not a question of which kind of insurance I should take out but rather that I should cancel the entire policy. Why? Dizzy spells were harassing me as a constant problem due to a stroke I had experienced some years back. The message was loud and clear: it was time to stop driving. My vertigo could cause me to get into an accident, hurting myself as well as endangering others.

Yes, I felt that I should quit driving, but then I was troubled with the idea of what to do with the car. To make a long story short, my friend Don came by the very next day telling me of his need of a used car for his son. He had no idea of the thoughts plaguing me. To make a long story short, he bought the car, making both him and me contented. Just coincidence? That might be a typical reaction, but I choose to say that God was behind it, which carried a small but important message to me of his personal concern.

I cite this incident simply to advance the idea that God works in ways beyond our imagination. He communicates, oftentimes in unusual ways, but always for our good. I don't have the slightest idea as to why He operates that way. All I can say is that He looks out for me.

I suppose it's all a matter of closeness to the Creator. The more intimate we are in our walk with him, the more likely we are to respond to his communication, because you see, we differentiate between messages that are divine and those our minds come up with. You probably won't believe it until you experience it, so I say that part of hearing God is the development of intimacy with him. It's the same regarding relations with anyone else; the closer we are, the more we understand each other.

A critical concern is that we recognize the futility of going our own way. Instead, we have got to give God a chance to direct us according to his ways. Perhaps by-passed because of his invisibility and therefore easily unnoticed, the Spirit occupies us for a specific purpose -- to guide us in our thinking and decision-making so that we flourish in everything we do. Yes, God wants that to happen, that we thrive, which means that He wills for us to be dynamic. Why do you suppose He indwells every one of us Christians? It's because He values each of us highly and wants to communicate with and through us for our joy and well-being.

Some of us may be so negligent as to be unaware of the Spirit's presence, while others may know of his indwelling only by having heard of it from someone or maybe having read about it at one time or another in the Bible. But the fact is that we tend to ignore him, to make him a reality, all to our disadvantage. Because you see, although God makes himself available to every believer, He is always gentle, never forcing himself on anyone. The Spirit is there, indwelling us and hoping we will acknowledge his presence, but He is of little benefit when left unheeded. That's the difference between us and God; we insist on making requests, even demands, while on the other hand He reveals his will and then stands back to see our reaction.

Relying on the Spirit's direction and power we leave behind mediocrity to be replaced by the dynamism God yearns for us. Yes, that's a part of Christianity. He could chastise us for neglecting his presence, but that's not in accord with his nature, which is one of patience and kindness as He hopes we will ultimately acknowledge the benefits of his divine blessing.

The first chapter ("We Are Special People") as well as the final one (#17, "Attuned to the Holy Spirit") offer suggestions on how to do that. They will revolutionize your life! But let's not get wrapped up only in those two chapters. Those in between talk about God's blessings, too, as well as on-going problems in the Christian life that prevent us from the dynamism God wills for us. The Holy Spirit is a prime factor in helping us overcome any hindering influences.

Chapter 2 ("We Are Included") and Chapter 3 ("We Are Forgiven") are brief reminders of God's inclusion of us Gentiles into his family as well as his sweet forgiveness of our past failings. They are short chapters but significant reminders of God's goodness, underscoring the fact that as Gentiles we were once left out (Chapter 2), even considered unworthy of God, but we are now included as his chosen people through Christ whose death accomplished a phenomenal forgiveness of all our sins (Chapter 3). So as Christians we are special in God's eyes, a fact that should joyfully affect us in daily living.

The book's next general division, <u>Understanding the Bible</u>, shows how to take steps to recognize God's voice specifically through Scripture, and most importantly, how to express it in daily living. Although sounding rather blasé, its chapter treats a serious problem that causes us to misunderstand and misuse God's written revelation -- the Bible -- all to our discomfort and harm.

You see, we find Satan attacking us subtly in various ways, even distorting our view of Scripture. That's seen in Chapter 4 ("The Bible: Two Religions"), whose primary message is that we must separate Judaism from Christianity to avoid the errors so many make in misapplying God's revealed truth. To misapply Scripture causes a lot of unnecessary misery as well as sending an erroneous message about Christianity. Let me explain.

In my early years as a Christian in the 1940s, I was a victim of such misapplication. It made Christianity personally burdensome. How it hurt when people, even the clergy of all things, preached legalistic rules and human-concocted ideas they told me to follow. Don't do this, or don't do that, they said with God-like overtones, which made me perceive Christianity as joyless rather than joyous. Of course, Scripture plainly tells us to avoid getting involved in many things, including toying with immorality. But being smothered by an endless list of man-made requirements that supposedly define spirituality makes us wonder just how much faith we should put in human-concocted ideas, even though those ideas may center around OT Scripture.

A common mistake is our failure to distinguish between Judaism of the Old Testament (OT) and Christianity in the New (NT). Many people succumb to crisscrossing the two, not only in mixing law with grace for salvation but in adding their own requirements as to what they think constitutes Christian living beyond salvation. Can you believe it? Adding ideas to Christianity that the Bible warns us not to do?

It's a matter of deciding which covenant to follow, the old or the new. I hope it's the latter, because you see, the NT declares the old covenant (OT Law) terminated, one that's been replaced by something far better -- Christ's crucifixion and resurrection -- the essence of the new covenant. In fact, the crucifixion and resulting resurrection are the most important events in the history of the world. They mark the beginning and ending of the two covenants -- OT and NT. Failure to differentiate between them hinders the blessed lifestyle that God wishes us to have, all of which causes undue woe and a distorted idea of God's will for humanity.

Those two testaments preach an entirely distinct message, the former centering around rules and regulations (slavery, as the apostle Paul put it -- Gal. 5:1) understandably to keep sinful man under control, while the latter freeing us from OT Law (including its erroneous application) to enjoy the freedom characterized by Christ's new plan for the world).

The beauty of the new covenant is that it's centered around the Holy Spirit who teaches us right from wrong and who makes it absolutely clear that God has put us under a new form of thinking, even as Scripture says, "If you are led by the Spirit, you are not under law," referring to the old covenant of the OT (Gal. 5:18). Yes, the Holy Spirit serves not only to direct us personally but also instructs us by divine inspiration through the timeless written words of the Bible. It all functions to ease our journey in the Christian life. Yet some continue to hold to those Law edicts and end up making Christians feel guilty by not complying.

Unfortunately, some of us tend to cling to burdensome OT dictates, making the assumption that we are obligated to keep those precepts simply because they were God-given, even though God has clearly declared them *passé*, rules designed in the past for the nation of Israel.

You may be thinking that the OT, a holy writ inspired by God, must never be abandoned. Certainly it's a document that teaches us many good things, but its mass of rules and regulations can interfere with God's new and generous work through Christ, so much so that we allow the law code to take a stranglehold on the joyful life that Jesus preached (we are saved by grace not of works). We deal in Chapter 4 with its subtleties, all a product of Satan our adversary who seeks every possible way to insert himself in order to lead us astray and even to make a mockery of Christianity.

The next section (Section 3, <u>Worship</u>), helps us appreciate the torment Christ went through on our behalf so that we give him the praise and adoration He deserves. Jesus' preoccupation with his coming crucifixion affected him terribly throughout his public ministry, which included frequent accusations that He performed miracles through the power of Satan. Can you believe it -- the Son of God healing the sick and raising the dead, and then being accused of performing those acts through demonic power? We deal with it in Chapter 5 ("Acknowledging Christ's Sufferings – An Appreciation of His Love") to give us a greater sense of the horrors He had to tolerate, all of which will instigate in us a greater sense of awe and worship of Christ who stood up against it all. He functioned exclusively as a dedicated servant for our benefit.

Chapter 6 ("Lifting Hands in Worship – A Contemporary Controversy"), deals with a phenomenon that has developed in recent times in many churches as it calls attention to the subtleties of incorporating new characteristics into worshipping God, such that may lead to disunity among worshippers to the extent of unconcern for their spiritual welfare. I'm afraid that many congregations think they are doing the right thing by incorporating new ideas into worship (keeping up with the times, so to speak), but they are splitting the congregation of believers, even causing enmity among worshippers, so much so that some even drop out of church and seek other churches to attend. It's a characteristic exactly opposed to the unity theme that Jesus prayed for. The essence of the chapter is to call for contemporary and traditional worshippers to come together to iron out their differences in their approaches to worship. which will bring about a surrender and submissiveness among both groups, not an easy task, but a necessary one to take.

The segment that follows, <u>Human Relations,</u> includes three chapters: "The Marital Scene" (Chapter 7); "Having a Servant Attitude" (Chapter 8); and, "Gift Giving and Receiving -- a Persistent Problem" (Chapter 9). All emphasize the importance of maintaining selfless attitudes toward one another. Believe it or not, such demeanor is hardly easy, simply because it runs against our human nature (we tend to look out only for ourselves). But the challenge is to overcome, because you see, although influenced by selfishness, we can push that negativity aside and experience triumph. But let's not forget that living a godly life is not merely a matter of knowledge but of willpower, too, which means that we ourselves have a role to play in Christian living. But God doesn't turn us into robots after we have been born again. He leaves choices to us. Hopefully we will make them under the Spirit's guidance rather than through our own manipulations

The first part of <u>Human Relations</u>, the "Marital Scene," underscores common errors that are destructive to a marital union. It calls attention to the incompatibility often seen among Christians in marriage relationships that often leads to disaster, even separation and divorce. Can you believe it -- Christian marriages running amuck? Where's the lifestyle change that's supposed to come about from the new birth? Application to loving other believers as well as people in general, as Jesus taught, is hardly possible if spouses can't do it in their marriage relationship. Or are we to deny the veracity of Scripture that commands us to love one another? Instead, we give in to society's answer to troublesome marital unions by resorting to divorce. It's an easy way out, and I'm afraid our culture supports it in order to facilitate separation and supposedly to keep everyone happy. I suspect that God has deep displeasure in the way we flippantly treat a marriage relationship, as if it were merely one of the many decisions humans make rather than being a very holy and decisive act in God's eyes.

God has designed marriage for closeness and happy living; however, the multiplicity of broken marriages among Christians today, unfortunately even among the clergy, attest to the fact that we selfishly ignore biblical teaching. God's cure centers around spousal *love* and *respect*, behaviors emphasized in Paul's letter to the Ephesians. Unfortunately, we allow selfishness to take precedence. The chapter discusses how love and respect show their potential in the marital union. In their absence, marriages run amuck and hardly represent Christ-centered lives. What a testimony it is to the world about the power of Christianity when two people agree to unite and love each other "until death do us part."

Chapter 8, on accepting a servant attitude, also reflects on spousal relations, but its main message deals with relationships between people in general. It calls us to assume a servant posture in our interaction with others, one that Jesus himself assumed as an example that we follow, not an easy stance to take in that it requires a great deal of fortitude. But when put into practice it produces spectacular results among both recipients and givers. After all, who doesn't react positively when given kind treatment? It's an influence the Spirit wields on us. Snuffing it out by ignoring it is a major mistake. In its stead, acknowledging Spirit-directed behavior allows us to serve one another in humility and love according to God's ways, which yields spiritual fruit in everyone. Furthermore, it helps us present a positive image to the world about the life-changing nature of Christianity, a message we all want to proclaim.

The next chapter on human relations entitled "Gift Giving and Receiving -- A Persistent Problem" (Chapter 9) will jolt you. It presents information that has long been suppressed, perhaps out of guilt and maybe embarrassment or even out of desire to protect family members and friends. It has become so pervasive that it demands addressing if we are to help gift recipients interact with their gift givers according to established norms of civility. Ignoring the problem won't make it go away; rather we must take steps to resolve it, even though stringent measures may be necessary. Too many people are being hurt, including young gift recipients themselves (oftentimes our grandchildren) who grow up failing to realize the harm they cause in human relations by blatantly failing to acknowledge gifts given them.

Section 5 on <u>Wisdom</u> and its accompanying chapter "Questioning God: Dangers and Benefits" (Chapter 10) carries a distinctly different theme, yet one that instigates in us an attitude of humility toward the Almighty. We tend to ponder thoughts regarding God's purposes simply out of a human mindset that makes us wonder why things happen the way they do. Granted, questioning of this sort can come across as sacrilegious, which is hardly its intent. Rather, it shows the thought patterns that many of us fall into at one time or another in questioning God's decisions. If done in a spirit of humility, however, our questioning can reap beneficial results. By all means we must not allow our questioning to take on negative overtones that turn us against the Creator.

Coming out of it is a recognition of God's boundless attributes compared to our limited thinking power. For example, have you ever wondered about the origin of sin that led to our fallen status, one that has interfered with human behavior throughout the ages, even from the beginning of the world? We wonder why God carried over Adam and Eve's disobedience to us, since we had nothing to do with it. Or how about going back even further by looking at the angelic rebellion against God that brought sin into the world, one that resulted in Lucifer and his followers being cast out of heaven? At one time or another we may wonder about the possibility of other angelic beings duplicating a rebellion against God at some future time. Such an occurrence is certainly remote, maybe even nonsense, nevertheless it enters our minds simply because the prince of this world, whether we like it or not, actively seeks to destroy any notions about faith in an all-powerful God.

Of course, such questioning can be judged as imagination running wild. We know that God is always in control of everything, which means that nothing happens of which He is unaware and doesn't resolve. But we question, nevertheless, simply because of our human makeup as seen through events occurring in our minds that we wonder about even though we have no answers. But good can come about through such questioning, because when done in an attitude of respect, it allows us to see our limitations and insufficiencies in contrast with the Almighty's supreme wisdom and power. That's an extremely important point, that our questioning be such that humbles us to acknowledge our limited ability to rationalize compared to that of the Creator.

It's possible that some might question God's actions in a proud and smart-alecky way, maybe even emphasizing their own ability to rationalize. Atheists do it all the time, often resulting in a flagrant show of superiority over God's wisdom, even causing a denial of God's existence. On the other hand, our questioning as Christians can allow good to come about -- a humble reflection of and deference to God's sovereignty. It recognizes his supreme wisdom over all creation, including us.

We can't give enough recognition to God's greatness as we see our limitations as created beings, which causes us to remember that although God blesses us with the ability to discern, He places certain restrictions on us. Wise people use the wisdom that God gives by taking on an attitude of humility, which is a recognition of our human insufficiencies in understanding everything that happens. After all, our understanding of the world, or for that matter, the universe, can't hold a candle to that of God and his supreme wisdom.

Stop and pause for a moment and think about the following: Who do we think we are to question the Almighty, Creator of the Universe, which includes us its inhabitants on earth, a tiny speck in the grandiose universe of which we are unable to fathom? Our thinking is so limited that we even aggrandize the idea of countries, the United States, for example, as if it were an important landmass amidst the innumerable number of planets in space. May it cause us to humble ourselves before an all-wise God by realizing that we humans are merely a tiny part of his creation.

Following up the discussion on how we handle wisdom is that of Part VI, Spreading the Gospel. The chapter on "Personal Evangelism" (Chapter 11) addresses how we converse with others about Christ, or witnessing, as some call it. It's a matter of concern since we so often abuse the privilege and cause a great deal of hurt and even rejection of God among those to whom we talk. Yet we often fail to see ourselves contributing to the problem. Instead, we blame others for their hard-headedness, which in itself underscores a weakness that we will want to correct.

Highlighted are the stances appropriate for everyone to assume in propagating thoughts about God -- *gentleness and respect* -- qualities that God has prescribed as critical for representing him to the world. In fact, we are to employ gentleness and respect not only in talking about God and his generous offer of salvation but in dealing with others on whatever the topic. And of course, they are God's characteristics and therefore necessary for application as we represent him through our discipleship.

I humbly cite some of my misguided attempts in trying to spread the gospel in my early years as a Christian. They serve as examples that we should clearly avoid. (I still shudder at the thought of my stupidities in those early days, and yet I ended up as a university professor, of all things). It shows how God blesses in spite of our past mistakes, even in ways we can't comprehend.

Gentleness and respect are not only nice qualities to assume; they are essential for sane living and, of course, for productiveness in displaying Christianity throughout the world. People are prone to listen to the gospel when they see good qualities in us. Scripture underscores gentleness, in fact, as a fruit of the Holy Spirit (Gal. 5:23), which should give us pause in considering whether we ourselves are behind gospel sharing or whether it's the Spirit working through us.

There's a difference, you know, in how the Christian message is given and how it's received. Our effectiveness in sharing the gospel depends on our recognition of those differences. Unfortunately, some Christians tend to exert control over talk about God, so much so that they make a mess of it, causing negative results. In other words, we allow our judgments to clash with those of the Spirit, which often leads to a faulty display of Christianity.

On the other hand, when we allow our conversations to be divinely guided, we show a respect for the Faith that can ultimately lead listeners to want to embrace it themselves. They see our words making good sense as well as having an aura of kindness, which is so because those thoughts are products of the Spirit who himself is gentle and respectful. Attending to those qualities allows us to represent Christianity in all its dynamism.

The section on <u>Undergoing Hardship</u> is reflected in Chapters #12 ("Suffering") and #13 ("Attaining Joy and Peace") to illustrate common problems that everyone faces in life. If at any time we need to lean on the Holy Spirit is when we undergo personal hardship, simply because it's a vulnerable time when Satan takes inroads to destroy our fellowship with God by making life miserable. Included is information of a comforting nature because, yes, we Christians do experience bouts of suffering that oftentimes involve horrendous afflictions causing a great deal of pain, both mentally and physically, all of which points to trusting God to deal with them in the way He decides, including his timing for relief. They are not easy decisions to make, but they exhibit the power to overcome whatever suffering that befalls us.

Sometimes our sufferings reflect issues that God in his wisdom chooses not to resolve, while at other times He deals with them in spectacular ways such as through miraculous healings. But holding fast in trust no matter what be God's decision brings about the much desired qualities of inner peace and joy of which Scripture so often speaks. They are characteristics of Christian living that help us not only endure hardship but to take steps to overcome its painful effects. It's what the Bible refers to as keeping in step with the Spirit (Gal. 5:25), because you see, the Spirit's job is to provide the help we need during those trials. There's no better way to reflect dynamic Christianity than to use the Spirit's power to overcome the negative occurrences that crop up in life.

The next section entitled <u>A Look Into the Future</u> involves three chapters: #14 ("Death"), #15 ("The Second Coming"), and #16 ("Heaven"), all signaling the glorious blessings awaiting us beyond our brief sojourn on earth. But they are not without problems.

The first points to an apprehension of death that's common to everyone, simply because dying is a discomforting experience that we have never faced. In fact, many of us actually fear the thought of it as we perceive death as a bitter experience to undergo, especially when preceded by a great deal of pain and suffering.

Christians throughout the ages have been hoping to escape death's reality by looking to the promise of Jesus' return. That concern carries over to the next chapter (15) about Jesus' second coming. It speaks of the glorious hope shared by all Christians of being taken to heaven at Jesus' appearance. Many tend to view it as an experience hoped for within their lifetime.

Jesus' return, certainly an event prophesied in Scripture, is muddled by various interpretations given it as an end-time happening. Lending to the confusion is the concept of the Rapture, one that many contend will be an event in which Christians are caught up into heaven prior to Christ's final appearance at the end of the age. It's a kind of escapism to relieve Christians from the horrors awaiting them through the massive disturbances in nature and the unimaginable evildoing among earth's inhabitants that Scripture talks about regarding end-times happenings.

There's no question about it -- being transported to heaven through a spectacular happening such as the Rapture has a far greater appeal than dying. Rather than taking a stand on its veracity, however, the chapter emphasizes our final outcome -- heaven. Our hope rests on that glorious experience with which the following chapter (#17) deals.

A number of mundane issues trouble us as we ponder heaven and our makeup there. In fact, heaven is so ethereal that we often fail to relish its blessings as reality. By that I mean that we tend to see heaven interfering with the joys of life on earth, so much so that we often hope for delay in going to heaven.

Some Christians, like those whose physical conditions cause severe pain and suffering, understandably wish to be transported to heaven immediately (life for them on earth seems to consist of nothing but pain and suffering), while others, imitating the apostle Paul, say they want to go to heaven to be with the Lord. We wonder about the genuineness of such a statement. Is it a declaration out of truthful yearning, or is it merely spiritual talk? Do we really mean it when we utter those words, or are we honest with ourselves by citing other pressing concerns about going to heaven, like being there with our spouses and children who may have died? But no matter how we perceive it, heaven is God's promise of rescue from life's adversities. It's an eternity of unspeakable wonders that can't in any way compare to whatever we might perceive as earthly pleasures.

However, consistent with our human nature, we continue questioning heaven's makeup and our role there. But we can put our curiosities to rest by trusting in a trustworthy God whose wisdom and care we will see taking place in our future home. So we accept the fact that God is really caring (the Bible tells us that He actually cares for us right now – 1 Pet. 5:7), not because the idea is something someone has drummed up to make us feel good. Scripture tells us that it's evident as we experience the comfort God renders as we undergo life's vicissitudes. That care, including his promise of eternal life, quickens us to hold fast in trust in a heavenly Father who has made us his children and who consequently loves us as family members. Consequently, we are challenged to await the time of togetherness in heaven in our new relationship as brothers and sisters in Christ and as sons and daughters of a caring heavenly Father.

Perhaps the best way to describe it is to refer to those who claim to have undergone the extraordinary experience of dying (often called near-death experiences) and then miraculously coming back to life again. They have written about being transported to a realm of joy and bliss that had such an effect on them as to remove the desire to return to life again on earth. We will examine those near-death experiences to see what we can learn from them.

Perhaps most importantly, the promise of heaven takes away the sting of death. The idea of heaven is in fact comforting as we see Scripture proclaiming the rapturous joy of our new life there.

The final section, <u>Dynamic Christianity Versus Mediocrity,</u> includes Chapter #17 ("Attuned to the Holy Spirit,"), a theme that runs throughout the book, one that serves to remind us to rely on the Spirit's wisdom and power as we attempt to live out the Christian life. We often rely on our own thinking based on a multitude of factors at play in our bodies that interfere with the Spirit's working. The trouble is that we are not always aware of them, so we plod along thinking that we are doing the right thing, only to find ourselves making a mess of the situation. Only by humbly leaning on God to take over can we expect to be victorious in all that we do and say, and more -- to enjoy life on earth to the fullest as God wills for us. It's all a matter of intimacy with God. The chapter suggests means to encourage that intimacy, which is a thriving spiritual life that rules out selfish motives. (of which we are often unaware). It allows for God's interaction with us toward the end result of a spirit-filled life.

<u>Reflections on Christian Living</u>, then, is a book on joy and of challenge as it guides us in recognizing the help available in the Spirit to make our Christian lives fruitful and meaningful. We really can't do it on our own, at least not in any meaningful way, but as we lean on God we then enjoy his blessings to the fullest. Once we begin doing it, we will attest to its life-giving power.

Describing God's unique care for us and the opportunity He gives us to magnify him causes a greater appreciation of what it means to be God's sons and daughters as well as his ambassadors on earth. We are indeed blessed by being made an integral part of his family as well as being given a unique status as his representatives. May we approach his blessings as dedicated servants.

Our Father in heaven cares for us as seen by his implantation in us, a provision that allows him to have a major role throughout our lives on earth. Our failure to submit to him leaves us to endure hardships unnecessarily, when actually He provides assistance to lead us through dark times that we all experience at one time or another as well as to give us joy throughout life. Hopefully, we will strive to put that help to use so that we take advantage of happy and vibrant lives while at the same time further Christ and his kingdom through dynamic Christian living.

You may wish to use this booklet for group discussion. I have included discussion guides after each chapter to facilitate thinking about key points in each chapter.

May God's blessings be upon you as you read and meditate on these thoughts.

I.

BLESSED BY GOD

One

WE ARE SPECIAL PEOPLE

D id you know that God considers us special, an honor He bestows on us for respecting his Son's sacrifice on the cross? He does so by showering us with special care, protection, and direction by means of embedding his Holy Spirit within us. It's a blessing that makes us unique from anything else experienced. Do we see it that way, or do we fail to recognize God's presence and instead plod along in our own strength and face the consequences of doing a pretty poor job?

Throughout the history of the world only Christians have had God permanently indwelling them, which indeed sets us aside as special, something to rejoice over, not with an attitude of haughtiness, but one that acknowledges God living in us as a helper to direct our operations. Can you imagine, God himself in us? And why not? He has made us his ambassadors. (You don't think He would do that without supplying the needed help to accomplish his purposes, do you?)

Scripture acknowledges that special status by saying, "you are a chosen people, a royal priesthood, a holy nation, a people belonging to God, that you may declare the praises of him who called you out of darkness into his wonderful light" (1 Peter. 2: 9). Chosen as a royal priesthood, holy, and commissioned to declare

3

God's message? You bet, and He shows us how to do it: "Show proper respect to everyone, love the brotherhood of believers" (v. 17). So you see, God's presence means responsibility, one that every Christian is to assume as we do it responsibly by showing respect through an attitude of love.

Love is something we have a hard time practicing, yet Jesus repeated it throughout his ministry as something we should heed. Are we up to it? Of course! Otherwise we wouldn't have been blessed with the Holy Spirit as a help in that endeavor. The trouble is that we often flounder about not knowing how to proceed.

Responsibility

In order to fulfill our God-given role, we must recognize that our special status carries certain obligations, among which is the critically important aspect of human interaction -- the way we deal with people, including fellow believers who have God living in them. Because you see, God declares *all* believers as special, not just a select few. That includes you and me. Its implications are the subject of this chapter.

Along with rejoicing over our special status, we need to keep in mind its responsibilities. It's something I pondered as a result of my involvement in a two-month government-sponsored project in India years ago. The trip's purpose was to foment student and professor exchanges among Indian and American universities in order to enhance increased understanding between cultures. As a university professor I was fortunate to be chosen by the National Association of Foreign Student Advisors (NAFSA) to be a part of that venture.

Standing out for me was the frequent use of the Hindi word *namaste* (pronounced "*nah ma stay*" and cutting all vowels short as well as accenting the final syllable), which I heard every time I was introduced to someone. (I'll put an accent on the final vowel as I refer to the word hereafter to remind you of its stress point).

I was sure it meant something nice, maybe even religious, since hands placed together in a prayerful attitude accompanied it. But I just had to find out its meaning. And guess what? *Namasté* loosely translated to something on the order of "I see God in you."

Wow! What a nice thought – to recognize God's indwelling in every believer we encounter. We will get to its implications shortly, but in the meantime I should point out that the expression has degenerated to serve as a mere form of greeting. (I doubt if Indian greeters really intended to convey any religious meaning but rather to use the expression as a means of merely saying "hello" or "nice to meet you.") That's the way greetings go. We use them in English by flippantly saying, "How are you?" which has degenerated oftentimes to "How ya doin?" without really wanting to know the truth as to how the person is getting along. In fact, we don't even expect a response other than maybe the customary "Fine, thank you," which in itself is generally uttered in habit-form fashion without any real meaning behind it. (Admit it. You automatically say it in spite of having a horrendous day.) If you dare make a truthful, detailed response, you may end up listing a number of annoying physical woes that no one really wants to hear. In fact, your listeners may think, "Why in the world is he telling me all that? I don't really want to hear it." But in order to show kindness, they listen anyway so as not to convey unfriendliness.

So let's think about the implications of *namasté* if we were to apply it to Christianity. Saying "I see God in you," and really mean it certainly would challenge our sincerity, wouldn't it? What possible carryover to Christian relationships could that Hindi expression have? Could we unflinchingly refer to brothers and sisters in Christ as having God in them? Well, I guess so, sort of, since Scripture tells us that He indwells every Christian. But what would be its implications regarding our true feelings and behavior toward them? Sure, the Bible indicates that the Spirit indwells us, which is nice, but so what? People have shortcomings in attitudes and behaviors that conflict with what we consider "proper living." In other words, they're not always the kind of persons we want to be around. How can we accept them according to the true meaning of *namasté,* that they are actually receptacles of God himself no matter their behaviors and attitudes?

And how about those who may be steeped in poverty? Do we care even in the slightest if they are in dire need of help? They may be desperate, even dirty and smelly, struggling to feed their families, for example, not knowing where to turn. We are sorry for their state of affairs, but we regard intimacy with them as something nauseous In other words, what's the difference between our attitude toward them and that which we hold toward God, remembering that God really lives within them? Or do we consider God's indwelling irrelevant?

Dave Burchett[1] has an interesting story in that respect.

> When we start looking down our spiritual noses at the lives of others, we are in dangerous waters. I saw a brutally honest T-shirt at a local amusement park. On the front it said, 'Jesus Loves You.' On the back it said, 'But I Don't.' We would actually be better off displaying that kind of frankness if our faith has no effect on how we treat those around us.

Christians often take one another for granted; that is, we often make no difference in our relationships between them and other people, as if our special status in God's eyes isn't to be taken seriously. We let little annoyances get in the way, sometimes showing a blasé and flippant attitude because of them. Could it be a violation of God's holy work in us? Review what Jesus said about criticizing others without recognizing at the same time that we also have faults. Do you remember? -- "How can you say to your brother, 'Let me take the speck out of your eye, when all the time there is a plank in your own eye?'" (Matt. 7: 4). We all have faults, some of them pretty ugly, so we need to recognize that our actions are often the result of traits we have developed over time.

Saints, Holy, Righteous

How does Scripture define our special status? One way is by calling us saints, holy people, and even righteous ones. Those words are found throughout the NT to describe believers in Christ. (See the beginning of many of Paul's epistles in which he addresses ordinary believers as "saints.") That's because the NT message says that God has declared us completely righteous for having applied the cross work of his Son to our lives. (Note that I didn't say *made* righteous, since we continue to sin as a consequence of our fallen nature inherited from Adam and Eve, but that God *declares* us righteous. In other words, He overlooks our sin-prone tendencies as humans by virtue of the fact that we have trusted in Christ's forgiveness.)

Since we inherited sin from our first parents in the Garden of Eden, we really can't help ourselves. Wrongful behavior and even ugly thoughts plague us unexpectedly, a situation to which Scripture speaks to point out how sin-prone we are as humans. But God steps in to help, and his attitude reflects his love and the value He places on us for having honored his Son's sacrifice. The upshot of the matter is that I see God wanting us to respect and relate to each other in line with his acceptance of us. And the beauty of it is that He offers us the power to do it.

Uh oh. Respect one another regardless of personal traits? Maybe we are feeling guilty already, because so many things crop up to endanger our relationships. But let's not despair. God is ready to fix it. Meanwhile, let's continue with the challenge Jesus gave about the way we are to treat one another.

During his earthly ministry Jesus continually emphasized that we deal with each other in love, which really carries the mutual relationship between us Christians even further than does the word respect, because we know we can respect others without really loving them. Consider his saying, "A new command I give you: Love one another. As I have loved you, so you must love one another" (John 13:34), which He followed up saying, "By this all men will know that you are my disciples, if you love one another" (v. 35).Obviously He wanted to emphasize the impact that love reveals about our seriousness in the Faith. Loving one another is a characteristic that underscores the reality of the Christian lifestyle. Onlookers are impressed when they see that quality in us.

I know that ugliness can easily enter into relationships as seen by the fact that fellow believers may say and do things that run counter to what we see as making good sense. In fact, their attitudes are often hurtful, which makes us question how we can love them when they behave that way.

Love is a concept we toss about loosely without giving heed to its true implications. In fact, I wonder if we fail to come to grips with its reality as often seen in marriage relationships that end up in divorce. If we can't love our spouses toward whom we have openly vowed to love "till death do us part," how can we love others?

Jesus' Example

Jesus never condemned any of his followers for failing to exhibit godly behavior.

I'm sure there were times when his disciples were ugly toward each other simply because of selfish human tendencies that were a part of their nature. James and John exhibited that fault when asking Jesus to allow them to sit on the right and left of him in glory, a very selfish request that riled up the other disciples when they heard of it (Mark 10:35-45). Everyone stumbles. That concept precipitated his teaching on exhibiting love toward one another. "Whoever wants to become great among you must be your servant," He said (v.43).

Selfishness is also seen in Peter's behavior when he went so far as to deny his relationship with Christ. Do you remember his negativity when questioned about being a follower of Jesus? He literally swore up and down that he didn't know the man. And how do you suppose the other disciples felt toward him when they found out about it? We are not told, but we do know that Jesus

8

approached him personally after the resurrection to tell him to buck up and not let his failure interfere with his discipleship. Although seeing human weakness that caused Peter to deny his Lord, the Master wasn't about to condemn or even chastise him. In fact, He predicted Peter's denial before it happened, which also impacted Peter when it actually came about.

Jesus understood why Peter acted the way he did. After all, He created him and knew his every move, seeing Peter's ugliness as well as his redeeming qualities. And Peter certainly got the message that turned him into a prime disciple.

Imagine how we would feel if a close friend refused to stand up for us. We would consider his disloyalty an affront, hardly condoning him as a true friend. But that wasn't the way Jesus responded toward Peter; rather it was that Peter should put the past behind him and go forward with Christianity. It's a message God wants all of us to practice. Why? Because He knows that although our human weaknesses cause us to fail him at times, He doesn't give up on us, rather He understands our imperfect nature and is always forgiving. And please note that the human trait of reprisal is not his characteristic. He actually sees potential in us in spite of our faults, just as He did with Peter. Buck up! We are not to live in the past with self condemnation. We all have potential that we will see blossoming as we turn our lives over to the Spirit and resolve to allow him to guide us in all that we do and say. It's important, then, to put aside our failures, not in the sense of being unconcerned over them, but rather to deny them the opportunity to drag us down to the extent of making life miserable for us.

We have got to realize that we are forgiven, that *all* our ugliness is paid for by Christ's sacrifice on the cross, a fact that helps us appreciate God's overall plan of rescue from our sinful dilemma. We are not to walk about guilt-laden when we make bad judgments, as if we didn't amount to anything worthwhile. God has made us perfectly clean, a state that permits us to spend eternity with him. But we don't want to lose sight of his expectations in terms of our relationship with other believers, or for that matter with anyone. So when we fail Christ, we confess it with all sincerity and then continue on, living and working for him with all our might. Why? Because He's a loving God who forgives us of all our ugliness and wants to see us thrive.

The fact that Jesus never condemns us for our shortcomings is a beautiful part of Christianity. I suppose that's so because He understands how we give in to all sorts of temptations generated by selfish motives simply because of our human deficiencies. At the same time, He challenges us to overcome ugly behavior.

Let's not kid ourselves. We are sinners, a fact we should recognize by the foolish decisions we make and the nasty effects they take on us. But praise God, we are sinners saved by grace, which means that: (1) we are made holy by Christ's shed blood; and, (2) we can weed out stupid behavior by hearkening to God's advice in the written legacy left us in Spirit-inspired Scripture. Can you imagine that we are children of a heavenly Father who has high expectations of us?

The Challenge of Love

The Bible provides teaching for you and for me to live together in harmony. But without the quality of love, a harmonious relationship becomes difficult, even impossible, simply because love is so essential for maintaining unity. Let it sink in.-- Jesus didn't say it would be nice *if* you loved one another. Instead, He said, "you *must* love one another" (emphasis mine) (John 13:34). Are you beginning to feel guilty? Don't despair! God's love for you covers your negligence. In his kindness He always gives us a second chance, and even beyond that. He is always forgiving of people who recognize his majesty and are serious about a relationship with him. Read on for your encouragement.

Practicing Unity

In an anguished prayer just prior to his crucifixion, Jesus cried out to the Father on behalf of his disciples: "that they may be one as we are . . . so that the world may believe that you have sent me" (John 17:11, 21). He was concerned about Christian unity, for He knew the powerful effect it would wield on cementing relationships among believers, and that it would likewise send a message to the entire world of onlookers regarding Christianity's claim of divine inspiration. In other words, we are *Christians*, not Catholics, Baptists, Methodists, Presbyterians, Pentecostals, or whatever. We are Christians, followers of Christ!

How do we show Christianity to be true amidst all the religions that claim truth? An important way, according to Jesus, is our treatment of one another. Seeing good behavior in us, people are apt to say, "Maybe there's something to that religion." However, we get an opposite reaction when mistreating one another. We might hear someone say, "How can I accept Christianity as relevant when its followers treat each other contrary to accepted moral principles?" We know they have a point there, because who's going to respect one's faith in Christ when human relations are not a part of it? Our proclamation of Christianity comes across as a sham; it goes against all accepted moral principles.

So by our actions we are in a position to uphold the truth of Christianity as well as to influence the world's opinion of it. The way we uphold society's moral standards in mutual relationships may not affect everyone (many probably don't have the slightest concern about behaving responsibly toward others), but it may cause some to reassess their attitudes about their relationship with God. The effectiveness of our witness does go beyond speech. I say that because I've learned that actions often display greater meaning than words; in fact, actions can either support our religious beliefs or deny them.

That's what I like about Christianity . . . its teachings reflect acceptable human relationships. Religions that fail to do that are suspect for their integrity and truth. Who's going to adopt a religion, like Islam, for example, that tells its followers to kill anyone who doesn't believe the way they do? It's attributing to God an attitude devised by humans that really amounts to mockery towards the Almighty. God is love and wants us to put that trait into practice as we deal with one another. True, He will judge those who reject his message of love through Christ, but He does not look to us to make such judgment.

Jesus understood that our disregard of how we treat one another would have dire consequences. So He called us to get serious about relating to one another as special people, spiritual kinfolk and family, if you will.

What parents wouldn't deal with their children in a very special way? We want the best for our sons and daughters by treating them with care and concern, and we hope that as they grow up they will be sensitive toward each other as well. God feels the same way. But could we fail to do so with fellow Christians whom God has declared our spiritual brothers and sisters, family members?

We may justify that neglect by saying that we don't really like a lot of things they do and say. In other words, we let their attitudes and behaviors conflict with our lifestyle. At the same time we fail to realize why they are that way, even failing to understand our own shortcomings. Unseemly attitudes often cling tenaciously to us by showing their sinful tendencies. Imagine the impact we have on relationships when we accept others as God accepts them. Or do we want to continue stubbornly in our old ways as we think that everything we do is the right way?

Special people? Yes! God declares us so. Since that's the case, might it not be a good idea to treat fellow believers as special? How productive it would be if each of us took corrective action to treat Christians in the spirit of Jesus' words . . . treating them as holy. Let's look into it.

A Holy Status

I grew up in a Pennsylvania community near a church bearing the name "Holy Family." I never gave any thought to its meaning until I started this writing. Then the name flashed across my mind -- a holy family. What a splendid idea!

Catholicism uses that name to refer to Jesus and his parents, Mary and Joseph, perhaps making that association in naming that Pennsylvania church. But suppose the people who met there considered *themselves* a holy family, and they treated one another accordingly. It certainly would cause some serious thinking about human relationships, wouldn't it?

Let's illustrate it with the following scenario: "Ladies and gentlemen," the pastor or priest announces. "We have a very special guest worshipping with us this morning -- the distinguished Senator from _____. Please give Senator _____ a very special welcome.

We are always careful to recognize special people in our midst. It's a common courtesy to show esteem for their position and accomplishments. We would do it for Billy Graham, Mother Teresa, or anyone else we recognize as extraordinary servants of God. They are special, and they deserve acknowledgment for their selflessness and dedication to humanity.

But others far less distinguished are special, too, perhaps not in the sense of having performed extraordinary acts that command public attention, but ones that hold special status in God's eyes nevertheless. Like who? Ordinary believers in Christ, like you and me, or the Smiths and the Joneses who attend church with us every Sunday.

Can we get through our heads that the idea of treating one another as special is an important outcome in God's eyes? By doing so, we are establishing relationships that can blossom into good things for all of us as well as for onlookers, not to mention the joy God gets from it. Unfortunately, we tend to take fellow believers for granted, regarding them no different from other people, while actually they are very important in God's eyes for having put their lives in the Father's hands through belief in Christ as Savior. I doubt that first-century believers took that kind of stance. They knew they were special by becoming Christians, including the life-threatening dangers that accompanied it. In short, they loved on another.

The Holy Spirit

We often overlook God's purpose in implanting the third person of the Trinity in us. That's a big mistake, since the Holy Spirit plays a role in treating us as special. The Spirit does many things, but let's look at a few of them, just enough, I hope, to cement in our minds the special status God wants us to enjoy as well as the status He wants us to give to every believer.

The Bible cites the honor that God bestows on each of us as He regards us as his holy temple (1 Cor. 3:16). You will remember that his temple under Judaism was a sacred place where man and God met, which is no longer the case, since God now lives within us, making his temple the Christian's body rather than a structure of wood and stone as in the past. So you see, it's not just your body that's holy, but every Christian's body.

Are you beginning to see the impact as the way fellow believers are to be treated? Do we realize that our poor attitudes we may have toward other Christians is a slap in the face of the Spirit who indwells them? In fact, do we realize that ways in which we abuse our own bodies are not in concert with the Spirit who indwells them? That means that we must do away with any destructive acts toward our bodies, like bad food and drink, tobacco and drugs, wrongful sex, unhealthy sleep patterns, or anything else that constitutes abuse. Let it be absolutely clear, God declares our bodies as sacred, to be treated with care as a fitting place for God himself to live. May we use our bodies to proclaim the intimacy we have with our Lord because of that indwelling. When we don't, my guess is that we grieve him terribly. But He doesn't leave us on our own, because once he declares us as his children He remains true to that decision, a responsibility that a father has toward his family members.

We often dismiss any idea of intimacy that God holds toward us. No other humans in the history of the world have had the privilege of carrying God within them. Could God have intended for us to show that unique indwelling in our relations with fellow Christians? The answer is obvious.

We see, then, the Spirit as a unifying force in making us God's children (Gal. 4:6 and Rom. 8:16), which suggests a family relationship -- sons and daughters of the Father as well as spiritual brothers and sisters of one another. Thoughts that often come to mind in that regard are: care; protection; and yes, love. Yet we often fail at their implementation, treating others as ordinary as we often neglect giving them even the slightest importance. Of course, God always keeps his part of the bargain no matter how badly we might act. He sees us as his children regardless of our disposition toward one another, which means that we are a part of his family, a holy family. The sooner we recognize that fact, the better off we will be.

Scripture teaches that since God indwells us and considers us holy temples as well as his sons and daughters -- very special positions -- then we ought to view fellow Christians in the same way. Why would I want to reflect an attitude different from that held by my heavenly Father? If I allow myself to be negative in my relations with other believers, I overlook God's personal indwelling and his regard of Christians as special. If I show anger or bitterness, I hear God crying out, "What are you doing? That's my son (or daughter) you're abusing." Further, I hear his voice resonating in my head, "That's your brother or sister in Christ that you're mistreating instead of honoring." The implication is that my treatment of fellow believers carries over to my attitude toward God. Does my esteem toward others coincide with the fact that they carry God within them?

Maybe we don't openly mistreat them, but the way we may ignore them sure calls for a change of attitude. Sometimes I wonder if God is even saying, "If you dishonor them, you dishonor me because I live within them." Can you catch its implications? We are family, which means that family members don't abuse or ignore one another but rather show care through sensitivity and concern, having a tie with one another that demands personal attention. Maybe we should see them as if they were being persecuted, even imprisoned or killed for the sake of their belief, which is actually happening in other parts of the world and which may even occur in the United States. Such thoughts would wake us up to the value of being a Christian, and I'm sure would affect the Lord's regard for us.

Sensitivity encompasses the word "love," a characteristic of the Spirit. So if we are to be true to the Spirit living within us we will want to demonstrate that love in our relations with one another. Hearken the teaching of Scripture: "God has poured out his love into our hearts by the Holy Spirit, whom he has given us" (Rom. 5:5). Also, love is declared to be a fruit of the Spirit (Gal. 5:22), a major ingredient of anyone claiming to be Spirit-filled. Or do we claim to be spirit-filled because of some extraordinary experience we had, like speaking in tongues, but which fails to reflect the true nature of Jesus' presence. I'm afraid we toss around the idea of being spirit-filled without understanding its true meaning, which is being *spirit-controlled*, that is, being dedicated to God in all aspects of life. Its effects are seen in the way we treat other believers.

The Holy Spirit and love? Do we make that connection? If we don't, we are cheating ourselves out of God's special blessing. You see, without reliance on the Holy Spirit we will never be able to love adequately and enjoy a relationship with other believers that God wills for us to have.

I'm sure you are now seeing that God wants us to esteem one another in the same way He esteems us. After all, why would we want to behave differently from that of God toward us? But please note that the Holy Spirit, although indwelling us, never forces us toward corrective behavior. We are always responsible for our actions, which means that even though God is love and wants us to behave in that manner, He leaves it to each of us to decide on the decisions we make as to whether we will demonstrate that love.

You see, God never treats us as robots, pushing himself on us; rather, He give us liberty to do as we please. The trouble is that we often abuse that liberty, which underscores the fact that ugly attitudes toward one another might be monumental and need immediate attention. Oh the woes of Christianity when we fail to heed the Spirit's guidance.

What a miserable lot are we, conceived in sin and continuing therein, even after becoming Christians. But sin does not need to ride roughshod in our lives. Through self discipline and dependence on the Spirit, we can conquer all negative thoughts and actions. That's why God has implanted his Spirit within us, to give us the help we need to overcome.

Eternal Life Guaranteed

We have seen that the Holy Spirit possesses each of us so as to underscore our special status before God. But let's look at another role of the Spirit that identifies the saved for the coming day in heaven. It's an identification made when we first believed the gospel. Here are the exact words: "And you also were included in Christ when you heard the word of truth, the gospel of your salvation. Having believed, you were marked in him with a seal, the promised Holy Spirit, who is a deposit guaranteeing our inheritance . . ." (Eph. 1:13-14).

The upshot of the matter is that we believers are set apart from the rest of the world by the Spirit's indwelling. God calls it a seal, a guarantee of eternal life, and because of it He regards us as saints or holy people. Forget about the usual meaning that society gives the word "saints." The Bible declares all of us as saints (holy people, or, as per the title of this chapter, "We Are Special People"), a privilege given us for our belief in Christ. All the more reason why we should treat one another as special. We will be living together in heaven some day where we will stand before the Lord Almighty who bought us with his life and who will look upon every one of us as holy and special, his sons and daughters, family members in Christ. How will we feel in heaven about that relationship if we disregarded it previously on earth? Well, in heaven we will have new mindsets which won't interfere with our relationships. But the question should cause us to think again about the way we relate with fellow believers while on earth.

This has had meaning to me as far back as my teenage years. After graduating from high school I worked on the assembly line at the General Electric plant. During our ten-minute rest break, I saw a young man down the line reading the Bible. I figured that anyone doing that under such circumstances had to be a Christian. Enthusiastic about my newfound faith, I approached him, eager to meet another believer with whom to identify, but to my astonishment, he didn't have the slightest interest in conversing or even in knowing who I was. I thought, "If this guy's a believer, what a gross inconsistency in reading the Bible in public and yet being rude to someone seeking friendship." I don't know why he acted that way, but from that day on I resolved never to view a Christian as common or ordinary. The world often rejects us. But a fellow believer?

Forgiving One Another

If Christians are special to God, shouldn't they be to us also? Granted that God is the ultimate forgiver, while we tend to hold grudges or at least find it hard to forgive and forget. We may try, but I think we all agree that sometimes it's hard to put into practice, especially when it suggests negative consequences in having to tolerate what might amount to continual abuse.

We do want to imitate God by forgiving whatever nasty habits practiced against us, but to forgive and forget continual wrongdoing requires a lot of fortitude. Yet we realize that we must grow spiritually in that direction. It takes resolve, which Scripture tells us comes about through self-discipline in meditating on God's Word as well as communicating with our Lord in prayer. Those good habits cause us to stop our rudeness toward Bob, our impatience with Sally, or our short-temperedness with Jim and Jane. We realize that we must get our act together if we are to claim true discipleship. We may even find the Spirit telling us to confess our bad attitudes to those whom we have wronged, which will take an awful lot of humility.

The apostle John defined discipleship in terms of love, but only in the sense of putting it into practice, that is, doing rather than just saying. You will remember his words when he said, "let us not love with words or tongue but with actions and in truth" (1 John 3:18). To do otherwise is to be grossly hypocritical as we fail to understand the true meaning behind "love" inspired by the Spirit within us.

One more concept regarding the Holy Spirit's indwelling is that it's not only the Spirit himself living within us, but the Father as well as the Son (John 14:23), something we often fail to realize. Father, Son, and Holy Spirit – a divine trinity, truly a mystery that our earthly way of thinking seems impossible to come to grips with. How can they indwell us while at the same time reign in heaven? Ah, that's the nature of God, one without restrictions.

That holy presence makes our bodies special indeed. In fact, Jesus cautioned against reviling against the Holy Spirit when He referred to disregarding the Spirit as a serious matter indeed (Matt. 12:31). Granted that his reference had to do with the way some people attributed the Spirit's acts to Satan, as did the Pharisees with Jesus' miracles (Matt. 12:24). But ponder the implications -- Do we really want to reflect little importance to the Spirit's indwelling by failing to acknowledge his special presence? We are to esteem his indwelling to such an extent that we honor the entire Trinity . . . Father, Son, and Holy Spirit. But I repeat again -- the Spirit is always gentle, never forcing himself on anyone. May we be equally tenderhearted in our attitude toward him.

Special people. That's what we are. God deems us so, and He wants us to reflect that same attitude toward each other, not just in talk but in action. It takes a lot of soul searching, but according to Jesus it demonstrates a dynamic Christianity that causes others to sit up and take notice. And of course, the way we treat fellow Christians will make an imprint on them as well, all to God's glory.

If you've been guilty of negative attitudes towards a fellow believer, don't despair. God understands our human proclivity toward such things. However, it's time to make correction by confessing it to the Father as well as to those we have wronged. What a time of joy that will ensue!

Personalizing

It's not a question of simply generalizing the fact that the entire body of Christians is special in God's eyes. We must personalize it, which includes you and me, which challenges us to reflect seriously on Jesus' prayer to the Father that showed his yearning, "That they may be one as we are one . . . so that the world may believe that you have sent me" (John 17:11,21). Consider the outcome -- outsiders always watch how Christians live. When they see us doing something distasteful, they are prone to condemn the Christian faith in general. In fact, people often do that simply as an act of hostility toward Christianity, often belittling it for no reason other than to trumpet their "wisdom." On the other hand, when they see us treating fellow believers positively in a very special and loving way, how much does that register with them, so much so that they may also want to identify with the Faith?

Christians maintaining unity with one another is not an idea applicable only to the first century when Jesus was on earth; rather it's a trait that has wielded tremendous ramifications throughout the centuries. If we want to influence people positively toward Christ, practice unity! And how do we do that? By being accepting of one another, just as we would toward Jesus as if He himself were standing in our midst. It's a silent witness to the wonders of Christianity, setting it apart as deserving of one's belief. Think about it: our role in accepting fellow believers is the same as if we were accepting Jesus Christ himself. The very thought of it should cause us to re-evaluate our relationships.

What, then, is our responsibility toward fellow believers? Some of them may have habits we dislike, so we think that shunning them is justified. But suppose the roles were reversed, that they saw habits in us that they disliked? What would be the solution? Throw our hands up in despair and give up on Christian living? Absolutely not! Rather, all of us have an obligation to fulfill toward one another to the extent that we treat each other as family members, special people. Being true to such a family relationship, we will have a role in bringing about the kind of fellowship that Jesus had in mind when He prayed for our unity. It's a healing balm that destroys troublesome relationships to which we must always give attention, that is, not just once, but continuously.

When we receive negative treatment from other Christians, how do we feel? When we are instigators of negativity, how do you suppose others feel? When God sees us abusing or ignoring people in whom He dwells, how do you suppose He feels? It doesn't matter how our puny minds justify the attitudes and treatment we give. We must overcome selfish tendencies to deal with others as God himself loves them.

These are challenges for all of us as we take a second look at Christian conduct and relationships. Let each of us fulfill our responsibility, which will change our lives by resulting in a dynamic discipleship that we never dreamed possible. And God will be pleased, and so will you as you see the love and respect that you render to others and receive the same from them.

A final note is that we step out to contact fellow believers whom we will recognize as special, maybe even to tell them so. When we do that, watch how relationships flourish. You will see God stepping in to create a union between you and your friends that will be astonishing. And you thought you didn't have a ministry.

Is this a discussion on "Special People" in terms of how we relate to one another? You may be saying, "I thought you were to show us how God miraculously turns our lives around by means of the Spirit's indwelling?" You are absolutely right! You see, the Spirit's hold on us takes effect starting with the way we treat fellow believers. If we push that aside by wanting more spectacular happenings, we are failing to give God a chance to develop us as his true servants.

The path isn't an easy one neither a glorious one that will show us as remarkable in man's eyes, but it's one that God desires, one in which He rejoices over because it renders love toward others. How do you suppose He feels when we exhibit such love? You're right! He's smiling over our willingness to give of ourselves, saying, "that's my son or daughter who's dealing rightly with a fellow believer." And God is glad.

DISCUSSION GUIDE

1. What does the fact that the Spirit indwells every believer have to do with our relations with other Christians? How does it change our perspective?
2. The Bible gives us examples of some of the Twelve (James, John, Peter, Judas, and Thomas) as those who in one way or another didn't stay true to Jesus. Yet they were among Jesus' closest friends. What message might that send to us as to how we must treat our friends with utmost care and concern in spite of any ugly actions they might display toward us?
3. The fact that the Spirit indwells us as Christians calls our attention to the importance of keeping our bodies pure. What does that mean in terms of daily living, and how might we discipline ourselves to keep our bodies under control? Are there any things that you have subjected yourself to that interfere with your body as a receptacle of the Holy Spirit?
4. God's forgiveness of our past mistakes makes us aware of the attitude we should have toward those whose actions have hurt us. How does the forgiveness idea challenge us? What effects might it have on others as well as on us?

Two

We Are Included

At one time God favored a specific group of people – Jews – while the rest of us were left out. In fact, almost the entire Old Testament (OT) concerns the Almighty's unique relationship with Israel. The Jewish people occupied God's thoughts and actions exclusively throughout those early recorded years. But things have changed. The whole world is now included through the provision of salvation through Jesus Christ.

Looking at the history of God working with mankind, we can go all the way back several centuries to his call to Abraham. That OT saint didn't have the slightest idea where he was supposed to go or what would be awaiting him. All he knew was to step out in blind trust of God who had communicated with him. Here was the directive:

'Leave your country, your people and your father's household and go to the land I will show you. I will make you into a great nation and I will bless you; I will make your name great, and you will be a blessing. I will bless those who bless you and who-ever curses you I will curse; and all peoples on earth will be blessed through you' (Gen. 12:1-3).

Abraham obeyed, but not without cost. There was a lot of wondering about God's direction, but perhaps the hardest part was to have to yield to God's demands later on in his journey to sacrifice his son, Isaac, as a burnt offering.. Why was God asking him to do such a terrible thing? Abraham was mystified. Killing his own son whom he and his wife Sarah had waited so many years to be born? But he still obeyed as he proceeded to take the necessary steps. Then God intervened at the last minute, saving Isaac, and then giving Abraham a blessing for his obedience.

'Because you have done this and have not withheld your Son, your only son, I will surely bless you and make your descendants as numerous as the stars in the sky and as the sand on the sea- shore. Your descendants will take possession of the cities of their enemies, and through your offspring all nations on earth will be blessed, because you have obeyed me' (Gen. 22:16-18).

Israel Established

The promise was fulfilled. Through Abraham's descendants emerged the nation of Israel that God saw as his special people. Although He didn't like their waywardness (they were always complaining and going their own way), He didn't give up on them, probably because as their Creator He knew their deficiencies. He continued to show mercy by dealing with them as an elect people.

Even at the time of Christ in the first century do we see his favoritism when Jesus sent out his disciples to minister exclusively to the "lost sheep of Israel" (Gen. 10:6). He actually prohibited them from going to the Gentiles (v. 5). Kind of horrifying, isn't it, God showing favoritism toward Jews? Suppose you, being a Gentile, were living back then. How would you have felt? But hold on! It was all a matter of timing. Things changed, and all the better for us Gentiles.

A New Plan

Christ's death changed the scenario – a radical switch, actually bringing Jews and Gentiles together as one people. Scripture, in fact, declared, "There is neither Jew nor Greek . . . for you are all one in Christ Jesus" (Gal. 3:28). Good news! Christ broke down the wall of partition between Jews and Greeks (Gentiles), making a new covenant that showed God accepting all of humanity without distinction. I like the Living New Testament translation of it, as it records Paul saying,

For Christ himself is our way of peace. He has made peace between us Jews and you Gentiles by making us all one family, breaking down the wall of contempt that used to separate us. By his death he ended the angry resentment between us, caused by the Jewish laws and excluded the Gentiles, for he died to annul that whole system of Jewish laws. Then he took the two groups that had been opposed to each other and made them parts of himself; then he fused us together to become one new person, and at last there was peace . . . Now all of us, whether Jews or Gentiles, may come to God the Father with the Holy Spirit's help because of what Christ has done for us. (The Living New Testament, Eph. 2:14-16, 18).

But we know that some first-century Jews rebelled at the idea of God changing his partiality toward them. They didn't like it one bit. They had been under Mosaic Law all their lives which declared themselves special, and in no way were they now to regard themselves differently. It didn't make sense that God would issue a holy proclamation (OT Law) to be revered and then to brush it aside, including its declaration of Israel being special. So they insisted that Gentile converts to Christianity keep those edicts, even as they the Jews had been doing, (although without sincerity). It was a revolutionary time, one they had trouble accepting, because you see, they must have wondered how an ordinance once proclaimed by God as holy was no longer valid.

25

Paul, who claimed a special revelation from the Lord, vehemently attacked their refusal to change. He would have none of their insistence that Gentile believers be circumcised according to Mosaic Law and to follow its edicts. Why was Paul so adamant in upholding non-partiality? To believe otherwise would conflict with God's new covenant, a pact that included everyone, including the entire Gentile world. Secondly, circumcision created a gender problem; it was only for males. Paul made it clear that God's new covenant rendered everyone equal regardless of gender, or even of race or of country of origin. In fact, Paul ripped apart all Jewish arguments about life centered around OT Law. (Read about it in the epistle to the Galatians.) A new era had begun, and although disruptive of Jewish thought, it ushered in a new act of God for humanity.

The Church

I am pleasantly overwhelmed by the new disclosure that makes me, a Gentile, equally accepted by God. But there's no stopping there. The next transition was the establishment of the New Testament (NT) Church, which came about after Christ's resurrection. Consequently, we are told that we are all one in Christ, an integral part of his church, which the NT declares as his body (Col. 1:18), which is in fact holy and without blemish (v. 22).

Application

The vast majority of the world's people, including me and probably you, too, are Gentiles. At one time we had no relationship with the Almighty. in fact, the Bible declared us as outcasts, without God and without hope in this world (Eph. 2:12). Christ changed all that (vv. 13-14). Quoting from Isaiah, Paul pointed to prophecy that said, "The root of Jesse will spring up, one who will arise to rule over the nations: the Gentiles will hope in him" (Rom. 15:12).

How strange that first-century Jews were unwilling to recognize that fact. Other verses in Isaiah refer to God's mercy on the Gentiles, so one would think that the Jewish religious leaders especially would have recalled OT Scripture predicting Gentile inclusion. For example, the Bible prophesies about what is to take place, saying, "I, the Lord, have called you in righteousness; I will take hold of your hand. I will keep you and will make you to be a covenant for the people and a light for the Gentiles" (Isa. 42:6). Also, it says, "I will also make you a light for the Gentiles, that you may bring my salvation to the ends of the earth" (Isa. 49:6).

I'm glad I've been included, since in God's eyes I as a Gentile was once nothing, non-descript, without hope, but through Christ I've been redeemed, accepted, and made a son of God. That's the whole idea behind the new covenant, which supplanted the old. Can you believe it, Gentiles, once of little importance now being God's children? Let's all rejoice in our acceptance, for in Christ we are now one – Jew and Gentile, male and female, slave and free – everyone equal. Once of no standing, now we are considered holy; once without hope, now we are promised eternity in heaven. The NT explains it vividly.

Remember that formerly you who are Gentiles by birth and called 'uncircumcised' . . . you were separate from Christ, excluded from citizenship in Israel . . . without hope and without God in the world. But now in Christ Jesus you who were once far away have been brought near through the blood of Christ . . . Consequently you are no longer foreigners and aliens, but fellow citizens with God's people and member of God's house-hold . . . Eph. 2:11-19).

Let's shout for joy we who were once without God. May it cause us to approach him in humble worship out of gratitude for his graciousness.

DISCUSSION GUIDE

1. How do you react in knowing that God has included us (Gentiles) as part of his holy family? Why should we pay much attention to it?

Three

WE ARE FORGIVEN

In this brief chapter I call attention to God's forgiveness of our waywardness, a sin that carried over from Adam and Eve's disobedience. I use the example of the apostle Peter's life since it holds a number of happenings from which we can benefit. It will remind us of God's constant love and blessings in spite of our inherent shortcomings.

Peter, along with the other eleven disciples, spent some three years with Jesus witnessing his power through miracles of healing, raising people from the dead, and feeding thousands of people with a tiny amount of bread and fish. Peter personally experienced the miracles of walking on water with Jesus and pulling in a boatload of fish after a long night of unproductive toil. Such happenings must have convinced him that Jesus was special, even the promised Messiah, which is seen in his vociferous answer to Jesus' question --Who do men say that I am? After hearing a litany of responses from his fellow colleagues, Peter declared, "'You are the Christ, the Son of the living God'" (Matt. 16:16).

Peter, along with James and John, were also privileged to witness the happenings on the Mount of Transfiguration: 1) they saw Jesus transfigured ("'his face shown like the sun, and his clothes became as white as the light'" – Matt. 17:2); 2) they saw Moses and Elijah talking with Jesus (v. 3); and, 3) they heard a voice coming out of the cloud saying, "'This is my Son, whom I love . . . Listen to him!'" (v. 5).

Yet in spite of these marvelous experiences, all wasn't positive in Peter's life. Showing his choleric temperament, he rebuked Jesus for talking about his coming sufferings and death (Peter vowed he would never let those things happen to Jesus). In his presumptuous humility at the Last Supper he refused to let Jesus wash his feet (but later recanted). He also declared that under no circumstance would he ever be disloyal to Jesus, but after the Romans took Jesus captive Peter ended up denying his Master, and three times at that. Of course, he knew he had done wrong, and He wept bitterly over it. At that time he recalled Jesus' brutal prediction that he would deny him (Matt. 26:34). All that must have left Peter in turmoil as he pondered his foolish behavior.

A pretty rotten picture of Peter, isn't it? Transfer it to your own past and see how you feel about yourself? All of us have to confess that we were like Peter in many ways, having done all sorts of horrible things. In the final analysis, Jesus forgave the apostle for his failings. The point is that we too are forgiven of all the stupidities of our past lives. Hurrah! In spite of our sinful natures, God has forgiven us, totally, which should put a smile of gratitude on our faces.

We tend to say that Peter should have known better, especially after seeing the miracles Jesus performed and hearing the wonderful things that Jesus taught. Surely he should have been convinced that Jesus was no ordinary human being. Isn't it odd how we do things that don't seem to make sense? So it was with Peter, who gave in to his own bodily desires, but in spite of it he was forgiven.

Peter is a good example of humanity, that is, us. We fail Christ in many ways, often deliberately, simply because of our sinful nature to which we often surrender. But let's not give up on ourselves. God understands our human nature and is always forgiving, which doesn't mean, of course, that we misuse his forgiveness by letting self predominate. (Out of weakness we often succumb to wrongdoing, which probably leaves Satan, our adversary, laughing up a storm.) We even repeat the kind of blunders that Peter engaged in, like claiming we would never deny Jesus, in spite of the convincing evidence of seeing Jesus perform miraculous happenings. But thank God, by confessing (owing up to) our waywardness, we have God's forgiveness (1 John 1:9), which is a way that God has provided to restore broken fellowship. Why did He make that provision? I repeat, He created us and thus understands our humanness to sin.

Forgiveness is a part of the wonderful plan God instituted through Christ. The Bible tells us of God's forgiveness (our past, present, and future sins) through the sacrificial offering of Jesus: "In him we have redemption through his blood, the forgiveness of sins, in accordance with the riches of God's grace" (Eph. 1:7). That's what makes the gospel so incredible; it wipes the slate clean by forgiving us of *all* our trespasses.

Now God tells us to go forward with him instead of looking back on our miserable failings before or even during our Christian lives. Just as he told Peter to forget the past and be God's witness, so He speaks to us, too. Like Peter, we probably wonder why God puts up with us, miserable creatures that we are. But the fact is that he does tolerate our misdeeds, and He gives us the promise of eternal life as well as his presence in whatever we do in his name. He even commissions us as ambassadors, that includes his power accompanying that commission, and that we will see his blessings as we spread his good news throughout the world.

Give thanks! We have a loving Lord who doesn't seek vengeance, although He has a perfect right to do so, given our proclivity to sin. He even considers us now as holy and makes us his representatives, but let's understand that we don't represent him on our own, in fact, by trying to do so we make a mess of things. That's why He said, "I am with you always, to the very end of the age" (Matt. 28:20). Jesus, the Father, and the Spirit stand with us as helpers in whatever we do, a lesson we take advantage of rather than to try do things through our own power.

The passage of time has a way of influencing our memory of God's intervention.

It did so with Peter, causing him to be so overwhelmed by the dilemma of Jesus' arrest, abuse, and finally crucifixion, that the many miracles Jesus performed earlier seemed to have escaped him. So it can be with us; we fail to remember God's miraculous hand of mercy in rescuing us from stressful situations that seemed impossible for us to overcome. Weren't there times when you were desperate, yet God provided relief? Isn't it strange how we remember our sufferings while at the same time fail to recall our blessings? Giving God thanks for his glorious interventions affects our attitude positively toward him and toward ourselves.

We are forgiven. We are truly blessed. Let's live positively to reflect those blessings!

DISCUSSION GUIDE

1. Do you have ugly memories of your pre-Christian life or even of some aspects of your life after you became a Christian? Why is it important to go forward with Christ rather than to dwell on past mistakes? How is it that we can rightly do that?

2. Can you remember a blessing that you received from God? Share it with others.

II.

Understanding The Bible

Four

THE BIBLE: TWO RELIGIONS

The title of this chapter may get you wondering. Two religions? In the Bible? It may even come across as sacrilegious. "I thought the Bible had to do with one God, not multiple deities," you may say. It does. One God who reigns supreme and who isn't intimidated by ideas we concoct about other gods. But we must take stock on how the Bible reveals God speaking to us? If we don't, we really end up endorsing two religions, OT Law and NT Grace, a stance that is totally incongruous with Scripture.

Law Versus Grace

It all stems on how you read Scripture; that is, to whom does the Bible speak, and why? By doing that, we will see the Bible talking about two distinct religious ideas. The trouble is that some of us tend to mesh the two, perhaps because the Bible is presented to us as one godly book, usually in one tome, Old Testament (OT) and New Testament (NT) combined. We think it all applies to us, when it addresses two distinct groups of people. What gets us into trouble is that we think the NT (new covenant) starts with Matthew, because that's the dividing line in our Bible between OT and NT.

I'm not talking about separating the OT from the New in order to recognize Jesus Christ as the Messiah. Jesus fulfilled prophecy as He came in the first century to replace the Law by establishing a new standard by which to live. We are pretty straight on that, knowing that salvation comes about exclusively through faith in Christ, a pact that reverberates in the way we order our lives. But we often use the Bible in subtle ways when we hold onto OT Law by connecting it with the NT. We often think that such reasoning makes sense by holding the OT as God's sacred revelation, which of course, it is. The problem is that we often don't know how far to go in upholding that idea.

The Bible emphasizes two major leaders -- Moses and Jesus -- each with his own mission. We see John the apostle calling attention to that fact by saying, "the Law was given through Moses; grace and truth came through Jesus Christ" (John 1:17). They represent two distinct ideas -- law and grace -- given through two different people.

The verse intends to contrast Mosaic Law (given to OT Jews) and grace (for all followers of Jesus under the new covenant). Scripture differentiates the two by emphasizing the superiority of grace over law. Grace, in fact, is now to have priority, not only in the sense that it comes as God's final redemptive plan, but that it actually cancels OT Law.

OT Advantages

That last part is awfully dogmatic, you may say. But hold on! Before you jump to conclusions, please understand that I am not saying that the OT is of no use to us. In no way do I disregard the OT's value, since it contains God's sacred revelations from which we can learn about him and his ways, even though they weren't addressed directly to us. Paul even upheld its importance by saying, "everything that was written in the past was written to teach us" (Rom. 15:4). So we learn from the OT, but we keep it in proper perspective, that God has now revealed himself in the form of his Son, Jesus. It has changed the way we are to have a relationship with the Almighty, not by following OT rules but by receiving his gift of grace through Jesus and letting it impact on the way we live.

The OT does indeed teach us a lot about godly living: the Psalms and Proverbs, are chuck full of wisdom about worship and morality; the lives of the prophets and of other OT characters are likewise examples for us; and, of utmost importance are the prophecies written hundreds of years B.C. about the Savior to come, even about his future appearance in end times. All of this supports the validity of Christianity and our trust in its proclamations. The entire OT is full of instruction by which we benefit and to which Jesus often referred, but we must take care to recognize its limitations, which unfortunately, some fail to do

OT Limitations

First of all, I must make it clear that the Bible doesn't uphold the idea of multiple deities which you may have mistakenly understood through the title of this chapter, "The Bible – Two Religions." We must recognize that even though the Bible teaches us of one supreme being, it's really a book of two religions -- Judaism and Christianity -- each with its own purpose and orientation. Jewish converts to Christianity in the first century had trouble differentiating between the two. Although they accepted Christ as the prophesied Messiah, they stubbornly held to their Jewish beliefs and even tried to influence Gentile Christians to follow them. In a sense we can understand their clinging to OT Law along with belief in Christ; old habits aren't easily relinquished, especially when ingrained in us from childhood with a distinct religious emphasis.

The New Covenant Reigns

Now it's a different story. The apostle Paul tells converted Jews that as Christians they are under a new covenant, meaning that they must recognize a new orientation, one they would contradict by merging the two testaments. They were especially at fault by singling out the rite of circumcision as a requirement for attaining God's approval. We can understand why they did that, since it was a part of OT rules issued by God, regulations they had lived by all their lives. Furthermore, the ordinance of circumcision was a symbol establishing them as special people belonging to God. Of course, as Christians they now believed in Jesus as their Messiah, an act that Scripture defines as faith. but they were guilty of mixing the two covenants by adding OT rules to their newfound faith. The OT declared those rules to be sacrosanct, that is to say, that they were to be followed no matter what. It's an addition that's easy to fall prey to simply because it underscores a major truism of life -- that we work hard toward attaining a goal. So we argue, that we are not to denounce OT rules and regulations in order to pursue the teachings of NT Christianity. We simply add Christianity to those OT edicts, and voilà, we believe we have a set of guidelines to follow. At least we think we do.

Paul's reaction to Galatian Christians who equated the two covenants was entirely negative. He pointed out that now that Christ has come, the Jewish act of circumcision was a worthless act that they were insisting on to put them in favor with God. "Mark my words," he said. "I, Paul, tell you that if you let your-selves be circumcised, Christ will be of no value to you at all" (Gal. 5:2). Why? Not that circumcision was a bad thing, but rath-er that they were making it a requirement for obeying God, even for staying in God's good graces, something totally contradictory to God's simple and generous plan to restore mankind exclu-sively through belief in Jesus. That salvation was one exclusively of faith, not one to be earned by doing things, a gospel truth we must always keep before us simply out of recognition of the fact that our enemy, Satan, subtly encourages additions so as to make us deviate from the gospel story. He knows that whatever he can get us to do in the name of religion will be to his benefit, caus-ing disturbances in the Christian faith that decry unity in Christ.

The result? Splitting Christians into disunity and even chaos by making them insist that their ideas are the right ones to follow.

Paul wasn't talking about circumcision as a health practice, which some claim to be the rationale for it today, but he was vehemently against it as a means of sealing one's relationship with God. The Jewish practice of adding circumcision as a necessary element to the gospel of Christ instigated Paul's condemnation, an act for which he made no apology.

Christ Plus Additions -- A Mistake

We might ask why a little physical act like circumcision conflicts with belief in Jesus. Can't we have both? After all, the OT shows circumcision to be a sacred rite that Jews insisted on both for themselves as well as for the people they conquered. But with the rise of Christianity, the apostle Paul declared that OT Law and NT Grace have nothing to do with each other. In fact, they are incompatible, diametrically opposed. Otherwise, by combining the two we give little importance to Christ's sacrifice, which was all inclusive for our justification before God. In other words, our relationship with the Father is bound up in what the Son did for us, not in what we add to it. Paul went on to explain by saying, "I do not set aside the grace of God, for if righteousness could be gained through the law, Christ died for nothing" (Gal. 2:21). You see, Christianity is not something that comes about in one's life by keeping rules but rather by relying totally on Christ's sacrificial death. In essence, salvation is a gift, something free, given out of God's generosity, not something we earn by working at it.

OT Law centered around following rules and regulations, so Paul was saying that we should stop relying on personal performance to gain God's favor. Jesus Christ has stepped in to remove any attempts toward self effort by declaring totally clean and acceptable those who believe in him. It was to represent a total transformation of our lives, something done out of God's goodness, not through our own manipulation.

39

NT passages indicate that we place a severe limitation on Jesus' sacrificial death by adding to it, be it circumcision or whatever. It really amounts to depreciating his sacrifice and in effect repudiating God's graciousness through his grand design of Christ's atoning sacrifice.

To reiterate the passage's condemnation of those who "set aside the grace of God," it's critical to point out that by including OT law we actually restrict grace by failing to appreciate God's new covenant. The simplicity of grace for salvation is nothing to be toyed with, which is exactly what certain Jewish zealots were doing, pushing OT Law edicts on new Christians by making them think that belief in Jesus wasn't enough, that they had to do something extra. They were even adding their own twists in interpreting the rules of the Law. We see Christians in Galatia getting swallowed up in that controversy.

Again, I repeat, that the transition from law to grace was not an easy one for Jews who had been under OT law precepts all their lives. Paul, who had a miraculous encounter with Christ on the Damascus Road and whom God taught the radical new idea of grace, preached that a whole new era had begun, one of grace over legal requirements. The transition was not easy for Jews to follow, but according to Scripture it was necessary, and for non-Jews like me and probably you, too, it was a blessing. It amounted to God stepping in to change the scenario completely so that the entire world could be saved through faith alone without being put under edicts previously given to the Jewish nation.

By the way, faith, or belief, has always been the way to please God, even in the OT. Remember Scripture that said, "Abram believed the Lord, and he credited it to him as righteousness" (Gen. 15:6). Of course, belief means dedication to the message that God gives you, which underscores the genuineness of your belief. I suppose that's what Scripture is saying throughout the NT gospels about showing your fruit in accord with what you believe.

Applying that to Jesus Christ, we see that God wanted to rescue humanity from its sinful state in the simplest way possible -- through faith in his Son. As we shall see later, that sacrifice on the part of Jesus unfortunately wielded such an impact as to cause him indescribable grief, suffering, and death. But, thank God, He went through with it out of love for his creation and his obedience to the Father.

Paul wanted Galatian Christians to rest in Christ's sacrifice rather than in following after OT edicts. Circumcision was one aspect of OT Law that Paul singled out that Galatian Christians were misusing, but he also referred to other Jewish rules they were inclined to hold on to: "You are observing special days and months and seasons and years." They must have been doing that as an addition to salvation in Christ, because he went on to say, "I fear for you, that somehow I have wasted my efforts on you" (Gal. 4:10-11). But no matter what OT elements they brought up, circumcision was the big one they felt obligated to keep.

There's nothing wrong with circumcision, a common practice today in the United States with newborn males. But OT Jews practiced it in obedience to God's OT command and, of course, to identify themselves as God's chosen people. Christians in Galatia mistakenly picked up on that idea, probably thinking it would improve their stead with God beyond belief in Christ. Little did they realize that Jesus' sacrificial work on the cross was not only sufficient to seal a godly relationship, but it was a complete and exclusive way, in fact, the only way (John 14:6). The beauty of it is that it included women who can't be circumcised as are men. We wonder why first-century Christians in Galatia didn't give attention to that fact. We are all one through our faith in Christ. The act of circumcision has nothing to do with it. Scripture tells us that we are neither male nor female in Christ, but that we are one! (Gal. 3:28). That's the way God looks on us and wants us to esteem one another.

Old Testament Law and Slavery

So Paul chastised them and even slammed OT Law as interfering with NT Grace. In fact, he argued that the Law contradicted Christian freedom with its tight rule-keeping system. Freedom from what? Freedom from a constant barrage of questioning as to whether we are doing enough to satisfy God. Emphasizing that freedom theme, Paul asked, "how is it that you are turning back to those weak and miserable principles? Do you wish to be enslaved by them all over again?" (Gal. 4:9).

"Weak and miserable principles?" "Enslavement?" Why would he use such derogatory language about OT Law? He did so because anyone trying to use the law code for gaining divine favor would be making a big mistake; it repudiated God's redemptive plan through Christ. When we do that we become bent on demonstrating self-effort, which the OT Law is all about and which is completely contrary to NT grace as a gift. No wonder Paul referred to the Law's make-up as "weak and miserable principles." Compared to the wonders of NT grace, there was no contest.

OT Law was God's temporary measure to keep sinful man under control. NT grace is final, sealing our salvation once and for all as a gift out of God's generosity. It's an act initiated exclusively by God, one that tells us to stop trying to make additions. In other words, stop trying to add to Christ's sacrifice by suggesting pious actions to perform. Salvation is free. We can't pay for it or work for it. It's a gift!

Application to Us

Beginning from the fist century onward, people have been making additions to Christian living. Today we find many well-meaning Christians doing the same thing, propagating rules to be followed that on the surface may appear complementary to Christianity but at the same time are befuddling and contrary to God's new covenant. They are often additions taken from OT Law, like mandatory giving of a tithe, or keeping holy days such as the strict OT Sabbath rule, even though they may both complement the church's function today and therefore be judged worthwhile.

Don't get me wrong. Giving financially to the work of the ministry and taking a day of rest are certainly laudatory traits. Where we go wrong is to pull those concepts from the OT to legitimize them as practices we are commanded to follow if we are serious about salvation or even serious about following Christian principles after salvation. Some throw a burden of guilt on people who disagree with following OT concepts. They often do that by quoting the demands of OT Law practices on tithing, for example, as follows:

Will a man rob God? Yet you rob me. But you ask, 'How do we rob you?' In tithes and offerings. You are under a curse – the whole nation of you -- because you are robbing me. Bring the whole tithe into the storehouse, that there may be food in my house. Test me in this, says the Lord Almighty, and see if I will not throw open the floodgates of heaven and pour out so much blessing that you will not have room enough for it (Mal. 3:8-10).

Church members' amen's and other enthusiastic shouts of approval whipped up by this emotional appeal are still ringing in my ears as I think back on my early days as a Christian. "It's God's word," they said. "We are obligated to follow it." What's wrong with this scenario? The congregation hadn't been trained, as Paul instructed Timothy, to correctly handle the word of truth (2 Tim. 2:15). As long as it's in the Bible, we've got to follow it, was their assertion. Context, in terms of whom the passage addresses, wasn't considered. Unfortunately, as a young impressionable believer, I got caught up in it to follow after its dictates.

Look again at the OT passage. It speaks of robbing God, and as a result being cursed, both of which are totally contrary to NT teaching. Being true to the Malachi passage, if you don't go along with its demand on giving, you are apt to experience shame, guilt, and condemnation for theft from God. Who wants to steal from God and lose out on his blessings? We have got to stop citing OT passages as pertinent to the NT when context shows them to be directed toward a specific group of people under a different covenant. Unfortunately, some today don't follow that truth, even some pastors and evangelists, which is indeed unfortunate because of the esteem we often give them. We do not have the freedom to chose which OT laws to follow. Scripture declares them all to be invalid under the new covenant unless they are reiterated in that covenant. Unfortunately, we allow other factors to offset that teaching, especially those ingrained in us from childhood, or perhaps those that we somehow defend as being appropriate to follow throughout life. We must come to grips with the fact that OT rules are cancelled, no longer in effect.

God's New Pact

What's all this talk, then, about a new pact? It deals with Jesus establishing a new covenant between God and humanity through his death on the cross. But we make the mistake of interpreting his cross-related effort only in terms of salvation, not the Christian life that follows. To be sure, salvation is the primary reason for Jesus' death, a fact that the NT speaks to exclusively in terms of faith.

A man is not justified by observing the Law, but by faith in Jesus Christ . . . by observing the law . . . no one will be justified. I do not set aside the grace of God, for if righteousness could be gained through the law, Christ died for nothing (Gal. 2:16, 21).

That passage makes it clear how God justifies us. Did you realize that the OT covenant established through Moses is no longer useful for maintaining a life acceptable to God, that it has been replaced by a new covenant? The writer of Hebrews backs up this change when he said, "By calling the covenant 'new,' he has made the first one obsolete; and what is obsolete and aging will soon disappear"(8:13). Will soon disappear? Does that mean that the Law would cease as a requirement for sealing a relationship with God? The NT declares that to be exactly what happened, bringing into being God's new plan for humanity through Christ.

Would to God that we would stop making Christians feel guilty by imposing certain OT rules on them that God has now declared invalid.

Erroneous Decision-Making

When some people hear these words, they feel threatened. Some even say, "If I don't have to follow OT commands, I guess I can do anything I want, which means that I don't even need to follow the generally accepted system of moral behavior advanced by the Ten Commandments." Some first-century Christians must have been saying the same thing, kind of like believing that since grace covers all sins we might as well take advantage of it by indulging in selfish behavior. Paul's reaction was, "Shall we go on sinning so that grace may increase? By no means! We died to sin; how can we live in it any longer?" (Rom. 6:1-2). You see, becoming a Christian is a transforming act resulting in a new way of living, one that exudes God rather than our own selfish desires. But I suppose that there will always be some who claim a belief in God but at the same time hold that they are not bound by restrictions as to how they should live.

We should note that those moral laws (the Ten Commandments) aren't to be completely chucked; they are repeated in one form or another in the NT for our benefit (except that of keeping the Sabbath as a holy day as peculiarly prescribed in the OT). We follow certain moral principles cited in the OT because they are a part of NT living, not because they are demanded by OT Law. Furthermore, we keep them because they infer a morality that we recognize as necessary for human relations. Who, for example, would not attest to the importance of honoring our parents? Neither would we agree to murder, adultery, stealing, lying, or coveting someone's possessions. Those OT concepts carry over to Christian living by being inscribed in God's new covenant, the NT which is governed by love.

We are not talking about ceasing from godly living. Both the OT as well as the NT give us plenty of ideas on setting our lives aright, behaviors we recognize as common sense for our own welfare. But what's critical is that we don't assume that certain OT commands are for us to apply when they're not endorsed in the morality of the NT.

When it comes to salvation, there's no contest between OT Law and NT Grace. And when it comes to Christian living after salvation, neither is there any contest between the two. God, in his good judgment, saw what was necessary for a Christian life-style by including it in the NT. Or do you think that God initiated a new covenant without explaining the demise of the old covenant?

Perverting the Gospel

Surely there have to be things we must do to please God in order to get eternal life or even to prove that we now have eternal life, we contend. That's the human way of thinking, that in some way we have to pay for something given us. We have company in that regards. Converts in Galatia and certain first-century Jewish Christians thought the same as they started tacking on requirements to the salvation process. Why did they want to complicate it?

We have a bad habit of adding things to salvation to make it more meaningful, as if to say that God allows us to rely on our wisdom to make salvation more sustainable. Some Jewish Christians influenced Galatians believers to start incorporating OT rules into their lives as necessary for salvation. Why not listen to them? the Galatians must have argued. Who knows better than God's chosen people to say how to direct godly living?

Well, they were mistaken. When Paul found out about it he told them, "I am astonished that you are so quickly deserting the one who called you by the grace of Christ" (Gal. 1:6). Deserting

Christ? What was it that they were doing wrong? They were applying circumcision as well as other OT mandates to a Christian lifestyle, all of which NT writers denounced as a perversion of the gospel. The gospel pure and simple is grace, which means that nothing can be added to it, no matter how good it sounds. It's something God does for us, not what we do for ourselves. All we have to do is receive it, and to do so seriously, with hearts of genuine appreciation.

How grateful we are to Paul, who learned of the special privilege of grace through revelation from God. He revealed that special gospel of grace in Ephesians, Chapter 3 as well as in Colossians when he said,

I have become its servant by the commission God gave me to present to you the word of God in its fullness -- the mystery that has been kept hidden for ages and generations, but is now disclosed to the saints. To them God has chosen to make known among the Gentiles the glorious riches of this mystery. which is Christ in you, the hope of glory (Col. 1:25-27).

Other NT writers, under the inspiration of the Spirit, agreed with him and preached the identical message.

Personal Application

Let's not make the mistake of seeing the error of some first century believers who circumvented grace without looking at ourselves. Talking only about erroneous practices of converts in Galatia can make us miss application to our own lives. Do we add to the salvation message, perhaps not intentionally but maybe in more subtle ways? For example, we may think we need to make the process clearer, still holding on to faith as a requisite but adding components to give it an air of genuineness.

So we resort to OT rules and regulations and even to practices we ourselves invent to lead us in the direction of what we consider holy living (remembrances of my early Christian days in which all kinds of man-made rules were placed on me). Yes, we have a bad habit of determining what we consider logical thinking as to the right way to live. How do you suppose God regards our efforts after providing a generous way of escape from our sinful condition? I repeat: it's a provision orchestrated completely by God, not something we add to. Accepting it as such, we orient our lives around living for God, not because *we have to* but because *we want to*. And we don't feel guilty over our failings, simply because God's salvation through Christ is unconditional, not in any way depending on our merits.

Legalism

As a young Christian I attended a church that was steeped in legalistic practices consisting of imposing OT Law practices as well as human-concocted notions on what was considered holy living. It gave a frightening view of Christianity. Do this and do that, or don't do this or don't do that, all of which was human-engineered, resulting in making life miserable for those who fell under its concocted rules. It amounted to prohibiting such things, for example, as movies, dancing, attending and participating in sport's events on Sunday, and even denouncing a day at the beach for a Sunday afternoon of swimming and relaxation. It was as if they were saying that you were not to have fun as a Christian, especially on Sunday.

Those are just starters. How many other man-made concoctions were imposed that supposedly were anathema for a spiritually-oriented Christian? I fell under that church's spell and as a consequence ended up as one very miserable Christian. What behaviors were to be performed? -- rules that would supposedly prove one's Christian sincerity. Who would take issue of them as good ways to live? It was as if God expected us to obey them simply because they were cited in the OT or that they were rules that religious people made up and gave some sort of relationship to the Bible. We failed to recognize them as OT rules designed for Jews to keep or even rules concocted by well- meaning but mistaken Christians.

That took place in the 1940s. Impose those requirements on Christians today and you will get reactions of unbelief that anyone would even have given ear to such regulations. But don't kid yourself; it's being done today. We pluck out of the OT certain rules that we think are spiritually legitimate simply because they are in the Bible. We even make up our own rules to follow because they in some way or another relate to OT edicts or to behaviors we devise that on the surface may seem to make sense but are absolutely contrary to the simplicity of God's new covenant plan of grace through Christ.

What's God's critical message in all of this? Stop applying OT regulations to NT Christianity, and even inferring certain practices to be followed that we ourselves have concocted. We justify them, like tithing, for example, a pervasive OT requirement (Lev. 27:30-34) that many churches and evangelical leaders foist on Christians in order to meet budgetary expenditures concocted out of human reasoning. Yes, we dream up all sorts of ways to minister Christianity to the world and then look to our congregations to pay for them even to the point of creating guilt feelings among people who don't or can't tithe. But we do it subtly by spiritualizing on it. On one hand we say, "The Lord will provide," while on the other we stigmatize our congregations into believing that it's their duty to support the ministry with their monetary giving, and of top of it insisting on a strict ten-percent rule of the OT. The latter, of course, insures a steady flow to the church's coffers to meet the church's expenditures concocted by humans. Sometimes we even make bizarre claims, like God telling us to initiate a certain kind of ministry no matter the financial cost and then pushing people to pay for it in spite of its hardship on them. Who's going to question that, especially when such a pronouncement comes from the clergy?

We can't argue about how money contributes to the work of the ministry, but when it comes to requiring a tithe, a strict ten percent, as was done in the OT, we are inserting our own ideas and giving them spiritual significance even though they are not even mentioned in the NT for us to follow. But if you are stuck on following them out of loyalty to the OT, you have got some radical revisions to make about Christian living. I repeat what I said earlier, that whether we are talking about salvation or about Christian living thereafter, we do not have the option of plucking ideas from the OT to apply to Christianity no matter how hard we try to justify it.

A good measuring stick is to insist on behaviors supported by NT Scripture. As for tithing, we won't find it as a NT principle. Instead, we are admonished to give cheerfully and as much as we are able. "Each man should give what he has decided in his heart to give" (2 Cor. 9:7). That means contributing as God moves us, which can result in giving enormous amounts simply because of being convinced of the importance and neediness of the situation. We seem to be stuck on a stipulated amount we are obligated to give, as if ten percent were a magic formula to follow today. Giving cheerfully and generously is what the NT proclaims as we allow God to communicate his will in meeting whatever be the need. We must come to grips with the fact that all our monetary resources are given us by God. So we hold nothing back, but we give freely in accordance with the Spirit's leading, not out of duty as instigated by someone's urging.

Combining Testaments -- A Misrepresentation

The OT is the Jewish scripture that contains the Mosaic Law found in the last four books of the Pentateuch (Exodus, Leviticus, Numbers, and Deuteronomy). We print the OT in our Bibles along with the NT to form a single tome as a handy volume of spiritual thought, and maybe even for publishers to facilitate sales (putting it all together under one cover to make it more attractive). Unfortunately, many who read the Bible fail to recognize the distinctiveness of the two divisions, which results in a failure to determine whom a given portion of the Bible addresses.

There's a tendency to assume that all of the Bible's writings are applicable to us today. Realizing it or not, by taking that approach we twist the simplicity of God's grace, as if to say, "Look God, we're merely applying your sacred words to life in Christ." So we end up applying OT rules to NT living by spiritualizing on them as appropriate no matter their contextual restrictions.

It's a common practice. "After all, the Bible, including OT and NT, is God's holy Word," we say defensively. "Who's going to diminish the importance of the OT? It must be upheld," we say. We may have come to understand how deplorable it is to take such a stance in connection with God granting us salvation, but when it comes to spiritual living after salvation we often uphold the OT as necessary to stringently follow.

The New Covenant and Christ's Death

The new covenant, brought about through Jesus' crucifixion, wasn't yet a reality during Jesus' early years on earth. Jesus talked about the crucifixion with the Twelve just prior to his death, as you will recall him lifting the cup of wine and saying, "This is my blood of the *covenant* which is poured out for many for the forgiveness of sins" (emphasis mine) (Matt. 26:28). He was referring to the New Covenant (New Testament) that He would institute shortly thereafter through his death. In fact, his coming death on the cross seems to have affected him to such an extent that He referred to it at various times during his public ministry. But it all seemed to go in one ear and out the other among his disciples. They didn't know what He was talking about, and even though not understanding, they were reluctant to ask for an explanation. They were looking to Jesus, the Messiah, to establish a new age in which He would rule the world. They saw the brutality of the crucifixion in erasing their hopes, but later they saw its beauty in saving mankind. Looking to Jesus to establish a kingdom over which He would reign on earth was perfectly okay. They just had the timing wrong.

The Cross – the Dividing Point

The NT's beginning, then? The Cross! It's important to remember it as the dividing line between the OT and the NT in order to keep things straight as to what belongs to the old covenant and what belongs to the new. It will cause us to read the gospels carefully, especially the synoptic gospels (Matthew, Mark, and Luke) to determine if we are to apply any pre-cross teachings of those gospels to us directly.

Also important to keep in mind is that OT Law, although God's Holy Word, had severe limitations; it was given to a special people for a limited time period. Paul underscored that principle by saying that the Law "was added because of transgressions until the Seed to whom the promise referred had come" (Gal. 3:19). The word "until" carries important implications. Let's analyze.

OT Law had a certain timeline -- until the Seed had come. The "Seed" was Jesus, the Messiah, promised way back in OT Scripture written hundreds of years B.C., which by the way, gives authenticity to the salvation story if for no other reason that it was predicted hundreds of years before it actually came to pass. It was Jesus, the Son of God, who initiated and fulfilled the new covenant of grace that voided OT Law. But we have to come to grips with the timing in which it took place.

OT Law was in operation until the Seed annulled it. Jesus did that, not by his birth, as some are inclined to think, but by his death. That differentiation in itself will clear up a lot of problems between Christian principles and OT Law. Through his crucifixion Jesus ended the Law (the old covenant) and introduced grace (the new covenant). As I have emphasized before, it's important to note that Jesus did it through his death (Luke 22:20), not his birth, or by anything else that He spoke about to inter-testament Jews who at that time were obligated to follow OT Law.

We tend to mix the two events -- Jesus' birth and his death -- as we celebrate Christmas and Easter, with emphasis on the former probably because it relays a beautiful picture of the birth of a child rather than the ugliness of death and sufferings of a man. But Jesus' birth and his life up to the time of his crucifixion were technically a part of the OT, which means that we must be careful not to attribute everything that was mentioned in that time period as NT doctrine. It was the latter, Christ's death and resurrection, that was the cutting off point that sealed our relationship with God and that teaches us about the Christian lifestyle.

By the way, the adjectives "old" and "new" that describe the covenants (testaments) in themselves are instructive. The "old" covenant is antiquated, no longer useful for the new life in Christ, having become obsolete and replaced by the "new." The writer of Hebrews uses that vocabulary to contrast the two covenants. "By calling this covenant 'new,' he has made the first one obsolete; and what is obsolete and aging will soon disappear" (8:13). It's a critical reference to keep in mind lest we ever get carried away with the idea that we can work our way into heaven, or at least keep in God's good graces by keeping rules and regulations of the old covenant.

The Gift of Salvation

Let it sink in! Salvation is a gift to bring us out of sin's captivity. There's nothing we can do to earn it; it's absolutely free of charge. That was undoubtedly the intention of the writers of the NT epistles when they referred to the great salvation effectuated by Christ. For example, Paul wrote to the Ephesians saying, "In him we have received redemption through his blood, the forgiveness of sins, in accordance with the riches of God's grace that he lavished on us with all wisdom and understanding" (1:7-8). In other words, the idea of God reaching down to us to cancel our inherited sinfulness is really beyond human understanding. Making us right without requiring anything on our part sounds preposterous, I know, but it underscores God's great love for his creation, a truly merciful act for which we should be ever grateful.

That's God's response to the question of sin that has befuddled humanity throughout the ages. He knew we weren't responsible for Adam and Eve's disobedience. Nevertheless, their sin, conspicuously carried over to every human being thereafter, needed to be dealt with. How did God do it? -- through his Son, Jesus, who went through the agony of the Cross and the misery preceding it in order to cleanse us from our inherited sinful condition.

All of this means that on receiving God's gift of salvation we undergo a fantastic change that previously we might not have deemed possible. God creates a radical revision in us, and we concur by following after his ways, which is a two-way street -- God and us working together to produce a new person.

Through the ugliness of my past legalistic experiences, I have determined never to impose or even suggest a legalistic requirement on another Christian. I do not have the authority to exert my will on anyone, even though it might have the flavor of a godly principle to follow.

OT Law Diminished

Christ's crucifixion brought about an astounding result -- *the cancellation of the Law* (Col. 2:13). NT writers viewed that act as extremely important as they saw so much negativity connected to it in its meritorious emphasis on doing good deeds. We see that as we look at some of their descriptors that pronounce the Law as: *temporary* (**Gal. 3:19**); *fading* (**2 Cor. 3:11**); *a barrier of hostility* (**Eph. 2:11-15**); *weak and useless* (**Heb. 7:18**); *weak and miserable principles* (**Gal. 4:9**); *enslaving* (**Gal. 4:9***); a burden and a yoke of slavery* (**Gal. 5:1**); *changed* (**Heb. 7:12**); *obsolete* (**Heb. 8:13**); and finally, *cancelled* (**Col. 2:13**).

Can you believe it? Such a battery of negatives about OT Law? Tough language about a set of rules that many churches foist on their members today. It's because of confusion between covenants. If it's in the Bible, they mistakenly contend, it's for us to obey. Context is pushed aside to give way to performing as prescribed by OT edicts, which amounts to a frightening requirement of self-effort.

We may see Paul as being pretty cruel in the way he talked about OT Law. He did it with a clear objective in mind -- to contrast it with the sheer beauty of new covenant grace. There was no comparison between covenants, and Paul came right out saying, "by observing the law no one will be justified" (Gal. 2:16). Why did he say that? Some of the Christians in Galatia were being influenced by certain recently converted and well-meaning Jews to start keeping the rules and regulations of their Law, as if those rules were still in place. Yes, they believed in Christ as their redeemer, but they tacked on other requirements as if to give authenticity to salvation.

When Christians play around with adding rules to grace, either their own or those of the OT, they set themselves up for all kinds of gospel twisting. Make one addition to faith, no matter how innocent it appears, and the ball keeps rolling to add others. It's like yeast, Paul said (Gal. 5:9). It spreads. Christians should be aware of it, otherwise we end up proclaiming a gospel full of rules and regulations that contradict God's gift of grace. That's what Satan, our adversary wants, because it's a misdirection of God's love.

We see that in its extreme in churches that emphasize a social gospel; that is, those that use nice sounding words about love and good works while at the same time fail to emphasize acceptance of Christ's sacrifice as the sole means of salvation to set us aright. But then, that's another gospel-twisting act that humans often undertake as they emphasize a social gospel at the expense of salvation. Somehow, the simplicity of salvation seems to be pushed aside to make way for a more intellectual approach, one that lauds human reasoning above divine direction.

The idea of trying to be a good person has constantly influenced human beings as the way to God. Ask people at random what they think will get them into heaven. Unless they are well informed biblically they will probably cite living a good life as the requirement. We can refer to that idea as a merit principle that has governed our lives since childhood. We have learned that we get what we work for, which is merit, and we think that God operates by the same system by rewarding us with salvation if we orchestrate our lives around being good. By so doing we overlook grace that the Bible defines as a gift from God. Being a gift, it's free, but at a great price for the giver, Jesus Christ, who suffered humiliation, torture, abuse, and death on the cross. (Do you remember his suffering and sorrow in the Garden of Gethsemane prior to his capture?) It was truly a horrendous experience. But He went through with it for our sake.

Christianity in the Bible

Where will we find Christianity defined in the Bible? Especially in the parts whose context is post-cross. That underscores the critical nature of the Crucifixion and the epistles that explain its accomplishment. We will also find Christian principles in John's gospel, especially standing out in Chapters 14 through 16 where the apostle shows Jesus teaching about the glorious new era to come that He would bring about through his death. That portion of John's gospel records Jesus speaking of such critical issues as: heaven ("I am going there to prepare a place for you" -- 14:2); his exclusivity ("I am the way and the truth and the life. No one comes to the Father except through me" -- 14:6); and, the coming Holy Spirit who will direct in matters of truth ("when he, the Spirit of truth comes, he will guide you into all truth" -- 16:13).

Of course, John's gospel contains other critical messages about Christianity, perhaps most widely cited are those in Chapter 3: "No one can see the kingdom of God unless he is born again" (v. 3); and of course, the very familiar verse that many of us learned in Sunday school -- "For God so loved the world that he gave his one and only Son, that whoever believes in him shall not perish but have eternal life" (v. 16).

We relish such passages, but at the same time understand that we can get into big trouble by applying others that run contrary to grace, even though Jesus spoke of them to his Jewish audience. See, for example, Luke 18:18-21, where a man asked how to inherit eternal life, to which Jesus replied by telling him to keep the commandments and to perform good deeds. What? Do good works in order to get to heaven? Not a surprising declaration if we keep in mind the context in which Jesus was speaking to a Jew still under OT Law. Unfortunately, some take it to mean living an exemplary life in order to attain heaven.

It's important to understand that the new covenant message of grace had not yet become a reality since Jesus had not yet been crucified. That's why we must keep in mind that *although all Scripture is for us, it's not necessarily to us,* which means that although benefiting from the OT and pre-cross teachings in numerous ways we would be making a major error applying everything therein as addressed to us, as if it were God's inviolable message. In other words, we are not always the object of its declarations.

Jesus' message to the Jewish inquirer was appropriate. The man was to keep the rules of the Law, since Jesus' crucifixion had not yet come about. The OT was still in force, and he was obligated to follow it. Surely he saw the beauty of the gospel and gave thanks when Christ was crucified and resurrected, and when the Holy Spirit revealed the simplicity of the gospel of grace by which everyone can be saved. Whether the man was still living at the time of Christ's death, we trust God to decide his status. In other words, we let God decide as He understood the man's heart.

In many ways we can learn from the Bible, but we must take care to apply it in its proper context. Critical questions to ask are: Who's the passage addressing, and why, and under what circumstances? In other words, context is critical. We use context to understand statements people make in dealing with one another in today's society, yet how important it is to apply context when it comes to understanding the Bible.

The Bible, a sacred book written to reveal God's involvement with humanity, is not designed only for Christians; it reflects two religions -- one for OT Jews, and the other for NT followers of Jesus Christ. Did God expect us to mix the two? Not in terms of salvation or even in terms of Christian living. In no way would He be happy with our perverting his all important message on how to get eternal life? And how about the Christian life thereafter? The message is a simple one that encompasses grace, which is a gift that God gives us out of great compassion for us his created beings. But dear reader, please remember what I said earlier lest you denounce me as being anti-Old Testament. The OT portion of our Bibles is an invaluable tool in support of Christianity, as it contains so many good things that we profit by, especially the re-inforcement it renders in terms of the Messiah who was fulfilled by Jesus Christ. As I reported earlier, the OT is full of gems about God's graciousness.

At one time we floundered about, not knowing how to please God. But then came the gospel of grace that we received through faith alone and that freed us from performing. Self-effort be-came a thing of the past, which is good, because as I've said so frequently, salvation is a gift, not something we earn by doing things, no matter how well-intentioned they be. In fact, we know our limitations in that we can't perform enough to merit God's blessing of eternal life.

The Bible, then, is a book of two religions, Judaism and Christianity. To apply it judiciously to our lives we will want to separate the two religions in order to uphold and respect Christianity with all the vigor we can muster. To do otherwise is to cause splits among fellow believers to give Satan leeway to denigrate the gospel of Christ.

DISCUSSION GUIDE

1. The Bible contrasts two covenants (testaments) – OT Law (issued through Moses) and NT Grace (brought about through Jesus Christ). How does the printing of the two covenants in one single tome of the Bible adversely affect the way we often see those covenants pertaining to Christianity?

2. Although the old covenant is cancelled by the new covenant in Christ, how can the OT be of use to us as Christians? Cite ways in which it can be helpful.

3. Why do you suppose Jewish converts in the first century held onto OT concepts and even influenced Gentile Christians to do the same?

4. What do you think was the rationale for Jewish converts in retaining the OT command of circumcision? Why was Paul vehemently against it as a requirement for salvation? How does he even cite circumcision as being a gender-related concept that has no business being attached to Christianity?

5. Where did Paul get the idea of the critical nature of grace over legal requirements? Can you suggest when God made that clear to him?

6. What other ideas did Christians in Galatia hold that made Paul say that he might have wasted his efforts on them?

7. Cite some ways that Christians can become legalistic either by transferring OT concepts to Christian living or by inventing their own spiritually sounding rules. Has this affected you personally in any way?

8. Which one of the Ten Commandments is not mentioned in the NT for Christians to keep? Can you suggest any reason why that commandment might yield practical results in our lives apart from being an OT commandment? Would you consider it a strict law for us to keep in accord with OT concepts? Why, or why not?

9. How do we recognize one's true commitment to salvation in Christ? What's the dividing line between performing legalistically and living a life governed by Christ?

10. Suggest some misconceived efforts in Christian living that diminish the effects of grace.

11. What's wrong with saying, "If it's in the Bible it's for us to follow?" Why do you suppose some Christians follow that line of reasoning?

12. We often interpret the start-up of Christianity by referring to Christ's birth, such as the Christmas story. Why is this a bad way to interpret Scripture for salvation as well as for the Christian life thereafter? What implications does it suggest for interpreting the gospels in the NT portions of our Bibles?

13. Why is the Gospel of John different from the three Synoptic Gospels regarding applicability to Christianity? Cite some instances in the Gospel of John that are directly applicable to life in Christ.

III.

WORSHIP

Five

ACKNOWLEDGING CHRIST'S SUFFERINGS –

APPRECIATING HIS LOVE

W e often think of Christ's sufferings only in terms of his cross death, but this chapter enlarges on that idea by citing instances in which Christ underwent several types of suffering preceding the cross that had an impact on his life. He accepted it for our sake, which gives us a greater appreciation of what He had to bear. But first we must consider grace, because that was the overriding feature behind it.

Grace and Salvation

Grace is a critical word for understanding God's message through Christ. It carries such import that NT writers were divinely inspired to refer repeatedly to grace. In fact, they used it more than one hundred times to declare God's critical message to humanity -- a pronouncement affecting our eternal destiny as well as our well-being on earth. If we are to show appreciation for anything given us by God, it's to acknowledge the meaning of grace.

The Bible defines grace as unmerited favor from God. Unmerited? Yes, it rules out self-effort simply because of its gift orientation. No one accepts a gift and the good-heartedness of the donor and then tries to pay for it. A gift means that the object associated with it is free, which says that the giver expects nothing in return, except maybe a show of gratitude by being thanked, which indeed reveals one's seriousness in accepting Jesus' gift of eternal life.

That's exactly how grace is measured. It's a gift from God that we receive with gratitude as shown by our changed lives. You will remember what Scripture says about the transformation that takes place as we receive God's gift through Christ – "Therefore, if anyone is in Christ, he is a new creation; the old has gone, the new has come!" (2 Cor. 5:17).

Our worship of the Almighty revolves around God's grace as we acknowledge what Christ went through on our behalf, which is a prime reason for our worship as we recognize the effect of Christ's sacrifice on our eternal destiny. How grateful we are for the gift of grace and its accompanying salvation, but at the same time we acknowledge the painful suffering and humiliation that affected Jesus in ways even beyond the cross.

Let's delve into that suffering. It will remind us of God's overwhelming goodness that we may frequently fail to acknowledge. Remembering what Christ went through will cause us to honor and adore him more than ever before.

The Suffering Jesus

One of the painful ways that affected Jesus was the thought of his oncoming death. It troubled him so much that He asked the Father to lift it as a requirement. (Do you remember his pleading with the Father in the Garden of Gethsemane?) But regardless of its horrors, He obediently completed the task because He knew it would usher in a new era for humanity to have a way out of its sinful dilemma.

Can you imagine, God wanting to shower his love on us to the extent of offering his own Son on our behalf? To drive home the message, think about sacrificing your own child (remembrance of Abraham's turmoil when instructed to sacrifice his only son Isaac as a burnt offering). As we reflect on the horrors that Jesus went through to fulfill his Father's wishes, we get a better appreciation of what He endured on our behalf. It was a sacrifice to restore our position with God, the Father.

Jesus' preoccupations over his coming death were frequent. When speaking to the Pharisees He said, "For as Jonah was three days and three nights in the belly of a huge fish, so the Son of Man will be three days and three nights in the heart of the earth" (Matt. 12:40). He didn't explain the meaning behind it, but it's implications to us now are obvious in that they show how death and suffering were so much on his mind. Looking back to the cross and then to his burial, we understand what He was talking about in saying He would be in the heart of the earth for three days. Then speaking plainly to his disciples He referred to being killed and on the third day being raised to life (Matt. 16:21). Likewise he told them of an incredible happening that was to come about.

> **'We are going to Jerusalem and the Son of Man will be betrayed to the chief priests and the teachers of the law. They will condemn him to death and will turn him over to the Gentiles to be mocked and flogged and crucified. On the third day he will be raised to life!' (Matt. 20:18-19).**

Apparently those words about horrendous mistreatment, dying, and being resurrected didn't register with the disciples, since they questioned among themselves what "raising from the dead" meant (Mark 9:10). Of course, it was an idea never confronting them before. They were mystified, failing to understand what Jesus was talking about. No wonder why they were frightened out of their minds when the Romans took Jesus prisoner and caused his abuse, humiliation, and crucifixion. All this talk that Jesus had made about his Father and about being the Father's Son, and then about establishing a kingdom on earth . . . none of it failed to make any sense to them now that Jesus was talking about dying. They were baffled over why the Son of God would talk about dying simply because they were expecting him to be the Messiah of the OT who was to establish the kingdom for Israel (Acts 1:6). They were hoping that Jesus would change the whole scenario and usher in that glorious new age. I suppose that's the reason why so many Jews (OT as well as those even today) reject Christ as the Messiah. They were expecting a conquering Messiah who would establish a glorious kingdom reign on the earth.

It was common for the apostles to think in that manner, but enlightenment came through the Holy Spirit after his death, resurrection, and departure to heaven. It's obvious that they didn't understand Jesus' atoning sacrifice on the cross, as seen in the behavior of Judas Iscariot, and even of Peter who denied him as well as Thomas who doubted Jesus' resurrection and who had to be given stark evidence of its truth by Jesus himself. (Do you remember Jesus telling Thomas to put his fingers in the holes of his hands?)

We may think that Jesus spoke of his coming death as if it were nothing special. But it seemed to be a theme continuously on his mind, apparently haunting him throughout his public ministry. It was a bitter thought He had to live with, one that tore him up terribly. We see his depressed mental state especially in the Garden of Gethsemane just prior to his crucifixion when He told his disciples, "'My soul is overwhelmed with sorrow to the point of death. Stay here and keep watch with me'" (Matt. 26:38), He pleaded. "Going a little further, he fell with his face to the ground and prayed, 'My Father, if it is possible, may this cup be taken from me . . . '" (v.39). Plummeting his face to the ground showed what great anguish He suffered. Why was He experiencing such things? For two reasons: (1) having taken on an earthly body He was overwhelmed with the thought of the physical horrors awaiting him -- the flogging, the jeers, the mental and physical pain (we can share that feeling as we think of us suffering in the same way); and, (2) as the Son of God He was distraught over the idea of taking on himself everyone's sins. Maybe that latter idea terrified him more than anything else. Think about it -- a sinless and perfect Son of God bearing your sins and mine. Sinless? Perfect? Not until we get to heaven will we completely understand the meaning behind those terms and what they meant for Jesus. No wonder He cried out to the Father that if possible there might be another way. It weighed heavily on him.

Who can understand the trauma that He, both divine and human, went through, one that insisted on him being infected with the sins of the entire world? Here was Jesus Christ, God, the eternal one, Creator of the Universe, becoming subject to the wickedness of his adversary, Satan. I suspect that we are unable to grasp the horrors of his capitulating to Satan. It makes us appreciate his willingness to do it, and all for *our* benefit.

The horrors of the crucifixion seemed to be constantly on Jesus' mind as seen in his statement, "'I have a baptism to undergo, and how distressed I am until it is completed!'" (Luke 12:50). He wasn't talking about water baptism (which He had undergone earlier with John the Baptist) but rather his death on the cross as seen also in his words, "'Now my heart is troubled, and what shall I say? Father save me from this hour? No, it was for this very reason I came to this hour. Father, glorify your name!'" (John 12:27).

The Father responded with words of comfort and encouragement, which Scripture says were heard even by the crowd surrounding Jesus. I am sure that the Father in no way was happy about what his Son was about to undergo. But He knew of its extensive benefit – canceling the sins of every human being who will accept it. It was God's way of restoring humanity. Wow! Thank you, Lord, because we recognize death as the ultimate sacrifice one can give for another, which points to us to accept it or reject it, even as Scripture holds us accountable as to our decision.

He came to that which was his own [The Jews}, but his own did not receive him. Yet to all who received him, to those who believed in his name, he gave the right to become children of God (John 1:11-12).

The fact that Jesus was so preoccupied over his crucifixion indicates the awful burden He carried throughout his earthly ministry. We think of it only in terms of a time lapse of some three years (the time period of his earthly ministry), but it must have troubled him even earlier, for example, during his teens and then even in his twenties. As the Son of God, He knew his destiny.

We see how terribly it disturbed him when He defended himself before the Pharisees. "'When you have lifted up the Son of Man, then you will know that I am the one I claim to be . . .'" (John 8:28). Of course, those Jewish leaders didn't understand what He was talking about when He said, "when you have lifted up the Son of Man." So you see, even though He didn't explain it (it came into focus for them after his resurrection), He couldn't rid himself of the thought of his impending crucifixion, an event that would cause some of the Jewish leaders ultimately to acknowledge his divinity.

Then we see Jesus again referring to his coming death when Mary poured expensive ointment on his feet. He said, "'It was intended that she should save this perfume for the day of my burial"' (John 12:7). So preoccupied was He over the frightful circumstances of his coming death that they seemed to haunt him at every turn.

Near the end of his ministry, Jesus sat with his disciples at what we call the Last Supper where He referred to the bread and wine as his body and blood, another reference to his coming death. The Last Supper took place just a few days before his crucifixion, and the disciples shared those elements with him without the slightest idea of the meaning Jesus was giving them. Recall how his disciples said, "'Where do you want us to make preparations for you to eat the Passover?'" (Matt. 26:17). Then at the table with the Twelve, He didn't refer to the Passover in Egypt (at least it's not recorded) but rather to his death, speaking of it in terms of his body and blood as symbolized by bread and wine (remembrance of the blood on the doorposts in Egypt as a sign for the death angel to pass by). His body and blood? The disciples didn't have a clue as to what He was talking about (their minds were undoubtedly occupied with the Passover in Egypt). But for Jesus, it summoned thoughts of his coming death experience at the hands of the Romans and spurred on by the chief priests.

Little did the Twelve know that their gathering together was a unique celebration of a new Passover, not one remembering God's rescue of the Jews in Egypt many years ago, but rather an event that would shake up the disciples as never before, one involving the offering of God's grace to all of his creation. It was a new Passover in the sense of God passing over our sins through the blood sacrifice of his Son, the greatest event in the history of the world.

We see Jesus constantly referring to his crucifixion when no one seemed to grasp what he was talking about. Can you imagine having to suffer without receiving any comfort whatsoever from your closest friends? It wielded a profound effect on him, as the ugliness of his approaching death affected him to the point of despair. Imagine what was going through his mind. The various references we have seen about his consternation tell us of the great travail affecting him.

We tend to take those references lightly, as if death were something He as God should be able to handle easily. I don't think we realize what it meant for a sinless Jesus to take on the sins of humanity. It put Satan temporarily in charge, and worse yet it caused the Father to temporarily turn his back on his Son (do you remember his words on the cross, "My God, my God, why have you forsaken me?" -- Matt. 27:46). Why did He say that? He knew He must die to take on himself the sins of the world, so it was not strange at all for him to see his Father temporarily ignoring his present ordeal. The Father was insisting that the Son go through with the process, just as Scripture declares, "without the shedding of blood there is no forgiveness" (Heb. 9:22 and Lev. 17:11). But in the end, it turned out for the good -- rescue for you and for me from the clutches of Satan. His obedience resulted in the forgiveness of all our misdeeds, which makes us absolutely clean in Gods eyes. Remember his last words on the cross -- "It is finished," which meant that our rescue from our sinful state had now been provided. Jesus' ordeal of being a sin offering was over. He had obediently completed the task in spite of the toll it took on him.

Did you ever wonder why Jesus didn't explain to his disciples his repeated references to his crucifixion? He spoke of it often, but He didn't explain it. I suppose it was due to the fact that the concept of grace was so beyond their comprehension that no amount of explaining would have done any good. Steeped in an orientation of OT Law principles (good works), they were in no position to understand grace. You would think that as Jews they would recall the various OT scriptures pertaining to Messiah's death. But God ultimately revealed it to them for their joy after Christ's resurrection.

Jesus' Healing Ministry – Unjust Accusations

Another aspect of Jesus' suffering that we tend to take lightly is the accusations about his miracles being products of demonic powers. We might even sympathize with the crowd's questioning as our minds go back to Pharaoh's magicians duplicating some of the miracles that Moses and Aaron performed prior to the exodus from Egypt (Exodus 7:10-12). But fast forward to the first century when Jesus called their bluff by casting out a demon and then saying, "'Any kingdom divided against itself will be ruined, and a house divided against itself will fall. If Satan is divided against himself, how can his kingdom stand?'" .' (Luke 11:17-18). In other words, Satan is not about to work against himself. Jesus was saying that his miracles were authentic, acts of God, not of Satan. The testimony of the demons themselves is worth quoting: "demons came out of many people, shouting, 'You are the Son of God!'" (Luke 4:41). They knew who Jesus was.

Nevertheless, we seem to be impervious to the accusations that Jesus had to bear when healing people of their infirmities. Being accused of performing miracles by the power of Satan must have really hurt. How do you suppose He felt after healing the sick and then being accused of doing it by demonic power? It's one of the many incidents that the Son of God had to bear at the hands of his accusers, the teachers of the law.

Unfaithfulness – Jesus' Disciples

One other aspect that must have left its mark on him was the unfaithfulness of his close companions: Peter denying any association with him, probably to save himself from Roman incrimination; Thomas doubting that Jesus had risen from the grave; and, Judas betraying Jesus to the chief priests for a measly thirty pieces of silver. How must Jesus have felt over the failure of his close friends to stand with him in that dark hour before having to undergo the cross?

How you would feel if those close to you failed to stand up for you in your hour of trial. Can you imagine your thoughts if you were condemned to death and then having your friends scatter rather than stay there in your support? They are sufferings that Jesus underwent that we tend to overlook, or at least ones we give little importance to, yet surely not easy for him to bear. Our remembrance of them makes our worship more meaningful, because we recognize that he endured it all on our behalf.

We are overwhelmed by the thought of Jesus undergoing such attacks, especially when we consider that He did it in spite of the human frailties of supposed friends . . . all to carry out the Father's plan of salvation for humankind. We praise and worship him for what He suffered on our behalf -- false accusations, jeers, humiliation, mocking, floggings, and much more. Finally,

He endured the disgrace of being pinned to a cross and the pain accompanying it, which was an act of generosity on his part that causes us to be ever so grateful.

Certainly we have great reason to worship. It challenges us toward a willingness to suffer ourselves if it be God's will, while at the same time rejecting sinful ways in which we used to participate. Scripture speaks to us on this latter theme.

Therefore, since Christ suffered in his body, arm yourselves also with the same attitude, because he who has suffered in his body is done with sin. As a result, he does not live the rest of his earthly life for evil human desires but rather for the will of God (1 Peter 4:1-2).

We are challenged to take on ourselves such an attitude. Praise be to God for the power to do it. We worship and adore Jesus who made it possible through his willingness to fulfill the Father's will. May the thoughts about his sufferings enrich our time of worship, but let's never forget that He did it for our sake, a matter of crucial importance, lest we put emphasis on his sufferings per se rather than on their outcome – our salvation (his dying on our behalf) and his absolute divinity (supremacy over Satan as well as the weakness of his followers). What we don't want to do is to allow Jesus' sufferings to overshadow their actual purpose. But they can help us better appreciate how He endured the agony on our behalf. That's the critical point – He did it for our sake.

DISCUSSION GUIDE

1. Define grace, and tell why it's important to you personally.
2. Why do you think Jesus spoke of his impending death throughout his ministry?
3. What other kinds of suffering besides his crucifixion did Jesus have to endure?

Six

LIFTING HANDS IN WORSHIP –

A CONTEMPORARY CONTROVERSY

I take up the challenge of addressing this topic because of its widespread appeal in many churches today. Why do I see it as a controversy? It's a question that addresses a possible breach in our dedication to obey Scripture in maintaining unity, a matter that Jesus so fervently prayed about (see John 17). We may not have thought much about it before now, but disunity caused by the idea of lifting hands in the air during worship seems to be getting worse and needs addressing. Let me explain.

Lifting hands has become a popular addition to the worship scene for many Christians, not only in charismatic churches but in others as well. The problem is that it's beginning to cause friction between hand raisers and those who don't participate in it. When there's controversy, it diminishes the dynamism of Christianity, not only affecting us in our relations with one another but as it relates to onlookers as well.

Those who practice hand raising argue for its acceptance as meaningful; they claim it increases intimacy with God. Being spiritually stimulating, they say, it's an aid to worship. Usually taking place during singing, hand raising takes place when special thoughts of praise are engendered toward the Almighty, but oftentimes the practice is unpredictable, cropping up at any time a worshipper feels the urge to engage in it.

But before analyzing its controversial aspects, it's important to discuss the setting in which it takes place, for it's the setting that seems to contribute to the problem.

Praising God through Music

We see the full force of praise when churches initiate what they call a contemporary service from the more traditional type. The music of that contemporary service, centered almost exclusively around praise, seems to play heavily in the physical movements of the singing congregation. Through its emotional appeal, the music elicits hand raising, sometimes through lyrics that actually tell worshippers to lift their hands in the air. Not everyone, of course, does it, in fact, only a small minority in some services, but since it's an outward manifestation before others, the practice may become a problem.

In contrast, the traditional service involves hymn singing without a display of body movements. Emotionalism is certainly present, but without accompanying physical acts. So as a starting point, it's probably a good idea to analyze the music of both services, traditional and contemporary, to see its effect on worshippers.

The Traditional Service

The music in this service deals with a vast number of different themes. Here are a just a few of them that I readily recall: 1) a challenge to live the Christ life; 2) God's sovereignty; 3) petitioning; 4) trusting; and, 5) yearning for heaven. I list off the top of my head a number of hymns that I remember pertaining to each category.

   A. Challenge to Live the Christ life.
     1. "All for Jesus" (dedication)
     2. "Be Still My Soul" (resting)
     3. "My Faith Looks Up to Thee" (trusting)
     4. "What a Friend We Have in Jesus" (divine support)

5. "Jesus Calls Us" (overcoming)
6. "Take the Name of Jesus with You" (available power)
7. "He leadeth Me" (directing)
8. "Draw Me Nearer" (reflecting intimacy)

B. God's Sovereignty
   1. "A Mighty Fortress"
   2. "Holy, Holy, Holy, Lord God Almighty"
   3. "Fairest Lord Jesus"
   4. "How Great Thou Art"

C. Petitioning
   1. "Guide Me Thou Great Jehovah"
   2. "Take My Life and Let It Be"

D. Trusting
   1. "I Am Trusting Thee, Lord Jesus"
   2. "Trust and Obey"

E. Yearning for Heaven
   1. "The Sands of Time Are Sinking"
   2. Thou Art Coming O My Savior"
   3. "Savior Come"
   4. "Some Golden Daybreak"

Granted, we can mentally inject a note of praise into these hymns, but the fact is that their content pertains to themes beyond praise as they depict worshipping God in a number of different ways.

The Contemporary Service

Here we see music consisting almost exclusively of praise choruses, ones that lead to hand raising as well as to other physical movements. They often cause friction between those who involve themselves in physical activity as they sing and those who don't. Standing is one of them, which seems to facilitate lifting arms in the air (although some may do it while seated when stirred, by something said from the pulpit). Then again, standing while singing has become popular apart from lifting hands in the air, I suppose as a means of honoring the Lord. In some churches, standing while singing goes on for twenty or thirty minutes, a distinct disadvantage for senior citizens who find it difficult to remain on their feet for that period of time. In fact, standing has become an automatic response to even the suggestion of singing.

Permit me to digress a bit further on the subject of standing while singing. One person stands up (usually up front where all can see) which precipitates the rest of the congregation to follow suit, perhaps stimulated by that person's compulsiveness, or maybe out of consideration that he or she not stand alone. Then again, they may get up in order to avoid being judged less spiritual if they remained seated. Those who don't agree with this spontaneous act also feel obligated to get up so as not to stand out like a sore thumb. I must admit, however, that at times I have refused to give in, simply because I have had enough of the up-down nonsense. I suspect, though, that as I remained seated I became the object of disapproving looks or at least wonderment from those who had joined the crowd.

Added to the ambiance is the influence of musicians called a praise team who, with a highly turned up audio system, creates high decibel music. For some, especially the elderly, the loudness is aggravating. Older folks say that loudness makes it impossible for them to worship, but the younger set seems to enjoy the high volume, even insisting on it perhaps out of influence of secular pop music to which many of them are accustomed (which may be the rationale behind holding a separate service for younger people). But problems ensue when a service with those characteristics is the only one offered.)

Traditional worshippers tend to get annoyed seeing hands lifted in the air; it's foreign to what they are used to. They wonder why hand raising is done. They also wonder about attitudes and judgments that hand raisers may hold against them for failing to participate. They feel that those who engage in the practice do so only to satisfy their own emotions without considering its effect on others (the reverse is also true when hand raisers wonder why others don't join in). Tensions rise and unity falls by the wayside.

Disunity

The newer trends for worship that lead to hand raising and its special style of music seem to contribute to disunity. I say "newer trends" because hand raising and high decibel music are a relatively recent phenomenon whose popularity came about in churches within the last half-century or so (although some will respond by citing hand raising not as a new trend but rather as a custom going all the way back to the OT). We will take up that matter later. But first, let's consider the effect of hand raising and its accompanying high decibel music on Christian unity.

Unity is an issue that compelled Jesus to pray so fervently prior to his death. Do you remember? He asked the Father "that all of them may be one," as He referred to those who would believe in him (John 17:21). But failure to show unity may not register with those bent on practicing hand raising and those who do not. Hand raisers see their practice as necessary for worship, believing that those who don't join in are failing to get the full benefit of worship. Full benefit of worship? As I have pointed out, hand raising is a relatively new phenomenon in today's society. Does that mean that those who haven't practiced it, like the millions of people of past years, have cut themselves short in their approach to worship?

Many traditional-type worshippers refuse to go along with the trend. They cite it as a practice that runs counter to worship styles in American culture, predicting it as a trend that will eventually disappear and that will be replaced by some new phenomenon that someone will think up and insist upon. Worshipping God, they contend, should not be relegated to trendy practices that pop up every few years. Who knows, they say, what new ideas will enter the scene in the future? They believe that to embrace new practices as necessary aspects of worship is a grave mistake, even when those trends are taken from the Bible, as occurring in hand raising among OT Jews. We will analyze shortly the phenomenon of hand raising in the OT.

Avoiding Controversy

A solution for those who strongly reject hand raising may be to avoid attending praise-oriented services in which hand raising dominates. Instead they might do well to gravitate toward the traditional-type service that's centered around hymns whose singing deals with a diverse number of themes beyond praise and without the conflicting element of loudness.

Complications come about, however, when a church offers only one service containing both contemporary and traditional characteristics in order to please everyone's tastes, or maybe even holding a single service given over completely to contemporary music in spite of its distaste by some church members. In either case, worshippers, troubled by seeing hands lifted in the air accompanied by high volume music, feel discriminated against. As a result they often seek out another church to attend. Too bad, because such a decision fails to acknowledge the purpose of church, not for satisfying personal tastes in song, but for encouraging one another in the faith -- a very critical concern out of dedication to caring for the spiritual needs of other believers and to growing in love toward them. It seems appropriate to question whether the clergy and its staff are willing to pay the price to bring about those purposes. The fact that members secede from the church should be a warning sign that things are moving in the wrong direction.

Could the absence of love and care toward one another be the cause of it all?

Could it be that a church may insist on a contemporary service, with its high decibel music accompanied by hand raising, regardless of those who find it distasteful?

Whatever be the case, tolerance and compromise seem necessary in a mixed congregation of those favoring hand raising and those who don't. It calls for a lot of soul searching and discussion to understand one another's feelings and to come to a decision that everyone can agree upon. Sensitivity toward fellow believers has always been the key for a strong and united church body.

It might be productive for the clergy to examine itself as it calls attention to the clashing of personal attitudes and the unhealthy feelings engendered. Or will the clergy stubbornly continue to design worship in accord with contemporary trends because of its drawing power of younger people into the church? (The younger are more apt to attend the contemporary service simply because it includes the ongoing music of present-day society.)

Again, I emphasize the unity theme that was so much on Jesus' heart. Do we dismiss the importance of unity by supporting practices that separate believers in worshiping the Almighty, or do we see unity only in terms of salvation without considering the totality of Christian living? It makes us ponder what Jesus referred to when he prayed so fervently for the bond of Christian unity. My guess is that He yearned for a united body of Christians in every aspect of the Faith, not just salvation, or the kind of music and its accompaniments that we insist upon to stimulate worship.

Mega-churches

Churches with huge congregations, like the so-called megachurches, consist in large measure of the younger set, let's say of some fifty years of age or less. Those who fall into that classification seem to be the ones who tend to favor contemporary characteristics in worship, perhaps due to the influence of secular music which has bombarded them. (We must admit that the secular music scene through radio and television confronts us at every turn, hence its influence on the music in church.)

Justification, then, is claimed for holding a worship service consisting of contemporary trends in that it has drawing power among younger people. But is it turning a blind eye to the problems it engenders?

Many churches surrender their reason for existence to growth in numbers, a fact that seems to run counter to the scriptural purpose of church. Are we really supposed to let numbers of people measure success of the church organization? It causes us to reflect on why we gather together in the name of the Lord. Certainly an increase in attendance seems to suggest that we are doing things right; we see people attending when they see their needs being satisfied. And the clergy relishes large congregations, making themselves feel successful because of the conversions to Christ seen among those attending, not to mention the increase of monetary giving that follows. But should the church's primary motivation be to attract new members to ultimately influence them to become Christians, or should the church function exclusively for believers; that is, to edify and encourage believers in the faith (Heb. 10:24-25) so that they grow in relationship with God and with one another. In other words, should the church be for believers' edification or should its efforts be evangelical? It's a dilemma. Both seem to figure into the contemporary worship service, which tends to make the church building the source of proclaiming the gospel.

Holding church as a means of evangelizing could become a major church focus, which makes gospel sharing by members outside of church to be replaced by evangelizing via the clergy through sermons. In other words, we may be establishing a religious culture in which everything centers around the church organization or building, often leaving individual members, who are really the church, devoid of responsibility to evangelize. Except in the case of a tiny minority, it can result in a non-functioning laity as far as personal evangelism is concerned. Balmer[2] suggests that most evangelicals talk about sharing the gospel more than actually doing it. He sees them hiring professionals to do the evangelizing for them, hardly a biblical example. Are we guilty of it?

As we look at the characteristics of Christians in the church of the Thessalonians we see Paul praising them for being "a model to all the believers in Macedonia and Achaia" . . . and that their "faith in God has become known everywhere" (1 Thess. 1:7-8). Would to God that we could duplicate that happening.

In contrast, the modern-day concept of church seems to reflect that everything be centered around the church organization or building, a kind of comfortable Christianity with little or no individual motivation. Maybe it's time to analyze our *raison d'etre* as a church and to follow through with it using examples in Scripture as a guide? It might cause us to come to grips with what seems to be the Bible's teaching on the purpose of the church – to build up believers in the faith so that they function with dedication and zeal both in and outside the church.

We begin our analysis of hand raising by referring to biblical references on it, first citing a NT passage that may be inappropriately understood and hence misinterpreted, and second, citing OT examples that may well be culture-bound in their application. We often refer to the latter without considering the role of Jewish culture that existed thousands of years ago before Jesus appeared on the scene. But first, a look into NT Scripture.

Hand Raising in the NT

Enthusiasts of hand raising often refer to scriptural accounts that they believe give legitimacy to the practice, often citing the NT in which Paul says, "I want men everywhere to lift up holy hands in prayer, without anger or disputing" (1 Tim. 2:8). Looking carefully at that statement, since it's the sole reference to hand raising in the entire NT, we must ask what message the passage really conveys. Three major parts constitute the verse: 1) hand raising; 2) prayer; and, 3) quelling anger and disputes. On which is the emphasis?

My examination of hundreds of internet articles based on the Timothy passage reveals authors giving unanimous support to hand raising as the sole idea being emphasized, perhaps because they themselves participate in its practice and hence read into the passage to justify their own behavior. None of the authors saw the passage emphasizing prayer. Neither did any of them see it referring to stemming inordinate conduct of anger and disputing (mentioned in the latter part of the verse as well as carried over from the context of the previous chapter, vv.3-4). Unfortunately, they may have ignored issues specified in the passage by being guilty of overlooking the contextual reason for Paul mentioning "lifting up holy hands." He seems to have seen it as a vehicle for prayer in order to combat the controversies that were cropping up. In any event, he wanted those controversies stopped.

What specifically were those problems? Christians to whom Timothy was ministering (the epistle is addressed to him) were engaging in false doctrines, myths, and misguided compliance to erroneous teaching. "Command certain men not to teach false doctrines any longer nor to devote themselves to myths and endless genealogies," Paul said (1 Tim. 1:3-4). Then he added that those practices were promoting controversies, and he insisted that they cease because, of course, they were endangering the Faith. How to do it? He urged believers to pray together, probably because he knew the benefits of engaging in group prayer when people are at odds with one another, especially when false doctrines begin appearing. He saw the idea of Christians sincerely praying together as a remedy to offset ongoing divisions. We must admit that continual group prayer, when done with sincerity, does have a way of uniting believers.

But wait a minute, you may say. You are forgetting Paul's mention of lifting holy hands. Right! And it's important to acknowledge. Why did he include it? The actual act of lifting hands doesn't appear to be the thrust of Paul's admonition. His saying, "I want men everywhere to lift up holy hands in prayer," when interpreted in a literal sense of advocating actual hand raising, causes us to miss his major emphasis -- to pray, not to lift hands. Why then, did Paul include hand raising? Possibly because he was acting out of cultural habit as a Jew (which I'll take up below).

I repeat, the major idea behind Paul's injunction seems more likely to mean praying together, not raising hands. Included, however, is the mention of "holy hands," which requires a brief comment.

Holy hands? Why not? He knew that the Spirit indwells every believer, which makes us holy in God's sight, an attitude we are in turn to carefully nurture in our treatment of one another. That drives home the idea of being concerned for fellow saints. In other words, treat other believers as holy, just as God does who made us holy. That causes some real soul searching in terms of our behavior toward one another, doesn't it? Or do we contend that there's justification for going our own way when others disagree with our manner of worship?

A Cultural Case

Now let's take up the point as to why Paul even mentions hand raising. He probably said it out of his Jewish custom of lifting hands, a cultural habit he associated with prayer and one he had undoubtedly practiced in his pre-Christian days as a zealous Jew (old habits tend to remain with us, especially those culturally ingrained over time). We must also realize that a bit of hyperbole is included in Paul's statement. Suppose he had said that he wanted men everywhere to bow heads in prayer. We certainly wouldn't interpret that to mean he was emphasizing the act of lowering heads, as we Americans are prone to do when praying. The real idea is actually to engage in prayer, which of course, causes us to take seriously our interaction with one another. He saw group prayer, when done with sincerity, as a means for participants to counteract ongoing controversies. We can't escape the fact that praying together from the heart has a way of uniting Christians.

Scripture, then, can be carelessly interpreted to say what we want it to say. If we are stuck on hand raising, we tend to grab hold of any passage that refers to it in order to defend its practice. Some Christians have gone that route with that single verse in Paul's letter to Timothy in an attempt to justify hand raising as a necessary NT procedure for prayer. An associated problem, however, is that we don't restrict hand raising to prayer, but rather that we include it in other activities also, especially in singing praise songs. So we establish our own rationale for lifting hands in the air. In fact, people do it whenever they feel like it, with no holds barred, which causes us to reflect on the effects of emotionalism.

I should mention that the verse in question is a unique reference to hand raising in the entire NT. Paul doesn't refer to it in any of his other epistles, nor do other NT writers, which in itself might tell us something about hand raising as a NT practice. That doesn't mean that Christians shouldn't practice it, but rather that we not allow it to become divisive when gathering with other believers in worship. We must always be concerned about how fellow believers are affected by our practices, whether they consist of hand raising or whatever. Are we forcing them to accept certain behaviors that they have trouble practicing? Perhaps "forcing" is the wrong verb. Hand raisers, I'm sure, don't intend to force their practice on anyone. But I repeat, non-hand raisers may feel that the act of lifting hands is an extraneous activity that actually interferes with their worship.

I cite one other reference to hand raising in the NT. Luke refers to Jesus lifting his hands as a blessing (24:50). The incident, however, is extraneous to our discussion on ways to worship. Only one verse in the entire NT, then, relates to hand raising as a worship activity. But it's seen in several passages of the OT, so it will be beneficial to look at hand raising as a practice in OT Jewish times which many refer to as support for its practice today.

Hand Raising in the Old Testament

In contrast to the scarcity of NT references on the subject, hand raising is portrayed more often in the OT. It was certainly a Jewish practice in worshipping God, which brings cultural implications into the picture. Perhaps it's legitimate to question, therefore, whether we should interpret ancient Jewish custom as something God expects us to follow today, a right way to worship so to speak. It runs counter to the appropriateness of transferring customs of one culture to another, or even from one age to another. Trying to carry over Israeli cultural traits of several thousand years ago to the present, we would end up applying OT references to worship in a variety of forms: (1) kneeling, accompanied by the sound of cymbals, harps, lyres, and trumpets (2 Chron. 29: 25-29); and, (2,) standing, lifting hands, bowing, and, prostrating oneself. Look, for example, at how the psalmist suggested praising God.

Praise him with the sounding of the trumpet, praise him with the harp and lyre, praise him with tambourine and dancing, praise him with the strings and flute, praise him with the clash of cymbals, praise him with resounding cymbals (150:3-5).

Accepting those OT Jewish ways as standards for praise, we would feel compelled to imitate them today, even though they run counter to current cultural norms. We might even view them as suggesting some special type of holiness. Worse yet, we might even perform those acts as if God demanded them, a right way to worship, for example. But then, we get smothered by certain actions, thinking they are the correct way of doing things simply because they've become habitual without our understanding of where they came from or how they got to that point.

I've never seen it done, but I wouldn't be surprised if some churches instituted praise to the Almighty with a background of trumpets, harps, lyres, tambourines, strings, flutes, cymbals and even dancing (Ps. 150:4), all out of imitation of the way people praised God in Jewish culture several thousand years ago. In fact, I recall getting an e-mail from a pastor who questioned a remark I made about dancing in church. "What's wrong with dancing before the Lord?" he asked. "We do it all the time in our church." He didn't explain how it was done or who did it, or under what circumstances, but I couldn't help visualize the congregation being affected emotionally to the point of dancing up and down the aisles.

That seems to have the earmark of a distinct cultural clash. I suppose it can become acceptable over time due to continual use (as well as other behaviors), but we might also question whether dancing in the OT was done in the temple or outdoors (the account of David dancing seems to indicate the latter). Regardless of where it's done, in the church building or outdoors, dancing before the Lord as a means of worship does seem inappropriate in twenty-first century America.

Why is it that people today copy OT Jewish customs? We sometimes reason that the practices of OT Jews, God's chosen people, are especially holy and therefore to be imitated. Also, a commonly distorted idea is that if something's in the Bible it's for our application without considering cultural appropriateness.

We accept the OT as God-inspired, just as we do the NT, but important to question is whether those ancient Jewish rites are cited for application to Christianity today. We have a tendency to apply to ourselves practices mentioned in the Bible without considering their cultural dimensions. Imposing them on believers oriented around cultural practices from a bygone era will automatically cause negative reactions.

David as well as other OT personalities lifted hands as a means of worship. But the question of utmost importance is whether they did it as a divine command or whether they simply allowed an ongoing cultural practice to influence them.

American Custom

I think back on my early years as a Christian, all the way back to the 1940s when I don't recall anyone lifting hands in church. But then I went off to college – Wheaton – an evangelical institution, of all things, where I never witnessed hand raising. It just wasn't done in those days. Neither could you find it practiced in neighborhood churches. As I look back on those times, I can't help but wonder what was wrong with those people. Were they missing out on something critical? And how about the millions of Christians in previous centuries who may not have engaged in hand raising or who may not even have considered it? Were they derelict in the way they worshipped? Did they fail to get the full benefits out of worshipping God?

I recently ran across an advertisement on Bible study material showing a hand lifted in the air on the cover of its booklet, probably to equate hand raising with worship. Another instance showed a woman on the front cover of a seminary advertisement with both arms lifted, perhaps to appeal to seminary prospects who favored the practice (a good public relations ploy to influence a greater flow of applications for enrollment in the seminary). It underscores the popularity of hand raising in Christian circles today, so much so that advertisers include pictures of it in their promotional material.

When did hand raising come into vogue as a Christian practice? I don't pretend to know, but whenever it started, I suppose religious programming on television helped speed its popularity. For example, we see it as a regular occurrence on a religious network where leaders as well as the audience raise hands in response to a variety of emotionally charged situations. That impelled me to investigate what might be behind the practice.

The Pop Music Scene

Since hand raising in the United States is a relatively recent phenomenon that has gained popularity within the past century or so, I wondered if the secular music scene wielded any influence. Flipping television channels brought up rock concerts that corroborated my suspicions: the entire audience (young people all) had their arms continuously in the air as they swayed back and forth during the musical performance. It was as if they were placing themselves under the music's spell. Then the music, loud and boisterous, consisting of high decibel sounds with extreme amplification accompanied by certain lyrics repeated over and over again, all combined to set an emotional surge. On top of it was an interesting observation – the audience stood during the entire concert. Chairs were provided, but I suppose only for sitting prior to and after the musical performance.

For the contemporary church service, then, the scenario is one of hand raising accompanied by a highly turned up audio system, including certain lyrics and melodies being repeated over and over again (another imitation of the secular music scene), all of which makes one wonder when it will all stop. It grinds on you if you are not used to it. Hand raising, deafening sounds, raucous drum cracks, repetitions of lyrics, and physical movements, like standing and swaying, create difficulty for some in worshipping. Are those characteristics a carryover of the pop music scene to music in the contemporary church service? We don't know for sure, but there does seem to be a relationship.

We have to admit that music and emotionalism do coincide. Kevin Reeves who had a leadership role in what he described as the hyper-charismatic movement, stated that "These days it is fashionable among many charismatic groups . . . to direct congregations into an intense state via music."[3] He continued his reference to the church music scene,

> Depending on the song, I could tell at a glance roughly how many times the chorus would have to be sung before it was felt the people had 'entered in' and we could move on to the next one . . . The longer the chorus droned on, or the more often it was repeated, the more time was allowed for the slower believer to shed the cares he'd come with and leave the mundane world behind[4]

None of this was done when I played the trumpet in the big band circuit of the 1940s. I know that some will claim that we just weren't "with it" back in those days. Yet I believe that anyone behaving back then as do pop concert goers today would have been out of their minds. Audiences always sat quietly during those concerts, which underscores the changing role of culture over time. We might want to be cautious therefore, in insisting on certain practices that are culture-bound to a specific time period, be they related to the secular or the spiritual. As for the latter, it seems important that we take care not to insist on practices simply because the Bible portrays them as examples of OT Jewish ways to worship.

Are the actions of standing and lifting arms in the air (and maybe swaying too) as done at pop concerts today reminiscent of activities seen in some evangelical services? And guess who does them? Generally the younger set. Few senior citizens get involved. When they do, it may be out of influence of the rest of the crowd, not as a form of worship that they themselves desire but as a means of fitting in with the rest of the crowd so as not to appear different or confrontational.

Could we be copying the secular music scene and then giving it spiritual overtones to fit into Christianity? Furthermore, do we bring certain biblical passages into play that speak of hand raising in an attempt to legitimize the practice in the church scene today?

Some justify imitating hand raising by making connection with certain OT references, citing David, for example, who said, "I lift up my hands toward your Most Holy Place" (Ps. 28:2); and, "I will praise you as long as I live, and in your name I will lift up my hands" (Ps. 63:4). Other references to the practice are seen in the following psalms: 77:2; 119:48; 134:2: 141:2: and, 143:6. Two other references that I've found are: Lamentations. 3:41; and, Exodus. 17:16.

Although we respect the OT as divinely inspired, an important guideline is to differentiate between its customs that are acceptable across time as opposed to those limited to OT Jewish culture. In other words, is lifting hands a peculiar cultural phenomenon or is it a spiritual act that God expects all people across time to practice? If the latter, then those who don't lift hands, like the millions of past centuries, are missing out on an important aspect of worship, aren't they? Worse yet, are they failing to realize how they may be falling short of pleasing God?

Emotionalism

A distinct characteristic of hand raising seems to be its emotional drawing power. I suggest that possibility because one show of emotion can lead to another, as often seen today in televised ministries in which preachers talk rapidly, sometimes shouting and screaming, pacing wildly across the platform, and even jumping up and down. Then there's the audience's reaction in raising hands accompanied by a continuous flow of oral insertions such as "amen," "hallelujah," and "praise the Lord" followed by an outflow of "tongues," standing, lifting arms, swaying, closed eyes and facial gestures conveying anguished and disturbing emotionalism (often seen among worship leaders and singers on the platform in today's contemporary church services). Worshippers attribute it all to the workings of the Holy Spirit. But could it be emotionalism gone wild, a blight on Christianity before the general public? Is the Holy Spirit an encouraging factor, or is it a question of something we have drummed up to justify an emotional and spiritual high?

Behaviors require standards regulated by cultural norms. Acting in unusual ways in the name of the Lord may invite antagonism from others. We have even seen people attributing crazy behaviors to the Holy Spirit when doing things like barking, shaking, twisting and rolling on the floor, actions commonly taking place among worshippers in relatively recent revival meetings. What might God be thinking about all this? And yet some people proceed as if they were obeying divine impulses that supposedly magnify Christ.

A no-holds-barred approach to worship causes emotionally charged actions of an extraordinary bent. I've even heard of removing one's shoes to imitate the scenario of Moses at the burning bush where God said, "Take off your sandals, for the place where you are standing is holy ground" (Ex. 3:5). We can follow that example in a trumped up atmosphere whereby the preacher creates a highly emotional situation in which he announces God's special presence. The carryover would be that we honor the Spirit through some form of physical manipulation.

Recall another situation that took place at the site of ancient Jericho, when an angel gave Joshua a similar order to remove his sandals (Joshua 5:15). Is it proper to transpose that command to contemporary living? Emotionalism has its merits (who would rule it out as we worship the Almighty?), but at the same time it can influence us to perform acts we might justify simply because the Bible cites them, although under extraordinary circumstances.

No one knows if the current idea of raising hands in worship will last. Will it quietly disappear, or will other ideas come into play to replace it? What we don't want to do is to create practices that we peg as necessary for communion with God in spite of the fact that those practices may cause disunity among fellow believers. We may be inclined to declare our approaches to worship as induced by the Holy Spirit when they really have nothing to do with the Spirit at all but rather are emotionally charged issues of human origin. We know that our adversary, Satan, will bow to no extreme to cause us to transgress the love relationship and unity that Jesus so fervently preached.

Excesses in Traditional Services

Remember Jesus' prayer to the Father to the effect that unity should reign among believers. And yes, that includes traditional-type worshippers who undauntedly may push their particular quirks on others as well. For example, I visited a church whose service was so highly liturgical that it forced rigid concentration on the participatory cues in the bulletin. It meant following a detailed four-page bulletin of prescribed written prayers read by the pastor followed by other statements that the congregation read aloud. Then there was a repeating of creeds, saying aloud and in unison a number of other readings, and a combination of standing and sitting according to the supposed appropriateness of the activity. The end result? It wore me out. And what was worse was that I went through a series of prescribed activity to keep up with everyone else without allowing my mind to concentrate on the Lord.

We are creatures of habit. As we engage in certain practices, we tend to believe they're the best to be followed without considering where they come from or the offenses they may cause among other people who are not used to them. We subject ourselves to certain practices whose performance becomes habitual without realizing the negative effect they may have on others Perhaps the injunction for all of us is that we come together to worship our heavenly Father in a oneness and unity of spirit that pleases him. He has given us his Holy Spirit toward that end, whose directions we will want to heed, even as Scripture says, "Since we live by the Spirit, let us keep in step with the Spirit" (Gal. 5:25). That implies following the Spirit's directions instead of our own emotional ideas that we've habitually established as a norm to follow.

In summary, how we interpret Scripture is critical in terms of our behavior. Do we practice hand raising simply because certain OT characters did it? Could it be a relatively recent phenomenon influenced by a combination of today's pop music trends and biblical hand-raising references that we unconsciously connect? And do we care if it's annoying to non-participants who may be so troubled by it that they feel their attempts to worship are undermined, maybe even seeing hand raising and all its accompaniments (high decibel music, repetitions, standing, swaying, etc.) as so upsetting as to lead them to seek other churches to attend? Do we really care?

Plucking passages out of their cultural contexts as often done with OT references on hand raising can lead to mistaken notions that cause damaging disunity across Christendom. And maybe worse, the world may view the gyrations of hands lifted in the air along with agonizing facial expressions and other accompanying movements as inappropriate to approaching God, which may influence an outright shunning or even ridiculing of Christianity. In that regard, I wonder how many people (both Christians and non-Christians) are turned off by the type of Christianity they see depicted on television where such behaviors are exhibited? Should we be concerned that we may not be providing a positive message of our faith? Or maybe we have an attitude that says, "I don't care what others think, I'm going to worship the way I want," a viewpoint that's pleasing to the Lord? In contrast, Scripture stresses humility and giving of oneself as we exhibit love and respect for one another.

An acceptable attitude is that we always be alert to whatever may cause disunity. Our adversary the devil can even use our approaches to worship as a means of splitting congregations in which he subtly inserts himself as an angel of light (2 Cor. 11:14). He has lost the first battle when we believed in Christ for salvation, and now he will work to cause us harm in a myriad of ways, even through our ideas on what we consider proper approaches to worship.

Finally, although we may see lifting hands as a meaningful way to approach God, we must recognize that others may not view it so. It's not my intent to discourage one or the other but rather that we be aware of practices that cause flare-ups among the brethren. Worship is a time for believers to come together to exhibit unified faith in a heavenly Father who has made us one in Christ. The Father loves to see us magnify his name, which we will do by being considerate of one another as we come into his presence. That includes both those who favor lifting hands and those who don't. I suspect that giving heed to such an attitude will cause a lot of supposed essential practices to eventually disappear. They will yield to practices in which everyone feels comfortable participating.

Trying to tie this all together, I will say that we must be concerned about our practices when we worship with other believers.

I suppose that what we do on our own in the privacy of our homes is another matter. (Or do we think that worship is only done in the setting of a church building?). We have an obligation to be concerned about the responses of others, which includes how they might react to hand raising, high decibel music, insistence on standing and swaying or whatever other habits we might practice. We are responsible for one another's welfare, which is the purpose of meeting with one another as God's church.

Obviously, both parties will have to unite to work out their differences, but one thing is certain – they must cooperate for the well-being of everyone. That will involve an open and honest meeting of minds and hearts to keep church unity on the right track. Such will happen only if the church leadership provides for open discussion on hand raising as well as on its accompanying characteristics of loud music and the like. Those who practice hand raising need to know how others who don't engage in its practice feel about it, and vice versa. For certain, there will be clashes of opinion. But to override them will be a true test of our faith. Let's face it: we often don't know why we do things the way we do them. Talking it out (and not necessarily in one sole meeting) will help us understand the rationale behind our actions. Above all, we must not lose sight of the scriptural admonition of maintaining love and unity through careful supplication to the Lord in prayer.

How must we agree with the way we go about worshipping God? The only answer I can give is that emphasized in Scripture – *love and unity* (see especially John 17). Both characteristics are those to which Jesus gave a great deal of attention, so He obviously wants us to incorporate them into our lives.

Without doubt, God will be pleased if we give priority to love and unity. When we insist on our own way of doing things, maybe even to the point of holding separately designed worship services, what statement are we making regarding unity in Christ? Aren't we all worshipping the same God? Is it not possible for believers to worship together without insisting on the inclusion of certain practices that turn some believers off? And how about when we are together in heaven? Will we worship the Almighty in different ways? I doubt it. We will be so overcome by the divine presence that we will be careful to guard our emotions lest they be offensive.

On the other hand, here on earth, when we are considerate of one another's feelings, the results will be astonishing: our concern for one another will increase; and, our witness about the truth of Christianity will impact unbelievers in ways never imagined.

DISCUSSION GUIDE

1. Contrast the music of contemporary and traditional services. Why is the music different? Would you suggest correcting it? How?
2. What physical movements among worshippers are influenced by contemporary trends? How do you react to those physical movements?
3. If you participate in hand raising, how do you react to others who do not go along with you? What judgments do you make?
4. What problems arise when a church holds one worship service that follows the contemporary mode? Why might this clash with the feelings of others?
5. How does a highly tuned up audio system affect older people? Why is it that younger people tend to favor high decibel music and the repetition of certain lyrics?
6. When does hand raising usually take place in a worship service? How do hand-raisers often regard those who don't go along with the practice, and how do non hand-raisers feel toward those who practice it?
7. How did Jesus emphasize the importance of unity? Could it be applicable to Christian disunity caused by the way we insist on worshipping God?

8. How does a church try to avoid controversy leading to disunity by holding separate worship services, traditional and contemporary? Are we really concerned about Christian unity, or do we yield to individual differences that we think keeps everyone happy?

9. Churches often emphasize contemporary worship characteristics to influence outsiders to attend and become Christians. How might that emphasis be at odds with the NT on the purpose of gathering together as a church body? What biblical passages might be appropriate to cite regarding the purpose of believers meeting together?

10. Churches often support hand raising by referring to the passage that says: "I want men everywhere to lift up holy hands in prayer, without anger or disputing" (1 Tim. 2:8). They see it emphasizing hand lifting rather than prayer, anger, and disputing. Why might that interpretation be erroneous? And since the Timothy passage is a unique reference to hand raising in the N.T., what might that suggest?

11. Many Christians refer to the O.T. to defend hand raising. Why might such a stance be challenged?

12. Hand raising in American churches is a relatively recent phenomenon dating back some 50 years or so. Why might this be a reason to question the validity of hand raising as a necessary part of worshipping God?

13. Some cite the American pop music scene as influencing hand raising in today's churches. What connections might there be? How do you see it?

14. Some say that hand raising is an emotional trend that leads to other emotional actions. What are some of those emotions often displayed in evangelical services as well as on TV? Although we recognize emotionalism as a characteristic of the human psyche, what expectations would be appropriate to insist on?

15. How might we go to excess in a traditional service? Might traditional worshippers view some of the practices in the contemporary service as excessive?

16. What are the implications of love and unity as addressed in John 17? What might be done to discourage disunity?

17. If love and unity are to be implemented, both traditional and contemporary worshippers need to meet together to iron out their differences. What do you suggest be the essence of those meetings? Have you thought about instigating such a meeting? What reactions do you think you might get?

18. To offset the possibility of disunity among believers in worshipping together, while at the same time not imposing restrictions on worship styles, might it be best to recognize hand raising as an individual matter to be practiced as a worship style in one's own home? How might that be, or not be, a solution to the problem of disunity among the brethren?

IV.

Human Relations

Seven

THE MARITAL SCENE

The Bible offers advice about successful marriage relations, but we often fail to put its good sense into practice. Could it be a selfish tendency for spouses to blame each other for not fulfilling individual responsibilities, or could it be that we look at scriptural recommendations with biased opinions and thus fail to understand their full import?

Spouses hate to give in to one another when there's a clash of opinions, even though they know that insisting on their own way could lead to discord. The human traits of pride and selfishness tend to reign to endanger the marital union. The following pages are designed to thwart such an undesirable outcome.

A Serving Attitude

The perfect union, Scripture declares, has to do with characteristics we don't like to face. That's because they call for a great deal of sacrificial giving as they call for spouses to serve one another. On the surface, that's an easy concept to mouth, but actually taking on a servant role involves a great deal of humility, self-sacrifice, and dedication. Paul emphasized the servant theme in his epistle to the Ephesians -- a long quote, but worth reading in its entirety to get the full impact.

Wives, submit to your husbands as to the Lord. for the husband is the head of the wife as Christ is the head of the church, his body, of which he is the Savior. Now as the church submits to Christ, so also wives should submit to their husbands in everything. Husbands, love your wives, just as Christ loved the church and gave himself up for her to make her holy, cleansing her by the washing with water through the word, and to present her to himself as a radiant church, without stain or wrinkle or any other blemish, but holy and blameless. In this same way, husbands ought to love their wives as their own bodies. He who loves his wife loves himself. After all, no one every hated his own body, but he feeds and cares for it, just as Christ does the church – for we are members of his body. For this reason a man will leave his father and mother and be united to his wife, and the two will become one flesh. This is a profound mystery – but I am talking about Christ and the church. However, each one of you also must love his wife as he loves himself, and the wife must respect her husband (5: 22-33).

Although containing several side issues, the quote cites love and respect among spouses as major concerns, which amounts to a stance of service by both husband and wife. The idea of spouses serving one another means looking out for each other's welfare, a characteristic that runs counter to feelings of self-interest. Failing at it administers a fatal blow to marriage relationships that often leads to those awful words of separation or divorce.

Divorce is relatively easy to attain in today's society; lawyers are always ready to step in for a fee. When the slightest thing goes amiss in the marriage relationship, divorce is made to be the answer, to the discomfort of all concerned. Even clergymen are sometimes guilty in subscribing to divorce, oftentimes unaware that their personal decision may set a negative example for others to follow. It's an easy way out, which can be justified in any number of ways, including the claim that it hinders one's ministry when discord between spouses is allowed to continue. So we resort to divorce as we think it's the best solution.

Did you ever wonder about the justification of Christian marriages ending in divorce? Jesus said that divorce was permissible only in case of infidelity (Matt. 19:9). We tend to override that teaching by bringing up selfish issues that we don't like to bear. At the same time Jesus teaching about loving one another in the same way that we love ourselves is sprinkled throughout the gospels. Now I know that we have trouble applying love to other believers who may have a multitude of peculiarities. but it seems a travesty to be unloving toward our spouses with whom we live day by day over a span of many years. I doubt that we can really love others, as Jesus taught, when we can't love our spouses with whom we live day in and day out.

Think about the commitment we made to our spouses at the time of marriage – to love one another no matter what may occur (in sickness or in health). Yet when things go awry, we come up with all kinds of justification for divorce. It's so easy in our present day culture where everyone does it, and our legal system supports it. I suspect, however, that God wants us to love our spouses even when we believe it deters the sacredness of our ministry, something we, as well as the clergy need to take note. Our responsibility is to give ourselves to our spouses no matter what, even if it means restrictions on a ministry in which we are dedicated.

Of course, our ministry itself may be the culprit, as we let it interfere with the marital union. We often justify our ignoble behavior by citing the harm our spouses cause toward the gospel, while the main problem may be that in our enthusiasm toward serving the Lord we render an inordinate amount of time and effort toward the ministry, which causes us to ignore the needs of our own spouses. Do you really believe that God looks with favor on divorce so that we might satisfy our own desires in the ministry?

Who do we think we are to rationalize divorce in matters other than infidelity of which Jesus spoke? There are reasons for marital discord, and it's up to us to handle them, even if it means personal sacrifice, or as the Bible says, serving one another. We are dealing with a sacred duty that is not to be taken lightly.

We get a better perspective of the marriage relationship when we understand that serving one another actually amounts to serving ourselves. That's so because when a husband deals tenderly toward his wife, there's a tendency for her to reciprocate. You would think that we learn by seeing how an act of tenderness works when put into practice, but we don't always realize a satisfying response immediately. Our short-sightedness in wanting instantaneous results prevents us from following through with it. When spouses continue to show negativity, they fall into the trap of retaliation, which only causes further resentments.

An unselfish attitude, on the other hand, does wonders because it's couched in tenderness, bent on making the marriage relationship work. But it's not easy to follow, simply because of the human tendency to look out for ourselves. When we get a rude response from our partner, we tend to retaliate, something which Jesus never did. (He got a lot of negative responses from the Jewish authorities who were steeped in their misguided attempts at following after God.) He even had trouble with his own disciples who were self-oriented. He was even accused by the chief priests of being in league with the devil by performing miracles of healing. Although He didn't allow such accusation to go unheeded, Jesus gave of himself to others, even making the extreme sacrifice of allowing people to abuse him and ultimately to crucify him. In other words, so intense was his devotion to fulfilling his role that he literally gave his life for it.

Jesus' Example

We see Jesus illustrating the importance of focusing on others when He washed his disciples' feet (John 13). Can you believe it -- the Master stooping so low as to wash their dirty feet?

104

Paved streets and sidewalks hardly existed in the first century as they do today. Dirt was everywhere, accumulating on people's exposed feet as they walked about using the sandal-type footwear common in those days. That's where servants came into the picture. It was their job to wash the feet of anyone entering a home, a menial task to be sure, but a cultural custom that was in effect in that day. Jesus picked up on the idea to underscore the idea of humility as a critical feature of serving, because you see, doing a servant's job to wash feet was a lowly, even repulsive act. Jesus actually performed the task toward his disciples to set an example of serving.

Foot washing is sometimes done on special occasions today as an act of humility, but it's significantly different from that of the Roman era. We don't do it as a necessary procedure; that is to say, it's not required of us nor is it expected. So it's not the foot washing act in itself that's commendable, but rather the giving of ourselves as servants to others. In a marriage relationship, it means knuckling under to give of yourself to your spouse, even if it's humiliating for you in the process.

Spectacular about a servant attitude was Jesus' refusal to allow his divinity to interfere. Being God, He could have gotten across the idea of serving in any number of ways, but He did it through an example of dedication involving utmost humility, one that would really impact their minds. Here's the passage together with it's application for us.

'Do you understand what I have done for you?' he asked them. 'You call me Teacher and Lord, and rightly so, for that is what I am. Now that I, your Lord and teacher, have washed your feet, you should also wash one another's feet. I have set you an example that you should do as I have done for you' (John 13:12-15).

When putting aside pride to engage in humble service toward others, even when it hurts, we send a clear message of discipleship. "I have set you an example," Jesus said, "that you should do as I have done." Critical in that role is our performing with an attitude of love, as the next verse confirms: "Love one another. As I have loved you. so you must love one another" (v. 34). It's a fruit of the Spirit (Gal. 5:22), one that requires our utmost co-operation and, of course, one that exemplifies being filled with the Spirit. That means yielding to the Spirit to direct us in everything. Let's investigate how we fail at loving one another and what we can do to correct it.

Practicing Love

The trouble with the servant idea is that although resolving to give of ourselves we end up practicing it only temporarily. Not that we intend to do so, but other issues enter the picture to affect our resolve. For example, we justify a non-commitment when we see our spouses exhibiting selfish behavior, which ends up in our retaliating, a behavior totally against Jesus' desire for us. Being a servant, according to Jesus, is a continuing attitude of persistence and humility, not a one-shot deal, nor is it one that places conditions on the other's actions. Wonderful principles, but do they work?

If I read my Bible right, God has the answer to a happily married life -- a continuous display of selflessness and humility no matter the partner's attitude. Consider the opposite in which we are prone to serve only when the other's actions seem deserving. It's always easy to be nice when someone is nice to us, but when their actions are ugly, we are apt to retaliate in kind, which only exacerbates the situation to draw us further apart. "Don't you correct me," one spouse says to the other. "You're hardly perfect in the way you act." It's an irrational retort that leads to defensiveness and disaster. How do you suppose people feel when reminded of their shortcomings?

The Golden Rule, based on Jesus' pronouncement about healthy relationships, is a familiar teaching that we often cite but fail to fulfill. Lest we forget, that exemplary rule doesn't say that we do to others as they do to us, but rather that we do to others *as we would like them do to us.* That throws an entirely different slant on the way we are to behave, which often includes our speech toward our spouses. Angry shouting matches have got to go. They only exasperate the situation.

In that regard, James reminds us of the tongue's destructive power (James 3). He then shows how hypocritical our speech can be: "With the tongue we praise our Lord and Father, and with it we curse men . . . Out of the same mouth come praise and cursing. My brothers, this should not be" (3:9-10). That should wake us up to our contradictory behavior.

We praise God, maybe in church where we delight in showing humility, while at the same time we behave unseemly toward our spouses at home. All of this makes me wonder why we go about endorsing the concept of love toward fellow believers when we don't put it into practice with our spouses. Broken marriages among Christians is a mockery. If we can't love our spouses with whom we share intimacy, how can we love others. The more I think about it the more I lean toward believing that divorce has no place among Christians other than that given by Scripture – "marital unfaithfulness" (Matt.19:9). Could it be that when things go awry, no matter how ugly they may be, we are to hold fast to our marriage commitment in spite of the sacrifice it requires?

Why is it that we can't love one another amidst all of life's problems? Simply because we can't come to grips with giving ourselves to our spouses. When a spouse is rude and ugly in behavior and attitude, we do the same, which of course only worsens the situation. On the other hand, when we show love in spite of the other's negativity, and continue to do it, we break down the barriers. May we learn to do that and continue to do it throughout our lives. But let me tell you right now; it won't be easy, simply because of our human nature, our proclivity to look out for ourselves.

Of course, Satan is behind evildoing. Recognizing marital discord as an act encouraged by Satan makes us see how serious we must be in our resolve. All the while he's laughing up a storm, even encouraging us to get even with our spouses. After all, he says, you can't let them get away with mistreating you.

The apostle Paul makes it clear that we are to "serve one another" *without conditions,* which we are to do regardless of our partner's attitude (Gal. 5:13). But given our weakness with its inclination toward selfishness, we plod on self-obsessed, only to our spouses' harm, as well as to our own also. Maybe we act that way because we hate to see them getting away with ugly behavior. We can't seem to get rid of retaliating, hoping it will bring them to their senses. But more, our pride has been damaged, and we want the offending spouse to acknowledge it. So what's the alternative? Stop the nonsense of insisting on our own way, and start serving each other! That's the biblical formula. It's not easy to practice, but consider the consequences.

Misinterpreting Roles

You, especially you husbands, may not like the next idea because it singles you out for the responsibility of keeping your marriage intact. Like it or not, the Bible places the greater responsibility to serve on the husband, since God ordained him "the head of the wife" (Eph.5:23). Then again, some women may be screaming at the top of their lungs at the mere thought of being cast in a subservient position. But then, there's even more, God calling the wife "the weaker partner" (1 Peter 3:7), which can cause even greater consternation as women interpret it as indicating an inferior role. It can likewise lead men to jump to erroneous conclusions about superiority -- "the head" and "the weaker partner" -- strong words often misinterpreted by both spouses. Yet they are God's words. What do we do with them?

Surrendering headship to the husband makes the wife feel inferior. She sees herself denigrated by being called "weaker," a regretful attitude because she misunderstands its basic meaning. More about that below. But ultimately, a wife will have to face scriptural admonition that goes far beyond it being a mere suggestion. It's a God-ordained edict, not for God's own pleasure but for our well-being. How is the wife to comply? Scripture puts it in a nutshell -- by respecting her husband.

What are the ramifications of that word "respect?" Could it be that husbands, because of the way God made them for the role of headship, have a built-in need for respect? I say that because some suggest headship as an inherent part of a male's nature. Of course, what goes with it is self-control and a great deal of giving, probably best summed up by the word "love." Love means kindness, a trait expected in any leader worth his salt. But the husband's practice of love toward his wife seems unlikely when she doesn't show him respect. Enter discord.

In-built emotions may apply to a husband's reaction when he's treated with disrespect. Eggerichs,[5] jumping on the idea that husbands have an inherent need for respect, suggests that the husbands' expectation of respect possibly results from cultural mores. Or is it an inherited characteristic that God implanted in the male psyche? Whatever the association, respect by the wife is high on God's list of requirements, as the Bible plainly states, "the wife must respect her husband" (Eph. 5:33). Wow! That sounds pretty one-sided, doesn't it?

Husbands, stop gloating! God also has a requirement for you, too, one that's hardly easy to perform -- to love your wives. Let's see what's behind that word "love" that we toss around so nonchalantly.

Love enters the picture as it shows wives having a special makeup requiring a need to be treated with kindness. Like the husband who looks for respect, the wife yearns to be treated tenderly with love, which may very well be an inborn trait among females.

Showing love toward their wives is a quality high on God's list for husbands (v. 33). When couples don't see good qualities forthcoming from each other, they end up in what Eggerichs calls the "Crazy Cycle," which he defines as a circular interaction that goes nowhere and actually spins out of control. We all fail by getting sucked into that cycle at one time or another, but what's critical is knowing how to get off of it. Hopefully we will realize that it requires an attitude that involves putting both traits -- love and respect -- into practice.

The Bible speaks of those behaviors as unconditional for a thriving marriage. None of this business of saying, "I'll respect him when he loves me," or, "I'll love her when she respects me." Love and respect have no conditions, none whatsoever, which makes it no easy task to put them into practice. We have got to stop asking who's going to start the process. The answer is "you," husband and wife, both of you, without conditions. Yes, I know, one of the spouses will undoubtedly fail to show respect or love at times and hence cause a serious break in a harmonious relationship. But if you retaliate, consider the consequences. Instead, you might as well face it . . . you will have to put up with some misery, maybe a lot of it, until your spouse comes to his or her senses.

It's tough maintaining good relations with people whose actions are ugly. Marriage is no exception. When a spouse does something we don't like, what's our resulting attitude? A flare up of anger? It's a human trait that we all have to contend with, which is why the Bible counteracts it with the qualities of love and respect. When anger is allowed to accumulate, it can lead to hate and even to the breakup of a marital union.

Now what about the wife's emotional makeup of being "weaker?" I'm sure women are screaming at the thought of being judged in that manner. But Scripture speaks of "weaker" as a laudatory trait rather than a negative one; that is to say, that women are exceptionally tender and caring in situations in which men in their masculinity often pay little heed and even fail to understand. At the same time, the wife is easily hurt by a harsh although perhaps unintentional remark from a more impervious husband. Let's face it: the makeup of women is different from that of men. And aren't we glad! Women have qualities that lend toward gracious living.

Unfortunately, husbands often refer to the female makeup in a lighthearted, even farcical way. "Women, who can understand them?" an utterance men often blurt out in jest about some ten-derhearted action that their wives take, one that they themselves would hardly perform. Tenderness and self-sacrifice by the wife in child rearing is a good example. Yes, we recognize the differ-ence between sexes, although unfortunately we males do so in a joking way.

We know that women can equal or even surpass men in many ways -- in business, medicine, science, law, politics, education, and in a host of other areas. Hurray for their abilities and exper-tise! Where they must be careful, however, is not to yield to the temptation of leaning on those accomplishments by demanding recognition from their husbands to the point of denying the ex-istence of male headship. Pride has a way of interfering with re-lationships. It's as if God were saying, "always maintain a servant attitude," which is a trait grounded in humility. Let's remember that both husband and wife are to be servants to each other, not an easy behavior to perform but one that's absolutely necessary for a thriving marital union.

Headship

Like it or not, we see God placing the greater responsibility of spousal relations on the husband. That seems to be God's way of making males responsible for the well-being of their wives. In fact, He commands the husband to "love his wife as he loves himself . . ." (Eph. 5:33), a big order indeed, but one that God deems necessary for a successful union. To fully understand that command, we must ask ourselves -- What man would pun-ish himself in the same way that he mistreats his wife?

Husbands, then, are to be considerate toward their wives in order to model Christ's sacrificial attitude toward all of human-ity (v. 25). In other words, God calls him to a headship position to be implemented by self-sacrifice, which is an exemplary pic-ture of Christ's sacrifice for us on the cross while at the same time pointing to Christ's headship over the church (Eph. 5:23). Husbands are to consider headship, then, in imitation of Christ, not as a power grab, but rather as self-sacrifice, just as Jesus did. There's no place for pride in leadership, since it's a responsibility that one can't truly fulfill when selfishness is allowed to reign.

Jesus was a leader, but he didn't hold that leadership proudly, as if He were to insist on others lauding him to make him feel good about himself. He was a servant, insisting that we follow suit, no matter how hard it may be to do it. I can't emphasize the idea enough, that God expects us to be servants to one another.

It's common, however, to misinterpret the meaning of headship. Sometimes a husband may mistakenly think he has God-given authority to rule over his wife no matter what. He may recognize his obligation toward being kind, that is, refraining from treating his wife harshly (Col. 3:19), but when he sees her walking away from a dispute uttering unkind words and even exhibiting hatred, he gets riled up and justifies his own tendency toward retaliation. "She's not fulfilling her role of submission to my headship," he says. There's no getting around it . . . when we see our wives behaving in ugly fashion, our tendency is to retaliate, thinking that it's the right action to take. She deserves it, we say to ourselves.

Husbands, look! The idea just quoted is merely an example of the myriads of things that can occur in a marriage relationship. Whatever happens, understand that you have a responsibility to show love to your wives unconditionally. In other words, the marriage stands or falls on your reactions to her behavior, which puts an awful lot of responsibility on you. Remember, God instituted you as the head, and with headship comes responsibility. And may I suggest that the best way to combat negative reactions toward our wives is through prayer. Am I incorrect in suggesting that prayer combats a multitude of negatives in our lives? Think about it!

Establish the daily habit of prayer for yourself and for your spouse It will be a good reminder of our responsibility to behave decently toward one another.

Husbands who try to justify their ugly reactions to their wives' conduct is a narrow view of headship. How much better it is to demonstrate authority through tenderness rather than through command. No one likes to be ordered, and furthermore, positive behavior influences positive reactions. We may not see the desired outcome immediately, but it eventually happens. It may even take a good deal of time, which understandably causes consternation affecting our pride and the desire for retribution.

We may think that by pointing out the wife's mistakes makes for a better marriage. However, such criticism hardly encourages her to accept his leadership, rather it erupts into rebellion that further separates them. And retaliation only aggravates the relationship. Yes, it's a matter of repeated surrender, and the responsibility to do that is placed on the husband, even if it requires surrendering numerous times. How's that for fulfilling the role of male headship!

Husbands, keep in mind that you are not to pervert the concept of headship for self-glorification. Headship requires dogged determination and dedication to the task of serving. That means you have to get rid of making demands; in their place, practice love and humility, which according to the Bible means gentleness and kindness.

Confessing to One Another

Let's face it: although our sins are covered by Christ, we are still sinners, and we need to do something about it. We react badly to situations on the spur of the moment simply because of our sinful dispositions that are not always easy to control. Although our sin problem has been paid for through the blood of Christ, it doesn't mean that we don't sin anymore or even that we should ignore sinning when it takes place. After having acted in ugly fashion, we realize our mistake, at which time it's important to confess it to our spouses and ask for forgiveness.

We are told that through our belief in Christ we are a new creation, which means that old things no longer control us, but rather that everything becomes new (2 Cor. 5:17). Those characteristics don't stop when we get married.

Confession of a wrong committed isn't always easy, but it's absolutely necessary for the survival of the relationship. We easily confess our faults to the Lord, but it's harder to do in a face to face encounter with a human being because pride enters in, which hurts one's self-esteem. I repeat, confession to our spouses is no easy matter, but it's one of absolute necessity for the well-being of a relationship. Don't just think that your spouse will forget the incident over time. You need to confess your mistake for the healing process to take effect. It won't be easy, simply because of the natural desire to protect oneself. (After all, leadership, or being the head, we think, demands respect.) But consider the ugly consequences of failing to approach our spouses by confessing our ugliness toward them. In fact, consider the positive outcome of humbly expressing your selfish behavior – overwhelming joy that draws one another in closer union.

I suppose that's the reason why Scripture encourages confession of sins to the Lord. Whether it's to the Lord, to our spouses, or to anyone for that matter, confession reaps beneficial results in that it teaches us to stop being ugly toward others. We know that we are plagued with sinful desires (it's part of our human makeup), and when we let that rottenness get out of control we must acknowledge it, which results in our trying not to repeat it. After all, who wants to continue with the same ugly behavior and having to confess it frequently to the one we have wronged? In fact, continued selfishness followed by continued confession suggests insincerity.

True confession has a rehabilitating effect on us, and it sends a sweet message to the person we have offended who looks on it as a positive trait that endears him or her to you. Since it's a human tendency to forget the nasty habits we have practiced, it's probably not a bad idea to review our lives at the end of the day in order to see where we have gone astray and then to confess it to our spouse as well as to our Lord.

By the way, reviewing our actions each day provides for substantial content of our prayers to the Lord. At times we may decide to skip our prayer time, when really we have a host of weaknesses to take to the Lord. The act of prayer not only calls attention to our stupidities, but it also serves to give us resolve not to repeat them.

An Orderly Relationship

God wants order, and He declares that it will come about only if marriage partners fulfill their God-given responsibilities of serving one another. That means for the wife to submit to her husband in the form of respect, and for the husband to be tender toward his wife in the form of love, traits that are primary needs of each marriage partner and that need to be carried out if the marriage is to flourish. But let's be realistic, they represent the ideal that we don't always see happening, since situations continuously crop up that interfere. Furthermore, a wife is prone to rebel when treated harshly, which she justifies because of her husband's failures. (The inverse, of course, is also true whereby the husband justifies his unloving attitude because of her failures.)

Our human tendency is to judge who's right and who's wrong, a reaction that runs counter to the instruction of the Ephesians passage that says,

> **Wives, submit to your husbands as to the Lord . ... Husbands, *love* your wives, just as Christ loved the church and gave himself up for her . . .. each one of you must also love his wife as he loves himself, and the wife must *respect* her husband (emphasis mine) (5:22-33).**

Trying to determine whose conduct is improper only aggravates the situation. What's best is to be giving, even though it hurts and makes you feel like a weakling. Our egos tend to take over to nullify our good intentions. Furthermore, taking time off to silently review the situation rather than responding immediately (giving God a chance to speak to you about it) can be helpful in stemming an ugly verbal response that may only exasperate the situation.

Although we can jump on the idea of our mate's submission, an action that generates love and respect, we must remember that those qualities are not conditional. Neither are they aimed exclusively toward Christians in Ephesus whom Paul addressed. He repeated the same instruction to the Colossians, saying, "Wives, submit to your husbands, as is fitting in the Lord. Husbands, love your wives and do not be harsh with them" (Col.3:18-19). We also see Peter saying it to Christians scattered throughout various regions. "Wives, in the same way be submissive to your husbands . . . . Husbands, in the same way be considerate as you live with your wives, and treat them with respect as the weaker partner . . ." (1 Peter 3:1,7). Aha! Respect is not only a duty of the wife toward the husband. The husband has the greater responsibility to keep things under control, and he must do it with humility leading to both respect and love.

How is it that both apostles, Paul and Peter, dealt with the same issues in the Bible? Because it's God talking, not Paul or Peter. Principles are being cited that work, even though they may be personally painful to put into practice. And we know that when we work hard at something, and then look back to see the fruit of our labor, we rejoice over it.

I know that some readers may think that all this talk about gender roles is ridiculous in that it contradicts the idea of self-esteem. There is the tendency to think that positions of subservience for women and headship for men are demeaning and go against personal welfare. It's a self-perpetuating response that feeds on one's ego, but one that, if followed, leads to marital disaster. Neither one of those roles are easy to perform, simply because they require utmost dedication by both parties. But if rejected and perceived temporarily as nonsense, they lead to disaster.

A workable marriage, then, is more than a give-and-take relationship, which some mistakenly suggest as a 50-50 proposition. Rather it places priority on giving oneself totally to the other in spite of his or her response. That's God's solution for a happy marriage relationship. It's the true meaning behind love and respect, a percentage proposition of one hundred to zero (100 to 0) that *each spouse assumes toward the other.*

You can be sure that there will always be negative responses by the other party simply because as humans racked by sin we have the tendency to err, to insist on our own way. We are beset with selfishness which the Bible categorizes as a human weakness that unfortunately affects all of us. That's why it's so important that we grow in intimacy with the Lord in order to subdue sin-prone tendencies before they erupt into hurtful outcomes toward our mates and eventually to ourselves. I think it's important to say, then, that *the way we act toward our spouses indicates our relationship with God.*

Here's the clincher -- ultimately the husband, according to the Bible, has the greater responsibility to keep the marriage relationship under control. How is he to do it? Not by insisting on headship as if it were a matter of words, but by actually practicing it as he loves his wife no matter the circumstance. According to Scripture, that's how he assumes the role of headship. The same idea even encompasses relationships outside of marriage in dealing with people in general. "Submit to one another out of reverence for Christ," the Bible declares in prefacing the marriage model in the epistle to the Ephesians (5:21). In other words, the way we treat people in general displays our seriousness as Christians. We are servants of Christ, which means that we give ourselves completely to the task at hand no matter the cost.

Let's not forget that God charges us to demonstrate discipleship no matter how someone else might behave. Quite a task, one that runs counter to pride and selfish inclinations. Yet we must try, and even persist in trying, although at times we may fail. But we don't want to take failure lightly. It may be helpful to think of failure toward our spouses as equivalent to failure toward the Lord, because if we don't have much of a relationship with our spouses, neither will we toward God. In fact, what may appear to be close fellowship with the Lord may be nothing more than a sham that Satan encourages us to continue in.

By the way, if outsiders see us behaving well toward our spouses, or toward anyone for that matter, what impression do you suppose it makes on them regarding their attitude toward Christianity? Likewise, when spouses openly mistreat one another, what image do you suppose arises? Probably something like, "Poor thing. How horrible that he (or she) has to suffer such demeanor! And they're supposed to be Christians?" God forbid that we ever be the object of such comments.

How true are Jesus' words: "By this all men will know that you are my disciples, if you love one another" (John 13:35). Those are important words for all of us if we are to demonstrate dedication in the Faith. Jesus spoke them knowing the outcome of true love, the beauty of which is that it actually works.

In his wisdom our Creator has presented a pattern for a satisfying spousal union that's centered around love and respect, the only way for maintaining a successful relationship. Remember, God instituted it, which makes it unquestionably true as it encompasses both the marriage union and relations with people in general. At the same time God understands that our inherited tendencies toward self interfere with his righteous ways, but He's always forgiving, spurring us on to new heights. His forgiveness is an important concept to consider, which is critical to lean on because our sinful nature so often erupts into selfishness that causes us to transgress.

We may think that our relationship with our spouses has deteriorated to such an extent that any attempt to put love and respect into practice will be useless. It's true that a broken marital union may seem impossible to reconstruct, but that's where a great deal of prayer and self sacrifice come into play. In the end, we must ask ourselves how badly we want to restore a broken marriage, or do we succumb to the easiest way out through separation or divorce?

We might portray God, then, as speaking to us as follows:

1. I'm interested in your welfare and want the best for both you and your spouse. I offer advice for both of you.

2. My recommendation involves your serving one another; that is, the husband loving his wife and the wife respecting her husband . . . a love and respect formula that works when both spouses perform their responsibilities unconditionally.

3. Remember that there are times when you will always exhibit ugly behavior toward your spouse. It's a part of human nature to which at times we surrender. Of course, Jesus paid for that weakness through his crucifixion, but you will want to acknowledge your wrongdoing by confessing it to your spouse. Just imagine the positive effect it has on you when your spouse tells you how sorry he or she is for having behaved improperly.

4. Strive to be servants to each other, and denounce the human tendency toward selfishness. It takes resolve, but it will be for your joy, and then you will represent me well before others.

Some people are headstrong and do just the opposite. I list below in italics some of their foolish responses, each prefaced by a scriptural citation on the positive way to carry out a marriage relationship. Some of the references relate back to our very first parents in the Garden of Eden. Hopefully, that timeline won't hinder us from accepting the wisdom of those ideas in the present.

A Fool's Definition of Terms

1. "Wives, submit to your husbands as to the Lord" (Eph. 5:22).

The fool's response (wife): *"Submit? That suggests slavery. I'm not his slave."*

2. "The husband is the head of the wife" (Eph. 5:23).

The fool's response (husband): *"You see, I'm the head. That sets me up to be the decision-maker, a position I glory in."*

The fool's response (wife): *"I'll go along with his decisions as long as I think they're appropriate. Anyway, head of the wife? Crap! Marriage is an equal partnership."*

3. "Wives should submit to their husbands in everything" (Eph. 5:24).

The fool's response (wife): *"In everything? You've got to be kidding. He often makes bad decisions, so I have to be ready to oppose them. Who knows what will happen to our marriage if I give in."* (And God is probably saying to her, What do you suppose will happen to your marriage if you don't give in?)

The fool's response (husband): *"There's no question about it. Scripture says that she's to submit to me. And she better start doing it."*

4. "'Your desire will be for your husband, and he will rule over you'"(Gen. 3:16).

The fool's response (wife): *"That applies only to Adam and Eve. Don't generalize."*

The fool's response (husband): *"See, from the beginning of creation the wife's responsibility is to knuckle under to her husband in everything without complaining."*

5. "They were submissive to their own husbands, like Sarah, who obeyed Abraham and called him her master . . ." (1 Peter 3:5-6).

The fool's response (wife): *"Master? Are you crazy? It's absolutely humiliating to submit to him as my master. That may have been customary in OT times, but it doesn't apply today, at least not in our culture."*

The fool's response (husband): *"You see, Scripture declares me as the Master, which means that she is to submit to me in everything, whether she likes it or not)."*

6. "She brings him good, not harm, all the days of her life" (Prov. 31:12).

The fool's response (Wife): *"It's reciprocal. If he treats me well, I'll treat him well. Marriage is a 50-50 proposition, you know."*

7. "The Lord God said, 'It is not good for the man to be alone. I will make a helper suitable for him'" (Gen. 2:18).

The fool's response (husband): *"See, it says she was created to be my helper, so she better start fulfilling her role."*

The fool's response (wife:): *"If he's too dumb to see the helpfulness of my actions, that's his problem."*

8. "Do not deprive each other except by mutual consent . . ." (1 Cor. 7:5).

The fool's response (wife): *"I have no desire for sex, nor will I give it to him until he starts changing his ways."*

The fool's response (husband): *"She's the one who deprives. She knows I need sexual release, but she doesn't care."*

9. "Husbands . . . be considerate as you live with your wives, and treat them with respect as the weaker partner and as heirs with you of the gracious gift of life, so that nothing will hinder your prayers" (1 Peter 3:7).

The fool's response (Husband): *"Since I'm superior I'll do what I deem best regardless of any mistaken notions she may have. Anyway, as a woman, she just isn't capable of thinking logically as do men."*

10. "Husbands, love your wives, just as Christ loved the church and gave himself up for her" (Eph. 5:25).

The fool's response (husband): *"I'll love her as long as she dutifully respects me."*

11. "Husbands, love your wives and do not be harsh with them" (Col. 3:19).

The fool's response (husband): *"Sometimes you have to raise your voice to let her know who's boss."* And finally,

12. "Do to others as you would have them do to you" (Luke 6:31).

The fools' response: *"Do to others as they do to you."*

God defines the wisdom that makes for happy marriages. The fools response, which is sometimes even that of the erring husband or wife, destroys marriages. As you have read the sample responses, you undoubtedly have seen destruction coming at every turn. You will want to make sure that you don't duplicate them.

The qualities of a good marriage are hardly practiced by people who are self-oriented. Because of human nature, we are beset with pride and selfishness, negative traits that cause our egos to get in the way. When not treated well, we tend to retaliate. That's why Paul and Peter pleaded that we look to humility and a giving spirit as important traits, which, by the way, were exemplified by Jesus in the foot-washing episode. Do you remember? The characteristic emphasized was that of being a servant. In other words, stop quibbling about who's right and who's wrong. Instead, determine to swallow your pride as you serve one another, just as you would serve Jesus. It might help to picture him as actually being in our midst, standing along side and observing our actions. Keep in mind that He sees our behavior by virtue of the fact that He is God, and of course, his presence within us makes it even more thought-provoking. Recognizing his presence can have a salutary effect on us simply because, as sons and daughters of God, and hence brothers and sisters to one another, we are special people. God has declared us special, so we need to respect that idea by putting it into action.

Respect and love -- God's words for a thriving marriage. They take courage and a lot of self-denial, not an easy route to follow for either party, but one that we can resolve by relying on God's help. Being God-oriented rather than self-oriented is the key to a joyous marriage.

A Strained Relationship

I give now an example of a strained relationship between spouses. I do so because Scripture admonishes us in right living without giving specific examples of what can go wrong. Of course, a myriad of examples could be listed simply because life is complicated, especially when it has to do with relations with another person. Anyway, how would you react if you were faced with the situation below?

Mary and John, a married couple in their 70's, are having trouble living with one another. Mary feels especially caring for her daughter's three-year old child, so much so that she frequently baby-sits the youngster while her Mom is at work, all to the consternation of John. Why is he upset? Babysitting takes place in his home where he relishes quietness and a wife whom he wants to recognize his needs. In its place is a noisy three-year old who constantly requires attention and disrupts life between the elderly John and Mary with whining and requests that are typical of children that age.

John understands his wife's concern for the child and her desire to be a giving grandparent, but he's troubled by the many situations that arise that impose on his well-being as a retired person. His wife, Mary, on the other hand, insists on babysitting while the child's mom works, even to the point of insubordination toward her husband's wishes. Sometimes, the child's mom takes advantage of Mary and John by leaving the youngster overnight at their home, which creates even further tension.

Whatever the reason for Mary's affection toward the child, she's doing it at the expense of her husband, insisting on continuing her relationship with the youngster and her mom in spite of John's feelings. He frequently calls Mary's attention to its intrusion on the well-being of their marriage, but to no avail. In fact, angry shouting matches frequently result.

So how do the biblical qualities of respect and love enter the picture? Obviously, Mary isn't respecting her husband, and John is failing to love his wife as seen by his angry outbursts.

Let's say that Mary stubbornly goes her own way while John decides that in spite of her disrespect he will try to put love into practice, to be tender toward her. How long will he be able to do so? Could it go on for months or even years, and does he have the stamina to continue showing kindness in spite of Mary's stubbornness? Flashing continuously across his mind is the image of her stubbornness in going her own way.

One might suggest that the answer lies in consulting a marriage counselor. In fact, Mary actually tried that, but she didn't like his suggestion to relinquish her babysitting, or at least to reduce its frequency. Consequently, she discontinued the counseling sessions (sometimes we have our minds made up to the point of rejecting whatever advice others offer even though it may come from a professional counselor and may make sense).

Can the problem be resolved? Will Mary eventually come to see that the stability of her marriage is being jeopardized? How long will John's attempt to endure as he tries to show love toward Mary? Might separation or even divorce be recommended for the benefit of both?

John and Mary's story is only one of many difficulties faced by spouses. We don't know why we act the way we do, but it may be a good idea to consider how past influences in our lives may enter in. Maybe the way we were raised, or perhaps the harsh treatment given us by our siblings, or perhaps peer pressures during earlier days of schooling, all of which can leave lasting scars that influence our behavior. Learning to come to grips with our past could be a challenge that might be necessary to face. A skillful counselor can be of great help.

The biblical teaching of a wife's respect toward her husband and his love toward her are critical qualities to be adopted for resolving marital conflict. Of course, seeking help from a skilled marriage counselor may be a necessary addition, but ultimately personal resolve must enter in. The latter will always remain critical for correcting or avoiding discord.

Love and respect, then, stand out as God's provision for a happily married life. It takes resolve to respect people and to love them regardless of their actions, not easy things to do, but in the end they are ones that quell a marriage relationship that could easily go astray.

Consider this important fact -- God has blessed us, his creation, with a marriage partner, including sex and children and all else that goes with it. We relish that blessing. but oftentimes we reject his communication as to how the relationship is to flourish. Hopefully, this chapter will remind us of our responsibilities in making the relationship thrive.

Gender Equality

Finally, there are questions to ponder as to whether the idea of a wife's subjugation to her husband (as stated in Ephesians) is a matter of culture rather than of biblical teaching. We have to agree with the fact that cultures change over time, which causes us to ponder whether the role of women in the first century should be carried over to today. There's a tendency in twenty-first century America, primarily influenced by the U.S. Constitution's stance on equality, to give equal rights to everyone regardless of gender, even in matters of sexual orientation (gay and lesbian marriages, for example). We can't argue the fact that society today is going in that direction, but is it in accord with biblical values? Unfortunately, society does not heed biblical values.

How does all this relate to a woman's role in the church today? Many argue that it's different from that of the first century and therefore the past status of women must not be subscribed to today. Left-leaning churches tend to endorse that idea, often leading to society's praise. I have taken the stance of husband/ wife relations as overriding time and culture; that is to say, that the Bible presents teaching on a successful marital union as applicable across time. I leave to you, the reader, to decide whether the carryover is relevant.

As far as the contemporary church scene is concerned about the role women play in the church, should we give women the authority to pastor and teach, or should their ministry be limited to that with women and children, as some might suggest or even as Scripture might suggest? It's not an easy problem to confront, but whatever be your stance, let it not be divisive in contributing to disunity. We are all brothers and sisters in Christ, and we must show respect for that standing through an attitude of love toward one another and toward God himself.

DISCUSSION GUIDE

1. How does being a servant affect the marital union? How do the elements of love and respect enter in?
2. In what way did Jesus exemplify the role of a servant? Why do you suppose he did it?
3. How does a dedication to love exemplify the Golden Rule? What is the Golden Rule anyway, and what is it not?
4. What are the implications of love as a fruit of the Spirit? What does it have to say about human relations in general?
5. How are the roles of husband and wife often misinterpreted? What does the Bible actually say about those roles?
6. What is the husband's responsibility in assuming headship? How might he misinterpret that role?
7. Why is it suggested that spouses confess to one another their bad attitudes and conduct toward each other?
8. Although spouses must continually be concerned about giving themselves to one another, who, according to the Bible, has the greater responsibility to keep the marriage relationship under control? What can restrain that responsibility?
9. How would you characterize Mary and John's attitude toward their marriage relationship? Why is it damaging?
10. How might the U.S. Constitution's stance on gender equality interfere with biblical teaching on husband-wife relations? What is the Bible's stance on gender equality in matters of the ministry?
11. Why is prayer important to maintaining a right attitude toward your spouse? How often should we pray, given our weaknesses in maintaining desirable spousal relations?

Eight

HAVING A SERVANT ATTITUDE

The idea behind this chapter is that we are to assume a servant role, whether we are married or single. There's justification for it, since Scripture makes such application for all to heed in whatever be the relationship.

I use the marriage passage in Ephesians (5:22-33) as a guideline for this discussion. I do so because, although talking about joint responsibilities of husband and wife, the passage applies to everyone, even as Scripture states (below) that we must all live in harmony with one another.

All of you, live in harmony with one another; be sympathetic, love as brothers, be compassionate and humble. Do not repay evil with evil or insult with insult, but with blessing, because to this you were called so that you may inherit a blessing. For whoever would love life and see good days must keep his tongue from evil and his lips from deceitful speech (1 Peter 3:8-10).

Married or not, then, we will all benefit from this discussion.

Selfishness

We may call one's attention to what we believe to be someone's improper behavior, yet at the same time we often err by responding with selfish inclinations. We expect the other person to assume responsibility toward realigning his or her misconduct as we fall back on selfish motives without giving thought to the role we really ought to take as servants. It's always easier to blame someone else rather than to take corrective action ourselves, isn't it?

So we tangle with the question of self-centeredness, a problem that often escapes us for its subtlety, yet one that takes a devastating toll on human relations. Scripture even calls it sin because of its hurtful consequences. In place of it, God asks us to give of ourselves "without grumbling" (1 Peter 4:9), that is, without complaining, which isn't easy to do when we feel that others are taking advantage of us.

God also exhorts us to "love each other deeply" (1 Peter 4:8). Love? Deeply? Words we commonly toss around without thinking of their implications. I try to apply them in my relations with my children and grandchildren, but loving others in general, even though they may be Christians, and loving them deeply on top of it kind of makes me uneasy as to whether I'm loving them enough. I think I love my wife deeply, but with others I'm not sure.

We don't have close relationships with everyone, which tells us that there's a difference in the kind of love we have toward them. We just don't love people in general in the same way we do toward our spouses, or maybe our mothers. They are people with whom we've had very close relationships, which naturally causes us to have deeper affections toward them. We don't seem to have intimate relations with other people, so it's obvious that the love of which Jesus spoke about loving other people is hard to grasp, let alone to put into practice.

The idea of love undoubtedly refers to giving oneself totally, to show true, unbiased affection. It even means overlooking others' weaknesses that's helped by close contact with them. You see, learning of someone's thoughts, including possible afflictions as well as triumphs, helps us understand what that person is going through and consequently allows us to express genuine love and concern.

Love was the tenor of Jesus' teaching ministry. Jesus spoke of its importance as He referred to a rich man whom He hoped would cease his self-centeredness by giving of himself (as well as his money) rather than indulge in selfish desires. Selfishness, a very human flaw, is a trait we have trouble with, but yet one we are called to control.

So how do we take the spotlight off ourselves and put it on others through loving behavior? We know it's more than a matter of generalizing the problem by blaming others for failing to love. We need to look at ourselves, which will invariably reveal our self-centeredness in ways we react to attitudes and even offenses that others hold toward us, whether we deserve their negativity or not.

When controversies arise, we tend to cast blame on the other person rather than recognize that we ourselves may be the culprits. Pretty hard to imagine, isn't it? Even in spiritual matters, we thought we did a good job in summing up the passage being discussed in Bible class the other day, yet other members of the class may have seen our summary efforts as offensive, something hardly reflecting a loving attitude. We often come across in an unloving manner even though it may not be our intent.

We may not always express ourselves in the best way, or maybe we see others doing the same also. But what's important is that we resolve not to condemn them but rather give them the benefit of the doubt, and perhaps even to suggest modifying what we said while at the same time not coming across as a proud know-it-all. If there's conflict, someone has to give in for resolution to come about, which means that I, claiming to be on top of the situation, must take the lead in subservience.

By the way, Paul speaks to the contrary of our human flaw of making unsound judgments by citing the characteristics of true love. Look at them below.

> **Love is patient, love is kind. It does not envy, it does not boast, it is not proud. It is not rude, it is not self-seeking, it is not easily angered, it keeps no record of wrongs. Love does not delight in evil but rejoices with the truth. It always protects, always trusts, always hopes, always perseveres (1 Cor. 13:4-7).**

Putting those qualities in the framework of a spousal relationship, or for that matter any relationship, we see our own shortcomings. But we have probably read that passage hundreds of times without being affected by its meaning. So I re-write it below by substituting "love" with the pronoun "I," which will cause the message to hit you like never before.

> **I am patient. I am kind. I don't envy. I don't boast. I am not proud. I am not rude. I am not self-seeking. I am not easily angered. I keep no record of wrongs. I don't delight in evil but I rejoice with the truth. I always protect, always trust, always hope, always persevere.**

Oh really? How do you feel about yourself after reading the passage that way? How do we personally stack up to each of those characteristics: patient; kind; not envious; not boastful; not proud; not rude; not self-seeking; not easily angered; not retaliatory; not evil-oriented but truth-oriented; always protective of others; always trusting; always hopeful; and, always persevering? If you're like me, you're in pretty miserable shape. We tend to gloss over the Bible's reference to loving people without thinking about how to apply it personally.

What I'm saying is that we tend to overlook those laudatory traits by failing to apply them directly to ourselves. "They're not realistic," we say. "After all, we've got to stand up for ourselves without letting others walk over us," an opposite stance to that taught by Jesus. By subjecting ourselves to others we will impact them in ways beyond imagination, perhaps not immediately, but sooner or later it will happen. In other words, we are to take on a servant attitude, one that takes on the characteristics of a selfless act of love. Furthermore, reflect on Jesus' teaching about love being the prime characteristic of human relations as it encompasses every desirable trait we can think of. The Corinthian passage quoted above is a pretty good reminder of how we fail. I'm afraid that we allow the Bible's continuous admonition about love to go in one ear and out the other, probably because its qualities are so hard to put into practice. We've got to get serious about it, to take measures to change the ugly scenario of our relations toward one another.

Love and Marriage

Let's zero in specifically on how this might relate to a marriage relationship, because if spouses can't love one another deeply they certainly can't practice it with others.

I'll use a made-up situation about Bill, Jane's husband, who volunteers to cook supper. "What an act of kindness," Jane says, "husband taking over one of my duties to give me some time off." But the pleasantry can completely change to one of phoniness. Here's how it could turn out.

Not used to the details of cooking, Bill forgets to wipe off the stove that he left awash in grease. To the wife's dismay, Bible class participants will be arriving shortly, some bringing refreshments into the kitchen for the group to enjoy afterwards. Since the messy stove is an embarrassment, the wife's first inclination is to tell her husband that he needs to clean up the mess that he left. She may gently call it to his attention, or she may tell him in an ugly, insinuating tone, maybe something like, "Cooking involves cleaning up after yourself, you know!"

Let's say it's the latter, which makes him retaliate by saying something on the order of, "I offered to cook out of a good heart, and now you're telling me I didn't do a good job. That's the last time I offer to do anything for you." Misunderstandings result, unkind words are spoken, tempers flare, all because the husband at the moment is easily angered over her response, especially since he acted with good intentions. He was hardly protective of his wife's feelings as he transgressed several salient features of love listed in the Corinthian passage above. Look at them again to review how he failed in his attitude toward his spouse.

But suppose Jane reacts gently by cleaning up the stove without saying a word. Her selfless response will have a way of resonating with him. Don't kid yourself, he knows she's cleaning up after him. But even if he doesn't respond properly, she still can be true to herself by giving selflessly in order to avoid a nasty scene, and more, to maintain good relations with her husband. When he does become aware of his negligence and of his wife's gentleness, he's more likely to see the foolishness of his error and then cement a loving relationship with her. What couple doesn't want such an outcome?

The Bible uses another word for "love" that we can apply to our behavior – "beauty." Beauty, Scripture says, "should be that of your inner self, the unfading beauty of a gentle and quiet spirit, which is of great worth in God's sight" (1 Peter 3:4). We see it in the wife's giving attitude, really a selflessness that applies to everyone, husband, wife, or whoever may be involved. So, we must ask ourselves whether we really have the inner beauty of a gentle and quiet spirit when dealing with others. Putting those traits into action brings us closer to the true meaning of love.

In another place the Bible addresses a desirable behavior as follows:

You were taught with regard to your former way of life, to put off your old self, which is being corrupted by its deceitful desires; and be made new in the attitude of your minds;

and to put on the new self created to be like God in true righteousness and holiness (Eph. 4:22-24).

"The new self . . . in true righteousness and holiness" versus "deceitful desires." The latter is the cause of self-centeredness, which creeps up on us unknowingly as it makes us think we are in the right while the other person is behaving wrongfully. Blaming others rather than looking at the nature of our own response is easy to do, especially when the other party acts in a grossly uncivil manner.

Think about the frequency of selfish blunders we've made, ones that are absolutely stupid and uncaring. We don't know why we acted that way, and it makes us disgusted with ourselves by allowing ridiculous emotions to rule over us. We even continue to repeat the same mistakes over and over again. In fact, we sometimes think we are in the right and the other person is in the wrong. It's a part of human frailty, always judging the other without looking at our own faults, hardly in tune with putting on "the new self" that the passage talks about.

We see that we aren't always in control, a fact that Jesus recognized when He said, "The spirit is willing, but the body is weak" (Mark 14:38). Our bodies are the fleshly part of our being that constantly cry out for attention that leaves us in a state of weakness. The good news is that we can overcome that weakness by leaning on God for help and at the same time resolving to do our part, which is how change comes about -- trusting in God while taking steps to exhibit self-control – all of which constitute a meritorious combination.

The Holy Spirit

Scripture speaks of self-control as a result of our response to the urgings of the Holy Spirit. Self-control, you know, is a fruit of the Spirit (Gal. 5:22-23), the result of which comes about through growth in spiritual intimacy. Two verses later we are presented with another challenge: "Since we live by the Spirit, let us keep in step with the Spirit" (v.25). None of this business of letting self-control get out of hand while at the same time claiming to be responsive to the Spirit. In other words, it's not just talk, but action.

Who's at fault in unpleasant disputes, and what perpetuates their continuation?

What must be our role as Christians towards others? Those are questions that impact life relationships and hopefully ones we will find answers to as we serve one another.

Being a servant, then, is God's message to us to live the Christian life as He portrays it, all of which takes gumption, sometimes even humiliation coupled with an attitude of humility. By getting control of ourselves as we practice being servants we see glorious results. It's the Spirit's way, one in which Jesus himself followed, so now it's up to us to follow through with it in our own lives. The results will be exciting

DISCUSSION GUIDE

1. How does selfishness contrast with love? How might we make the love passage in I Corinthians 13 personally meaningful? How do you feel you stack up to it?
2. How does the example of Bill and Jane show resulting misunderstandings? What would you have liked to see Jane do to defuse the situation, and what might it have accomplished in the way Bill reacted? Why is it a good example behind the meaning of love?

Nine

Gift Giving And Receiving –

A Persistent Problem

Have you ever given a gift and not been thanked? When that happens, we suspect ingratitude on the part of the gift recipient. It hurts.

Here's a personal episode of non-acknowledgment of gifts that I shared with others, only to be told that I wasn't the only one facing the problem.

I had been feeling sorry for myself, but when I found out that others were experiencing the exact same thoughts, I got a better slant on the problem. I think the entire message bears addressing, that it should be brought out into the open to discourage its continuation.

Early Training

I set the scene by going back to my early years growing up in the Depression Era. Those were tough times, including a lot of poverty and even people going hungry. Money was scarce and was used for basic necessities, not for gift giving. Christmastime, however, seemed to be an exception. As poor as we were, we always gave each other some kind of gift, and my parents taught me always to show appreciation when I was the recipient.

We see an entirely different scenario today, maybe because we now live in an age of prosperity, at least in the United States. For many, saying "thank you" has fallen by the wayside, but not without consequences. Consider the outcome of an unacknowledged gift and its destructive toll on givers, especially when it becomes habitual. Of course, we can brush off a lack of response by questioning our own motives in gift giving in the first place. Maybe we should be generous without expecting anything in return, which is indeed an important principle to apply to helping people in need, like those who are hungry and without food. My guess, however, is that when we step in to help a destitute person, we will be shown appreciation. But it's different with gift giving that involves someone who doesn't really need the gift, one whose status in life doesn't require generosity on our part.

What I'm referring to as gift-giving has nothing to do with needs of the recipient. I give gifts regularly to my grandchildren -- on birthdays, Christmas, and other special occasions such as graduation from school or college. They really don't need my gifts; they come from fairly well-to-do families that provide for all their needs. But I must admit that I'm troubled by their frequent failure to acknowledge my kindness.

The problem may stem from the fact that my gift giving involves mailing. That's because I live in another state than do my grandchildren, and hence gifts across distance aren't always acknowledged as they would be if given in person. I suspect that a similar situation exists among other grandparents and grandchildren.

At first I felt hurt, but then I thought that maybe I was being an old fuddy-duddy, feeling sorry for myself. But failure to show appreciation intensified, making me feel increasingly worse. That's when I decided to find out what others were experiencing, to discover perhaps something important to apply to my own situation, so I dashed off a letter to friends in different parts of the country to see what they were experiencing. I found out that the problem is widespread and needs serious attention. I cite below their replies.

Responses

1. "Today in Sunday school class, I mentioned your letter. Wow! Did it open a can of worms. The message? Your experience is very common."

2. "Ditto on your experience. I've wondered why there's such a lack of gratitude in this generation. I suspect that some of it may be because kids have always had everything; they really haven't had to be without. It's obvious that the more needy you are, the more you will appreciate a gift."

3. "A few do acknowledge the gift, while others more often do not."

4. "After waiting a couple of weeks, we had to follow up with a call asking if they got our money gift."

5. "We suspect a change in cultural values. Yet this should not affect us who are expected to follow unchanging Christian principles."

6. "Lack of sensitivity is not only restricted to grandchildren. My nephew and his wife never acknowledged my wedding gift. That made me feel awful because it was a sacrifice to give them that money. How anyone could be so rude really got to me. I understand how a husband might leave the writing of a thank-you note to his wife. But neither of them responded.

7. "All those years of sending money without a response! Even the oldest at 28 was guilty of not thanking me. I realize that my grandkids are scattered, but they all have cell phones to call me with. Well, I've become hardened. So from now on I'm going to be a mean old grandma and send only a card. Maybe that will cause them to question why no $100 bill was included. I'll wait and see."

Do these comments strike a chord? Failure to acknowledge gifts seems to be a common occurrence today, especially among younger people. Maybe, as one respondent suggested, values change in a culture that's permeated by plenty. But it leaves the gift giver dismayed and unappreciated. Could there be a lesson here for parents to teach their children to acknowledge gifts, to be sensitive to the givers? That seems especially important to someone who gives gifts out of great sacrifice.

The following responses take on a somewhat different thrust; that is, why non- acknowledgment of gifts exists and ways we might use to correct it.

8. "Maybe they don't respond because they don't really appreciate the gift. When no gift comes at the next holiday, they or their parents may ask why? This is our opportunity to explain that since no word of appreciation was received, the gift may not have had much meaning to them."

9. "How about being upfront with them (and their parents) about your feelings? Then proceed from there."

Running throughout the above reactions is a feeling of disappointment and uncertainty as to steps necessary to take. Without question, the problem isn't easily resolved, yet it begs addressing lest we be guilty of overlooking insensitivity toward the good will of others. It's a question of insisting on good character. Bad habits left unchecked tend to persist and maybe even multiply later in life, perhaps causing undue woe in terms of relationships. It can happen even with grandchildren who enter adulthood and continue to lack graciousness in their relationships with peers, or for that matter with anyone.

Jesus' Example

Whatever the occasion for a gift-giving celebration, thanking the giver is an expected courtesy in human relations. Even in the Bible we see Jesus expecting it after healing ten lepers from their devastating disease. But what happened? Only one of them bothered to thank him, so Jesus asked, "Were not all ten cleansed?

Where are the other nine?" (Luke 17:17). How do you suppose He felt after showing such spectacular kindness and then being treated with indifference? He expected a show of gratitude. And why wouldn't he? It had to do with a devastating disease whose healing was unheard of in those days. Without doubt, showing appreciation is just as relevant today, since the Bible exemplifies it as a commonly expected trait. Thanking people for their generosity is an expected behavior.

Part of the problem today may be geographical. As I alluded to earlier, young children live with their parents while gift givers, like grandparents, may live elsewhere. When receiving gifts from their own parents, young children are more likely to express thanks simply because they live in the same house. On the other hand, when it comes to others who may reside in another city or state, distance may influence their failure to respond. But as mentioned in one of the surveyed responses, considering today's technology of cell phones and computer e-mail, we wonder if non-contact is a valid excuse. Could a non-response be due to laziness, or maybe a take-it-for-granted attitude when receiving a gift, or even because of today's affluent society, as one of the respondents suggested: "Kids really have always had everything; they really haven't had to be without."

Perhaps Jesus' statement best summed it up when He said, "Do to others what you would have them do to you" (Matt. 7:12), a golden rule that permeates society.

Who doesn't relish a word of thanks? It doesn't cost anything other than a bit of time for making contact, yet its effects are far-reaching. I wonder if we should begin reminding young people (with whom the problem seems to predominate) to say, "Thank you for your generous gift." How nice it would be to hear it, and maybe even with an added response such as "You are so kind to remember me." Such expressions of gratitude have a golden ring to them as they cheer the gift giver and strengthen relationships.

Taking Action

Now what to do about it is the big question. We certainly don't want to continue with the status quo while at the same time alienate friends and loved ones. A delicate expression of concern is obviously necessary, and when flowing from a spirit of gentleness, it can certainly do wonders. How about something like: "Would you let me know when you receive my gift? I want to be sure it arrived." That might do the trick in getting a response, but if not, we might take a more stringent measure. I say that because there's the temptation to simply give up as we tolerate the situation while at the same time continue hurting. But is it not perpetuating a wrong by failing to address it? We want our gift recipients to learn graciousness in relationships in order to mature in sensitivity toward others.

A softening expression of inquiry may help get them on the right track. But then it may not. I say that because I used it last Christmas in sending $100 checks to each of my ten grandchildren. I got seven acknowledgments. Obviously I will have to use a different strategy with the other three, maybe one that temporarily rules out gifts, as one person suggested in my survey. Would that wake them up to the fact that something's wrong? But by taking such action, I wonder if the motivation to acknowledge gifts would be more pecuniary than affectionate. But that's another matter; we look for a response, no matter the attitude behind it.

On the other hand, maybe I should continue giving gifts without requiring acknowledgment. Could that be a sacrifice I should assume? We know that the passage of time in itself has a way of changing attitudes to eventually bring about a change in behavior. The trouble is that grandparents have the desire to get a response while still alive.

Indeed it's a delicate problem, but one we have to tackle if we hope to pass on good habits of personal relations. Certainly we mustn't succumb to the temptation of verbally chastising irresponsible gift recipients. Rather, operating in the spirit of kindness and love is undoubtedly the best approach for helping them grow into responsible adulthood.

By all means, we must always maintain a Christian attitude toward those who fail at it, even if it comes to our personal suffering in feeling unappreciated. Didn't Jesus teach the same? Also, Scripture teaches us to do everything in an attitude of gentleness and respect (1 Peter 3:15). We often want those qualities heeded by the younger toward their elders. But may they not be shown in the reverse? After all, what better way to help young people follow Christian principles than for their elders to set the example? Gentleness and respect are behaviors we must never lose sight of in spite of the difficulties of putting them into practice.

This brief survey coming out of my personal experience suggests that unacknowledged gifts continue to be a widespread problem. Perhaps you, dear reader, have at some time or other felt its brunt, but hopefully the discussion will influence both the giver and the recipient toward responsible attitudes and actions; otherwise, we are faced with a serious problem of human relations that could escalate into broken relationships. And no one wants that hurdle to be thrown at them.

DISCUSSION GUIDE

1. Cite your own experience in gift giving without receiving a response. How did it affect you, and what did you do about it? What were the results?
2. What example does Jesus cite to underscore the importance of acknowledging a gift? Do you suppose Scripture cited the incident as a lesson for us to learn today?
3. Why might part of the problem today be geographical (you and the recipient living in different cities or states)? What suggestions would you make to defuse the situation?

V.

Wisdom

Ten

QUESTIONING GOD: DANGERS AND BENEFITS

I must make it clear at the outset that this chapter does not discuss questioning God about personal salvation, as if we were unsure of its premise. Rather, it's a chapter for Christians who are secure in their faith but who from time to time wonder about issues for which there are no answers. Questioning of this sort underscores human limitations that impose superiority of knowledge and the ability to figure out life's complexities.

So here we go. Have you ever thought about God's operations in life, maybe wondering why He decided to take certain actions the way He did? Wow! Questioning God? Do we really want to do that, pushing aside his supremacy?

Whether we want to or not, we still do it, because our minds automatically go in that direction as a part of our human way of thinking. But I suspect it's all mental and hidden from others, that is, we don't do it out loud, which allows us to tolerate it by excusing ourselves from intentional blasphemy. Nevertheless, we can't help thinking about why certain things happen, while at the same time justifying our thoughts as perhaps being more logical than God's ways. But we smother our thinking by not bringing it out in the open. (I suspect we may do that to maintain a semblance of humility before an all wise and knowing God; some may even experience shame for even having entertained those thoughts in the first place.) The danger involved in questioning God is that it can tear us away from him, which of course would cause us undue misery and woe.

We Christians are taught to accept God's ways by humbly submitting to our inadequacies; that is to say, that as created beings we are in no position to understand all that takes place in the world or even in the universe. After all, we realize that we are mere creatures of God's grand design; that is, He being the Creator means that He's totally omniscient in knowing why everything happens the way it does. We accept the Bible's instruction on God's actions and pronouncements in accord with his divine wisdom as we remind ourselves that his judgments are always the best, replete with wisdom and understanding, ones that can't even get close to human reasoning. It's a lesson in humility we have learned throughout the years in recognizing our human deficiencies. But still, we seem to have an inbuilt tendency to wonder why God allows certain things to happen, especially when they affect us personally. Let's face it: our minds question God's actions, even though we don't like to admit it.

It's not my position to condemn such questioning but rather to use it for good, which is the purpose of this chapter. Questioning can bring us closer to our Creator out of humble recognition of his awesome divinity.

Origin of Evil

Let's start out thinking about the origin of evil, since it's not unusual for us to question it. Scripture tells us that it resulted from rebellion in heaven by Lucifer and a body of angelic supporters who tried to overpower God in a takeover attempt. The Creator ultimately squelched it by throwing them out of heaven. But we silently wonder why He didn't destroy the insurgents right then and there, which would have allowed his future created beings (Adam, Eve, and us) to enjoy the bliss of living without the effects of evil in the world. Furthermore, had God done that, He would not have needed Christ to sacrifice himself on the cross, saving him a lot of misery and woe (memories of Jesus praying in the Garden of Gethsemane where He said, "'My soul is overwhelmed with sorrow to the point of death . . .'" -- Matt. 26:38 -- and then, "being in anguish, he prayed more earnestly, and his sweat was like drops of blood falling to the ground" -- Luke 22:44). Obviously Jesus was greatly troubled over having to take on himself the sins of humanity. Had God obliterated sin from the very beginning, we counter, salvation would have been a non sequitur, since our lives would not have been corrupted by evil, and hell's existence would have been unnecessary as well, since no one would be banished there.

In other words, earth would have been like heaven whereby humanity would enjoy the delights of a sin-free life. Was God derelict in not recognizing that possibility? Surely not, we declare, as we recognize that He is God, the all-wise and all-knowing. But for some reason, such a declaration fails to satisfy our innermost probing.

Questioning God's decisions oftentimes plagues us when we are alone in our silent moments of meditation. His verdict that sin infects all peoples on earth seems to run counter to what we see as common sense. We didn't have anything to do with the origin of sin, we say, so why should we be punished? It mistakenly gives us the impression that our inherent ability to reason allows us to understand all things as it makes us god-like, reminiscent of Satan's ploy with Eve in the Garden of Eden that she would be like God. She gave in to that subtle suggestion and must have suffered mentally and physically the rest of her life because of it. We don't want to let that happen to us.

In all of this, we must remember that God created mankind with freedom to choose, which is exactly what Adam and Eve did, disobeying God and then suffering as a consequence. But no matter how we try to rationalize, ultimately we have to come to grips with our humanity and its limitations.

Our Limitations

As created ones, we are really deficient in trying to look into the mind of the Creator. We struggle as we fathom our limitations while at the same time our earthly minds tell us we have unlimited capacity to reason. That causes grave concern, because sooner or later, if we are honest with ourselves, we see that many of our calculations are really indefensible.

Consider, for example, the various declarations humans make that must later be reexamined because of new findings, something that happens in the scientific world all the time. We constantly come up with new theories that we think explain certain universal phenomena only to abandon them when we get new information. It's an ongoing struggle -- declaring certain events to exist and then making new calculations when the old ones prove inadequate.

If you are a scientist, admit that you dogmatically believed in certain aspects of life, only to change your mind as new information came into view. What does that say about future findings and your attitude? Obviously we continue learning (and who knows what new discoveries will be made after we are gone?), which should influence us toward a stance of humility in recognizing our limitations. At this stage of thinking, we are tempted to throw out the idea of a God who is in charge. But hold on! We don't want to arrive at quick decisions for which we'd be sorry.

I suppose our limited thinking in itself suggests our inadequacies. A case in point is when scientists renounce their preconceived ideas on atheism by a change in mindset in which they declare belief in God (which has happened among some of them). They come to recognize that their ability to understand all things through scientific discovery doesn't produce satisfactory answers to life. Sometimes it takes a spectacular event, like a near-death experience, to jolt them out of their comfort zone, one that causes them to declare a change of mindset about the Almighty's existence. So near-death experiences can be helpful, although in defending them we might go so far as to erroneously ascribe all of them to the working of God.

That's why I prefer to bank on God's declarations rather than to rely on my own wisdom to figure things out. Standing out in that regard is the OT reference repeated in the epistle to the Romans: "'Who has known the mind of the Lord? Or who has been his counselor?'" (11:34). Pretty humbling questions, aren't they?

Applying human reasoning to the transfer of Adam and Eve's sin to us, we question our suffering as a plague owed to their wrongdoing. We ask, why would God create two human beings when He knew the disastrous consequences that would come about? Surely, being God He could foresee the future. To be sure, God did endow them with free will, a quality likewise passed on to us. But I guess that's why we question; we justify that creative act by saying that God never intended to create robot-like creatures who couldn't think for themselves. Yes, we have free will, but we know that trying to exercise it beyond our human limitations may be going too far. It takes a humble stance to declare our inability to know everything, doesn't it?

Just look at the history of humankind and its thinking about what transpires in life. We constantly change our minds as new information becomes available. But we plod on, putting the spotlight on new developments as we aggrandize our abilities rather than recognize our former mistaken manner of thinking. I wonder if God looks down on us saying, "When will they ever learn?" In spite of our accomplishments, our reasoning ability remains minuscule compared to that of the Creator.

Free Will

The concept of free will creates problems that lead to questioning. It can get us into trouble when applied to the spiritual. For example, it causes us to wonder whether the concept of free will actually exists in heaven, just as it did with Lucifer and his supporting angels in the past. Might it occur even in the future with the angels still in heaven? And how about us? Does the Bible's revelation of our eternal security in heaven abolish free will? Or could the present angelic realm, and maybe even we, too, possibly repeat the rebelliousness of Lucifer and his followers once we are there? Does it put the question of eternal security and heaven in jeopardy? Or maybe the answer to it is that once transported to heaven we are given new bodies including a new mindset apart from what we have to tolerate in our present sinful condition. In other words, maybe our heavenly state will be so distinct that any type of questioning God (free will) will be non-existent.

Let's look at what free will did for Lucifer and his followers -- banishment from heaven to ultimately undergo unending punishment (Rev. 20:10). That's another decision that doesn't seem to make sense for us -- unending punishment of the rebellious angels. Why unending? Why didn't God just wipe them out right from the start? Look at the evil they are engaged in by being allowed to harass humanity in many different ways. It certainly would have changed the whole scenario of creation, including that of man. It's the human mentality versus the supreme wisdom of the Creator. Which do you favor?

Questioning of this sort haunts thinking persons. But maturity in the faith teaches us to face such ideas without wavering in trust in a sovereign Creator. In other words, there comes a time when we must simply throw up our hands in despair as we acknowledge our human limitations compared to the mind-boggling attributes of God. It's something Eve failed to do as she succumbed to Satan's trickery. Certainly we don't want to follow in her footsteps.

People have been struggling with unrestricted human ability ever since, an issue that has been to mankind's harm. We tend to rebel at the idea that we can't figure things out for ourselves, which gets serious when we let it get so out of control that we begin substituting self-reliance apart from God. Why do we do it? Pride in our ability to reason may be one answer. If something doesn't make sense according to our way of thinking, we declare it so, even if it runs counter to God's judgment. Atheists have been doing that for years on end.

End Times Interpretation

I can't help mention a phenomenon created by God that's been troubling me, and maybe you also -- interpreting what appear to be end-time events. Biblical scholars have been at each other's throats on scriptural interpretation in that regards, which may be to the disgrace of Christianity.

Certain issues that Jesus dealt with seem to contradict themselves, at least the reporting of what He said seems to imply contradiction. For example, his teaching oftentimes seems to relate to end-time events while at the same time hinting that they may have already taken place within the first century. All three of the Synoptic Gospels, for example, have Jesus speaking to his disciples about what will seemingly occur in the last days. But, then, He included is his statement that the happenings discussed would take place within that very generation. Scholars, jump on the word "generation" by saying it has different meanings in terms of time. Others hold that it means exactly what it says – the span of one's life, which is generally the interpretation we give it -- that if correct would annul Jesus' previous sayings that seem to relate to end-time events. Hanegraaff[6] takes the approach of relating it to the first century. In fact, he sees Mathew 24:1-35 referring to the first century, and that its teaching must not be taken literally as applying to end-times. But we still are unable to agree on Scripture's meaning of the last days, which leads to various camps of interpretation, and unfortunately dogmatic stances.[7] That seems to be the way of human beings; we studiously try to figure things out and then are dogmatic about our ability to reason.

In the end, we remain confused. Oh that all things were as simple as God's plan of salvation, we say. Yes, God made that historical event extremely easy for everyone to grasp. He wanted

to make it so simple, in fact, that even the most lowly or unedu-
cated person would know what He was talking about. Of course,
people run in the other direction by stating that the biblical plan
of salvation is too simplistic to be credible. So the world tends to
reject the whole idea of God reaching down to rescue mankind
from our sinful dilemma. How bewildering. We strive for simplicity while at the same time reject it -- a decidedly puzzling picture.
There's no question that sin has taken such a hold that it causes
us to go about declaring our own thinking to supersede the wisdom of God.

This makes us wonder if we should refrain from dogmatic
interpretation of certain scriptural concepts that go beyond
the basics of salvation and its effects on Christian morality, especially that which heralds future events. Our human proclivity is to want to understand certain biblical issues in detailed
fashion, which is okay, otherwise they wouldn't be included in
the Bible. But we let that desire get out of control, resulting in
fierce verbal combats on different viewpoints. Such in-fighting
leads to serious divisions among Christians, causing lack of
unity and even lack of love for one another, matters that define the essence of Scripture and even those that Jesus himself
emphasized.

Faith Justified

Christians may be accused of living in a state of make-be-
lieve as we acknowledge our inability to answer life's complexities. Some say one thing while others assert an opposite opinion,
which makes us wonder whom we are to believe. What is dangerous is when we fail to regard the Christian life as one of faith in
an omniscient Creator who wants us to realize our inadequacies
so that we trust him in everything. Paul's words are appropriate
here: "But who are you, O man, to talk back to God? Shall what
is formed say to him who formed it, 'Why did you make me like
this?'" (Rom. 9:20). Just thinking about those statements makes
me realize how inadequate I am in my questioning. I am a being

created by God and hence must recognize my inadequacies compared to the wisdom and finality of my Creator.

God doesn't expect us to understand everything that takes place. He tells us certain things through the medium of the Bible to inform us of what has happened or what is about to happen, but not always describing it in its totality. He doesn't always provide detailed information, and even if He did, we would probably question it, simply because our earthly minds can't fathom its complexities.

To question is part of human nature, which is not necessarily bad but rather can be a strengthening process in helping us realize our limitations. At the same time it causes us to have faith in the Creator's supreme wisdom. But what we don't want to do is to question in such a way as to cause friction with other believers whose thinking may go in a variety of directions. Nor do we want to question in such a way as to tear us away from God. I suppose that Satan in all his subtleness tries to make that happen, to which we must always be astute enough to put our foot down to say, "No, I will not allow it!"

So we question with caution, hopefully with humility, that is, without dogmatism, so as not to give our adversary inroads to destroy our reliance on God's wisdom and understanding. Otherwise we put ourselves in a position of allowing Satanic manipulations to destroy our ability to understand life's complexities. And that ultimately leads to dissatisfaction as we see our inability to get answers through human reasoning, and more, it may have such a disastrous effect as to cause us to question even our faith in God.

We experience the joy of living as well as the confidence of inheriting life beyond the grave, all stemming from an unwavering belief in the good judgment of a loving heavenly Father. We don't understand all his ways. In fact, we wonder why in the world He decided to sacrifice his Son to rescue us miserable creatures in the first place. But that underscores the difference between the Creator and us. As created beings we have incomplete understanding of the desires and decisions of an eternal God. Obviously, we fail to understand the love behind his actions.

Humility

Wrapping this up, then, we use our God-given ability to question and to reason, but always within the scope of humility in the positions we take. I don't think I can stress that stance enough. It's a characteristic that Jesus emphasized when washing his disciples feet. Why did He do such a base thing? To set an example for them and for us, that we should live humbly before our God. God loves humble people, and so do we, because it gives an aura of trustworthiness, a quality we desire for ourselves.

Practicing humility will help us clear up a lot of questions about Scripture and about God's ways in general. That doesn't mean we should stop trying to understand the complexities of life, or even of Scripture, like those pertaining to the end times, for example. (Let's face it: Christians promote a multiplicity of ideas about happenings, often doing it so dogmatically without concern for the feelings of others.) But to approach the task in a spirit of humility in which we recognize our limitations, and by all means, showing tenderness toward one another, will always prove superior over haughtiness and pride toward our reasoning ability.

The temptation to become proud in being able to figure things out causes us to demean those who fail to agree with us, and worse yet, doing so as if it were God-inspired. As Christians we have got to stop the nonsense, for example, of claiming the Spirit's guidance in our biblical interpretations of the last days, ones that obviously were never intended to be understood in detailed fashion, such as knowing the exact time of Christ's return. For example, one man makes declarations supposedly in the Spirit regarding the last days, while another emits contradictory ideas that he also claims in the name of the Spirit. We contribute to the problem by taking sides and letting our own thinking interfere with that of God.

Humility seems to be the key word that God wants us to grab hold of in our attempts to explain things. Some events we will never understand by human rationalization. Yet we make declarations, even with supposed Scriptural support, by comparing one passage with another, as if we had complete understanding of the phenomenon, a definite human tendency that we let get out of control. It leads to different interpretations and stances and unfortunately puts us at odds with one another.

We act as if it were our responsibility to understand everything in detail by emphasizing our natural ability to discern. Our dogmatic interpretations obviously reveal our mistakes. Could it be that Scripture includes end-time information, for example, simply to confirm in us God's mighty operation in the last days, that He's always in control of everything? And about heaven, we don't know everything other than it's a promised home that will delight us, and forever at that. Furthermore, dying is something Christians have been facing for the last two thousand years. Why put emphasis on trying to delineate end-time events of Christ's return and our transport to heaven when the reality of death faces us every 70 to 80 years or so? As if every one of us were to still be alive when Christ returns for his church, and that because of it we feel we must know exactly what is to transpire. We seem to have a proclivity for wanting complete and absolute details, which may be okay in some instances while not so in everything.

Acknowledging our limited ability to comprehend all that God sets before us, be it through questioning his decisions in general or through understanding all that will occur in life, is to place proper emphasis on God's supreme wisdom and our walking humbly before him. That's emphasizing love, not knowledge, the latter I suspect we allow to get out of control. It makes a mess of things and causes ridicule from onlookers, even to the point of distrusting anything we have to say about the Bible.

DISCUSSION GUIDE

1. What is the danger in questioning God's decisions? On the other hand, why might questioning help us strengthen our relationship with him?
2. We sometimes find Scripture difficult to understand. What do you suggest we do to resolve the problem?

VI.

SPREADING THE GOSPEL

Eleven

PERSONAL EVANGELISM

Looking at the title, one might react by saying, "Another bunch of urgings to get us to witness." Hold on! This writing goes beyond that. You will find it instructive.

Sure, we are concerned about spreading the gospel, in fact, the Bible charges us to do so, but how we go about it may require some soul searching. Many of us mess up by doing more damage than if we kept our mouths shut, since our strategies, or maybe best put, our inadequacies, often cause people to get mad and embittered. We hear them saying that they don't want to hear any kind of God talk, an unfortunate situation indeed, which causes us to reassess our methods of communication to make them positive-oriented and more likely to be received.

Human Relations
I got thinking about how I shared my faith with others in my younger days, .as ugly memories of gross missteps surrounded me when I forced people to listen (at least I thought they were listening). Although I spoke out of sincere devotion, letting my emotions as well as my erroneous thinking influence the way I spoke, I pushed myself on them only to justify it as a godly act from which they would benefit. Here are two characteristics I

failed to acknowledge, yet they are ones that Scripture clearly advises us to heed:

1. Show proper *respect* to everyone (1 Peter 2:17);

2. Always be prepared to give an answer to everyone who asks you to give the reason for the hope that you have. *But do this with gentleness and respect* (emphasis mine) (1 Peter 3:15).

Standing out is the practice of gentleness and respect. Gentleness, of course, is a fruit of the Spirit (Gal. 5: 23), which along with respect must be recognized as critical in our communication with others if we are to experience any good coming out of it. In our zeal to share the gospel with others we may ignore both qualities, as I did, and thereby misuse the opportunity to be a positive witness.

Nobody wants to be spoken to roughly and with disrespect. And should we think that it was only Peter who wrote about it, we need to be aware that it was also on Paul's mind as he said to believers in Philippi, "Let your gentleness be evident to all . . ." (Phil. 4:5), then following it up by adding, "the peace of God, which transcends all understanding, will guard your hearts and minds in Christ Jesus" (v. 7). In other words, gentleness toward others leads to an inner peace, one that goes beyond human wisdom. And I'm not talking about those with whom I discuss spiritual concerns; I'm talking about myself. I personally had no peace over my conversations, but I continued on in spite of it, thinking that my lack of tranquility was all a product of Satan's manipulations. I suppose we can push ourselves to such an extent of being unaware of our own bungling.

The apostles Peter and Paul wanted us to surrender to God's ways in spreading the gospel rather than to rely on our own wits. It's an undertaking that must be done delicately, one guided by God's Spirit, because it's only then that we will have a peacefulness to which the above verse refers. You see, our message is one that changed our own lives, and now it's one that we want others to experience. How we conduct ourselves, that is, whether we operate under our own manipulations or whether we submit to the Spirit's guidance, determines its effect on people.

Our Motives

The problem hinges on mistaken zeal. We may be so taken up with getting salvation commitments that we forget about acceptable patterns of human behavior. It makes us wonder about our true motivations. Are we really interested in people's welfare, or are we more interested in chalking up points to add to our résumé? Forced commitments are not always true commitments.

Do we talk about Jesus out of sincere concern for others, or do we have hidden motives, ones that maybe glorify ourselves? Have we considered the possibility of inappropriate motives, maybe ones that may cause us simply to testify in church that we've engaged in witnessing to someone or that we have succeeded in winning a certain number of souls? We often succumb to glorifying ourselves for having shared the gospel; it makes us appear so spiritual. But we hide the dumb ways we go about it and therefore don't seem to realize how upsetting our approaches may take.

Imposing ourselves on others at the expense of their feelings automatically produces reactions of disgust. We often hear people say, "I don't want to hear your religious views, and I don't appreciate your pushing them on me." Some may be considerate enough not to voice it, yet they commonly think it.

The late Paul Little,[8] a dear friend of mine who was a dynamo with Intervarsity Christian Fellowship, had some interesting thoughts about communicating the gospel. Referring to his own experiences of his younger days, he said the following with great regret.

I wish I'd learned this lesson about communicating with people sooner. About once every six months the pressure to witness used to reach explosive heights inside me. Not knowing any better, I would suddenly lunge at someone and spout all my verses with a sort of glazed stare in my eye. I honestly didn't expect any response. As soon as my victim indicated lack of interest, I'd begin to edge away from him with a sigh of relief and the consoling thought, "All that will live godly in Christ Jesus shall suffer persecution"- (II Tim. 3:12). Duty done, I'd draw back into my martyrs shell for another six month's hibernation, until the internal pressure again became intolerable and drove me out. It really shocked me when I finally realized that I, not the cross, was offending people. My inept, unwillingly rude, even stupid approach to them was responsible for their rejection of me and the gospel message.

I may not have imitated Paul Little exactly, but I came mighty close. The message for me to remember is that without practicing human relations I'll get nowhere. At the same time I do untold damage, since people rarely listen when treated disrespectfully. In fact, they turn away in disgust. Let's not kid ourselves. They know when we are pushing a personal agenda rather than showing genuine concern for their welfare.

In place of all that nonsense, how about talking in such a way as to make our listeners feel respected? When feeling that way, they are more apt to take our words seriously, even to the point of allowing Christ to take charge of their lives. We might counter with the argument that they are sinners who have done horrendous things and hence don't' really deserve our respect. But I caution you to acknowledge that, in spite of our own sinful state, God treated us with tender mercy by forgiving us.

Without doubt, that's the gist of the story of the story of the prodigal son. Lest you think that Jesus told it to portray the son's foolishness of having squandered his inheritance in riotous living, ponder the implications of his brother's selfish concerns, and then apply them to your own life. Here is the main message. **The older brother became angry . . . . So his father went out and pleaded with him. But he answered his father, 'Look! All these years I've been slaving for you and never disobeyed**

your orders. Yet you never gave me even a young goat so I could celebrate with my friends. But when this son of yours who has squandered your property with prostitutes comes home, you kill the fattened calf for him. (Luke 15:28-30).

The whole idea concentrates on God's gracious forgiveness, not on our stupid behavior. We are to relish that forgiveness rather than have negative attitudes towards others, something the older brother failed to do.

Guidance by the Spirit

A major part of the problem is our self-centeredness; that is, we fail to turn control over to the Holy Spirit, our helper and guide, one who's opposed to selfish interests. At the same time He doesn't force himself on anyone. For example, we can have hidden motives in proudly wanting to claim conversions for personal benefit rather than to allow the Spirit to work in ways acceptable to his will. We fail to realize that aligning ourselves to the Spirit's good work frees us from worrying about the outcome, or even whether the comments we make in talking about Christ are appropriate.

I was always plagued by such thinking in my younger days. "Did I say the right thing," I wondered.? "Were my explanations clear?" Such thoughts haunted me after every encounter, which clearly indicated that I was centering my operations around self rather than relying on the Spirit's work. But I didn't see it that way, simply because I wanted to see the results of my efforts right then and there. I failed to recognize that maybe people might not respond in accord with my desires. I needed to come to grips with the fact that my listeners might even need to reflect on God's salvation offer over time. The gospel of Jesus Christ is certainly a life-changing experience, but not everyone is ready to accept it instantaneously. A lot of factors enter in that cause us to push the good news of the gospel aside for another day.

I personally experienced that phenomenon simply because of having heard the gospel message in bits and pieces without thoroughly understanding its personal application. Hence, I trod on without realizing my flawed relationship with God. Not until later, in fact, much later, did the gospel message hit me to the point of making it personal. Maybe I was a slow learner, I don't know, but the fact is that I was not ready to accept salvation until it became an obvious and necessary decision for me to make. Isn't it strange how we all have different experiences in heeding gospel truth? But the Lord doesn't give up on us, does He? Thank God!

Now as we proclaim the lordship of Christ, we are hampered in many different ways, for example, through books and seminars we learn how to deal with typical arguments people make to disprove the gospel. Although the authors of those materials cite arguments in good faith for careful application, we often misuse their ideas for the task of confrontation; that is to say, that we pound away at their objections to talk about God as if our job was to win arguments. No one wins arguing about God. We may think we have bested our opponents, but how do you suppose they feel afterward? Humiliated, and maybe even angry? They will hardly be disposed to seek God's answers to life simply because of the confrontational way we go about talking to them. Egos tend to possess us, whether we like it or not.

Of course, it's important to be prepared to handle a defense for belief in Jesus, but to do it always with the right attitude. Would that had registered with me in my earlier days when I was full of enthusiasm but unfortunately ridiculous in my approach. I relied on my own wits rather than on what really mattered -- the Spirit's gentleness as well as his power to bring about qualities He wanted to display about God. Without relying on divine backing I might as well have been speaking to a stone wall. You see, the Spirit indwells us as a helper, and when allowed, He will perform miraculous things. Learning to rely on his good judgment, not on our own wits, is our challenge.

The implication is that the Spirit is always kind and considerate, just as Jesus himself is. Carrying out those traits will do wonders in creating a consciousness about God among those with whom we speak. But there's something else to consider -- believe it or not, at times I have sensed the Spirit telling me to keep my mouth shut, of all things. The reason? Conversation was not flowing in the direction appropriate for me to bring up spiritual issues, and to forcedly insert them would have been disrespectful to the Spirit as well as to my listeners. It would have been a case of ignoring God's better judgment of people's disposition to listen.

Do we understand how that might happen? How often have we done more harm than good by following self-induced inclinations rather than to rely on the Spirit to work as He best understands the situation? Remember, the Spirit works in accord with the Bible, which means that we are always to proclaim his message with gentleness and respect.

What this says to me personally is that I had better look back on my own life, both in regard to salvation and then to how I shared it with others. I must not dismiss my erroneous ways by plodding on unconcerned, but rather to learn from them.

Let me put it bluntly -- I don't mean to say that we can't insert a notion about God or the Bible into the conversation. But it must always be done with the backing of the Spirit, with gentleness and respect. If it's strained and even obviously a ploy on our part to bring the conversation around to religion, then it's probably wrong. God expects us to be his emissaries with the Spirit's backing, not through our own devices. We may not like keeping quiet if that's what the situation calls for, but we've got to get rid of the idea of pushing ourselves on others as if we had failed God by not talking.

Changing Times

I think we have to recognize that people react differently to the gospel today than they did in the first century. Nowadays, they don't want to hear talk about Jesus, even though they really may not understand his message. The blinding power of Satan, our adversary, is in motion to cause people to turn a deaf ear to any talk about sin and salvation. It's a personal matter, they say, and they don't want anyone forcing religious views on them.

Two thousand years ago, on the other hand, Christianity was new and often supported by miracles to convince hearers of its veracity. Seeing diseases disappear and dead people resurrected, for example, people were shaken up over the seriousness of the accompanying message. It may have been God's wisdom to accompany the salvation message with extraordinary happenings simply because the message, being new and perhaps radical, needed such support.

It's obvious that God chooses not to operate in the same way today, at least not in the United States where the gospel has been preached for many years, even though people don't really understand it. That leads us to take an approach that's decidedly supportive of human relations. In other words, we speak always with the understanding that God knows the situation and deals with it as He sees best, which will always be with kindness and genuine concern for the listeners' feelings. Results may not necessarily come about immediately (sometimes the Spirit's message carries into the future when a series of events will cause listeners to give it serious attention).

God elicits our cooperation in that undertaking, wanting us to remember his charge that we go about it in a friendly manner. In fact, He doesn't want us to forget that He esteems us so greatly as sons and daughters that He commissions us to be his emissaries, even calling us ambassadors (2 Cor. 5:20), a position we are to revere as we consider whom we represent. Ignoring his leading, we can misuse the office and cause untold damage.

I don't mean to imply that our application of gentleness and respect when speaking about Christ is a sure-fire way of eliciting desirable responses. We must realize that we are talking about a life-changing event that our formidable enemy, Satan, will do his utmost to oppose. Furthermore, we must realize that not everyone is ready to respond positively to our message. Rancor can develop, simply because the message is about sin and can be viewed as personally offensive. When that happens, there's no need to blame ourselves for wrongful approaches. If we have spoken of Jesus under the Spirit's guidance, we should not look with guilt upon an undesirable outcome.

Accepting negative responses isn't easy, but it's sometimes necessary. We just don't know what the future holds for the people with whom we are speaking. But let's not forget that it's the Spirit's job to cause people to think seriously about their relationship with God, not our own efforts, which means that we need to butt out and let God take charge in his good wisdom and timing. Forget about any idea of self-glorification. If any credit is due, it belongs to the Father, not to us.

Clamming Up

On the other hand, we see those who silently pass up opportunities to share their faith when given opportunity to do so. They may clam up in order to maintain a "good ole boy" or "gal" image, so as not to lose popularity with friends. Too bad, because a spiritual comment can often fit nicely into the flow of conversation to make positive impact. But God never forces it. The message we proclaim is life-changing among those who receive it. Do we really want to clam up for selfish reasons? It's a delicate matter, and we must approach it with genuine trust.

Refraining from talking about God unfortunately is characteristic of many Christians, probably because they fear that any sort of "God talk" will make people uncomfortable. Best to pursue it only when others bring it up, we argue, which unfortunately may be never. In fact, we may take the silent route by throwing all responsibility on God to instigate a show of inquisitiveness among listeners. We fault him when that doesn't happen. It's a dilemma. Which is it? Are we really depending on him, or are we relying on our own resources? We don't know when to keep quiet and when to speak up. By accepting God's role in our lives, however, we experience his personal directives that tell us when spiritual insertions are appropriate. Our job is to be open to those directives and then to comply with the Spirit' s urging, even as Scripture says, "Since we live by the Spirit, let us keep in step with the Spirit (Gal. 5:25).

That doesn't mean that we be so uptight that we don't know when to speak versus when to remain silent. Placing ourselves under the Spirit's control allows us to loosen up and be ourselves rather than to be so hesitant that we end up muted and withdrawn. We have a message that everyone desperately needs, but to give it with good sense is of critical concern. When doing that, we can be assured that God is behind it, which means that whatever the circumstance, He will use the conversation for his glory. That's relying on him to do his work, which releases us from the anxiety as to whether we are representing him properly.

When Jesus commissioned his disciples to preach the gospel to all nations, He was aware of their human foibles. That's why He reminded them of his help: "I am with you always," He said (Matt. 28:20), which undoubtedly meant that they could lean on him for help, even in ugly circumstances. You don't think that He made that statement without knowing the consequences, do you? Looking at the disciples' encounters, we see people reacting in different ways, some glorying in the salvation offer while others rejecting it outright. But regardless of outcome, the Twelve plodded on, even in spite of personal suffering, and so must we, always being dependent on God's input, not on our own resources.

Witnessing without Words

One other thing -- getting people attuned to Jesus doesn't come about solely through verbal influence. Attraction to Christ can result through positive traits people *see* in us -- gentleness and respect -- characteristics cited at the outset of this chapter. Through the way we live, those characteristics often speak louder than words as they cause listeners to remark, "There's something different about you. What is it?" It's a challenge to always maintain an expression of joy reflecting our inner peace.

Witnessing for Christ isn't always a matter of words. It's the way we reflect Christ in our lives that others can plainly see and appreciate.

And let's not make the mistake of thinking that people won't be saved unless we take charge of the situation, as if their decision rested on our operation. Our listeners may not be ready to respond to the gospel at that moment. Forcing it would only get in the way. We just don't know what's going on in their lives behind the scenes. In other words, in some instances it may be best to consider our role as a preliminary one that may lead them to make a decision at another time or maybe under someone else's influence. In other words, get rid of the idea that everything necessarily depends on us. God is at work, and we must be willing to allow him to proceed as He sees fit. Forget about seeing immediate results. It's God who's in charge. That's walking in faith, an experience about freedom in Christ that Scripture so loudly proclaims.

Simple Explanations

I make one more point about evangelizing that I pull from my miserable attempts at it in the past. In addition to my failure to implement critical qualities of gentleness and respect, I mistakenly talked about Christ by trying to give an erudite explanation, thinking that by so doing I would give the message greater credence. After all, a college graduate should be able to do more than render a personal testimony, I reasoned. Instead, how effective I might have been had I simply told my own salvation story. Little did I realize that telling why I became a Christian would be more effective than any academic approach.

That makes me recall Philip Gulley's conversation with a friend about someone he referred to as his "life coach." He "helps me maximize my potential. He enhances my life performance," the friend said. Gulley didn't have the slightest idea what he was talking about, so he simply retorted by saying, "Plain English, please."[9]

How often do we fall into that trap, especially when talking to people with university backgrounds or those of special influence in society? Speaking eruditely to impress them makes no sense whatsoever. I repeat Gulley's reaction, "Plain English, please."

I'm reminded of the apostle Paul's words when he thought about how he had approached the Corinthians with the gospel. "When I came to you, brothers, I did not come with eloquence or superior wisdom . . . My message and my preaching were not with wise and persuasive words, but with a demonstration of the Spirit's power . . . " (1 Cor. 2:1,4). So Paul spoke plainly and simply in the language of the day, and so must we. Remember, it's the Spirit's power behind the message, not our own devices or manipulations, a power we will want to take advantage of in proclaiming the gospel, and thus see its effect on our listeners.

Do you wonder why people fail to respond to God's generous offer of salvation? Accepting the biblical account of creation -- humanity straying from its originally created state -- helps us understand why people tend to shy away from God's generous remedy. Unknowingly they are affected by their own human state of affairs in acting the way they do as they are influenced by selfish ways emanating from mankind's initial disobedience. We all have hang ups that keep us from looking to God for answers. It's a part of our human nature.

There's no escaping the ridiculousness of human behavior that leads to fighting, wars, theft, rape, and a host of other negatives you can think of. In addition, all die rather than experience God's original intent that we enjoy life on earth with peaceful hearts, to say nothing about life after death that God promises those who put their faith in him.

How sorrowful He must have been to see his created ones stray from a once perfect state in the Garden of Eden, yet He generously provided a way of escape through personal sacrifice, one that made humanity again acceptable to the Father and that brought us back to sanity with ourselves. But those who take Jesus' experience lightly, or even reject it by pride or by insisting on their own way, remain in a state of disarray, distress, and discomfort over life's vicissitudes, especially when it comes to thinking about death and its consequences.

Anger

I cite anger as an unhappy characteristic in sharing the gospel because I fear that many of us actually justify it through scriptural example. For example, Paul got fed up with people (the Jews) failing to recognize the goodness of God in providing salvation. I can picture him getting mad at their reaction as he stormed out of their presence saying that if they refused to take God's offer seriously he would go to those who would listen (Acts 13:44-46). Maybe he did that out of obedience to the Holy Spirit, but his example may not be one that we should necessarily imitate today, simply because we don't know the motive behind it. The setting may be different, which should cause us to ponder the correctness of using certain scriptural examples in support of our imitation of them. Again, I suggest listening to the Spirit's guidance in whatever we do, which is the safe way, yes, the best way of ministering to others. We can save ourselves a lot of grief by doing that, to say nothing about its damaging effect on others. In other words, approach the whole matter of relaying the gospel message with deep humility rather than to allow any sort of pride or self esteem to control us.

Our Challenge

Having chosen to accept God's remedy for our sin-oriented lives, we have restored our relationship with our Creator. Scripture says that "to all who received him, to those who believed in his name, he gave the right to become children of God" (John 1:12). Having a family relationship with the Father through belief, then, we have his encouragement to help others realize the same. It's God commissioning us to rescue them from what they erroneously consider an acceptable path of living, yet one that's tainted by attitudes and behaviors that conflict with

God's ways. "Go and make disciples," Jesus said, and then adding an assurance of assistance, saying, "I am with you always" (Matt. 28:19-20). I suspect He attached that final declaration partly because He knew of our tendency to rely on ourselves rather than on him to get the job done. But please be reminded of the fact that He does not force himself on us, rather He makes himself available to us to help proclaim his message as He sees fit.

Perhaps the greatest consideration of all is that we ourselves have received the joy of God's grace when someone took the time to tell us about it. Aren't you glad they didn't hesitate or make excuses? They let God do it in his timing and in his good way.

Being God's messengers, we have a task to be welcomed "with the joy given by the Holy Spirit" (1 Thess. 1:6) as did the Thessalonians, for example, in spreading the good news that so miraculously changed their lives. Following their example, we can be "a model to all the believers" so that our faith in God "becomes known everywhere" (vv. 6-8). After all, why wouldn't we want others to enjoy God's blessings just as we have experienced them? The way we go about that privilege will tell how serious we are about following God's ways rather than our own.

I make one further plea about taking the salvation message to others. It has to do with us as older people who seem to approach witnessing differently than do the younger. It may be that we have less contact with others beyond our families, which leaves us with less opportunity to carry the salvation message. Since many of us are retired from the workplace, we use our more sedate lifestyle as an excuse for inactivity in spreading the good news of the gospel, but I suspect we may carry that notion too far, as we limit our outward spiritual activity to Bible classes, as in Sunday school or in other church group meetings, for example. But in situations in which we meet with people outside of church, we use the excuse of having more pressing concerns, like maybe declining health that causes all kinds of discomfort, or the welfare of our spouses, or the needs of our children and grandchildren, or whatever other ideas we drum up. We let ourselves fall into an inactivity that keeps us from speaking up for Christ when opportunities clearly arise, only to make selfish excuses. Leave it to the younger, we say. But then, if younger people conduct themselves the way I used to do in my youth, we are faced with a pretty grim picture. As I've said earlier, in my mistaken zeal I did all kinds of crazy things for which I now have deep regrets.

Anyway, sharing the good news of Christ can serve as an antidote to the multitude of excuses we often come up with. It's invigorating for us and, of course, it can cause great joy among those with whom we talk. I suppose that the way people respond in large measure has to do with characteristics they see in us. Let's remember that we represent Christ through our lives, not only through the things that we say.

I don't say any of this to create guilt feelings, but hopefully to challenge you to improve on your discipleship. Whether it be through verbal explanation of the gospel or the way we live day by day, we have a hand in reflecting God before others.

Approaching people with gentleness and respect, the essence of this writing, suggests that we *share* our faith with others, not *impose* it on them. That places a lot of responsibility on us, doesn't it? Let's stop abusing the privilege of sharing the gospel by shoveling it down someone's throat. That means that we approach the matter gently and then allow the Spirit to do his work as He sees fit.

We often operate contrarily through scare tactics about hell, punishment, and maybe telling our audience that their stubbornness makes them responsible for Jesus' crucifixion. Our job is to proclaim the good news, not to use gimmicks to cause people to make emotional decisions, oftentimes, insincerely. It's all a matter of allowing the Spirit to do the convincing. Certainly it's not a question of shenanigans that we do, perhaps to aggrandize ourselves, like counting the number of people we forcibly influence in making decisions.

We are to tell the gospel story in the way God wants it told, and we leave it to the Spirit to do the rest. That's proclaiming the good news as it's supposed to be proclaimed.

I would be remiss by stopping here. I don't want to leave you with the impression that we are to share the gospel of Christ as if our witness were demanded by God. It's possible to assume that feeling by applying to ourselves Christ's ambassadorial charge to his disciples (Matt. 28:18-20), as if it were directed to us personally and hence requiring compliance to the point of being an obligation. Salvation in Christ is an event that frees us from ourselves. God has relieved us of good works for attaining eternal life. Consequently He doesn't require us to assume other obligations that would deflect on the joy of receiving his most precious gift.

Yes, first-century converts shared their faith with others. But they didn't do it as a requirement but rather out of joy in wanting others to experience salvation just as they have. God forbid that we weigh ourselves down by propagating Christianity out of obligation. God's gift of grace has set us free to look at life as something to enjoy. We attune ourselves to that inner quality in whatever we do, always maintaining the vibrancy of a changed life in Christ, including sharing the good news with others.

DISCUSSION GUIDE

1. Comment on any behaviors you had in sharing the gospel for which you are now sorry. Why do you think you acted the way you did? How have things changed?
2. Why might we sometimes fear talking about God in a group conversation? What care must we take in respecting others, and how might we carry it to extremes?
3. What's the difference in witnessing through our own ability versus relying on the Spirit to lead us? Can you cite ways in which you transgressed?
4. How is it possible to be a witness for Christ without saying a word? How does that coincide with the adage, "actions speak louder than words?"

5. Why is it that we must not be concerned about giving erudite explanations about the gospel? What have you found to take the place of it?

6. Why do you suppose Jesus emphasized his presence with his disciples as they went into the world to share the gospel?

7. Why is it that older people may feel disadvantaged in witnessing for Christ? How do you feel about your own life in that respect?

8. How might we get so uptight about sharing the gospel with others that it affects us negatively as an obligation to perform? How might we counteract it?

VII.

Undergoing Hardship

Twelve

SUFFERING

Life is full of unpleasant happenings, even for Christians who have the promise of God's care. We not only undergo various kinds of persecutions simply for declaring ourselves Christians but we also suffer a host of physical and emotional disorders that commonly erupt, all a product of our adversary, Satan, who loves to make our lives miserable.

Many of the maladies we have to face radiate great discomfort. Recall your reaction the last time you suffered either physically or emotionally. Were you mad? Did you have ill feelings toward God, or did you just accept it as something you didn't understand and must endure?

The nature of this chapter is to discuss how suffering came about in the first place, and then to suggest some ideas for overcoming it. As Christians we may face undesirable circumstances that affect our lives in many different ways. But it's not a gloomy picture; God has provided a way out. If you have already learned to apply God's wisdom for overcoming those circumstances, hurrah! If not, read on, because this reading can change your life. But whatever your state, I think you will find what I have to say as invigorating; it will help you rejoice in God's provision for you to flourish.

The Beginning of Suffering

Our very first parents, Adam and Eve, decided to go their own way rather than to obey God, a rebellion that left its mark on humanity throughout the ages, causing Adam and Eve to relinquish their blissful state for a life of survival by the sweat of their brow. The final outcome, death, took its hold on them as well as on all humanity to cause great sorrow and grief. All because of the sin of two people? Is that fair? Many complain about it as totally unreasonable as they ask, Why should we have to suffer the outcome of Adam and Eve's disobedience, since we didn't have anything to do with it?

Scripture shows the initial rebellion as follows:

To Adam he said, Because you listened to your wife and ate from the tree about which I commanded you, 'You must not eat of it,' Cursed is the ground because of you; through painful toil you will eat of it all the days of your life. It will produce thorns and thistles for you, and you will eat the plants of the field. By the sweat of your brow you will eat your food until you return to the ground, since from it you were taken; for dust you are and to dust you will return (Gen. 3:17-19).

Wow! What a horrendous result! It's a picture of the agony of human life today that ultimately takes us to the grave. But it reveals even more -- discontent with our human limitations toward the end of wanting to know and control everything. How did that come about?

Now the serpent was more crafty than any of the wild animals the Lord God had made. He said to the woman, 'Did God really say, You must not eat from any tree in the garden? . . . You will not surely die,' the serpent said to the woman. 'For God knows that when you eat of it your eyes will be opened, and you will be like God, knowing good and evil' (3:1,4).

Referring to Satan who takes the form of one of the Garden's creatures, a serpent, whom God allows to speak to Eve as he tempts her to doubt God, then to disobey him, followed by getting her to influence Adam to follow suit. The result? Catastrophe! It's the cause of all hardships and sufferings in life that Scripture declares are passed on to us.

We don't understand why God allowed the rebellion of two people to affect us throughout the ages, yet it continues today among all of earth's inhabitants. Because of it, we suffer diseases including all sort of painful infirmities, even natural disasters such as earthquakes, tornadoes, and hurricanes that seem to come out of nowhere. God declares our hardships to be due to that initial sin that left its mark on the world. We don't understand why He allows the carryover, but we do know that things aren't right in this world, either in our personal welfare, in human relations, or in natural disasters that affect our well-being. Humanity lost its initial blessing through rebellion against God, and as a result the Bible declares us "a prisoner of sin" (Gal. 3:22).

The Power of Evil

Our first reaction is to say, "God, you didn't have to allow that to happen. You could have crushed wrongful inclinations right then and there so that they wouldn't affect us so negatively." But that would be *our* solution, not God's. There's a power behind sin, a very formidable personage called Satan, whose strength, of course, is not greater than that of God who controls all things. Why God permits him to exist is beyond our understanding. He certainly is doing a great deal of harm to us as well as to non-Christians. But someday, when in heaven, we may grasp the rationale behind it. For now we must accept it as per God's wisdom. The big problem facing us is to determine how are we going to cope with the suffering afflicting us.

The Power of God

God chose a remedial path to our frustrations -- the death of his Son – his solution to our sinful dilemma, a simple proviso that He holds out to the world as a remedy for the frustrations of our sinful state. In fact, the Bible states that Christ was chosen from the creation of the world to come to earth to redeem us (1 Pet. 1:20), which tells us that God in his omniscience was aware that his created ones would rebel. Did you realize that God foresaw mankind's rebellion and provided a remedy even before our rebellion came about? We can come up with all kinds of solutions that God could have taken, but that's the difference between us and God; we are incapable of such heady issues, even of knowing the mind of God. The fact is that He did provide a solution, a remedy that's easily accepted simply through a matter of belief or trust in him, the grand Creator of us all. Coming into a right relationship with him is the starting point in our understanding of life.

Unpleasant happenings continue to plague us throughout life. God responds, sometimes in the form of miraculous healing while at other times through special helps so that we might endure whatever the unpleasantness being faced. As Scripture says, "The Spirit helps us in our weaknesses. We do not know what we ought to pray for, but the Spirit himself intercedes for us with groans that words cannot express" (Rom. 8:26). Apparently those groans have an effect on the Father for our blessing.

Yes, we have a loving God who is well aware of our plight and shows his mercy in various ways. The trouble is that we don't often like his ways as we think our ideas of relief are better than his, and we wonder what kind of God is He who doesn't think "logically" as we do. We tend to get caught up in a pride that we think reflects true wisdom for dealing with life's complexities. Are you beginning to see the carryover of Adam and Eve's desire to be like God?

Our Tendencies

So we proceed to respond in our own ways to the vicissitudes that crop up in life. We rejoice in God's provision of salvation, but always putting it on the shelf as something pertaining to the future, that is, our life after death. We are concerned about right now, because we are hurting. Succumbing to the weakness of the flesh, we question why we have to put up with our present hurts. They are painful -- diseases, accidents, financial difficulties, natural disasters, death, you name it. Our human reaction is to cry out, "Why God?" We even get mad at him because our patience runs out for lack of relief. Yes, we want an immediate explanation, as we think the Almighty should prevent suffering from coming about, or at least when it does, that He keep it from continuously affecting us. After all, we say, we Christians are God's sons and daughters, and accordingly special people, so why should we have to undergo the sufferings that non-Christians face?

D'Souza speaks to it with tongue-in-cheek.

If He [God] is all powerful, He is in a position to stop evil and suffering. But we know from experience that evil and suffering go on, scandalously, mercilessly, without even a hint of justice. Thus, there cannot be an omnipotent being capable of preventing all this from happening, because if there were, He surely would. Therefore, God does not exist.[10]

D'Souza doesn't believe for a moment the idea of God's non-existence. He wrote it to illustrate the mistaken notions of those who take an anti-God stance. But we Christians are guilty of reacting in similar ways. We blame God for everything. "God, if you're good, why did you let it happen?" "Why are you doing this to me?" "Why don't you intervene?" "Where are you when I need you?" "What kind of a God are you to let me suffer like this?" And on and on it goes. Do we really want to blame God for everything that happens? Well, who else are we to blame? He's a good scapegoat who is in charge of everything that takes place, we say.

When hurting, sometimes seriously, we tend to throw the blame on God, at least temporarily until we come to our senses. Put yourself in the shoes of Jews in Germany during the holocaust. Their tendency was to cry out with the usual, "Why, God?" The scenario was truly ugly -- starvation, death camps, rapes, and all manner of repulsive torture techniques. How would you have reacted if you were there undergoing their suffering, especially if you had the Jewish mindset of a caring God? My guess is that you also would be perplexed by what seems to be his absence . . . thousands of Jews, including women and children, brutally murdered.

We can be thankful that such a scenario is not part of the contemporary American scene. But it does show the ruthlessness of the human race and the need for a caring mindset. It's one example of the multitude of atrocities that humans commit toward one another. Yes, people can be ugly toward their own species, especially when they grab control of government and are in a position to exercise deadly force, as did Hitler in the 1940's. Millions, if not billions, of earth's inhabitants have been slaughtered throughout the centuries by the ruthlessness of supposedly intelligent human beings who have taken over governments to exercise their power. The mindset even exists today, in the twenty-first century, as seen in the insane threats repeatedly issued by Iran to "wipe Israel off the map." Slaughter an entire nation? That seems to be the Iranian desire, full of hatred and vengeance toward those who make up the Israeli nation.

There's no question that when the chips are down, mankind throughout the centuries has shown itself to be concerned only with its own agenda no matter its cost on human life. Inherited sinfulness reigns even to the point of mass murders of those who contend against ongoing corrupt policies. The irony of it is that mankind continues to spout platitudes about its own goodness in an effort to squelch the Christian viewpoint of sinfulness.

Is it any wonder why we ponder God's absence in human affairs? Yes, we do question what appears to be his withdrawal;

however, questioning doesn't necessarily mean a loss of faith. We question our sufferings out of confusion caused by the hurtfulness of the situation, since it's a human tendency to wonder why we have to bear conditions that seem beyond our control.

There's no question that we must now bear the vicissitudes of life on earth. Bible personalities of past centuries also became despondent over circumstances they had to face, including Abraham, Elijah, Joseph, and other OT figures, as well as John the Baptist and Jesus' disciples in the NT. We even see it in the incident of Lazarus when messages were sent to Jesus about his friend being about to die. Jesus arrived late, after Lazarus had already died, to which Martha responded, "If you had been here, my brother would not have died" (John 11:21), a typical response reflecting the human desire of timing. We want God's *immediate* help, and we expect him to resolve the problem *right now.* Of course, in the case of Lazarus, timing didn't matter. Jesus still raised him from the grave, and in front of all the onlookers at that.

Life in this world isn't always a rosy picture. Scripture speaks of it by saying, "Now for a little while you may have had to suffer grief in all kinds of trials." But in answer to life's unpleasantness, Scripture continues: "These have come so that your faith, of greater worth than gold, which perishes even though refined by fire -- may be proved genuine and may result in praise, glory and honor when Jesus Christ is revealed" (1 Pet. 1:7). Does that mean a good outcome can result from suffering? I think that's what the Bible is saying, even though we don't always see it immediately or even within our lifetime. Ugh, that latter thought certainly isn't to our liking. Who wants to bear unpleasantness throughout life and then to die in the process? But read on to see how God deals with it.

By the way, Peter (quoted above) is not the only one predicting hardship. Jesus likewise told his disciples, "In this world you will have trouble" (John 16: 33), and then He followed it up with a consoling message about overcoming: "I have told you these things, so that in me you may have peace" (v. 33). Peace? "Wait a minute, Jesus, please don't confuse the situation by bringing up irrelevant issues. When hurting, we don't want to hear any suggestion of peace." Yet it's an inner quality that Scripture claims to be God-given for easing our pain in times of hurt. When accepted, peace isn't a one-shot deal; it provides for overcoming a multitude of ugly situations. We are challenged to grab hold of peace because it affects our entire being as it leads to inner qualities of contentment and joy. We will deal more with those characteristics shortly.

In the meantime we see the apostle Paul entering the fray by noting how everyone suffers, including Christians, but emphasizing the fact that as believers we will ultimately be released from this world's horrors. Scripture declares, "We know that the whole creation has been groaning as in the pains of childbirth right up to the present time. Not only so, but we ourselves, as we wait eagerly for our adoption as sons, the redemption of our bodies" (Rom. 8:22-23). So we are reminded of life beyond the grave as an antidote to our present hurts, which is certainly reassuring, but it doesn't deal with our immediate concern about getting help right now, does it?

The writer of Hebrews reminds us of some interesting facts about how OT saints suffered in the past.

Some faced jeers and flogging, while still others were chained and put in prison. They were stoned; they were sawed in two; they were put to death by the sword. They went about in sheepskins and goatskins, destitute, persecuted and mistreated -- the world was not worthy of them. They wandered in deserts and mountains, and in caves and holes in the ground (11:36-38).

A pretty horrible picture, isn't it? Few Christians, especially those in the United States, have to put up with such mistreatments. Granted, it was persecution that caused the suffering of OT saints, not illness or anything else, which reminds us of how fortunate we are to live in a country where Christians don't have to bear such horrendous treatment, at least not presently. Who knows what the future holds? If we are to believe the prophetic words of Scripture, there will be great hardship for Christians in the end times, and I suppose that includes us who are living in the United States.

But we do suffer in many ways right now, including slanderous and harmful accusations that take their toll on us. Disgracefully, they are uttered even by Christians, perhaps with good intentions, but only to cause great despair. What am I talking about?

Unsavory Statements

When undergoing suffering, we may become the butt of statements by other Christians that, although perhaps well-meaning, are not easy to take. "There's something in your life that's obviously displeasing to God," they suggest, while others might say, "what you're undergoing is probably a form of God's punishment." (memories of Job and his "comforters"). Still others might say, "God wants to teach you something that will draw you closer to him." And then there's the often quoted reference from Paul's letter to the Romans that's hardly what we want to hear when hurting -- "All things God works for the good of those who love him" (8:28). Such statements may be well-intentioned, but they're demeaning and hurtful. In times of distress we look for comfort, not criticism or correction.

God's Sovereignty

What attitude should we take when undergoing suffering? We know how difficult it is to experience hardship without signs of relief. We also know that trials and tribulations confront us that don't seem to make sense, and we wonder how God enters the picture. Scripture reminds us of our mortality that actually makes it impossible for us to comprehend the thoughts of God. It's always good to be mindful of the gulf between divine wisdom and ours. Remembering the saying, "The secret things belong to the Lord our God . . ." (Deut. 29:29), which keeps us humble in recognizing human limitations. We are incapable of knowing everything, a notion we might reject, but we will always have to accept the fact that many situations occur for which we have no answers. It's a hard lesson to learn, but it's one that reminds us of our human limitations. Hopefully we will recognize our position as we quit trying to appear God-like in our thinking.

The OT continues to refer to our limited understanding of the world and the happenings therein, as it states, for example, "As you do not know the path of the wind, or how the body is formed in a mother's womb, so you cannot understand the work of God, the Maker of all things" (Eccl. 11:5). Notice that the verse depicts God as being over everything -- "the Maker of all things."

God continues to say, "For my thoughts are not your thoughts, neither are your ways my ways . . . As the heavens are higher than the earth, so are my ways higher than your ways and my thoughts than your thoughts" (Isa. 55:8-9). It takes a good deal of humility to accept those ideas. But to do it in the spirit of humility is what God wants of us, even as Scripture says, "with humility comes wisdom" (Prov. 11:2), and wisdom tells us to put our trust in the Master of the Universe to handle whatever problem that comes our way. The NT likewise offers advice about humility when we contemplate God and his ways.

> **"Oh, the depth of the riches of the wisdom and knowledge of God! How unsearchable his judgments, and his paths beyond tracing out! ' Who has known the mind of the Lord? Or who has been his counselor?"' (Rom. 11:33 -34).**

The answer to Paul's question is self-evident -- no one. Hopefully, you agree.

The upshot of the matter is that we are incapable of thinking in the same way as our Creator, who is above all things and in control of everything. Think of his omniscience, for example. He hears all the prayers of believers worldwide, and He does so all at the same time. We wonder how that can be. How can he hear the petitions of millions of people, and when they pray simultaneously at that? Then consider his omnipotence, when he makes things happen not only in the world but throughout the universe. The man Job, who suffered immeasurably, questioned God about it only to face a series of sobering questions to bring him to his senses. Look what God said to him.

Brace yourself like a man: I will question you and you will answer me. Where were you when I laid the earth's foundation? Tell me if you understand. Who marked off its dimensions? Surely you know! Who stretched a measuring line across it? On what were its footings set, or who laid its cornerstone -- while the morning stars sang together and all the angels shouted for joy? Who shut up the sea behind doors when it burst forth from the womb, when I made the clouds its garment and wrapped it in thick darkness, when I fixed limits for it and set its doors and bars in place, when I said, this far you may come and no farther; here is where your proud waves halt? (Job 38: 3-11).

God's response continues throughout the book of Job as it deals with a host of other matters, but I hope we understand that God is the ultimate power and authority. His footings are so enormous that trying to make comparisons between our knowledge and his makes no sense whatsoever. We need to wise up to the fact that we are created beings incapable of making comparisons between our wisdom and that of the one who created us.

But let's try. It might cause us to understand things better. Consider God's wisdom and knowledge to equal all the world's waters; that is to say, oceans, lakes, rivers, streams, and even underground reservoirs. Compare it all to our own wisdom and knowledge to which we'll assign one sole drop of water. In other words, so enormous is the difference between the two that any attempt at comparisons is ridiculous. Think about it! -- One measly drop of water as opposed to the world's water supply is like our wisdom compared to God's, and then the difference doesn't even come close. It's utterly impossible and even insane to try to match the attributes of God. Are we willing to accept the fact that we are mere created beings? Trying to impose our judgments on the Creator of the Universe is hardly appropriate, yet many do so, only to find that the answers they come up with hardly satisfy their questioning.

Free Will

Some think that God is the cause of all suffering simply because He is God, in control of everything. Yes, He is totally omnipotent, but for some reason or other He allows certain conditions to come about that we don't fully understand. Ruling over a bunch of robots is certainly not a part of his agenda. He has given mankind the ability to make choices, some good and some bad, but for which we must accept the consequences.

For example, He doesn't restrain us in our individual selections of food and drink. That's because He's given us free will to decide whether we want to eat healthfully or destructively. Neither does He control offenses we make against society that obligate us to suffer punishment through fines and even imprisonment. Then again, the way we care for our bodies is a choice we ourselves make. Some people allow tobacco, drugs, liquor, and sex to take a terrible toll on their lives. Likewise we are often lazy by failing to exercise, even though the Bible warns us against the neglect of our bodies as holy temples of God's Spirit. In other words, we may be the villains who cause ourselves untold damage, even though we have God's instructions on healthy living. We decide what to do, and we say that God has nothing to do with it. But then we suffer the consequences of our own shortcomings, even when undergoing feelings of depression, as so often happens to the elderly in their later years of retirement, we may experience a loss of purposefulness. Sometimes such feelings also come about at the loss of a spouse that causes us to flounder about, not knowing what to do with ourselves or how to survive. We face feelings of uselessness and ambiguity.

God doesn't cause such suffering. We do, by failing to follow his simple recipe for healthy living -- a reordering of our mental state and an absolute trust in a loving and all-powerful God who is in control of everything. Yes, He relates to every circumstance we face as He understands our grief, but He wants us to let him step in to ease the situation, all a matter of faith or trust in him.

I hope you are beginning to see that we have a role to play in overcoming the evil effects of suffering. God is there to help, but always in accord with our trust in him as well as in our own dedication toward personal discipline. So let's stop moaning and groaning over our present condition, but instead let's free ourselves from its ugliness and come out smelling like a rose! I know that as of now you are not quite sure how to do that. Stay with me, and I'll try to clear it up.

Silent characteristics may also crop up in our lives that are contrary to good sense. I bring up one of them -- pride -- a huge one indeed, one that can govern our lives in such a way as to cause disaster. Wise Solomon warned, "A man's pride brings him low" (Prov. 29:23). Likewise, God states that He hates pride and arrogance (Prov. 8:13). Why do you suppose? Pride isn't only offensive to God, but it also has a way of devastating us who insist on operating under its selfish principles. It makes us believe we are in control when actually we are unable to help ourselves. Pride is destructive; its consequences ultimately take their toll on us.

Stemming pride as well as the many ugly characteristics associated with it that go unmentioned are corrective measures we can take when reading the Bible seriously. The Bible gives us instruction to cherish, a guide for sane living, one that God has provided and preserved over thousands of years for our wellbeing. Our attitude toward Scripture, then, has a lot to say about our seriousness in listening to God. We can be sure that the world will not agree with us, because according to non-Christians, trusting in the message of the Bible is nonsense. But then, we are not vying in a popularity contest as to what actions are the right ones to take. We might as well face it: we cannot expect the non-Christian world to agree with our belief and actions. How can unbelievers understand our confidence in God when they themselves reject him?

Benefits of Suffering

It's not my intent to cause despair in analyzing our hurts; suffering can bring about good things that we would otherwise miss. First of all, suffering builds character, causing us to rely on the Lord for help in time of need, which influences us toward self-discipline to behave in accordance with God's Word. That in itself teaches dependence on God, which includes a greater intimacy with him and a desire to persevere in whatever circumstances that befall us. It drives us to the Holy Scripture, making its words come alive so that they speak to our unique needs to give us comfort. Yes, we ultimately have to come to grips with the fact that the Bible's words are timeless as they apply to whatever and whenever the situation. The apostle Paul speaks to the benefits of suffering.

> **We also rejoice in our sufferings, because we know that suffering produces perseverance; perseverance, *character, and character, hope.* And hope does not disappoint us, because God has poured out his love into our hearts by the Holy Spirit, whom he has given us (emphasis mine) (Rom. 5:3-5).**

By persevering in suffering, we have seen how it produces character, which tells us how important it is to remain steadfast in trust. We can attest to the character-building aspect of steadfastness as it reinforces determination and furthermore supports our trust in God, which Scripture characterizes as a hope we can rely on.

Helping Others

When undergoing suffering, we are naturally taken up with ourselves; we are hurting, and we look for pain's demise. However, with the right attitude, we learn a lot through the experience, even the ability to comfort others who are also undergoing hardships. We can ease their plight by helping them rely on God's grace to endure even as we are doing. Look at how Scripture talks about it.

Praise be to the God and Father of our Lord Jesus Christ, the Father of compassion and the God of all comfort, who comforts us in all our troubles, so that we can comfort those in any trouble with the comfort we ourselves have received from God. So just as the sufferings of Christ flow over into our lives, so also through Christ our comfort overflows (2 Cor. 1:3-5).

Our sufferings, then, have an outlet in helping others who are distraught, perhaps not in identical fashion to what we have to put up with, but suffering nevertheless. For example, God admonishes us to "Remember those in prison as if you were their fellow prisoners, and those who are mistreated as if yourselves were suffering" (Heb. 13:3). In other words, we put ourselves in their shoes in order to understand what they are going through.

We can moan and groan over our aches and pains, but to what avail? Better to get our minds off of ourselves, and instead to think in terms of aiding others who are suffering, which makes me reflect on our role in caring for one another. There's something about that kind of personal resolve that helps us override our own hurts and in turn makes us dispensers of good toward others. We cannot dismiss the psychological effect that a positive attitude has on us as well as on those to whom we minister. By trying it you will undoubtedly see how caring for other sufferers takes the focus off of yourself and thus relieves you of your own hurts.

If nothing else, suffering gives us a proper perspective of death and eternity. After all, isn't that the grand outcome of life, one that we want to share with others? Paul states his opinion about it when he says, "I consider that our present sufferings are not worth comparing with the glory that will be revealed in us" (Rom. 8:18). Elsewhere, he states,

Therefore we do not lose heart. Though outwardly we are wasting away, yet inwardly we are being renewed day by day. For our light and momentary troubles are achieving for us an eternal glory that far outweighs them all. So we fix our eyes not on what is seen, but on what is unseen. For what is seen is temporary, but what is unseen is eternal (2 Cor. 4:16-18).

The ultimate outcome of whatever suffering we face wields an unmatched attitude to face life with joy as well as rewarding us in eternity. Aren't those reasons challenging to us not to lose heart? Putting our minds to it, we can override anything and be happy about it, to say nothing about its resurgence in heaven when God lauds us by saying, "Well done, good and faithful servant."

Comforting Without Words

Sharing experiences we have undergone, however, isn't the only way of helping others who experience similar hurts. We can have a positive effect on those people without even saying a word. For example, our presence in itself can be a healing balm. We often succumb to the idea that when visiting suffering people we have to present a verbal message. Let's remember that our rationale for helping others is to comfort them, which doesn't necessarily mean to talk. Our presence in itself can be comforting. In fact, the sufferer may be undergoing such intense pain that we may not know how to respond adequately in speech (remembrance of Job's suffering being so great that his three friends who came to comfort him were so taken back that they could hardly recognize him in his disfigured state, all of which resulted in their sitting with him several days without saying a word). Just sitting there, then, maybe holding the sufferer's hand, will send a message of sincere friendship and concern that may do more good that any words we might utter.

The biggest mistake is to fail to be there. Busyness and sometimes the distaste of having to view the sufferer in his or her misery often keep us away. It's a terrible mistake to react that way. The sufferer needs our presence, and our being there in itself is an assurance to him or her of our love and concern.

Put yourself in the shoes of the sufferer and see how much you crave visitations. The very thought of people coming to see us in our distress is so meaningful that it goes beyond description. It tells us that they care.

I can't help but remember the time when my wife was enduring great pain and discomfort in a nursing home prior to her death. I visited her daily, but oftentimes she was so distraught that she didn't want me to leave. The nurses praised me for spending long hours at her bedside each day, telling me how selfishness often rules among the married toward their spouses who had been committed to nursing homes. The nurses informed me that many disastrous marriages are caused by spouses abandoning their mates during periods of extreme suffering, which makes me wonder whether some of us look for excuses to free ourselves from our marital commitments. Selfishness often reigns. Do you remember your marriage vows, one of which was loyalty either in sickness or in health? Thinking about how we would like to be treated can energize us to give ourselves to do the same toward others.

Sufferers need a visible assurance of love, which we as God's messengers can render. I'm reminded of the scriptural passage that states that if anyone "sees his brother in need but has no pity on him, how can the love of God be in him? Dear children, let us not love with words or tongue but with actions and in truth"

(1 John 3:17-18). Operating out of love, we are guided in what to say and do. Whatever that may be, we rest in it without worrying whether we said or did the right thing. That's relying on the Spirit within us to operate as He sees best.

I hope you've seeing the need to be supportive to suffering people. It requires unselfishness in taking the time to visit them, and while there, to give of ourselves in whatever way that's needed. Are we willing to do that, putting aside busyness, finances, selfish inclinations, or whatever other hindrance in order to serve the sufferer? Remember, being supportive toward others who are suffering not only helps them but helps ourselves too. Whenever we do good, it renders to us a joy of having done the right thing.

Overcoming Hurts

We have talked a lot about enduring suffering in general and even helping others endure. Now we must look at what gives us to the ability to stay the course when we ourselves are suffering. It's about time we are getting to that, you may say. I've left personal suffering and its effects on you until now, but I caution you to give it your utmost attention, for God's remedy isn't easy. To override suffering we must give it our utmost dedication and trust in God.

The desired outcome that Scripture proclaims is for sufferers to have faith that God will deal with their hurt in *his* way, a step that leads ultimately to the desirable outcome of inner peace. We would like immediate relief, and our prayers often make such requests, sometimes even demands. God understands why we act or pray the way we do. Please understand that He recognizes our desire for immediate help while at the same time He wants us to wait on him for relief in accord with his timing.

Time is a human concept that God wants us to replace with faith. That's hard to do since it's so contrary to human ways. We want relief. Why doesn't God step in? we ask. But it calls us to reflect on the foolishness of comparing human understanding with divine wisdom.

At times we see God's help coming about for some individuals through physical healing, which makes us want the same to happen to us. In fact, we see in Scripture that healings were prevalent at the start up of Christianity, and we wonder if something's wrong with us when we don't see them happening today, at least not in identical frequency and fashion. Scholars talk about this phenomenon, especially in the sense of dispensational belief that healings were done in the first century to provide a sign of Christianity's validity. But its massiveness, they say, existed primarily as a sign for people to believe Christ's salvation message in the first century. They quote John's gospel in support of their stance.

Jesus did many other miraculous signs in the presence of his disciples, which are not recorded in this book. But these are written that you may believe that Jesus is the Christ, the Son of God, and that by believing you may have life in his name (20:30-31).

Some disregard the idea that healing isn't carried over to today. Instead, they push for God's power to be revealed among all the sick, oftentimes putting their faith in so-called "healers" who may or may not be legitimate but who sometimes make their practices questionable by their constant requests for money and other dubious behaviors, like pressing you to feel that you've been healed when nothing of the sort happens. Such deceivers will ultimately have to answer to God for their skullduggery.

Whatever form of relief God gives is one in which we are obligated to take seriously. It may be instantaneous healing, or it may be healing over time. Then again, it may not be healing at all, but rather an overcoming of inner peace, a quality that tells us that no matter our hurt, God is concerned and gives us the ability to bear it. Again, I must repeat, that whatever happens, we are in no position to make demands on God or even attempt to understand his actions, a stance of humility on our part that He favors and ultimately will bless in one way or another.

If we are to look at his usual operations in our midst, we will have to admit that He operates that way in most people. I wish I could say otherwise, but I'm not one to dictate to God on how to perform. Yes, in the final analysis we are constrained to think in terms of trusting God for our deliverance, which He will do in the way He sees fit, and of course, which will be for the best.

Why do we have to continue hurting, we ask, when we know that He's capable of giving miraculous and immediate relief? It's a typical question that we often ask, but at the same time we fail to realize that God may have other plans, like maybe wanting us to bear the suffering as a means of molding us in ways that we would otherwise never experience to our benefit. In fact, many believers have verified such happenings taking place in their lives that have granted them great intimacy with their Lord. They relate their joy in life to that intimacy.

Peace

Peace (an inner feeling of tranquility) is something the Bible talks a lot about, such as Jesus' reference to it when He said, "Peace I leave with you; my peace I give you. I do not give to you as the world gives. Do not let your hearts be troubled and do not be afraid" (John 14:27). Jesus also said, "I have told you these things, so that in me you may have peace. In this world you will have trouble. But take heart! I have overcome the world" (John 16:33). Those sayings were intended, I'm sure, for whatever suffering we face. (Note that He said we will have trouble in this world.) The effect of inner peace is a quality that the world cannot give, only God can. As for our part, we must be willing to receive it by ceasing to insist on God lifting our suffering in accord with our dictates.

Peter, Paul, and John, all three of them, remind us of the importance of peace as they make a point of including it at the outset of each of their epistles. For example, a common greeting they gave was to wish grace and peace on the recipients of their letters. They didn't do it as if they were following customary ways of greeting, that is, making nice sounding statements without any meaning behind them. When they spoke of peace, they meant it, that their readers would experience that inner quality as a sustaining force in whatever trial or tribulation they were facing. And you can be sure that in the first century they suffered at almost every turn, because being true to Christianity was not easy in those days where any ideas related to the one supreme God were scorned and even ridiculed.

To be sure, peace is an obvious quality that each of us was blessed with initially as we believed in Christ for salvation. We have peace about eternal life that God promises us, which takes away the fear of death. But biblical writers were also concerned about peace beyond that initial blessing of salvation, one that takes over the Christian life to allow for meeting all types of circumstances. Paul even went so far as to say, "May the God of hope fill you with all joy and peace as you trust in him . . . " (Rom. 15:13). Note how he emphasized the idea of a two-way street; that is, God doing something in us (filling us with joy and peace) while in turn we act upon it by trusting him in our suffering. The passage includes "joy," simply because it's a natural outcome of a peaceful heart. Who doesn't yearn to have peace and joy in all matters?

He also describes joy and peace as fruits of the Spirit (Gal. 5:22), which attests to the importance of those qualities. We can be sure that anything related to the Holy Spirit is of prime importance for us to have. Put it into practice! Otherwise, we are failing to take advantage of the Holy Spirit's divine presence in us.

Paul likewise stated: "The peace of God, which transcends all understanding, will guard your hearts and minds in Christ Jesus" (Phil. 4:7). Yes, we have inner peace about our future, now that we have trusted in Christ for salvation. But the other kind of peace that Scripture alludes to is one that deals with trusting in God's help in all circumstances, even when it doesn't seem to make sense. Other people can't understand our forbearance because it's a spiritual quality that we have learned to assume, although we admit that our learning oftentimes comes about painfully through kicking and screaming.

God, then, does provide peace, but as with any good thing, it's application is up to us to receive no matter how great the pain we may have to experience. It seems to emphasize the mind exerting control over the body so that we can overcome whatever ill that comes our way. Why do you suppose peace is constantly expressed as something we have a part in attaining? It seems to be a quality engendered by God in connection with our own resolve to have it as it applies to all circumstances, not only ones we may presently be suffering. It's a balm that provides the ability to withstand and even overcome no matter how unsavory the situation.

Another Bible passage that comes to mind is one I memorized early in my Christian life. I want to share it with you. Although its main message relates to overcoming temptations, it also can be applied to suffering in general. Temptation, of course, is a form of suffering that we all undergo, especially as we resist it. It often causes such discomfort that makes it hard to bear. Scripture tells us that we are tempted by our own evil desires. (James 1:14), but there's no getting around it, temptation hurts. We know that we must stand firm against it, but we also know the reality of the suffering involved. So the connection is not far-fetched. As you read it, substitute the idea "suffer" in place of "temptation," as I have inserted.

No temptation [suffering] has seized you except what is common to man. And God is faithful; he will not let you be tempted [suffer] beyond what you can bear. But when you are tempted [suffer] he will also provide a way out so that you can stand up under it (1 Cor. 10:13).

Also note a critical idea that you might otherwise have over-looked, simply because the New International Version (NIV) from which the verse is quoted begins the sentence with the conjunction "And," ("*And* God is faithful"), which tends to divert attention from the important message of God's faithfulness, as if it were something inconsequentially tacked on. That God will never abandon us to whatever be the suffering is a critical concept for us to remember, an idea that throughout the ages has been a healing balm to the host of sufferers in both Old and New Testaments.

Attitude

I emphasize the role that attitude has to do with our well-being, no matter the nature or intensity of our suffering, which is seen in part in the prayer of a confederate soldier during the war between the states. Here's how he approached God and in turn benefited.

I asked for strength that I may achieve;
He made me weak that I might obey.
I asked for help that I may do great things;
I was given grace that I might do better things.
I asked for riches that I might be happy;
I was given poverty that I might be wise.
I asked for power that I might have the praise of men;
I was given weakness that I might feel the need of God.
I asked for all things that I might enjoy life;
I was given life that I might enjoy all things.
I received nothing that I asked for, all that I hoped for.
My prayer was answered.

The prayer contains the kinds of foolish requests we so often make. Mull over them and see how they apply to you. We can include suffering, pain, and hurt, and our attitude toward them, all of which makes us ponder the extent of our trust in God to meet whatever situation that may arise.

David expressed another kind of sentiment about receiving benefits from God.

I waited patiently for the Lord; he turned to me and heard my cry. He lifted me out of the slimy pit. out of the mud and mire; he set my feet on a rock and gave me a firm place to stand. He put a new song in my mouth, a hymn of praise to our God. Many will see and fear and put their trust in the Lord. Blessed is the man who makes the Lord his trust . . . (Ps. 40:1-4).

Trusting for divine help was the psalmist's answer to suffering. May we remain true in the faith to receive God's assistance to do just that. It's a miraculous help, one that comes in different forms but that puts a new song in our hearts.

The Holy Spirit

I emphasize the role of one of the triune godhead, the Holy Spirit, in dealing with our hurts, who comes into play simply because He personally indwells us and knows what we are experiencing. Yes, He understands our dilemma and wants to help, which He does in a very unusual way.

The Spirit helps us in our weaknesses. We do not know what we ought to pray for, but the Spirit himself intercedes for us with groans that words cannot express. And he who searches our hearts knows the mind of the Spirit, because the Spirit intercedes for the saints in accordance with God's will (Rom. 8:26-27).

And we thought we were alone in our sufferings. Far be it! The Holy Spirit out of love constantly intercedes for us before the Father. In fact He actually feels our hurt. I know it's hard to understand. But who are we to contradict the veracity of Scripture? The Spirit is concerned for each and every one of us to the extent that He undoubtedly weeps (groans) over our discomfort. Knowing that God Almighty cares about what's happening to us, may we be comforted in our individual trials and tribulations to the point of realizing that He will render help.

In some circumstances, we suffer terribly. God is aware of it, and He operates together with the help of the Holy Spirit to relieve us of its burden. That Spirit spells power and gives us joy, not necessarily to relieve us of the pain, but to endure it, just as Paul told the Christians in Thessalonica: "our gospel came to you not simply with words, but also with power, with the Holy Spirit . . . in spite of severe suffering, you welcomed the message with the joy given by the Holy Spirit" (1 Thess 1: 5-6). I repeat, power is an attribute of the Holy Spirit, and that power is in us and is our source of joy no matter the severity of our suffering. And please understand that there is no rationing of the Spirit's power. He functions in such a way as to be mindboggling.

Such teaching is nonsense to non-Christians, simply because they don't have the Spirit indwelling them to affect their attitude toward life. They can't understand suffering for lack of discernment that the Spirit gives (1 Cor. 2:14). We, on the other hand, have him indwelling us, but we would be mistaken to let him lie dormant without depending on his power, which unfortunately many of us do. Paul talks about the Spirit in that context. Power for what? So that Christ may dwell in our hearts through *faith,* so that we might experience the wonders that God is able to perform in us.

Are we beginning to see the importance of faith or trust? No matter how badly we suffer, Scripture encourages us to endure with trust in God and in his provider, the Holy Spirit, by which means we survive whatever horrors that afflict us. We do it with joy that leads to inner peace, not an easy route to follow, but it's God's way, and of course, the best way. It takes our utmost resolve to put it into practice, but by following the formula of trust we can overcome whatever vicissitudes life throws at us, which has been the experience of Christians throughout the ages and hopefully will be yours, too.

There's no question that it takes dedication, or maybe you see it as self discipline or self-control. Whatever your perception, may you determine to trust God for his resolution and thus experience the joy of intimacy with him. Otherwise, God becomes an abstract being unconcerned about our welfare.

A Personal Note

I wish to call to your attention that the ideas behind this writing are not theoretical, as if they proceeded from an academic study of the problem of pain. I offer them out of personal experience in undergoing a physical affliction taking place in my aging body, especially over the past year to impair my ability to function as I would like. I'm learning the beauty of the scriptural admonition to be filled "with all joy and peace as you trust in him" (Rom. 15:13).

It's not easy to continue trusting as you debilitate. It's not reality, we say. But consider the alternative of angrily denouncing the circumstance that's affecting you and in the end feeling miserable about it. By doing that, the toll it takes on one's body is beyond imagination. It's a matter of remaining steadfast, trusting in the Lord no matter the outcome, a stance that produces joy and peace. We know that although for some reason or other we might have to continue suffering, God will ultimately take us to his heavenly abode where He will say, "Well done, good and faithful servant!" (Matt. 25:21).

You see, He has a reason for everything, even though our earthly minds are not adequate to understand. We may not understand his role in our lives until we find ourselves in heaven with him.

At present, I must admit my ignorance of the full meaning behind God's unwillingness to override the negative circumstances I'm facing. But I suspect that someday as I hear his words of commendation reflecting his joy over my steadfastness, I will more greatly grasp the reality of his love for me.

Peace and joy, qualities that cannot be matched by insisting on our own ways. In whatever circumstance we suffer, may we experience that peace and joy! The following chapter takes up those matters in greater detail for our benefit.

In summary, let me try to pull together the various thoughts I've mentioned in this chapter to challenge us in our sorrows. In the final analysis we have to accept the fact that we don't really know what will ultimately happen to us in our suffering. It helps us maintain a humility to rest in God's decisions even if they are not to our liking. That doesn't mean we must waste away and be bitter about our situation, but what it does mean is that we humbly accept the fact that we don't know why God chooses not to heal us, and with that in mind we are determined to override our suffering with every ounce of stamina that we have. That means that we have a job to do, to exert ourselves to the point of doing everything we can to overcome our misery. It's a question of personal resolve and of receiving God's help in the process.

In your case, it's important to be specific about what you can do. I list four actions that I believe are critical to take.

1. Get a new mindset that says you will live positively each minute of the day; that is, that *you* are in control, not the hurt that's gripping you.

2. Ask God daily, maybe before you get out of bed each morning, to help you maintain a positive outlook on life, an act that recognizes your need for divine mercy to overcome the negative thinking that Satan will continually throw at you. The alternative is to be negative and to say "woe is me," which of course, only exasperates the situation to make you feel worse.

3. Continue to be open to the decision that God will make about your suffering without being gripped by thoughts of future healing. (if healing comes, you will rejoice in it, but you won't count on it, rather you will leave it up to God).

4. Focus your energies on being God's servant to others (in whatever way your energy allows) rather than being concerned

about yourself. In other words, maintain a life in which you make yourself available to help others rather than to be preoccupied with your own hurts.

Those four principles tell us to buck up and take control, an attitude that God continually addresses throughout the Bible. We call it personal resolve. We can do it, but it involves perseverance and a relying on the Spirit to help us, which amounts to saying that we are trusting God to step in so that we be victorious over the negatives. We and God combining forces -- an unmatched combination.

Here's one final thought I have found helpful -- when we decide to follow through on the list above, we face Satan's subtle attacks to give up on our commitment. He moves against us in all sorts of ways to make us change our minds and to surrender to him. I have found that communicating with others about my resolve is a good way to fight him off. So, you might want to tell family members and friends about your determination, asking them to continue praying that you be strong in staying the course. After all, what you are about to do is a huge undertaking, so you will need all the help you can get.

May God's blessings be upon you as He fills you with joy and peace. Your resolve will be a fulfillment of the following biblical passage:

Do not be anxious about anything, but in everything, by prayer and petition, with thanksgiving, present your requests to God. And the peace of God which transcends all understanding, will guard your hearts and minds in Christ Jesus (Phil. 4:6-7).

"Do not be anxious," and "present your requests to God," all of which will wield a peace that "transcends all understanding." God's words of comfort and of power.

Peace and joy – attributes that are ours for the asking. But it's not only a matter of God blessing us, but also of personal resolve to overcome the situation mentally.

For more insight on the qualities of peace and joy, continue reading the next chapter.

DISCUSSION GUIDE

1. In what way has Adam and Eve's disobedience affected us? What remedy did God provide, and how do you feel about it?

2. Scripture tells us that God is not oblivious of our sufferings but that He has provided relief from it's devastating effects through the Holy Spirit. How does that Spirit respond, and in what ways is He helpful?

3. We often protest our sufferings by blaming God. Why is such an approach irrational? Could we be responsible for our suffering by the negative ways in which we live?

4. How may we err in the accusations we sometimes make toward believers who undergo painful situations, even though those statements may be well-intentioned? Job's friends reacted to Job's suffering in similar fashion. How did God respond to Job, and what lesson does it hold for us?

5. How is it that suffering can produce personal benefits? Can you give an example in your own life?

6. How does care for others who suffer have a beneficial effect on them and perhaps even on us as well? Can you cite a personal example?

7. We often think that comforting a sufferer must be done verbally. Sometimes, however, we don't know what to say. By what means can we still be a source of comfort?

8. How can an inordinate and selfish emphasis on time hinder us from caring for a sufferer? What is required in its place?

9. Although as sufferers we have a perfect right to request healing from the Lord, what attitude must we take in the absence of healing?

10. Why does the Bible regard peace as a direct result of trusting God? What is peace anyway? Can you explain it?

11. Why can temptation be a form of suffering, and how do we deal with it?

12. What role does the Holy Spirit play in helping us with our hurts? Although we may not be aware of it, what effect do you suppose it has on God?

13. How does personal resolve help us overcome the evil effects of suffering? What are the four recommended steps for putting personal resolve in motion?

Thirteen

Attaining Joy And Peace

Joy and peace are character traits we strive for, and Scripture is filled with references on attaining them. Yet we know that circumstances crop up to counteract their becoming reality, and furthermore, we say, it's not realistic to think that we can always be happy and have peaceful hearts. Ugly situations eventually arise to take their toll on us -- financial problems, life-threatening illnesses, broken relationships, and a string of other difficulties that cause worry, anxiety, and frustration. Of course, we take those problems to the Lord, but we don't always seem to get a reply, at least not the kind hoped for. They have a way of destroying the joy of living.

Learning to Trust

The trouble is that we think joy and peace are qualities easily acquired without requiring much effort. We pick up on the Bible's requirement of faith without understanding what it entails, and then when seeing it non-productive in terms of expectations, we judge it as simplistic, even an insult to our intelligence. It doesn't work, we say. Nevertheless, Scripture tells us that the key to realizing joy and peace is *trust,* a critical stance of *dependence on God to overcome whatever negative circumstances that arise.*

Putting trust into practice isn't easy, primarily because it doesn't always bring about immediate results. That's the problem, we don't like waiting when we're hurting. Oh, so we are supposed to trust and then grit our teeth while waiting to bring about joy and peace? It's a typical reaction of those whose relationship with God may be shaky. It's not reality, they say. Let's see what it's all about.

Most important is to determine whether we are going to believe God as trustworthy in providing a solution to our ills. As Christians, we are reminded that God cares for us and that He knows how to stem our suffering, but He wants us to trust him for it. We try, only to discover that our suffering continues. When one action we take doesn't work, we sometimes abandon it and then wring our hands in despair. So what are we doing wrong?

Our problem often stems from expectations that God will come to our rescue in ways that we ourselves have prescribed. And timing? We want relief, and we want it now! Okay, we are willing to wait a couple of days, maybe even a week or so, but not months or years, or maybe even a lifetime.

Timing is important to us because we are hurting. After all, we remind ourselves that our earthly lives are stuck with only a short span of years. But an eternal God doesn't operate on a time schedule. Do we really expect him to succumb to our way of thinking? Dictating to God is utter foolishness. He operates in his own inimitable way, which may not necessarily be in accord with our wishes.

The OT Story of Joseph

Joseph, in the OT, is a splendid example of continued trust in spite of circumstances. Do you remember his years of suffering prior to his ascendancy to the rank of number one man in Egypt next to Pharaoh? Earlier he was betrayed by his brothers, sold into slavery, jailed under false accusations of sexual misconduct by Potiphar's wife, and abandoned to even more prison time after interpreting his fellow prisoners' dreams. It must have taken its ugly toll on him, even though Scripture is silent about it. We do tend to get waylaid by intervening thoughts about not getting relief, which could have happened to Joseph, too, as he waited years for God to rescue him. Yet in the long run he remained faithful. Wow, Joseph, you are some kind of guy to endure years of negativity without giving up. To be sure, his humanness must have caused him to wonder at times why he had to continue bearing such trials, a trait that affects us all.

God speaks continually throughout the Bible of the link between trust and its resulting benefit, "joy," and then follows it up with its cousin "peace," critical qualities for coping with problems that negatively affect us in daily living. Joseph faced them too, but he had to wait on God to act, not just a few days, but several years. All that time of suffering and hoping God would come to his rescue? Well, there were intermediate periods of blessing; at times he felt things were going well for him, but at other times, disaster. We don't know the reason, but we do see God ultimately blessing him in ways unimaginable, all as a consequence of trust. But I suspect that in the meantime he was learning invaluable lessons that he looked back upon and for which he gave thanks.

For one thing, God cared for him by giving him clues of divine involvement along the way. As mentioned earlier, he was sold by his brothers (a caravan was passing by headed for Egypt that served as an easy way for his siblings to get rid of him). We don't know what was going through his mind then, but it must have been horrendous. Imagine the pain of being sold into slavery, and by your own family members at that. They were fed up with him and his cocky, juvenile attitude, which I'm sure he was sorry for as he looked back on his relations with them.

Anyway, things got better after being carried away into slavery in Egypt. The Bible says, "The Lord was with Joseph and he prospered" (Gen 39:2). The result? He was put in charge of Potiphar's household, which made him believe that his life was on an upward swing. But then came the crash -- accusation of foul play (sexual misconduct) by Potiphar's wife, which landed him in prison again for several years. Then a reversal -- the Lord showed him kindness by granting him favor in the eyes of the prison warden who put him in charge of all the prison inmates (Gen 39: 21-22). But events turned negative again. Having interpreted the dreams of two of Pharaoh's servants who were presently incarcerated, Joseph must have been wondering why God wasn't stepping in to help him. One of Pharaoh's servants was eventually restored to his initial position, just as Joseph had told him would happen, was apparently awash in relishing his restoration to the point of forgetting about Joseph, leaving Joseph to face the ugliness of continued imprisonment,

In the end, we see God coming through with great blessing. Pharaoh had a complex dream that none of his court could interpret. It caused the restored servant finally to inform Pharaoh of Joseph's skill in interpreting dreams, just as Joseph had done for him. So Joseph interpreted Pharaoh's dream and was rewarded. Pharaoh said, "'Since God has made all this known to you, there is no one so discerning and wise as you. You shall be in charge of my palace, and all my people are to submit to your orders. . . I hereby put you in charge of the whole land of Egypt'" (Gen. 41:39-41). Indeed, it was a blessing that brought a happy ending to the unpleasant and alternating events that Joseph experienced.

Think about its implications. Throughout many years, Joseph suffered, then he was blessed, then he suffered again, and back and forth it went. Yet he continued to trust God, even though out of his humanity he must have wavered in faith at times. We are not told what was going on in his mind, but we do know that through his continued steadfastness in trusting God, he was eventually rewarded for it. So let's ponder what it means to trust.

We are not going to trust anyone who hasn't earned it. If we do, and it doesn't turn out the way we expected, we are prone never to do it again. We look for clues to confirm trustworthiness. We observe others, hear their words, and see the outcome of what they say, which gives us a pretty good idea as to whether they really deserve our trust. But when applied to an invisible God, determining trustworthiness requires a different perspective. With him we follow a route apart from sight and audible speech, and to make matters worse, the outcome of trusting God doesn't always meet our expectations, like maybe in intervening periods of suffering (as per Joseph's experience). We want God's help right now, and we even specify how it's to be done. Not getting immediate help, and in the way we envisioned, we tend to entertain negative thoughts that contradict trusting.

Here's another possibility to ponder. Has it ever occurred to you that our initial trust may not have been reality but rather one of simply going through the motions, maybe just mouthing the idea? When expectations don't come about as hoped, especially after long bouts of waiting, they endanger the entire process.

So what's the answer? Trusting God for being in charge of the situation no matter how He chooses to deal with it sounds awfully simplistic. Are we to blindly trust in an invisible God whom we can't see or even hear audibly? Are we willing to do that? I agree that it's not our way of problem solving., but the Bible makes it clear that it's God's way. How in the world are we to accept it, since we are hurting and looking for relief?

Steadiness in holding fast, doggedly fast, to God's trustworthiness results in inner peace over a given situation, which allows us to conquer destructive worries and anxieties that tear us apart to cause great misery and woe. You see, God operates in accord with his divine wisdom that doesn't always reflect our mentality, our human way of doing things. Why is that? We know that He is capable of relieving us of the suffering, even though we lapse in trusting him at times. But in the end, we reap his benefits. It's a testimony of so many people, even of Joseph, the end result of which is great rejoicing.

A cursory look at Scripture shows hundreds of references on trusting God. Why do you suppose people trusted? First of all, they developed a relationship with God that supported their confidence. They knew He was trustworthy because they tested it and saw the results that confirmed their trust. But it took time to see it unfolding.

Secondly, they believed in God's sovereignty, that He was in charge of everything and consequently knew best how to deal with their situation. That's the hard part, because it often requires a lot of waiting, during which time all kinds of detrimental thoughts undoubtedly entered their heads to distract them from trusting. The same happens to us, a decidedly human trait – doubting -- especially when a lot of waiting is involved. Always remember that God doesn't look at time as we do.

We see admonitions on trusting God throughout the Bible, especially notable are the Psalms that speak of trusting in whatever circumstances that come our way. Perhaps all encompassing is the thought that often confronts us when we face fearful circumstances, ones we think will end up even causing our death. Look at Scripture . . . "When I am afraid, I will trust in you" (Ps. 56:3), the psalmist said. Trust is an antidote to fear. What does it accomplish? When supported by sincerity, no matter how massive the problem, in the end it produces joy. "When anxiety was great within me, your consolation brought joy to my soul," the psalmist added (94:19), which was his actual experience, not something he had concocted.

Let's look at how our minds work: we are hurting while enduring our suffering, but having a mind that is fixated on God on whom we wait, we seem to be able to overcome the pain simply because we believe that God is dealing with it. Of course, waiting is the hard part, as I've suggested earlier, but it's a part of trusting.

Everyone wants joy, yet so many things crop up to interfere. One day we are happy, the next day sad, our emotions moving up and down like a yo-yo manipulated by a string of circumstances we can't seem to control. Sometimes those happenings so overwhelm us that they have us think of life as joyless rather than joyous. The culprit is our impatience, which says that we are hurting, either physically or mentally. We don't like the idea of waiting on

God over a lengthy period of time. If help is to be rendered, we say, it should come about quickly. Hey God, we're hurting!

Okay, so you say that God produces an antidote. Let's see what it is.

The very first step -- believing or being born into Christ -- is an experience unmatched by anything the world can offer. As Christians we have taken that step. We recall the angelic message at the birth of the Savior: "I bring you good news of great joy." It's the Christmas story we all know so well, a life-changing event about a Savior being born to change the course of events. That message brings joy to our hearts, but does it last? Does it carry over to the ravages of life after we believed initially for salvation? Not necessarily. And I'm not only talking about other people, I'm referring to myself as well. We all falter, just as any Christian who has his or her bouts with hurtful circumstances. You may be aghast at hearing about their frequent failures.

Having joy and peace is a learning process we grow in over time as we experience different situations that cause us to question their ugliness. We wonder if the circumstance will disappear on its own or whether it will need God's involvement. Some things, like minor physical ailments, often take care of themselves, although I'm not about to suggest that we exclude God from little happenings. But we have to admit that serious afflictions force us to approach God for help. The trouble is that we cop out when not experiencing immediate relief.

The Helping Holy Spirit

Although God expects us to do our part in overriding the negatives that crop up, He does provide help and encouragement. Scripture continually refers to the helping role of the Holy Spirit, the one who intercedes for our well-being (Rom. 8:26-27). Again, we might say, it's not the kind of helper we are used to because of his invisibility. We can't see him or touch him, even though the Bible tells us that He lives within us, which of course suggests all kinds of communication possibilities.

Divine Communication

Now I've got to make this personal. At times I have found him speaking to me inwardly in such a way as to uniquely signal his divine message. At other times I have seen him direct me through other persons or situations. Then again, others have found him communicating differently. The lesson is that when God has a message for us He may communicate it in a multiplicity of ways to which we aren't accustomed but that impact us in unusual ways. I have found that sometimes they are quiet ways, maybe through the influence of his words in the Bible (words of the Spirit, divinely inspired by God himself) or through talking and listening to him as I pray. We can't forget that those are ways God has established for mutual communication in the place of visible confrontation. To be sure, they aren't what we're used to, but they are ones He has decided on. And they are powerful, leaving a distinct imprint on our minds. Remember, He is the Almighty Ruler of the Universe who has no equal. Surely we will want to acknowledge our insufficiencies compared to his wisdom and mighty power. But what's important is to hold fast in our resolve to trust. Why? Because God has his own timetable. Recall God's dealing with Joseph that gave him hope that things were turning around for the better, only to bring up new problems to cause further distress. Maybe it was a time of testing, but the end result was joy.

We may want a face-to-face encounter that would verify God's involvement. But sorry, that's not how He operates. We have got to accept his way as a helping step toward relief, or, we can moan and groan over the circumstances troubling us, a choice we have to make. God doesn't treat us as robots. Instead He gives us free will to decide which way to go. So what will it be, his route or our own.? Those who elect the former affirm it as the best way, in fact the only way that makes sense.

Forget about getting help at the snap of a finger. God doesn't usually operate that way. He may give instant relief, but don't count on it. Okay, so we say that we accept his way. What's next?

Paying attention to his silent voice within us allows us to attend to his direction. It's that communication that's reinforced by the Bible, by prayer, or maybe by other circumstances, even by other people. By the way, I don't expect to hear God communicate if I'm not meditating on the thoughts He has provided in Scripture. His revelation is timeless, applying in one way or another to all of life's situations. It makes sense to see the foolishness of trying to deal with our hurts when we brush aside the communication provision God has already given us.

Yes, I know, the Bible is full of teaching, that makes us wonder where specifically to look for instruction on our peculiar problem. There we go again. We want direct and immediate help, not dilly-dallying around with long term propositions like growing spiritually, which we acknowledge doesn't come about in a moment. But we really want to be led to the particular scripture that pertains specifically to our problem. We are hurting, and we have got to resolve the intrusion right away, we add. But God isn't necessarily interested in immediacy. He wants a relationship, one that He wants to build while at the same time one that takes time because we tend to be slow learners who often deviate from his ways. We may not be ready to receive God's help at that particular time. Developing intimacy with him in the long haul helps us see things we never anticipated. In short, by contemplating on his Word we become God-oriented rather than self-oriented.

Are you seeing the importance of delving into Scripture on a daily basis? The Bible is tantamount to God speaking expressly to us, although doing it through the medium of all kinds of situations.

We see, then, a growth that God wants, and of course that we want too, but it's not easy to come by, simply because of the distractions brought about by our adversary, Satan, who operates to frustrate us to the point of doubting God's involvement. His favorite trick is to tell us how ridiculous it is to blindly trust in an invisible God. Unless we are careful, we are likely to get sucked into that way of thinking. Of course, we don't attribute such thoughts to Satan (we think they came about through our own reasoning). We delude ourselves into thinking that our rationalizations are a product of our own minds when actually they are implanted there by our adversary.

Listening to the Spirit, on the other hand, acknowledges our dependence on God, which gives us the strength, perseverance, and character to accept whatever be his answer or timing. God can certainly zap us in a spectacular way to allow an immediate escape from our unpleasantness, but He doesn't usually work that way. He seems to want to mold us over time rather than to pull us immediately from our particular discomfort. We who have undergone that route can testify to its validity, even though we have given up oftentimes in spite of our better judgment. In the final analysis, as we continue trusting him, in spite of temporary lapses, we triumph, which brings joy. Joy mingled with inner peace are outcomes of trust.

All that by trusting in his divine way of working when we can't see him or hear him speak audibly? Yes, I'm sorry if it comes across as cruel, but it's God's way. Of course, people may consider us crazy to follow such a line of thinking, but then, they unknowingly take that stance because they themselves haven't experienced God's voice speaking through the Holy Spirit and seen its good results. That's why our pronouncements about trusting God come across as foolishness to them, which includes trusting God for salvation. If they can't understand our talk about getting saved, how can we expect them to accept our declarations about God's guidance in daily living? Look at what Scripture says about it.

For the message of the cross is foolishness to those who are perishing, but to us who are being saved it is the power of God. For it is written: 'I will destroy the wisdom of the wise; the intelligence of the intelligent I will frustrate.' Where is the wise man? Where is the scholar? Where is the philosopher of this age? Has not God made foolish the wisdom of the world? . . . For the foolishness of God is wiser than man's wisdom, and the weakness of God is stronger than man's strength (1 Cor. 1: 18-20, 25).

The passage calls attention to the foolishness of those who contend with God by leaning on human wisdom. Unfortunately, to their detriment, many get sucked into relying on their philosophical and supposedly scholarly way of thinking. Comparing our wisdom with that of God has no merit whatsoever. We who have trusted him in our trials and tribulations are able to understand the Spirit's message -- faithfulness in trusting God brings about joy and inner peace – which is not just with help involving a circumstance facing us at the moment but one that carries over to new circumstances that may crop up as well.

I should point out that we tend to be slow learners when it comes to trusting God. Even when we reap the benefits of trusting in a given situation, we may not continue to do so in new circumstances. Our adversary continues to work on us to surrender to what we deem rational thinking instead of calling attention to how we trusted God and found his help in previous situations. We have short memories, and God as our Creator understands our inconsistent way of thinking. The message that we must always come back to is, "Don't let Satan befuddle us; continue to trust in the Lord no matter what!"

Fruits of the Spirit

Joy and peace, by the way, among other things like love, patience, kindness, goodness, faithfulness, gentleness and self-control, are what the Bible states as fruits of the Spirit (Gal. 5:22), a mysterious process that comes about through a combination of God's help and our dependence on him. We want that fruit beyond our salvation experience, but it doesn't come about automatically. Scripture tells us that the key to getting it is through a dedicated trust in God as He communicates through the third person of the Trinity. Little wonder why the Bible puts so much emphasis on trust or faith; it's the key to a thriving Christian life.

A big challenge, then, is that we "keep in step with the Spirit," a scriptural admonition that we must never push aside (Gal. 5:25). It bears repeating -- we can't see him or hear him speak audibly, and although we rely on sight and sound to determine trust in people, in the spiritual dimension we have to approach God without those proofs. It's important to remember that He personally cares about our discomfort, just as Scripture says, "Cast all your anxieties on him because he cares for you" (1 Pet. 5:7). Believing that fact is a critical step in beginning to realize positive living. God cares about us, a fact that I can't emphasize enough. We just have to let him work the way He wants, the way He deems best, because you see, God is our Creator and we are merely created beings. He knows and understands all things, and we don't.

A mistaken notion that often arises is that God's too busy to bother with our particular aches and pains, which causes us to plod on in a depressed state as we wonder why we have to bear such hurt. Oh sure, we display a semblance of faith, like when mixing with fellow believers we make it appear that everything's okay. But we know we are playing games with ourselves as we allow negative circumstances to get the best of us. "Oh God," we cry out secretly. "Why do you let these things happen to me? I thought you were a caring God." -- typical reactions of people who say they are trusting God but who are ready to give up for lack of immediate results.

Someone once said that few things come about without some form of accompanying annoyance that we must overcome. That may well apply to the stance we have to take in dealing with ugly circumstances. In other words, hold fast in trust no matter what happens, because God rejoices in seeing us do that, and He rewards us for it.

The Origin of Suffering?

We suffer all kinds of afflictions, many of them extraordinary. Does God cause them? We can't deny that He allows them, but it would be presumptuous to say He's their instigator. Yet in all of our hurts we often blame him for initiating them. Let's remember that sin is a very real part of this world, going back as far as the Garden of Eden when Satan, whom Jesus described as the Prince of this World, was responsible for much of the evil we bear. I say "much of the evil" because some of our problems are a result of our own negligence. Of course, Satan gets involved when he sees the opportunity, but we are often guilty of causing our own hurt, such as through carelessness in maintaining our bodies as pure receptacles of the Holy Spirit. We get addicted to certain foods and drink, for example, and we even experiment with tobacco, alcohol, drugs, and sex to our harm. Then again, it may not have anything to do with substance intake but rather to foolish behavior regarding finances. Money woes contribute to a lot of the suffering that goes on with people, Christians not excluded. Let's think about how easy it is to get sucked into money matters that lead to financial despair.

Money

Life is full of temptations that lead to poor judgment on spending. God blesses us financially, but we often ignore good sense in the way we handle it, as we get caught up in buying beyond our means. The lure of possessions overwhelms us to the extent that we glibly justify our spending habits by saying, "What's wrong with buying things on time? Everyone's doing it," and all the while credit card debt is mounting, mortgages are in trouble, car payments are going unmet, feeding the family becomes a strain, and even giving to the Lord's work ceases, all of which often sneaks up on us unawares.

But there's hope. God doesn't give up on us but rather guides us to rectify our foolish behavior by encouraging us to take corrective measures, to begin whittling away at the causes through self-correction. Do we have input? Yes! You don't think God is going to do everything without exacting something on our part, do you? It's even true with salvation which, although free, still has to be accepted (received) and done with sincerity.

Are we going to put an unshakeable trust in God, no matter the hardship? Yes, we may have to undergo some serious soul searching as to the causes of our despair. Correction may take time, sometimes requiring a long and dreary wait, but the secret of Christian joy and peace is at stake. So we must ask ourselves -- How badly do we want help? Maybe we have gotten so used to living without personal discipline that we expect God to come to our rescue without any corrective measures that we ourselves. take. I can't help remembering Paul's words to Timothy, when he said, "train yourself to be godly" (1 Tim. 4:7). In other words, we don't become godly overnight; it takes training, which involves personal discipline.

We don't want to be guilty of merely talking about a relationship with God instead of experiencing its reality. The apostle Paul reminds us that joy and peace result from trusting, that is, having faith in God's help while at the same time being willing to take steps to help ourselves, perhaps better said, to *cooperate* with our Lord. Here's the passage to grab hold of or maybe even to memorize in order to keep it constantly before us: "May the God of hope fill you with all *joy* and *peace* as you *trust* in him . . ." (emphasis mine) (Rom. 15:13). He, as well as we, provide input, a two-way street that involves our *trusting*, which means pushing aside everything that interferes, and *listening to him* about the role He expects us to play.

Adopting that scriptural attitude puts an all-important smile on our faces as we never give up hope. It not only wields a positive impact on our demeanor but on onlookers as well, many of whom will begin to view us differently from other people. They are likely to say, "There's something different about you; you don't seem to be shaken by negative circumstances." Or maybe it's a comment like, "She's a delight, standing apart from everyone else. How in the world does she do it?"

Would to God that such comments be made about us. People notice exemplary attitudes; they know what's good and what's bad as they connect with those who demonstrate the positive. They may even step up to say, "You are so different from others. What makes you like that?" . . . which of course gives us a chance to tell our story.

And God is glad.

Do we want inner peace that leads to joy? God's provision is that we simply trust him to bring those qualities about and to cooperate with him as He outlines his remedies.

DISCUSSION GUIDE

1. When God doesn't seem to answer our requests for relief, what negative attitudes do we often have because of it? What is God's remedy, and why is it hard to put into practice?

2. Why is Joseph's life in Egypt a good example of trust during suffering? What did it have to do with the timing of happenings in his life?

3. How does a determination to trust God result in inner peace? What negative ideas come about to deflect that inner peace? Cite your own experience to that effect.

4. Joy is often cited as a by-product of inner peace. Why is that so? How does God provide help through the Holy Spirit to override the negatives that crop up in life?

5. Instead of a face-to-face encounter with God, as did Moses at the burning bush, we see God revealing himself in more quiet ways. How have you experienced such personal communication, and what effect has it had on you? How do you look on others who may have not had a similar experience?

6. An intimate trust in God's communication is often ridiculed by others as foolishness and devoid of reality. Why do you suppose they take such a stance? Have you ever imitated them? If so, how do you feel about it now?

7. Money often controls our lives. How can the wrong emphasis on it rob us of peace and joy? If you have been a victim of a wrong emphasis on money, in what ways did it affect you? What message can you share with others for avoiding that trap?

8. A common reaction to suffering is to expect God to rescue us immediately. Why do we do that, and why doesn't God meet our requests as we expect him to?

VIII.

A Look Into The Future

Fourteen

DEATH

Death, ugh. Its sound brings shudders, mystery and maybe fear, even though we have God's promise of life beyond the grave. That's because dying is something new, something we have never experienced, and hence troubling. It's uncomfortable even to think about, probably because of its finality of life on earth, the end of everything we are used to. What's more, we don't like the idea of being put in the ground, which will result in our rotting away and turning into dust (it's horrible just to think about it). And we wonder about what lies ahead, even though Scripture tells us that we will be with the Lord. To overcome its fear requires a new mindset of absolute belief in a trustworthy God.

We have to face the fact that death reverberates all around us as one funeral after another seem to crop up with family members and other loved ones. Dying occurs due to human rebellion against God's edicts all the way back to the garden of Eden where Adam and Eve in their disobedience heard God telling them: "dust you are and to dust you will return" (Gen. 3:19). Then we see the NT following it up by saying, "just as sin entered the world through one man, and death through sin, and in this way death came to all men" (Rom. 5:12). What an outcome!

As a man in my 80's, I lament having seen so many of my loved ones die -- my parents, siblings, and my late wife who provided me with so many years of joy and happiness. It seems that we have to put up with an endless stream of people dying, which of course causes great sadness. Only memories remain. Some even have to bear the death of their children, which I'm sure is awfully painful.

Without question, death is ugly, but at the same time it reminds us of God's remedy through Jesus Christ. Yes, we are happy over that remedy, but at the same time we flounder about with feelings of great discomfort at the death of a loved one. Furthermore, we don't like the idea that it will eventually happen to us as well.

Paul tried to cheer up Timothy by telling him that there's hope beyond the cruelties of this life. He reminded him that Christ "has destroyed death and has brought life and immortality to light through the gospel" (2 Tim. 1:10). We recognize that death has no hold on Christians; nevertheless, it's a sorrowful time that we hate to bear, and worse, regardless of God's promise of redemption, death remains a mystery, something we don't like to face.

Near-death Experiences

We read about people having died and then returning to life, called near-death experiences, a confusing term because we wonder about its reality. In other words, did those people really die, and what's more, did they really experience the heavenly bliss they claimed having? We would like to believe their experience of a blissful state from which they didn't want to leave. But let's face facts: Scripture fails to give much description of life after death other than to say that it involves a place replete with God's blessings. We look for details, but we wonder if claims of near-death experiences are more a matter of emotion than reality.

We know for a certainty that as Christians we have inherited eternal life simply because God promised it in Scripture. Too many facts exist to deny its reality, in prophecy written hundreds of years B.C.; in the historical evidence of Jesus' life, crucifixion, and resurrection; and, in our personal communion with God . . . all of which supports our belief in an afterlife prepared for us by a loving heavenly Father.

I suppose I react to near-death experiences with some degree of skepticism as I wonder how it's possible for one to experience heavenly bliss while at the same time reject a belief in Christ as Savior, as some have done. I recognize that I'm stepping into a matter for which I can be highly criticized. "How dare you," some might say, "to project yourself into a God-like position to decides who goes to heaven?" All I can say to such accusation is that I follow scriptural declaration in which Christ himself said, "I am the way and the truth and the life. No one comes to the Father except through me" (John 14:6). Anyway, to say that everyone who has undergone a near-death experience actually went to heaven, may be stretching it a bit. But wait! You may find that I'm not as negative toward near-death experiences as it may seem.

The entire Bible centers around Christ as God's exclusive way of rescuing mankind, including the host of OT prophecies pertaining to the Savior to come. Furthermore, God did provide us with written instructions (preserved throughout the ages) on how to ensure life after death. Should we not question the veracity of near-death experiences that fail to uphold Christ as Messiah, who Scripture proclaims as the one and only way to heaven?

I recognize that God may cause near-death experiences among non-believers as a means of bringing them to the truth of Christ as Savior. However, I question the claims of those experiencing dying when they contradict scriptural assertion of Christ being the only way to heaven. Such claims don't seem to make sense when they reject Christ as God's remedy for the world's state of disarray. But then, who am I to judge? Near-death experiences may in some way be a wake-up call that God himself has orchestrated. People who experience them must come to grips with the reality of their relationship with God.

An interesting question to ponder about the rash of near-death experiences published within recent years is whether they support the divine message of an afterlife or whether they are merely a figment of one's imagination. We know that our minds can play tricks on us, causing uncertainty over the veracity of thoughts engendered by mental states that may have been altered by extraordinary circumstances. For example, could we transpose thoughts we have read in the Bible to something experienced in a near-death situation, such as seeing streets of gold that the Bible talks about in projecting a spectacular scene (which may be intended to be more figurative than literal)? On the other hand, maybe those experiences are a wake-up call engineered by God to remind society that life indeed does exist beyond the grave. Certainly the way the world is headed with its anti-God declarations lends support to the idea of God communicating in unusual ways to wake up humanity to the fact that He exists. At least, it seems a logical possibility.

Interesting is the fact that Paul way back in the first century was caught up temporarily into paradise (2 Cor. 12:4) where he was given a supernatural vision. But it was one he didn't dare explain, which unfortunately doesn't tell us anything about heaven's make-up. His contemporary, John, likewise stated seeing a heavenly scene when he was "in the Spirit" (Rev. 1:10), but his description pertains to heavenly persons (the Lamb of God, angels, and worshippers) and to their reactions of things to come. By not delving into personal feelings as to how they regard heaven, their accounts leave us wondering about the make-up of life there. It would be nice to have more information, since heaven will be our eternal abode after life in this world, but then, there's a reason for the Bible's scanty explanation of life after death, which I will suggest in the latter pages on the topic of heaven. So please be patient until I get to discussing heaven.

Trust

In our younger days we didn't think much about death, perhaps because we were given over to meeting the challenges of life on earth. Our bodies were young and vibrant. Dying, although recognized as inevitable, was a long way off and didn't concern us, but as we grow older and hence closer to our heavenly home we begin to wonder what it's like to die. In the absence of details, we put our trust in Christ who Scripture proclaims having destroyed the pangs of death (2 Tim. 1:10) by making dying an experience of gain rather than a negative and fearful one (Phil. 1:21).

The psalmist trusted God about heaven saying, "you will take me into glory" (73:24), but he didn't describe it other than to suggest the inadequacy of comparing heaven with earth. "Whom have I in heaven but you? And earth has nothing I desire besides you," he said (v. 25). That was truly a declaration of faith in the future, an apparent outcome of intimacy with his Lord. He saw being in God's presence more appealing than anything the earth could offer.

The psalmist's relationship with his Lord challenges us to a similar closeness, which obviously comes about through personal interaction with God. But we are headstrong, wanting details about the hereafter. In their absence we are left with confiding in God about heaven by means of trust.

Scripture implies a trustworthy Father, but in spite of it we are still haunted by the thought of having to experience the grave, indeed a very human reaction, simply because we have never experienced it.

Walters[11] reminds us of the harassment of human thinking that causes uneasiness over death. "Trust doesn't eliminate fear and sadness and pain of dying, nor does it necessarily help us look upon death as a friend," he says. I suppose it's because trust involves a personal intimacy with God, a challenge that affirms his trustworthiness, something we need to make a part of our being. We will want to strive for that intimacy to annul whatever negative thoughts that harass us about dying.

In the final analysis, we have God's assurance of a spectacular place awaiting us after death. But I suppose that even if we knew the details of our new life, we might still question the future as we look for supporting evidence. Unfortunately, Scripture doesn't provide much of it other than to say that our heavenly home will be glorious. God wants us to accept his trustworthiness. What does it require? -- a complete abandonment of self to make way for a confidence in the Almighty. Enter faith, which we carry over from the time we first believed the gospel message for our salvation. You don't believe that faith ended at the time of your acceptance of Christ for salvation, do you?

The thought of being ushered into eternity becomes more of a reality as we grow older. It's an astounding part of God's salvation plan that takes the sting out of dying. Even Paul back in the first century proclaimed, "Where, O death is your victory? Where O death is your sting?'" (1 Cor. 15:54-55). In other words, he was saying that death loses its ugliness when we accept the Savior's sacrifice. Paul then ended the passage by saying, "Therefore, my dear brothers, stand firm. Let nothing move you. Always give yourselves fully to the work of the Lord, because you know that your labor in the Lord is not in vain" (v. 58). That's certainly a comforting thought we will want to take hold of.

I believed that promise early in life when I accepted Jesus as my Savior. But now that I'm older and face major difficulties, as perhaps you too may be experiencing, I wonder about the make-up of heaven. Not that I put my eternal destiny in doubt, but I can't help wondering what it's going to be like. Our minds seem to focus on details, which we will get into with the chapter coming up on "heaven."

In the first century, some Christians seem to have wavered in faith over God's promise of heaven, so Paul reminded them of its reality, assuring them that their loved ones who had already died won't be abandoned but will rise from the grave when Christ comes. It's a promise that we cling to.

Brothers, we do no want you to be ignorant about those who fall asleep, or to grieve like the rest of men, who have no hope. We believe that Jesus died and rose again and so we believe that God will bring with Jesus those who have fallen asleep in him . . . For the Lord himself will come down from heaven, with a loud command, with the voice of the archangel and with the trumpet call of God, and the dead in Christ will rise first. After that, we who are still alive and are left will be caught up together with them in the clouds to meet the Lord in the air. And so we will be with the Lord forever. Therefore encourage each other with these words (1 Thess. 4:13-18).

Jesus Christ's spectacular return to earth is an event that all Christians anticipate. We aren't sure when it will happen, and we wonder if we will be alive when it does occur, but we hold fast to God's promise of a glorious eternity with him. We deal with Christ's coming in the very next chapter.

DISCUSSION GUIDE

1. The idea of Christians leaving this world by dying can be discomforting. Why is this so, and why is growth in intimacy with God a necessary countermeasure? Explain what you see as necessary for that intimacy to take place.
2. God instituted death as an outcome of Adam and Eve's sin, but He chose to provide a remedy for it through his Son's death. We are, of course, grateful for that remedy, but we wonder why He chose to retain dying for all of humanity to experience. Discuss the idea.
3. Discuss the topic of near-death experiences. Do you regard them as credible? Do you suppose God orchestrated

them as a wake-up call to humanity regarding life after death? What do near-death experiences mean for you as a Christian?

4. New Testament personalities (Paul and John) experienced descriptions of heavenly scenes. How do those descriptions leave us wanting about what we will experience in heaven?

5. How might dying be a positive experience for Christians? At the same time, how might death be discomforting or even fearful?

Fifteen

THE SECOND COMING

Theories abound as to when Christ will return, which is often spoken of as the "Second Coming." It's a glorious hope, an outcome of belief in the Savior that will usher in a life that will never end. But no one knows when it will happen, although throughout the ages prognosticators have been falsely setting dates for its occurrence. Such thinking is contrary to Scripture and is confusing to many, since Jesus himself declared, "No one knows about that day or hour, not even the angels in heaven, nor the Son, but only the Father" (Matt. 24:36). In spite of that declaration, some people continue to tinker with end-time dates as if there were a secret code in Scripture to be unraveled. I suspect it's done to aggrandize the people behind it.

We can understand why we oftentimes get frustrated over the promise of Christ's return. Throughout the ages we have been waiting for that day to arrive, but to no avail. Life continues to plod on as before. Two thousand years, and still waiting, and who knows how much longer before it happens? We find hope, however, in Scripture that prophesies of the foolish attitudes of some who ask, "'Where is this coming he promised? . . . everything goes on as it has since the beginning of creation'" (2 Pet. 3:4).

At the same time, we are reminded that, "With the Lord a day is like a thousand years, and a thousand years are like a day" (v.8).

In other words, time, on which we put so much importance, is hardly of any significance with God. Why should it? God has no beginning nor end, having always existed. He will fulfill his promise to return, just as he has with everything else, but He will do it in his timing, which He has chosen not to reveal, only to give some general signs of it approaching.

Signs of Christ's Return

Let's face it: as humans we are stuck on clocks and calendars, while in their stead we are challenged to remain true to Scripture that admonishes us "to live holy and godly lives as you look forward to the day of God . . . " (2 Pet. 3:11-12). We have got to forget about our inclination towards time. However, God does understand our makeup by giving us some clues as to when He will fulfill his promise to return.

> **People will be lovers of themselves, lovers of money, boastful, proud, abusive, disobedient to their parents, ungrateful, unholy, without love, unforgiving, slanderous, without self-control, brutal, not lovers of the good, treacherous, rash, conceited, lovers of pleasure rather than lovers of God -- having a form of godliness but denying its power . . . (2 Tim. 3:2-5).**

But we might say, What else is new? That's supposed to be a sign? People have been acting selfishly throughout the ages. We might want to ponder if the passage is talking about happenings occurring during a brief period just prior to Christ's return or whether it relates to an extended period covering several centuries. The latter might be so, since He spoke of deceivers who would proclaim themselves as "the Christ," as well as the proclivity of "wars and rumors of wars," and even "famines and earthquakes in various places" (Matt. 24:5-7).

Another prognostication pertains to Jesus' telling his disciples that they "will be handed over to be persecuted and put to death" (v. 9), which actually happened in their lifetime. But his other words may be in force especially in the future, when He said, "You will be hated by all nations because of me" (v. 9), which may be interpreted as referring to Jews in general (note that He was speaking to Jews).

There's no question that animosity toward Jews has existed throughout the ages, but it seems heightened today, especially toward the nation of Israel that came into being in 1948. That milestone may play a significant role in Christ's return, since hatred toward Jews seems to be on the increase, especially seen in the followers of Islam. Iran, for example, has declared its intention to "wipe Israel off the map." Enmity between Jews and Muslims is obvious.

But back to the Matthew 24 passage that states that "At that time many will turn away from the faith and will betray and hate each other" (v.10). We don't really see much of that taking place today, but on the other hand our time frame may be geared toward the United States where we don't see much of that happening (those events may well be occurring in other parts of the world). We tend to apply Scripture to the United States as if America were the object of its declarations. Who knows if the U.S. will even exist at Christ's coming. Does that frighten you?

We are left to ponder ideas commonly perpetrated regarding the end times: the rapture, the antichrist, the tribulation period, Jesus glorious appearance, the millennial kingdom -- all of which make us wonder about the progression of events to occur in the last days. Scholars have been debating those events for years as they insist on the correctness of their positions, as if they were endued with all knowledge and wisdom to figure things out. That's one of the shortcomings of the human mentality. Although Scripture gives some indications about the occurrence of the second coming, we studiously compare Scripture with Scripture using our intellect to make prognostications that we dogmatically defend and probably cause a great deal of harm when they prove false.

Our time on earth is short, and we crave to see things happening that imply Jesus' coming; however, we must resist setting dates. Sure, we like the idea that it may occur within our lifetime. After all, it will be a glorious happening. But we must stop the nonsense of making predictions or even talking about his coming in a general sense, like saying it will happen within our lifetime.

If God wanted us to know when Jesus was to return He would have told us. In the meantime, we look for clues, not in the sense that they suggest his coming within our lifetime but rather as general indicators of it approaching. We who are older know that some have allowed themselves to get so caught up emotionally as to suggest the Lord's return by setting a specific time for it to happen. Yet they, too, have died, and life goes on and will continue to do so until the Father decides on the appropriate time for Jesus' return.

Lending to the confusion are repeated biblical references of Christ's coming as "near" and "soon" (Phil. 4:5) (Jas. 5:8) (1 Pet. 4:7) (Rev. 1:1, 3) (Rev. 3:11) (Rev. 22: 6,7, 10, 12, 22). The use of those adverbs is perplexing as they transmit the idea of an event to occur shortly, even within one's lifetime. Could that faulty language use cause us to reject the idea of Christ's return? In place of such a conclusion we might want to view the timing of the Lord's return as an undefined future event to which Scripture speaks in non-specific terms ("With the Lord's day is like a thousand years, and a thousand years are like a day" -- 2 Pet. 3:8).

It's unfortunate that biblical translators used the terms "near" and "soon," since those words add to the confusion over timing. Interesting is the fact that none of the hundreds of computer articles on the second coming offer an explanation of the translation of those terms. In the final analysis, we should not allow ambiguous wording to destroy our faith in Christ's return. Jesus said He would come back, but we have to admit that its exact timing is not for us to know. In the meantime, let's not get upset over the Bible's wording of Jesus' return. We are not sure what timing is really behind those words.

The Rapture

A typical idea advanced by evangelicals stems around what is referred to as "The Rapture," an event that many support as relating to Paul's epistle to the Thessalonians.

> **For the Lord himself will come down from heaven with a loud command, with the voice of the archangel and with the trumpet call of God, and the dead in Christ will rise first. After that, we who are still alive and left will be caught up together with them in the clouds to meet the Lord in the air. And so we will be with the Lord forever. Therefore encourage each other with these words (1 Thess. 4:16-18).**

The passage doesn't use the word "rapture" but speaks of believers being "caught up," an action many interpret to mean a rapture as an end-time happening. An entire dogma has been established on that idea to mean that Christians will be lifted up to heaven as a surprise event followed by what many believe will be seven years of terrible tribulation on earth under the rule of one (the antichrist) proclaiming himself to be God and then followed, they say, by the return of Christ accompanied by his saints (us) and the establishment of a millennial kingdom on earth.

The idea of a Rapture gives evangelical Christians solace as to something that will happen within their lifetime, perhaps even in the twenty-first century (Some present-day evangelists continue to proclaim the immediacy of Christ's return within their lifetime, which certainly stimulates their audience to listen more intently.) The final sentence of the Thessalonians' passage tells us to "encourage each other with these words," which is certainly a comforting thought if we are to be rescued through a Rapture and to escape the horrors of a supposed Tribulation Period and even suffering leading to death. But hold on, a rapture of believers as an end-times happening may not be reality.

Origin of the Rapture

I should point out that the idea of a Rapture came about in the nineteenth century by the preaching of John Nelson Darby, a British evangelist,[12] which means that Christians over the course of nineteen hundred years were not "enlightened" about it as an end times happening. That in itself may have something to do with its credibility. What a pity! -- nineteen hundred years passing us by without leaving any notions of a Rapture. But then we don't want to be dogmatic one way or another. We simply have to wait to see how things unfold.

Rossing[13] takes a different view on the Thessalonians passage, debunking the whole idea of a Rapture.

A closer look at this passage in the overall context of the letter shows that it is not about Rapture, however, but about resurrection from the dead at Christ's second coming. The Thessalonians apparently feared that some family members who had already died before Christ's return would be left behind in their graves when he returned – and they were grieving that separation. Paul wrote to the church in Thessalonika to reassure them that those who have died will also be raised to meet Christ, 'and so we shall always be with the Lord.' He wrote the letter in order to give comfort and encouragement, using the assurance of Jesus' resurrection from the dead to give assurance of resurrection also for us.

Rossing also claims,

Most Christian churches and biblical scholars condemn rapture theology as a distortion of Christian faith with little biblical basis. Critics represent the whole spectrum of churches, from conservative Missouri Synod Lutherans to evangelicals,to Roman Catholics, and liberal Presbyterians [14]

She may be stretching it a bit to get her point of view across. I say that because many evangelicals believe in the Rapture.

I don't assume the correctness or incorrectness of a pre-tribulation rapture, or even as some think in terms of a mid-tribulation event (after three and one-half years of the seven-year tribulation period). But I wish to say that the theme suggests happenings that would prove extremely spectacular, a fact that to my knowledge no one really talks about regarding its ramifications.

What are some of those ramifications? If Christians are caught up (raptured) as a second coming event, it will cause unprecedented happenings throughout the world. The United States, if still existing as a nation at that time, may be the country in which turmoil primarily exists, since it's heavily populated by Christians. But other countries where believers live will undoubtedly be affected. (We know that Christian populations are growing by leaps and bounds throughout the world, which may lessen the attention presently given to America.)

The book series "Left Behind [15] suggests crashes of cars, trains, planes, boats, and other modes of transportation operated by believers (supposedly in the United States) who will be automatically caught up into heaven. The situation suggests widespread chaos (imagine operators in charge of transportation being caught up; it makes us wonder about the safety of those they are transporting). But it may be only the tip of the iceberg.

If a rapture actually takes place, a gigantic financial situation will undoubtedly accompany it to cause considerable distress and even rebellion among those unfortunate to be left behind. Those people will surely contend for a claim of the wealth of family members who have disappeared. Widespread upheaval could take place. In any event, the situation suggests chaos due to people's zealous regard for money.

Financial Holdings

What do you suppose is going to happen to the bank accounts, savings plans, property, and a host of other possessions of the countless number of Christians throughout the world who have disappeared from earth? Literally trillions of dollars, and maybe more, will be up for grabs, which will cause great disarray. I suspect that governments, perhaps poverty-stricken as existing today in many European countries, and maybe even in the United States, will appropriate the riches left behind to help solve their economic woes. It will be a vast problem never before experienced. Family members of those who have disappeared will rebel at the government's appropriation of the riches. It smacks of extraordinary turmoil, which may put the veracity of a Rapture in question. Then again, some may see it as verification of a Rapture, holding it to be an event that adds to the many upheavals taking place in the end times.

In Support of the Rapture

Believers in the Rapture refer to the absence of the Holy Spirit during that time, which will cause a period of great lawlessness to occur and which will usher in the reign of the antichrist over the world. They cite Scripture that presumably refers to the Holy Spirit -- "For the secret power of lawlessness is already at work; but the one who now holds it back will continue to do so till he is taken out of the way. And then the lawless one will be revealed . . . " (2 Thess. 2:7-8). If indeed the passage refers to the Holy Spirit as a restraining force, widespread evil will undoubtedly occur once the Spirit is removed. Certainly a plus factor for belief in the Rapture will be that Christians, by virtue of having the Holy Spirit indwelling them, likewise will be removed (raptured). If that be the case, we may not want to dismiss the veracity of a Rapture. But then we are faced with another obstacle, that of the Holy Spirit being withdrawn from the non-Christian world leaving lawlessness to reign among non-believers, but not necessarily among Christians. I must admit, however, that the argument is somewhat flimsy.

Questioning the Rapture and Other Dispensational Ideas

Lest we get caught up in the veracity of these ideas, we might want to ponder whether they relate to the end times. Based on the Mathew 24 passage, some agree with Hanegraaff [16] that the language used is figurative (for example, referring to Isaiah 13:9-10 in which the writer declares that the sun will be darkened, the moon failing to give its light, while stars fall from the sky and the heavenly bodies are shaken). Supposedly the prophet is pronouncing judgment on Babylon. In other words, it may be a mistake to think of it referring to Jerusalem in the end-times, they contend.

Then again, a few verses later we see Jesus making an astonishing statement: "This generation will certainly not pass away until all these things have happened" (Matt. 24:34). This generation? What is Jesus referring to? According to the meaning of "generation" today, it has to do with a period within one's lifetime (although some scholars see it as a biblical reference of some 40 years, perhaps because it was unusual for people in the first century to live beyond the age of forty). Yet the verses that follow the Matthew 24 passage do not seem to refer to an event that had already happened but rather to Jesus' future coming, all of which creates a conundrum for the reader. Interesting is the fact that the Living New Testament omits the use of "generation," stating simply, "Then at last this age will come to a close" (Matt. 24:34).

There's no question about it: the translation of biblical texts into modern day languages may cause problems in meaning. Furthermore, after two thousand years, do we really know the exact meaning behind statements made in the original language?

Perhaps the best approach to take is to recognize the difficulty of making exact predictions about the end times and simply to rely on being transported to heaven upon death. As for the timing of the Lord's coming, it may be wise to heed Jesus' own words about it: "Therefore keep watch, because you do not know on what day your Lord will come" (Matt. 24:42).

The notion of a rapture, as popular as it may be, may hardly be a definitive answer to end-times happenings. Tim La Haye,[17] contending for the Rapture, compares what he sees as distinct differences between The Rapture and the Glorious Appearing of Christ – two separate occurrences. I list them below for you to decide on their merits.

Rapture	Glorious Appearing
Christ comes for his own	Christ comes in the air with his own to earth
Believers taken up	No one taken up
Christians taken to the Father's house	Resurrected saints do not see the Father's house
No judgment on earth	Christ judges the inhabitants of earth
The church is taken to heaven	Christ sets up his kingdom on earth
Imminent: could happen now	Can't occur for at least seven years
No signs for the Rapture	Many signs for Christ's coming

For believers only	Affects all mankind
A time of joy	A time of mourning
Occurs before the day of wrath	Occurs immediately after the Tribulation
No mention of Satan	Satan is bound in the bottomless pit for one-thousand years
The Judgment Seat of Christ	No time or place for the Judgment Seat
Wedding of the Lamb	His Bride descends with him
Only his own see him	Every eye shall see him.
Tribulation begins	A thousand-year kingdom of Christ begins

Scripture indicates that in the end times massive wickedness will reign, I suppose even to the extent that rational thinking will be shoved aside to make way for personal pleasure or even illogical thinking. If the Rapture is indeed true, those left behind undoubtedly will come up with all kinds of irrational thoughts as to what happened to the missing. A popular idea may be that aliens from outer space caused the disappearance of Christians.

The fact is that life in the end times will not be the same as we see it now. Minds will be affected in such a way as to accept events taking place as normal. Rational thinking will fall by the wayside, as Scripture declares to be characteristic of non-believers at that time: "God sends them a powerful delusion so that they will believe the lie (2 Thess. 2:11). Who knows what preposterous theories people will come up with in an attempt to explain end times happenings.

Concern for people will apparently decrease, as Scripture says,

Because of the increase of wickedness, the love of most will grow cold (Matt. 24:12). . . For then there will be great distress unequaled from the beginning of the world until now – and never to be equaled again. If those days had not been cut short, no one would survive, but for the sake of the elect those days will be shortened (vv. 21-22).

Will we be a part of that scenario, or will we have been taken to heaven prior to it as many rapture-leaning Christians claim? In spite of the abundance of prognostications, no one really knows. Could people be living in a dream world with their continual references to an escape from current events? What we do know is that God's promise of eternal life will indeed take place, but we just don't know when it will happen. Whatever be the timing, we look forward to its realization.

Since humanity has been experiencing birth and death throughout our existence, it may be more proper to fixate our hopes on eternal life *upon dying* rather than on a one-time event of being caught up to meet the Lord in the air while still alive. In other words, it may be more sensible to gear our thinking in the direction of death that results in an immediate transformation to a new life in heaven. After all, Christians have been dying over a period of some 2,000 years, so it makes sense to emphasize hope of eternal life at the time of death rather than at a one-time spectacular event of a rapture, whose timing is uncertain and maybe even delusional.

Judging by the often-spoken verbal references to Christ's coming, people like to see it taking precedence over dying, perhaps because it's far more comfortable to think in terms of a spectacular rescue from the ugliness of the grave. But we know that death awaits us all. Fortunately for the Christian, death carries the promise of eternal life in heaven, and if any comfort comes with it, we should be thinking of it taking place simply within the blink of an eye, a happening that transports us immediately to heaven rather than a drawn out trauma of unpleasantness to be endured. Oh I know that we are troubled by the fact that our bodies will rot away in the ground. But we must never forget that eternal life has to do with our souls, our real selves, not our physical bodies. Anyway, God has made the provision of giving us new bodies in heaven, ones that will never die or suffer pain (Rev. 21:1-4).

The next chapter delves into that subject -- heaven and its characteristics -- including the many questions we have about it. May we find solace in its promises.

DISCUSSION GUIDE

1. Why is it a mistake to think of Christ's return in terms of happenings to take place solely in the United States? We know that Christians in other countries are undergoing great persecution, even death, because of their faith. It seems to take place especially in Arab countries where Muslims kill Christians as an act supported by God. Should we view those acts as an end-time event, or should we accept them as inevitable outcomes in an evil world?

2. Discuss the Rapture that some Christians declare as an end-time event. When did the idea originate and why might it cause us to question it's veracity? Why is it that some put greater emphasis on death as an alternate happening?

3. What is Rossing's position on the Rapture? Why might it be credible or not credible?

4. Review Matthew 24 in its reference to the end times. Discuss the possibility that part of it may have happened in the first century. Include Jesus' referral to "this generation" (v. 34). What does it all mean?

5. How does the Holy Spirit's supposed departure from earth support the veracity of a Rapture? Why might his departure not be entirely true?

6. What position should we take regarding the many biblical references that refer to Christ's coming as "near" or "soon.?" How might that terminology affect one's belief in the inerrancy of the Bible? What solution would be logical to uphold?

Sixteen

Heaven

What is heaven all about? Sure, as Christians we know it will be our ultimate destination where we will live with God forever, but we have to admit having a barrage of questions about it.

The Bible does talk somewhat about our future home, but unfortunately does so in ways that don't really deal with the specifics that cross our minds. Of course, we know that whatever God plans for our future will be for the best, just as we trust him for salvation that annuls the horrors of death and hell, so we trust him for a spectacular life in heaven. Yet we continue to be inquisitive as we ponder heaven's characteristics.

I must admit that the older I get, the more I wonder about heaven's makeup. My body's aches and pains cause me to zero in on that future home where suffering will be nonexistent. I can't help thinking about leaving my physical woes behind to take on a brand-new body and mind. You bet I'll relish it.

At the same time I don't really know much about life in heaven. In fact, I wonder about a lot of things that the Bible doesn't mention. Because of Scripture's relative silence about heaven, a lot of people see it as a rather dreary place, something they can't get excited about. How many times have we heard a description that someone made up about sitting on clouds and playing harps all day long. Who wouldn't be bored stiff doing that? Of course, it's all nonsense, but we have to admit that the Bible gives little information about heaven. So we remain somewhat uneasy about it, not necessarily skeptical of its reality but at least wondering what it will be like.

Constraints on Heaven's Description

Could it be that heaven's details are so distinct from our earthly experience that even if explained we wouldn't understand them? Would we really know what heaven is like if it were outlined in detail? I doubt it, because earthly minds are incapable of grasping explanations about a heavenly realm that's distinct from anything we've known. We must come to grips with the fact that God created us with earthly bodies and minds to meet the requirements of living on this planet. So, any attempts at describing heaven would be far beyond our perceptions. Some have tried, claiming to have died (called "near-death experiences), but their explanations are naturally couched in earthly language, which restricts them from conveying their true experiences. Some who claim to have undergone a near-death experience actually say that they don't have the words to explain what it was like, which may be actual fact simply because their explanations are tied to earthly concepts Their feelings went far beyond description, so they refrained from delving into them. More about that later.

Paradise

Knowing that everything about God is so far beyond our imagination, we concede that his abode may defy description. It takes a great deal of humility to accept our human limitations, and I suspect God has refrained from describing life in heaven simply because its magnificence goes beyond human description. After all, Jesus did refer to a future place that He described to the thief crucified next to him as paradise. Paradise? Try defining it. It suggests all kinds of exquisite feelings we find difficult to explain. A place of unending happiness and exhilaration, we might venture a guess in saying. But I suspect that such a description merely scratches the surface. It's the abode of the Creator of the Universe; it has no limitations. Our earthly bodies are incapable of understanding all that's involved in the word paradise. But let's not despair, for God will lavish us with heavenly bodies with which to enjoy our future home to the utmost. After all, how can an earthly body and mind designed to understand earthly things function to comprehend the heavenly realm?

Scripture does give us some indication of heaven that we can understand, describing it as a splendorous place containing streets of gold and a fantastic display of jeweled structures. Whether that description is literal is open to debate, but it does appeal to human senses in painting a spectacular scene, which may be the rationale behind it. I call attention to Don Piper's experience in heaven after his car crash and supposed death in which he identifies the streets of gold as literal.[18] It may cause us to question the reality of what he claimed seeing. (Could he have been influenced by biblical references to heaven's streets of gold which he had read earlier?) But we might be cautious in making that judgment since we know that someone else also experienced a heavenly visit -- the apostle Paul (2 Cor. 12:2-3) -- which underscores the fact that God does allow select humans to get a personal glimpse of our eternal abode. Different from Don Piper, however, Paul declined to delve into the specifics, saying that "He heard inexpressible things, things that man is not permitted to tell" (v. 4). Have you wondered what they were?

Perhaps more convincing is the impact Don Piper's experience has had on so many people accepting Christ as well as the comfort it has given to broken-hearted people at their wits end in suffering. There's no question about it, Piper's experience was breathtaking; it challenges us about the splendors of heaven. Could it be that his vision of heaven was given as a means of reminding us of heaven's magnificence so that we not fear death but rather accept it as a stepping stone to a glorious life beyond? I must confess that it reinforces heaven as a place awaiting me, one consisting of eternal bliss beyond imagination to which Scripture seems to allude. My guess, however, is that words don't approach the full reality of heaven's splendor. Don Piper said, "I can't begin to put into words what it looked like, sounded like, and felt like,"[19] probably because heaven's description is beyond human language. In other words, any attempts at describing heaven would probably fall by the wayside. We would have to experience it in order for it to register. And then it would be impossible to explain with an earthly language, since the way we feel about something and our ability to express it through words seem to be distinct characteristics. But whatever be heaven's physical properties, they will undoubtedly dazzle us with their magnificence.

We don't have a clue as to our perceptions and feelings about our eternal home.

We know it will be wonderful, but we have no idea of its effect on us, simply because the change from earth to heaven will undoubtedly be totally contrary to any human reaction. We may get some notion of it from people like Don Piper as well as from others who claim to have died and then come back to life again. But one impression stands out -- they were so overwhelmed with blissful feelings that they wanted to remain there rather than to return to earth. That in itself tells us that their experiences seem more than breathtaking; they influenced them in such a manner as to make them unwilling to return to their former lives. Now that's something, isn't it? -- wanting to cancel out everything about life on earth, including the memories of spouses and family members, in order to feel the bliss of heaven. Hmm, it sounds like something never before experienced, doesn't it?

I used the word "bliss" in referring to our perceptions of heaven, probably because it's the closest I can get in describing my feelings about it. The dictionary defines bliss as extreme happiness, joy, even ecstasy. I would go so far as to say that it's a feeling difficult to express.

No one in his right mind would limit God, Creator of the Universe, in the glories of his abode. When talking about heaven, who would be so ridiculous as to put restrictions on it? It's contrary to anything we have experienced. I would go so far as to say that heaven is limitless. Furthermore, ponder the implications of created beings imposing an earthly language system on the one who created us. Where do we get the audacity to do that?

Language Limitations

So heaven's characteristics must surely extend well beyond anything we have experienced. Have you ever been so overwhelmed with the beauty of nature that you couldn't find adequate words to explain it? You tried, fumbling with adjectives but ended up saying something like, "It was so breathtaking, I really can't describe it." Yet we had a feeling of wonder and astonishment that overwhelmed us. Could it be that heaven is so spectacular and overpowering that its description goes beyond our human expression system?

I suspect that our earthly communication systems can't even get close to describing God's abode, which may be the reason for the Bible's limited description of heaven. A hazy picture predominates, but always suggesting grandeur that will never lose its appeal. So we trust God about heaven being spectacular beyond our ability to imagine. But more important than its physical make-up is the fact that we will actually be there, and for all eternity at that. Can you imagine, being reunited with loved ones, not to mention being in the presence of the Lord of the Universe who understands our yearnings and who meets every one of them?

As a former language professor, I can understand the deficiencies of an earthly language system as well as our earthly makeup in describing the heavenly realm. Although language is a remarkable system of communication, it undoubtedly can't get close to describing the abode of the great God of the universe, a situation in which we presently can't comprehend, simply because we are tied to an earthly culture. It's all we know, and our language and thoughts are tied to it, which I suspect is the reason for Scripture's relative silence on heaven. We have severe limitations in our earthly bodies and minds, so I suggest that as created beings we have the capacity to understand happenings only within the context of life on earth. Understanding heaven is another matter, something far beyond our human ability to imagine. Maybe that's why Jesus didn't go into detail in talking about heaven as well as why He implied that we would experience a transformation with new bodies in heaven.

While on earth, Jesus did mention one of heaven's physical aspects. He told his disciples he was leaving to prepare a home for them. Naturally they were curious about what He was saying, but they didn't understand the import of it all. Wasn't He to establish a kingdom on earth, something they knew that Scripture pointed to about Messiah's coming? That's what they had been thinking all along, and they were right, except that Messiah didn't come in terms of their expectations as a glorious conqueror to establish his earthly kingdom immediately. They couldn't get rid of the idea of timing, as seen later after his resurrection and personal appearance before them when they asked, "Lord, are you at this time going to restore the kingdom to Israel?" (Acts 1:6), to which He replied, "It is not for you to know the times or dates the Father has set by his own authority" (v.7). It's true that scoffers will jump on the fact that it hasn't occurred within the past twenty-one centuries. Scripture prophesied of such faulty reasoning:

You must understand that in the last days scoffers will come, scoffing and following their own evil desires. They will say, 'Where is this coming he promised? Ever since our fathers died, everything goes on as it has since the beginning of creation' (2 Peter 3:3-4).

Jesus limited his description of heaven simply by saying, "In my Father's house are many rooms" (John 14:2). Now that doesn't really sound like much, does it? But I suspect that the disciples were curious and thus wanted Jesus to describe his Father's house in greater detail. The Bible doesn't get specific in explaining it, but it does imply heaven to be a place of unimaginable and everlasting joy. Would God contradict that idea when talking about an abode where we will spend eternity, one in which we have been putting our hopes while on earth, a life eternal after death?

A Wedding in Heaven

What was important for the disciples was that Jesus was leaving earth to make preparation for them in their new home. We would expect that preparation to be a glorious surprise. After all, Jesus is depicted as a bridegroom and we his bride, so what bridegroom wouldn't be concerned about doing his utmost in preparing for his loved one? Having a deep-seated love, one so intimate and intense that includes a willingness to die for her, Jesus would surely want to surprise his bride (us) with blessings beyond imagination. When will that happen? Jesus said that no one knows, only the Father. I can't help visualizing a scene in heaven in which the Father tells the Son seated at his right hand, "Now's the time. Go get your bride!" That will be a time of emotionalism and celebration by both bridegroom and bride.

NT writers under divine inspiration did pick up the banner to explain heaven somewhat, but their disclosure was wanting. They were human just as everyone else, lacking the ability to truly relate heaven's essence. It did reveal an important point that all humanity yearns for -- a release from our present suffering, which includes the removal of pain and the creation of bodies that won't debilitate. Ah, good news, especially for those of us whose bodies are racked with all kinds of infirmities that drag us down.

But all that registers around what won't be -- the negatives, which we clearly understand, simply because we have been suffering them all along. The positives are hardly mentioned, probably because they go beyond earthly mindsets. How can we presently understand heavenly things with earthly minds? That may be the reason for the Bible's relative silence about our future home.

But let's continue with the negatives, our sufferings, for a moment. NT writers also spoke of the non-existence of unpleasant experiences in heaven, ones that continually crop up in life on earth, like increased consciousness of death as we enter our senior years. Death is the one thing we hate to face, probably in one sense because of the pain that often precedes it, but in another sense, the fear, or perhaps better said, the discomfort it engenders simply due to being an unknown that we've never experienced. Furthermore, the idea of being separated from family members troubles us, even though that separation will be for a brief period of time.

Unfortunately, death has been passed on to everyone as a result of the sin of our forefathers, Adam and Eve, a negative that God for some reason has chosen not to remove. We are loaded with sinful tendencies, not able to help ourselves. But thank God He has provided a way of escape through the cross work of his Son (putting humanity at a decision course to either accept or reject it). We rejoice in that provision, because we know that no one dies in heaven; it's an eternal abode. The fact of the matter is that death on earth for Christians is a fleeting moment, a pause in which we are transported from earth to heaven at the blink of an eye. But to be fair, we have a bunch of other concerns.

One that looms large is our physical makeup. What will it be like up there? Or is it down there? Wherever. Our minds entertain a number of thoughts about the kinds of bodies we will have. So let's delve into that idea.

Glorified Bodies

Scripture says we will get new bodies, different from what we have now (1 Cor. 15:40), which makes us wonder what form those bodies will take. How about age, for example? We depend on appearances in order to recognize people we have known. Certainly we can't have a scene of crawling infants interacting with adults in heaven, so we ask if we will be of different ages, which without doubt is an earthly way of thinking that must be put aside. Paul tells us that we will experience a transformation (Phil. 3:21), probably inferring that we will be able to identify people regardless of their age. It's something God will make happen, even though it defies human logic, but I suppose our human mentality prevents us from understanding the transposition that will take place. Earthly ways of thinking are hardly the kind of experiences that await us in heaven; instead, new minds not restricted to time nor to past experiences will be ours.

We can be assured that in his divine power God will know our yearning to see and recognize long-deceased family members and they toward us. We look forward to seeing loved ones with whom we delighted on earth, and thus God will make it happen. For example, will I recognize my mother who died when I was a mere lad of twelve? It's been so long that I can't remember much about her, and I wonder how she will recognize me, a man now in his eighties? Knowing the importance of earthly relations, God will surely see to it that such problems don't occur. But my mind continues to wonder how Mom and I will locate each other amidst the millions (maybe billions or trillions) of heaven's inhabitants. You see, I'm still thinking in earthly terms.

And how about Dad, my three siblings, and my late wife? Will I be able to find them, or will I be so caught up in the glory of God himself that earthly relations will be unimportant? It's one of the mysteries on which the Bible is silent but which still haunts me. Of course, I'm aware of it being a question of trust in God who will take care of such matters for my joy. Yes, I'm sure that my trust in a trustworthy Father is of absolute importance, out of the fact that He knows my earthly mindset and the things that are dear to me.

Disappointments surely won't exist in heaven. I have to remember that our God is a miracle worker who will see to it that all my yearnings are completely satisfied. Knowing who God is, I have a hunch that He will go way beyond human feelings in making heaven a joyous experience. I have no idea how He will do it, but I know it will happen simply due to the fact that I know He is one who understands and cares for me and sets things in motion out of his unlimited power. After all, we are talking about one without beginning and without end, the King of the Universe, one beyond description, just like his heavenly abode.

What will God do about human relations in heaven? I suspect He will honor our past remembrances and do so by transforming us in such a way as to recall our loved one's characteristics. Don Piper in his near-death experience suggests that possibility as he talks about seeing people in heaven he had known before their death, including his great-grandmother who "stood strong and upright, and the wrinkles had been erased from her face . . . I sensed that age has no meaning in heaven,"[20] he said. Of others, he explained,

> They were of the same age they had been the last time I had seen them – except that all the ravages of living on earth had vanished. Even though some of their features may not have been considered attractive on earth, in heaven every feature was perfect, beautiful, and wonderful to gaze at."[21]

Whether or not Piper's experience is real, we have to conclude that our God performs miracles that are personally meaningful to each one of us. He understands our thoughts and wishes, and He makes things happen to satisfy our longings.

Prevailing Attitudes

An overriding concern has to do with *when* we want to go to heaven. I'm not talking about when life is snuffed out at death, which all of us will ultimately experience. When I say *when*, I'm thinking about our *attitude* as to timing, that is, when we are actually ready to leave earthly things behind. Kind of ridiculous, isn't it, wanting a delay in going to heaven? But that's what we often want, because as earthlings we are tied to experiences that are earth-connected. Being stuck with an earthly orientation, we have absolutely no idea of the marvels that await us in heaven. That makes us uncommitted to our timing of wanting to go there; that is to say, that each of us has different priorities that may not make heaven our immediate yearning. Earthly experiences surface to make us want to be a part of them, really a delay tactic, as we cite hopes to live longer with our spouses, children, and grandchildren. Or maybe we are influenced by other material wants, like buying a home, advancing in a job, or earning money to buy things we have always wanted. Think about it: do we yearn for such experiences before going to heaven, so much so that we are wanting time to live them out?

We are so preoccupied with life on earth that we lose sight of the ecstasies of life in heaven with God. Those delights make earthly experiences of absolutely no import. But of course, we don't realize it, simply because they are not a part of our earthly mindset. If you were to ask Jesus about them, you would more than likely hear him say, "I can't describe it to you, because even if I tried, you wouldn't grasp it's impact. All I can say is, trust me! Your heavenly home will be beyond anything you can imagine. It will astound you. I can assure you of it."

Wanting a delay in going to heaven? Kind of ridiculous, isn't it? Yet we get some degree of joy from earthly tangibles as seen in younger people who dream of future careers, marriage, or procreating children. They want to see those desires fulfilled, and until they become reality I suspect that many of them will say, "heaven can wait." You see, our minds are earth-oriented, which God understands. We are ruled by sensory impressions that have been implanted in our earthly bodies. Without doubt our makeup will be radically different in heaven, where we will think as heavenly beings, not as earthly sojourners.

Without question, we are stuck with an earthly-oriented mindset that interferes with a desire to go to heaven right now. Of course, we want to experience life beyond the grave, but not right away. First, we want to undergo what we deem as satisfying earthly experiences.

That kind of thinking is reflected in a church survey I took a few years back in which respondents indicated looking forward to heaven, but their timing varied. No one, in fact, wanted to go immediately. Can you believe it? I suppose that would have changed had they been undergoing devastating health problems that would understandably lead them to want immediate release from their suffering (the younger set generally doesn't usually have to face debilitating physical problems, which probably makes a difference between them and their elders in yearning heaven). But it also underscores the major difficulty in coming to grips with heaven's makeup -- our earthly minds can't conceive of a place that's better than or radically different from our present experience.

I hope we are beginning to see that heaven is so unlike any earthly experience that a new mindset must come into play to affect a yearning to go there. Comparisons between our present state on earth and life in heaven will be ridiculous. Scripture suggests that we will be totally overcome by experiences that we would never have dreamed possible. Here's a foretaste of it.

I saw the Holy City, the new Jerusalem, coming down out of heaven from God, prepared as a bride beautifully dressed for her husband. And I heard a loud voice from the throne saying. "Now the dwelling of God is with men, and he will live with them. They will be his people, and God himself will be with them, and be their God. He will wipe every tear from their eyes. There will be no more death or mourning or crying or pain, for the old order of things has passed away." He who was seated on the throne said, "I am making everything new!" (Rev. 21:2-5)

Then one of the angels said,

Come, I will show you the bride, the wife of the Lamb. And he carried me away in the Spirit to a mountain great and

high, and showed me the Holy City, Jerusalem, coming down out of heaven from God. It shown with the glory of God, and its brilliance was like that of a very precious jewel, like a jasper, clear as crystal . . . The wall was made of jasper, and the city of pure gold, as pure as glass. The foundations of the city walls were decorated with every kind of precious stone. . .The twelve gates were twelve pearls, each gate made of a single pearl. The great street of the city was of pure gold, like transparent glass . . . The city does not need the sun or the moon to shine on it, for the glory of God gives it light, and the Lamb is its lamp. (vv. 9- 23).

It's not just a matter of what we will see in heaven, but what we will feel. Why do you suppose that those claiming near-death experiences didn't wish to return to their former lives on earth? In spite of the close ties they had with family and friends, they were gripped with the rapturous joy of being transformed into new ways never before experienced.

Without question, many of us are stuck with an earthly oriented mindset that interferes with an immediate desire to go to heaven. The statement that many make –"I can't wait to go to heaven to be with Jesus" -- may be simply a fabricated repetition of the apostle Paul saying that he prefers heaven more than he does life on earth. It sounds so spiritual to think that way, and I suspect we may imitate Paul's statement to impress others with our supposed spirituality, or at least to say it without giving it much thought. I understand why Paul said it -- His personal relationship with Christ was so intimate, so intense that he regarded mundane earthly experiences hardly worth banking on. Do you remember his encounter with Jesus through the spectacular miracle on the Damascus road? That happening, and many others, created an intimacy between him and Jesus that must have made him yearn to be with Jesus. No wonder why he said that he wanted to leave this life to enjoy the fellowship of the one who communicated with him so intimately during his earthly sojourn.

But how about us? Do we really mean it when we say that we yearn to be with Christ? Is going to heaven to be with Jesus our true motivation, or do other factors concern us? God understands honesty, and He wants us to be true to ourselves. For many, part of that honesty is to confess our yearning for heaven while at the same time hoping for delay. That's because earthly experiences tend to bind us to such thinking. For others, being with Jesus may not be the main focus, but rather that of being with spouses and family members who have already died. We are stuck with an earthly mindset that prevents us from yearning heaven with the idea of being with God. But let's not feel guilty about it; that's the way we are made, and God understands, because you will remember, He created us and knows all our thoughts, desires, as well as our limitations.

Being honest with ourselves, we admit our dependence on earthly experiences. But we also recognize that a life in heaven is of far greater worth than what we presently enjoy. Although we may presently lack the intimacy with God that places him as our prime motivator in wanting heaven, we will undoubtedly see God as our prime reason for being in heaven, which will than cause us to understand that all that happens to us relates to his divine love and care. So don't despair about distinguishing your present feelings between earthly loved ones and God. In heaven we will have new mindsets that allow us to honor earthly ties as well as those pertaining to God.

Heaven's Permanence

Let's shift gears momentarily to concentrate on heaven's permanence, which may figure into our attitude about our future home.

We are well aware of the fact that many things in this world don't last, as seen in our constant discarding of worn out items for new ones. Even nature offers no constancy: flowers bloom, then fade and die; leaves sprout showing their spring freshness followed by their autumn splendor, only to eventually wither and yield to winter's harshness; and, trees, those magnificent towering specimens that often outlast humans, likewise die. All this is contrary to the characteristics of heaven, because the Bible describes our eternal home as a place that will never spoil or fade (1 Peter 1:4). Heaven means permanence, and how glad I am for it.

I recently took my wife, Deleta, to the Grand Canyon on our wedding anniversary. As we stood there peering into that deep abyss and then looking at the high cliffs surrounding it, we were awed by the Canyon's splendor. I suppose, however, that had we looked at it for several days straight we wouldn't be quite so impressed. Boredom would set in.

In no way will heaven's spectacle be boring, simply because our bodies won't be programmed with that earthly trait. The Bible is clear in teaching that our new and glorified life will experience only exhilaration. We will be incapable of boredom and indifference. Why? Because an understanding and wise heavenly Father will transform us to make our perceptions different from earthly ones. Remember, we are talking about one who has absolutely no limitations, one who has always existed and who created us in the first place and consequently knows all our thoughts and desires by making them come about as reality. And that's just one aspect of it. I suspect that heaven will be of such magnificence that it will awe us beyond our wildest dreams.

Surely what lies ahead is something we can look forward to in spite of having to undergo the temporary experience of death on earth or maybe the suffering that precedes it. I say temporary, because death's hold is for a fleeting moment, if we are to believe Jesus' declaration to the repentant criminal crucified next to him that he would be with him in paradise that very day (Luke 23:43).

As for our sufferings that we've been experiencing throughout our existence, we give testimony to the fact that God provides the inner peace that allows us to tolerate them. At other times He performs miracles of healing to relieve us of the pain and anguish. Whatever route He decides to take, He will perform it to our satisfaction. But we will always fulfill our responsibility of maintaining trust in him to help ease our pain.

Priorities

I have a confession to make. I don't put myself in Paul's shoes in looking forward to death and then to heaven as he did. Does that bother you? I make such a confession because I haven't experienced what Paul went through, like hearing God speak audibly and through visions. I suppose had that happened it would instill in me a greater desire to be with God because of its unquestionable demonstration of personal communication.

Neither have I experienced God's power to perform miracles as did Paul, nor have I received God's comfort in the same way as had Paul through imprisonment, shipwreck, and the many other physical abuses he suffered. So I confess that my motivation to be with God is not like that of that first-century man of God. He experienced miraculous encounters that undoubtedly influenced his yearning to be with his Lord, which doesn't suggest that God doesn't care about me, but rather that life's vicissitudes have been uniquely different for me, just as they have for everyone else. Can you identify with that? Anyway, Paul expressed his sentiments about dying and going to be with the Lord, but he didn't expect us to have identical feelings.

I have to admit that in my early years my attitude about going to heaven was reflected in some degree of fudging. I didn't really want to reveal my hesitancy about leaving earth, maybe out of guilt of having my spirituality questioned. I admit having earthly ties that I hated to give up, but also, I'm not sure if my main rationale for going to heaven was to be with Christ, as was Paul's declaration (Phil. 1:23).

What an admission, you may say, perhaps thinking that it's blasphemy. Sure, I'm comforted with the idea of heaven as the place for continued living, and for eternity at that. But I suspect my early priorities may have been tilted toward other things, like being with deceased family members, a spouse, for example, with whom I've lived joyously for forty-six years. Oh, I'm aware of the descriptions of God's presence and the joy that our togetherness will produce, but the picture is offset by current realities on earth, so much so that heaven's spectacular characteristics didn't really register.

To some degree, then, I find it hard to comprehend life in heaven, simply because I think as an earthling, finding it difficult to transform my earthly thinking to a heavenly one. But I know that God understands and doesn't take me to task for thinking that way. As Creator, He knows all that takes place in this puny mind of mine. Through all my interaction with him, I remain certain of the miraculous change He will perform in me, one I will revel in with thanksgiving. Maybe you, too, can share those thoughts.

Continued Relationships

Let's carry this one step further by looking at an earthly marriage, because I think it can affect our outlook on heaven. As widows and widowers, it would be natural for us to wonder how our relationship with deceased spouses will affect us in heaven. It becomes even more complicated when we remarry, as I have done after my late wife's passing, which causes me to ponder whether compromising affections will exist. Will I delight in being with her, or will I favor my present spouse?

The same holds true toward deceased parents versus step-parents. Will prejudices exist for one over the other? Somehow, favoritism doesn't seem appropriate in heaven, does it? It's a dilemma that God in his sovereignty has to resolve simply because we are in no position to deal with it with an earthly mindset. In fact, we are presently incapable of realizing a lot of things, which means that we depend on God to resolve all our human feelings and questionings. He is a miracle worker capable of doing things far beyond anything we can imagine.

Jesus did describe relationships in heaven by answering the Sadducees' question about marriage (Matt.22:23-32). He told them, "At the resurrection people will neither marry nor be given in marriage; they will be like the angels in heaven" (v. 30), an answer that dispels any notions we may have about relationships in heaven, be they about marriage or otherwise. In their place, we will have a new mindset, one like that of angels, which doesn't mean that intimacy will be non-existent, but rather that it extends toward everyone, not just our loved ones. Currently, we can't understand how that will happen. That's what heaven is all about -- a perfect state of intimacy among everyone that's beyond human understanding. So let's not worry about how it will take place. Our heavenly Father will see to it.

We experience the joys of living with our spouses on earth, which increases our love for one another. Carrying that over to life in heaven, we think that physical interaction with one another is necessary to enhance our relationship. But according to Jesus, none of that applies. We don't even understand our feelings toward God. While on earth we strive for a spiritual relationship with him, but we know it doesn't come about in the same way as do the physical. God understands our human dilemma, that our relationship with God is based on faith in the messages He conveys in the Bible. He looks to us to grow in faith as we reflect on the potency of his words, which will impact our love relationship and desire to be with him in heaven. But in the final analysis, we are hopelessly stuck on earthly experiences produced by a human mindset, no matter the extent of our spiritual relationship with Christ.

I cite these ideas not to suggest having an improper perspective toward God or even to create guilt feelings among you the reader. Surely God understands how earthly habits tend to control us. Like it or not, we are presently tied to the realm of the physical. And we can be sure that He understands. As I have said earlier, Scripture doesn't address many of the questions we have about heaven, not because God is unconcerned but rather because in our present state we are incapable of grasping the magnificence of heaven as well as understanding God's way of making it meaningful to us. In his usual quiet way, He is saying, "I'll take care of it. Trust me!" And like any other circumstance in which we trusted God (salvation, for example), that of heaven will be extraordinary, even mind-boggling.

A Spiritual Orientation

We may be reluctant to admit a lack of priority about going to heaven because we don't know Jesus in terms of the sensory impressions of sight, touch, audible communication, and other physical characteristics that we are normally used to. Does their absence interfere with our spiritual relationship? What might we do to improve our ties with Christ other than to search for miraculous experiences such as visions or other unusual encounters that we hear some people claiming to have?

The Bible seems to indicate that the desire to be in heaven relates to having a spiritual perspective. In other words, an individual's yearning to be with Christ seems to be a matter of spiritual growth, which makes us consider the vast difference between now and our younger days as Christians.

Think back on your early Christian days. They remind us that spiritual growth and maturity take place over time, the extent of which depends on our habits of personal discipline in the Christ life. How might we apply that discipline to our lives now and then counsel others in it? Growth in Christ helps us beyond our insecurities to a point of complete trust in our Heavenly Father to take care of everything. And I mean everything.

The Problem of Pain

I would be remiss if I ended this section without delving into our present consternation over physical suffering, although I've mentioned it off and on throughout this writing. Of course, when undergoing pain we look forward to relief in heaven. However, in the meantime, although outwardly we waste away (bodies falling apart with sickness or with age), we experience God's inward renewal so that we replace physical desires with spiritual ones, which keeps us going so that we not lose heart. We expect the possibility that we may "groan" and "be burdened" with possible sufferings while awaiting the final outcome of being transported to be with the Lord, but the end result will be a marvelous realization of togetherness with him.

Scripture addresses our problem of discomfort by telling us that in heaven we will be changed (1 Cor. 15:52), which infers alteration of our physical state to eliminate crying, pain, and death (Rev. 21:4). Yes, suffering and death will be no more; new bodies, functioning perfectly without wearing out, a fact that will be especially joyous for those who have undergone great physical hardship on earth. And by the way, we can forget about wheelchairs, prostheses, hearing aids, implants, and other human-concocted devices. They won't be needed.

Celebration

Another thing is that we are told that we will participate in "The Wedding Supper of the Lamb" (Rev. 19:6-9). Who's getting married, and what's behind the idea of a wedding? We are, to Jesus our bridegroom. It causes us to ponder the way Jesus thinks about us.

Did you ever wonder whether Jesus really has deep, special feelings toward us (each one of us) for whom he sacrificed himself on the cross? Sometimes I get the feeling that we look at his sacrifice merely as a necessary duty he had to perform, rather than one He was eager to accomplish for us in spite of the personal humiliation and pain accompanying it. I suspect that most of us don't really recognize the intense love Christ has for us, to cause him to be willing to undergo the extreme suffering of the cross and all the horrors leading up to it. We talk a lot about it, but I suspect we don't really understand the love motive behind it. How can He love everyone, and intensely at that? I suspect that God's love is a quality that we can't measure, along with a host of other matters on which we are humanely deficient.

Let's make it personal. Scripture refers to you and me as Jesus' bride, indicating that as a bridegroom He's anxious to unite with his loved one, which underscores his great love for you and me, one somewhat compared to that of an earthly husband toward his new bride. However, it's a love so distinct and pure that I'm incapable of comprehending it. I'm human, stuck with an earthly mindset, so I don't have the capability of completely understanding divine love. But what a great day of rejoicing that will be for me as well as for Jesus when united together as husband and wife I will see all human restrictions erased.

The marriage supper of the Lamb, a celebration of husband (Jesus) and wife (us) together. Aren't we glad we've been invited? And why wouldn't we? We are his bride whom He has come to claim as his own. It will be a time of pure joy for both male and female when we unite to partake of the marriage supper in honor of our reunion with Jesus, the bridegroom.

How will we react in the presence of the greatest being in the universe, not only one who has the characteristic of grandeur, but who is actually the *Creator* of everything? Yet He is one who relishes intimate communion with those whom He created. Were you aware of that fact being applied to Jesus? Scripture speaks of him as "the Word" who participated in the creation of the world. "In the beginning was the Word, and the Word was with God. He was with God in the beginning. *Through him all things were made; without him nothing was made that has been made*" (emphasis mine) (John 1:1-3).

That's our bridegroom, our husband. Jesus, who participated with the Father in the creation of the world, and because of it we will surely be overtaken by his majesty. In fact, I suspect we will be totally awestruck. But perhaps most startling is that above all his splendor He is concerned about you and me, something we find difficult to grasp, especially when relating it to one whose majesty is so incomprehensible as to make him concerned about individuals. Yet that's a part of his love, which we will fully understand when we get our heavenly mindsets.

Heavenly Scenes

No wonder the Bible depicts heavenly scenes of people prais-ing God. We won't be thinking about ourselves but instead will center our thoughts exclusively on God, not only to show our gratitude for being in his presence but being overwhelmed by his glory. It will be an event never before experienced or even imagined. The book of Revelation gives us a glimpse of it, start-ing with praise and honor for the Son and then extending to the Father. Here's a part of it.

And they sang a new song: 'You are worthy to take the scroll and to open its seals, because you were slain, and with your blood you purchased men for God from every tribe and lan-guage and people and nation. You have made them to be a kingdom and priests to serve our God, and they will reign on the earth.' Then I looked and heard the voice of many angels, numbering thousands upon thousands, and ten thousand times ten thousand. They encircled the throne and the living creatures and the elders. In a loud voice they sang: 'Worthy is the Lamb, who was slain, to receive power and wealth and wisdom and strength and honor and glory and praise.' Then I heard every creature in heaven and on earth and under the earth and on the sea, and all that is in them singing: 'To him who sits on the throne and to the Lamb be praise and honor and glory and power, for ever and ever!' (Rev. 5:9-13).

Never before had we seen such a scenario. We will be breath-less in witnessing it.

The description continues.

I looked and there before me was a great multitude that no one could count, from every nation, tribe, people and language, standing before the throne and in front of the Lamb. They were wearing white robes and were holding palm branches in their hands. And they cried out in a loud voice: 'Salvation belongs to our God, who sits on the throne, and to the Lamb' (7:9-10).

We see here a uniting of the world's Christians, including ourselves, all of distinct languages and race. How will we understand what's going on? Not to worry, because God, the miracle worker, will take care of it. Language, skin color, and cultural customs won't have anything to do with it. We will understand and glory in him who made it possible for us to be in that setting.

Listen to what is said in praising the Almighty.

We give thanks to you, Lord God Almighty, the one who is and who was, because you have taken your great power and have begun to reign' (11:17).

'Great and marvelous are your deeds, Lord God Almighty. Just and true are your ways, King of the ages. Who will not fear you, O Lord, and bring glory to your name? For you alone are holy. All nations will come and worship before you, for your righteous acts have been revealed' (15:3-4).

I heard what sounded like the roar of a great multitude in heaven shouting: 'Hallelujah! Salvation and glory and power belong to our God, for true and just are his judgments . . . ' **(19:1-2).**

We are then reminded of that glorious event about to come, the wedding of the Lamb.

'Let us rejoice and be glad and give him glory! For the wedding of the Lamb has come, and his bride has made herself ready . . . Blessed are those who are invited to the wedding supper of the Lamb' . . . (19:7, 9).

Aren't you glad you've been invited? Heaven is God's pledge to all who have trusted in his Son as Savior, a promise He will fulfill, for He never goes back on his word. But we must confess that we don't understand all its ramifications, simply because God has not revealed them, probably because He knows our present inability to understand heaven's splendor -- a totally new experience, even an explosive one that earthly minds are incapable of grasping. As I intimated before, its overall effect might be inexplicable in human language and therefore go unexplained in the Bible. Get ready for the big surprise. It's coming.

The message that the Bible seems to suggest is that earthly pleasures will be miniscule compared to heavenly experiences. Yet we often feel guilty in wanting to cling to earthly joys, a human tendency that God understands, for He knows they are a part of our humanity. In the meantime, we see the need to improve our focus on heavenly experiences rather than on earthly involvements.

As Christians we can give thanks for the rapturous joy awaiting us. Although we may have trouble grasping its full meaning right now due to human limitations, we accept Scripture's pronouncement that heaven will be indescribably splendorous, a scenario beyond any human imagination. Let's never forget that our God is a miracle worker who will see to it that our joy in heaven will far surpass any earthly mindset. I don't know how He will do it, but I do know that He will take care of everything for our joy.

I'll see you there, where together we will enjoy each other's presence, including that of our Savior, the King of the Universe.

DISCUSSION GUIDE

1. Discuss possible reasons for the Bible's meager description of heaven.

2. Scripture alludes to a wedding in heaven. Who are the bride and bridegroom, and how will the wedding supper take place with the millions, billions, or maybe trillions of people in attendance? Could the idea be figurative rather than literal, or must we resist imposing earthly thought patterns on God? Finally, react to the uniting of

the bridegroom (Jesus) and the bride (us) by citing the feelings to be had by both.

3. How will our physical makeup in heaven be different from that on earth? Why might age or change of appearance cause problems in identifying loved ones in heaven? What might be the solution?

4. Why is it that some Christians, and maybe you also, want a delay in going to heaven? List experiences you hope for on earth that might cause you from wanting to go to heaven immediately.

5. Christians often feel guilty in wanting to unite with spouses and family members in heaven. Why is this so, and how do you suppose God looks upon it?

6. Picture yourself in heaven, and tell what your demeanor might be in worshipping the Almighty. Might it be different from your style of worshipping him while on earth?

7. Why might we be at a loss for words in describing heaven's magnificence? Can you cite an earthly experience that you had difficulty explaining?

8. Refer to the experiences of John and Paul regarding their glimpses of heaven. Do they leave you wanting? Why?

9. Growing in intimacy with God reduces our yearning for earthly experiences. How might that spiritual growth come about, and how would you counsel others toward attaining it?

IX.

Dynamic Christianity Verses Mediocrity

Seventeen

ATTUNED TO THE HOLY SPIRIT

This final chapter defines the supernatural force, the Holy Spirit, whose wisdom and power every Christian has available in whatever we do or say. I have left discussion on the Spirit as a separate chapter in order to emphasize the critical nature of that third person of the trinity in our lives.

We certainly don't want to do anything for Christ without grasping the Spirit's helping role, since trying to live for God apart from the Spirit can lead to mediocrity and even harm. In its stead, we want a dynamic Christianity, one we can rest upon with the assurance that all we say and do has God's approval and backing.

I'm sure you realize that we can operate on our own without giving heed to the Spirit's power. In fact, we probably have been guilty of doing it at one time or another. The tragedy of it is that by doing so we miss out on divine blessings that we would otherwise experience. As Scripture says, we can extinguish the Spirit's fire through which we would otherwise benefit (1 Thess. 5:19).

So how do we commit to the role that God wishes us to have? The overriding issue is to develop an intimacy that calls us to depend on God in place of self-centeredness. Doing things in accord with our own efforts is out; it has no place in our lives if we are serious about being God's representatives and receptacles of his blessings. In a word, we are to strive for intimacy!

Disciplinary Measures

Intimacy? How do we get it? There are many issues on which God will deal with us along the way. To be sure, they consist of instructions that are distinct for each individual, even too numerous to try to list. The starting point, and that's as far as I intend to go in this discourse, is that of personal discipline, one in which we establish critical habits that allow for intimacy with God to take place.

That means getting serious about *Scripture*; that is to say, taking a disciplined approach and attitude toward the Bible and seeing it as God's manifest wisdom preserved throughout the ages for our benefit. No one who seriously approaches Scripture will be haphazard in the way he or she goes about treating it. In its place will be a dedicated effort to read, study and make personal application. Let's keep in mind that the Bible, although inspired thousands of years ago, addresses issues that are applicable to everyone today, probably because it represents God's wisdom addressed through the Holy Spirit that applies to whatever situation that may crop up in life.

Most importantly, the Bible helps keep us centered on God's ways. How often had I experienced the desire to indulge in temptation and sin, which was deterred by recalling scriptural passages I had read, meditated on, and even memorized. The psalmist clearly addressed the question, "How can a young man keep his way pure? By living according to your word . . . I have hidden your word in my heart that I might not sin against you" (Ps. 119:9,11). There's no denying it: Scripture has the power to help us triumph over fleshly desires, which is so simply because it's a product of God's inspiration. How grateful I am that I was taught to discipline myself in respecting the Holy Word of God; it was the help I needed in shaping my entire life. But let me be clear about one thing – self discipline in the Word of God is not necessarily a miracle-inducing action. We can discipline ourselves to read and study the Bible, but those actions can become so mechanical that the process (getting into it) takes precedence over the message (what it does for us). In fact, nothing we do produces automatic results, but getting immersed in Scripture is a help against the powerful wiles of the devil. Without the help of the Holy Spirit, we could never fight off Satan successfully.

Look at another of the psalmist's declarations -- "How sweet are your words to my taste, sweeter than honey in my mouth! I gain understanding from your precepts; therefore I hate every wrong path" (119:103-104). That was the psalmist's reaction to God's Word thousands of years ago, which can be ours, too, but perhaps even more so now that we have experienced the appearance of Jesus Christ.

The other aspect of discipline that I have found is *prayer.* Since God has made us his sons and daughters, He allows us to communicate with him, actually desiring us to do so. We may wonder what to talk to him about, so Scripture tells us to pray on all occasions (Eph. 6:18), which underscores the fact that God knows our human weaknesses that cause us to face the myriad of problems for which we need help. Prayer gives us the opportunity to voice those concerns. You see, no Christian need stand alone in confronting discomforting situations; we can always count on God to help no matter what be the problem. But to do so requires the personal discipline of talking with him about the problems vexing us.

Of course, prayer involves far more than approaching God with needs, as if we were to abuse the privilege by asking him to give us things we need or even things we would like to have. Prayer also provides a means of communicating with our Lord for many different reasons. For example, who would converse with someone only to ask for things, especially when those petitions are self-centered? If we allow it, our entire prayer life can go in that direction, although God certainly wants to hear those requests out of personal concern for our well-being, He also wants to have a relationship that comes about through means other than requests. Everyone yearns to be told how much they matter and then to be thanked for their support, and so I imagine that God does also.

Those are starters. The key to the relevance of both the Bible and prayer is the Holy Spirit who is implanted in our bodies. That's God himself occupying a place in us with the hope that we will use his presence as a help in whatever we do -- working for him, praising him, and thanking him. You see, prayer is a means of developing a love relationship with God, a communion He wants and one that will benefit us also.

I've suggested in previous chapters that our effectiveness for God will depend on our acknowledgement of the Spirit within us (Rom. 5:5). We see that happening beginning with the first chapter of this book that talks about us as special people, then in our relations with one another as discussed in other chapters, followed by manifesting God through our speech and actions as well as when we undergo hardships, and finally, as we look forward to God's promise of heaven. As for the latter, God tells us that the Spirit serves as a seal or deposit that guarantees our inheritance in heaven (Eph. 1:13-14), a promise we can grab hold of right now. We have a wonderful surprise awaiting us beyond this life on earth.

Believers who are serious about a relationship with God are aware of their responsibility to give the Spirit free reign instead of fulfilling selfish desires. You see, God has several motives for indwelling us: (1) to identify us as his sons and daughters (Rom. 8:15-16), a family relationship that makes us aware of his loving care; (2) to remind us that He considers us holy for having honored his Son (He actually calls us saints, which tells us of our responsibility to care for our bodies as temples in which He dwells) (1 Cor. 6:19); and, (3) to keep before us the existing unity of the Trinity, an example for us to realize that we have a responsibility for a God-given unity in our relations with other believers (Eph. 4:3).

May these thoughts inspire us to a dedicated life in Christ Jesus, one in which we allow God's power to exhibit itself in all that we do and say. With that in mind, we will not only experience the joy and peace of which Scripture so often speaks, but we will please God in the way we conduct ourselves.

DISCUSSION GUIDE

1. In what ways do we develop an intimacy with God that attunes us to the Holy Spirit's direction? Cite your own experience in that respect.
2. Since the Bible is a product of the Spirit's inspiration (God speaking to us), what attitude should we assume toward it?
3. How does prayer figure into intimacy with God? What are some ways in which we can wrongfully use prayer?
4. Since the Spirit indwells our bodies, what responsibility does it suggest for the way we treat our bodies?

Notes

Chapter 1

1. Burchett, Dave. *When Bad Christians Happen to Good People* (Colorado Springs: Waterbrook Press), 2002, 88.

Chapter 6

2. Abernethy, Bob, and William Bole. *The Life of Meaning* (N.Y.: Seven Stories Press), 2007, 231-32.

3. Reeves, Kevin. *The Other Side of the River* (Silverton, Oregon: Lighthouse Trails Publishing), 2007, 160.

4. Ibid., 159.

Chapter 7

5. Eggerichs, Emerson. *Love and Respect* (Detroit: Gale Cenage Learning), 2010.

Chapter 10

6. Hanegraaff, Hank. *The Apocalypse Code* (Nashville: Thomas Nelson), 2007.

7. See Sproul, R.C. *The Last Days According to Jesus* (Grand Rapids, MI: Baker Books), 1998.

Chapter 11

8. Little, Paul E. *How to Give Away Your Faith* (Downers Grove, Ill.: Intervarsity Press), 1962, 32.

9. Gulley, Philip. *Porch Talk* (New York: Harper Collins), 2007, 24.

Chapter 12

10. D'Souza, Dinesh. *What's So Great About Christianity* (Washington, D.C.: Regnery Publishing), 2007.

Chapter 14

11. Walters, Kerry. *The Art of Dying and Living* (Maryknoll, N.Y.: Orbis Books), 2011, 4.

Chapter 15

12. Rossing, Barbara R. *The Rapture Exposed* (Boulder, Colorado: Westview), 1989, 22.

13. Ibid., 175.

14. Ibid., 21.

15. LaHaye, Tim and Jerry B. Jenkins. *Left Behind* (Wheaton, Ill.: Tyndale), 1995.

16. Hanegraaff, Hank. *The Apocalypse Code* (Nashville: Thomas Nelson), 2007.

17. LaHaye, Tim. *The Merciful God of Prophecy* (Warner Books), 2002, 162.

Chapter 16

18. Piper, Don. *Heaven is Real* (New York: Berkley Praise), 2009, 24.

19. Piper, Don. *90 Minutes in Heaven* (Grand Rapids, MI: Revell), 2004, 33.

20. Ibid., 26.

21. Ibid., 27.

The Author

D r. Theodore Kalivoda, Professor Emeritus of Language and Applied Linguistics, University of Georgia, taught at three major universities (University of Georgia, Oklahoma State University, Louisiana State University) over a period of 40 years. During that time he wielded a profound influence across foreign universities where he directed projects in Asia, Europe, and Latin America under governmental and university sponsorship. His efforts facilitated professor and student exchanges leading toward increased international understanding and good will.

Professor Kalivoda has also tackled the problems and needs of foreign language teaching in our schools and colleges. Through his prolific writings he champions the exclusive use of the second language in the classroom in order to provide for a solid oral experience for learners, something that is not always forthcoming, mainly due to an early emphasis of the written language and its literature. Although valuing literature, Dr. Kalivoda sees it deflecting on oral language acquisition through its early introduction in the curriculum. He calls for a radical shift in instructional planning and implementation on the undergraduate level so that aural-oral goals take precedence over literary study by means of innovative oral experiences.

Since his retirement, Dr. Kalivoda has been actively involved in lay ministries, including evangelizing and Bible teaching in U.S. prisons where he has influenced hundreds of inmates toward an intimate relationship with their Creator and a dedicated life of service to God and humanity.

He lives with his wife, Deleta, in Saint Charles, Missouri.

Dr. Kalivoda welcomes contact with readers to discuss whatever questions or comments you may have about this book. He may be reached via e-mail: **tvoda1@sbcglobal.net.**

Made in the USA
Charleston, SC
31 May 2014

The Abuse of Beauty

THE PAUL CARUS LECTURES

PUBLISHED IN MEMORY OF

PAUL CARUS
1852–1919

Editor of
The Open Court
and
The Monist
from
1888 to 1919

THE PAUL CARUS LECTURE SERIES 21

The Abuse of Beauty

Aesthetics and the Concept of Art

ARTHUR C. DANTO

Open Court
Chicago and La Salle, Illinois

THE PAUL CARUS LECTURE SERIES 21

To order books from Open Court, call toll-free 1-800-815-2280,
or visit our website at www.opencourtbooks.com.

Open Court Publishing Company is a division of Carus Publishing Company.

First printing 2003
Second printing 2004
Third printing 2005
Fourth printing 2006

Printed and bound in the United States of America.

Library of Congress Cataloging-in-Publication Data

Danto, Arthur Coleman, 1924-
    The abuse of beauty : aesthetics and the concept of art / Arthur C. Danto.
        p. cm. — (Paul Carus lectures ; 21st ser.)
    Includes index.
    ISBN 0-8126-9539-9 (alk. paper) — ISBN 0-8126-9540-2 (pbk. : alk. paper)
    1. Aesthetics. 2. Art—Philosophy.   I. Title. II. Series.
BH39 .D3489 2003
111'.85—dc21

                              2003005374

Sublimity Triumphant over Beauty?

With his *Onement I* of 1948, Barnett Newman
posed an aesthetic of sublimity against an aesthetic
of beauty. "The invention of beauty by the Greeks,
. . . their postulate of beauty as an ideal, has been
the bugbear of European art and European aesthetic philosophies," Newman wrote. Free from
the weight of European culture, a few Americans
could now express their relation to the Absolute,
undistracted by the pursuit of beauty, the fetishism
of perfect quality.

For David Reed and Sean Scully,
as well as to the memory of Robert Motherwell,
and of course for Barbara Westman

Beauty is the promise of happiness

STENDHAL

Contents

Preface

It is a curious fact that while my philosophy of art aspires to the kind of timelessness at which philosophy in general aims, it is so much the product of its historical moment that it can easily be considered to have relevance chiefly to the art that occasioned it. The art itself was the product of various avant-garde art movements of the early 1960s, mainly in and around New York City. Most of the art, moreover, could hardly have been made at a much earlier date. Consider the celebrated *Brillo Box* of Andy Warhol, which has figured so prominently in my thought and writing. It was made and exhibited in 1964, and appropriated the format of a commercial shipping carton, which pre-existed it for little more than a year. The designer of that carton, himself an artist, drew upon stylistic paradigms from contemporary abstract painting. "Brillo" itself was the name of a recently invented soap-pad, held to be particularly effective in brightening aluminum ware. It had only a few years earlier been introduced to the American market. *Brillo Box* could hardly have pre-dated what gave it its meaning. It is possible to imagine that an *object* could have made a century earlier, which resembled it exactly, though it could not have drawn upon the associated meanings that gave life to *Brillo Box* as a work of art. Not merely could the same object not have been the same work of art it was in 1964, it is difficult to see how, in 1864, it could have been a work of art at all. It was difficult enough even in 1964 for many to accept it as art, but by then space had opened up for at least a certain segment of the art world to accept it as art without hesitation. And the question that initially concerned me as a philosopher was what made it possible for something to be a work of art at a given historical moment when it could not have had that status at a much earlier one. At the very least this raised the issue, at the most general philosophical level, of what its historical situation contributes to an object's status as art.

Somehow, the timelessness that belongs to philosophy has tended to inflect the way the objects of philosophical concern are themselves thought of as timeless. But I have always found it philosophically instructive to imagine objects, which are locked into their historical moment the way *Brillo Box* was, transported back to a much earlier time, as Mark Twain famously imagined a Connecticut Yankee conveyed to the court of King Arthur. For the cover of my book, *Beyond the Brillo Box*, the clever painter, Russell Conner, replaced the cadaver with *Brillo Box* in Rembrandt's famous *Anatomy Lesson*, making it appear as if Dr. Tulp's eager seventeenth-century auditors are listening to a discourse on mid-twentieth-century avant-garde art. We are used to the idea of passing from the gallery devoted to seventeenth-century Dutch art to the one dedicated to twentieth-century American art in today's encyclopedic museums. We take in our stride the juxtaposition of works from various centuries and cultures in a single gallery, in which they are allowed to "communicate" with one another, as curators like to say. But those for whom Rembrandt painted would have had no way of accommodating *Brillo Box* under their concept of art. In 1917, Marcel Duchamp undertook to enter an "assisted readymade"—in effect a urinal—into an exhibition which was to have had no jury, where it was rejected by the hanging committee on the explicit grounds that it was not art. There were sectors of the 1917 art world hospitable to Duchamp's ready-mades, but the hanging committee of the Society of Independent Artists, which sponsored the exhibition, was clearly not part of it. In much the same way, there were large parts of the artworld of 1964 for which *Brillo Box* was not art. But there were not and could not have been any parts of the artworld of Paris in 1864—or Amsterdam in 1664—in which *Brillo Box* could have fitted. It is true, of course, that the concept of art was beginning to loosen up sufficiently that Manet's *Déjeuner sur l'herbe* was accepted as art in 1864, though for most who had seen it in the recent *Salon des refuses* it was a perversion of the very idea of art. Heinrich Wollflin wrote that not everything is possible at every time. In that sense of historical impossibility, *Brillo Box*, while just possible as an object, was not possible as art much before the moment it was made. (One has to remember that *Brillo Box* was made of industrial plywood, which may not have existed in 1864, let alone 1664, and was painted with silkscreen ink, which almost certainly did not. Philosophers

FIGURE 1 Russell Conner, *Cover image for* Beyond the Brillo Box
Content may be lost in temporal transit.

are exceedingly casual when they perform such "thought experiments." An object like that in which *Brillo Box* consists might have elicited astonishment, much in the way in which coconut shells did when they washed ashore in medieval Europe.)

These considerations throw some doubt not only on the timelessness of art, but, in a more immediate way, put in question how works of art are to be approached critically and aesthetically. It must be an assumption of formalism, as a critical approach, that everything relevant to addressing a work of art must be present and accessible at every moment of the work's existence. There is, so to say, a position in the philosophy of art analogous to Internalism in the philosophies of mind and of meaning. Works of art, of course, change physically over time, sometimes in radical ways—pigments fade, statues lose appendages like arms and legs. And information relevant to the identification and interpretation of a work is sometimes simply forgotten: we no longer know the identity of persons in old portraits; the individuals who knew the keys to reading certain signs and symbols have died without passing that knowledge on to others. We simply don't know how to read Pieter Breugel's prints the way his contemporaries, or some of them, presumably could. There are words whose only known occurrence in English is in one of Shakespeare's plays, so that if the manuscript were missing, even specialists would have no way of knowing what the missing words were. The relationship between the play and the manuscript is metaphysically delicate, but certainly not a matter of strict identity. So the changes that works of art as physical objects undergo are really merely contingent. It is with reference to the work of art, to the degree that it can be distinguished from the physical object, that one refers when one says that nothing outside it is relevant to understanding it critically and aesthetically. Internalism in art is the position that everything relevant to appreciation is ideally available to the critic's eye at any moment, and nothing beyond that is relevant to experiencing the art as art.

It is the work of art in this curious sense, as distinct from the physical object, that I am imagining transferred to some earlier historical moment—*Brillo Box* as a kind of formal design. But what will have been lost in this imagined transit is what I have spoken of here as the meanings that give the work life. For meaning is based on art's connection to the world, and the relations between the design and the world are historical. The name "Brillo," for example, designates a household product, invented and patented at a certain time. Before that, it was just a noise, or, a written design—or at best a word in some form of dog Latin. On *Brillo Box*, there is a mark that consists of a circle with a "u" inscribed in the center. This is a logo used to mean that the product that bears it is certified as kosher by the Union of Orthodox Rabbis in Jerusalem, which was established after the state of Israel came into being. Brillo was kosher in 1964, but is kosher no longer, so the Brillo cartons in the supermarkets are no longer entitled to display the logo. Is the logo part of the design or not? This is something I shall leave to formalists to worry about. A much more important consideration is the fact that, as already stated, *Brillo Box* itself, as a work, stands in the relationship of "appropriation of" to the cartons in which Brillo was shipped from factories to distributors and thence to supermarkets from the mid-sixties until the late 1990s, when the design of the cartons changed. But even more important than that, the interest and importance of *Brillo Box* is very much bound up with attitudes toward art that prevailed in art in early to mid 1960s, especially in Manhattan. Part of what made it possible for it to be art at the time was the fact that this atmosphere of history and of theory defined what was historically possible. In 1964, when I published "The Art World" in the *Journal of Philosophy*—the text in which the first outlines of my philosophy of art were laid out—my thought was that, in order to see *Brillo Box* as art, one would have had to have known something of the history, and something of the theory that defined the relevant art world of that moment. There were many art worlds, even in New York, at that particular moment. I don't want to relativize art to art worlds, but only at this point to emphasize that *Brillo Box*'s status as artwork depended upon external factors which were not in place much earlier than 1964.

I want to say something about the degree to which these historical considerations belong to the concept of art, but I had better interject a few words about the concept of concepts itself. It has often been noted that the Greeks, with whom the philosophy of art began in the west, did not have a word for art in their vocabulary. But they certainly had a concept of art, which included in its extension a great many of the same kinds of objects we would consider works of art today. A definition of art that excluded Greek sculpture or Greek dramas would ipso facto be unacceptable. At the same time, they were aware that certain properties, characteristic of these objects, were not part of the concept of art, even if they were widely present. I refer in the first instance to mimetic properties: Greek statuary was believed to resemble its subjects, in much the same way that Greek tragedies were believed to resemble certain historical episodes in the lives of their heroes. The technique of resemblance indeed defined a progressive history in the main mimetic arts that have come down to us—sculpture and drama. It was a progress defined in the direction of life-likeness, from archaic figures of Apollo to figures so close to the way human beings look that there was a genuine possibility of illusion. This possibility must have played an important role in Greek forms of life, especially in religious worship, where statues of gods and goddesses were so compelling that one might believe oneself in the very presence of the deities themselves, especially in the dark, smoky atmosphere of temple interiors. In Nietzsche's account of early tragedy, there was a moment in which the central actor was believed by celebrants actually to be possessed by a god, so that the chorus could feel that Dionysus, for example, was there among them. It is not implausible to suppose something like this could have been believed of statues of the gods in temples dedicated to their cult. After all, the "mystical presence of the saint in the icon" has been widely subscribed to in Greek Orthodoxy, where it played a central role in the fierce iconoclastic controversies of eighth-century Byzantium. There was no implication that artistic quality was indexed to differing degrees of life-likeness—no sense that Aeschylus was Euripides's inferior. So Socrates, in his famous polemic, was able to imply that life-likeness was no part of the *concept* of art, though widely prized in his own age. It was, however, central to the Greeks' concept that art should represent things. But degrees of life-likeness in mimetic representation were matters in part of taste, in part of function, and it was clear to Plato that there were modes of representation other than mimesis, whatever degree of life-likeness the latter might have. Their notion of representation was fairly abstract and general. And so of course is mine, when I have proposed representation as part of the definition of art. I emphasized representation in considering how one would distinguish as art something that deeply resembles something that is not art at all. My concern was occasioned by the art of the 1960s, but it is meant as universal and timeless.

Here is another example. From the eighteenth century to early in the twentieth century, it was the presumption that art should possess beauty. This was so much the case that beauty would have been among the first things people would think of in connection with—well—*les beaux-arts*. When Roger Fry organized his great exhibitions of Post-Impressionist art at the Grafton Gallery in London, in 1910 and 1912, the public was outraged not only by the disregard of life-likeness, which characterized so much of the modernist movement, but by the palpable absence of beauty. In his defense, Fry argued that the new art would be seen as ugly *until* it was seen as beautiful. To see it as beautiful, he implied, requires aesthetic education, and that the beauty would be seen in the course of time. Undoubtedly we sometimes do come to see beauty that evaded us at first—but suppose we don't? Is it because we are blind to the beauty—or is it because we have wrongly taken it as a given that art *must* be beautiful? What I shall speak of in this book as the Intractable Avant-garde abjured beauty. I mean in the first instance Dada, which refused to make beautiful objects for the gratification of those they held responsible for the Great War. In his Dialogues with Cabanne, Duchamp is dismissive of the whole idea of what he calls "the retinal flutter," which art since Courbet was suppose to induce in viewers. He was keen on an intellectual art, with no sensory gratification whatever. I regard the Intractable Avant-garde as having taken an immense philosophical step forward. It helped show that beauty was no part of the concept of art, that beauty could be present or not, and something still be art. The concept of art may require the presence of one or another from a range of features, which includes beauty, but includes a great many others as well, such as sublimity, to use another feature much discussed in the eighteenth century. For the moment, I'll call these *pragmatic*, to contrast with the *semantical* ones, which mimesis exemplifies, borrowing this vocabulary from Charles Morris's Theory of Signs, which played an important role in the heyday of Logical Positivism. Pragmatic properties are intended to dispose an audience to have feelings of one sort or another toward what the artwork represents. Morris says in passing that what he calls pragmatism was called rhetoric in earlier times, and rhetoric was one of the defining disciplines of the classical age. It may be the pragmatic function of beauty to inspire love toward what an artwork shows, and the function of sublimity to inspire awe. But there are a great many other cases, such as disgust, to inspire revulsion, or ludicrousness, to inspire contempt. Or lubricity, to arouse erotic feelings. In a way, pragmatic properties correspond to what Frege speaks of as "color"— *Farbung*—in his theory of meaning.

The range of pragmatic features is far wider than anything really compassed by the canon of writings in aesthetics, just as the range of semantic features includes far more than mimetic representations. But my concern here is simply to have picked out a few of the components that figure, or could figure, in the conceptual analysis of art, and to make clear how narrowly that concept has been construed in the philosophical and critical literature devoted to art. A philosophical definition of art has to be cast in the most general terms, in order for everything that has ever or could ever have been a work of art to be covered by it. It has to be general enough to be immune to counter-examples. And while I cannot pretend that I have achieved a formulation that meets such a condition, that is what has governed my philosophy of art as an undertaking from the beginning. But it is precisely that which dealing with the art of the mid-sixties has made possible. For that was a period in which so much that had been felt part of the concept of art had fallen out of consideration entirely. Not merely beauty and mimesis, but almost everything that had figured in the life of art had been erased. The definition of art would have to be built on the ruins of what had been thought to be the concept of art in previous discourses. This returns me to my paradigm.

The issue which concerned me immediately in connection with *Brillo Box* was not simply what made it art, but how, if it was a work of art, objects exactly (or exactly enough) like it were not, namely the multitude of cartons designed for the transport of Brillo pads. It doubtless belongs to the interpretation of this segment of Warhol's oeuvre that it uses logos from commercial art for purposes of art. But in truth, Warhol could have made art of anything, so long as what he made it of belonged to the domain of objects that were not works of art. In 1964, he used, for example, police photographs of "Most Wanted" criminals, as well as newspaper photographs of plane crashes, suicides, and automobile accidents. There is something we can speak of as Warhol's "style," which determined which, among the vast number of things he could have made art of, he did make art of. All that I required of his art, however, was that there should exist examples of things that were not art, so long as they and the art should look as much alike as *Brillo Box* looked like the ordinary Brillo boxes. This gave me the idea of indiscernible pairs, one of which was an art work and the other not, so that I could then ask on what basis one of each pair should be an artwork and the other just a thing. This turned out to be a powerful tool for the conceptual research I needed. But it hardly suggested itself as a tool much before the possibility actually existed in artistic practice.

Now in truth, I could have found examples of these pairs everywhere in the art world of the 1960s. *Fluxus*, for example, used food as art. Minimalists used sections of prefabricated buildings and other industrial products. Pop artists like Lichtenstein enlarged the cartoons on the inside of bubblegum wrappers, and presented them as paintings. The Conceptualist Dennis Oppenheim dug a hole in a mountain near Oakland, California, and offered it as a sculpture which could not be transported to a museum. By 1969, the Conceptualists were ready to consider everything as art, and were prepared to consider anyone an artist, much the way that Joseph Beuys was shortly to propose. Examples could be found in dance, especially in the Judson Group, where it was possible for a dance to consist in someone sitting in a chair; and in avant-garde music, which challenged the distinction between musical and non-musical sounds. The 1960s avant-garde was interested in overcoming the gap between life and art. It was interested in erasing the distinction between fine and vernacular art. But by time the decade was over, there was very little left of what anyone would earlier have thought was part of the concept of art. It was a period of spectacular philosophical erasure. Bliss was it in that dawn to be alive!

There can be no question that my philosophy was itself very much part of that moment, though I was aware only of part of what was taking place, and even more is it the case that none of those in the artworld—or in the set of overlapping artworlds of the time—were aware of my philosophy at all. Only recently has the 1964 "The Art World" begun to appear in anthologies of documents for the art history of those years. But the structures with which I was working were very much those of analytical philosophy. My book, *Analytical Philosophy of History* was in press in 1964, and the ideas of that book inflected the way I thought about everything. In that book, for example, I argued, through a kind of truth-condition analysis, that the meanings of historical events are invisible to those who live through them. That was the Externalist kind of thesis that I followed in the analysis of the concept of an artwork—that what makes an object an artwork is external to it.

But let us return to the philosophical situation of that moment in art. Once one reflects on what made that moment so unique, two things have to become clear. The first is that, once it is seen that anything can be an artwork, there is little point in asking whether this or that can be artworks, since the answer will always be yes. They may not be works of art, but they can be. So the second thing is that the question now became urgent of what must be the case if they *are* to be works of art. That means that a theory of art is all at once imperative in a way that it had never appeared to be before. It is also transparent that no previous theory of art could be of great help, since none had been formulated in the kind of situation that defined the art world of the 1960s, namely, that in which anything, however banal, could be a work of art. One could only achieve the generality that philosophy demands against the extreme latitude that the sixties made vivid. So it was a great time to be a philosopher of art.

My own work in this marvelous field has been inspired by two interconnected thoughts of Hegel. The first is his thought that the philosophy suited to a form of life can only properly begin when that form of life has grown old: "When philosophy paints its gray in gray, then has a form of life grown old," he writes, elegaically, in *The Philosophy of Right*. I think that only when the history of art comes to its end can the philosophy of art fully begin. It can do so because, until then, philosophy does not have all the pieces it needs to build the theory. But that connects with the second thought I have, based in a way on Hegel's masterpiece, *The Phenomenology of Spirit*. That book has the structure, as the American philosopher, Josiah Royce once suggested, of a *Bildungsroman*. Spirit, or *Geist*, as Hegel terms his subject, undergoes in the course of the book the education through which it comes to discover its own identity. That is the kind of *Bildung* that Hegel was concerned with, and that we are all concerned with in coming through experience to learn what we really are. I like to think of the history of art as a *Bildungsroman* in this way as well, in which *Kunst* discovers bit by bit *its* own identity. Philosophy is the changing consciousness of this history in the sense that at each stage, a piece of the puzzle emerges which philosophy supposes is what *Kunst* is. But, as with the *Phenomenology*, this is often partial and often wrong. It is not a smooth progress. *Kunst*'s adventures, peradventures, and misadventures, make up not the history of art, which has been the province of art history as a discipline, but *the philosophical history of art*, which in effect is the history of the philosophy of art. That history reached a new level in the 1960s when it at last became clear that everything was possible as art. The end of art, as I have used that phrase, means this. It is now possible to give an answer to the question of *Kunst*'s identity which we know cannot be overthrown by the further history of art. That is what must be true of every philosophical definition.

In this preface, I have mentioned two conditions which help specify that identity. One of them is that to be art, it must represent something, that is, it must have some semantic property. A good bit of my book, *The Transfiguration of the Commonplace* is addressed to establishing this. I would like to say that having some of what I have here called pragmatic features is a second condition, but I am not sure this would be true. I am not because I am uncertain what role if any pragmatic properties play in the art of today. They have, however, played an overwhelming part in the art of the past, and were held to give an answer to the question, were anyone to ask it, of what the point of art is.

If I am of my own historical moment, that would explain why I have neglected to raise, let alone attempt to answer this question, and in the fact that I have rarely considered in the analysis of art the role if any of beauty and the like. This in part is to be explained by the historical circumstances under which my philosophy of art originated: the avant-garde art of the 1960s turned its back on aesthetics almost as resolutely as the avant-garde philosophy of that period turned its back on edification. Both aspired to be "cool." I think this was, in the philosophy of art, a healthy move. It helped separate the philosophy of art from aesthetics, which has always been such a muddle. I think we have now built up sufficient immunities that we can again consider what after all makes art so meaningful in human life, and that is my current agenda. Protected by what I have learned, I can begin once again to pick up, with the long forceps of analytical philosophy, such toxic properties as beauty, sublimity, and the like. There are probably good reasons why beauty has been the paradigm pragmatic property in the history of art, and its entrenchment in the discourse more than justifies the emphasis I shall assign it in this book.

When I began to think through the project of framing a definition of art, the philosophy of art was dominated by two main theses: that no such definition was possible, and that no such definition was needed. The latter was largely a Wittgensteinian response to the former. But as so often with Wittgenstein, his position presupposed a stability in the set of things called by a given term—in this instance "work of art"—so the speakers of the language can be expected in general to recognize instances of art works for the most part. The former position, meanwhile, was based on the immense pluralism that was beginning to prevail in art: so many things became possible as works of art that no definition seemed any longer possible. The conservatism of the Wittgensteinian view was beginning to be threatened almost at the moment it was enunciated. What we now know is that only when the radical pluralism was registered in consciousness was a definition finally possible. It must consist in properties which must always be present, however various the class of artworks turns out to be—as in the Whitney Biennial of 2002 for example. That pluralism was evidently not discernible even as late as when Wittgenstein's philosophy began to be applied to the philosophy of art by his followers. Only when pluralism itself becomes established is it finally possible to do the philosophy of art in a transhistorical way. So one can aim at last at a timeless philosophy of art only at a moment like the present one, which is after all unique in the history of art. Only by paying the closest attention to the art of my historical moment, have I been able to hope for a philosophy of art valid for all historical moments.

This brings me to a third thought of Hegel's. We are all children of our times, he writes—but it is the task of philosophers to grasp their times as thought. Since the 1960s, and compulsively since the 1980s, I have tried to turn my experiences in the art world into philosophy. One can only do that if one lives the times in question, and that makes this book more personal and confessional than philosophy is expected to be, and more abstract than confessions commonly are. There is a tradition of meditative confession in the literature of philosophy, but mainly one must not regard this book as pretending to any kind of scholarly authority. Its authority, if it has any, lies elsewhere. I have dispensed with footnotes, which, except in the most scholarly of writing on art, constitute a *façade* of craved authority. Read it as an adventure story, with a few philosophical arguments and distinctions as trophies brought back from my encounters with the life of art in our times.

ARTHUR C. DANTO
New York City, 2002

Acknowledgments

The Paul Carus Lectures, named after the editor of *The Open Court*, the Open Court Publishing Company, and *The Monist*, are sponsored by the Foundation established in his memory. Generally, the lecturer is invited to present a series of three lectures at a meeting of one or another of the three divisions of the American Philosophical Association, and at three-year intervals. The series I know best is C.I. Lewis's 1946 *An Analysis of Knowledge and Valuation,* which I read as a graduate student, and which, for better or worse, defined the way I thought and in many ways still think, not only about the theory of knowledge but almost everything else. Lewis's was the Seventh Series—the first was John Dewey's *Experience and Nature*—and both of these are far too substantial as volumes to represent a mere three lectures. It is understood that the lectures are to be published as a book by Open Court, but that means that the manuscript will finally contain a fair amount of material not in the lectures themselves. And so it is in the present case. Nothing can be considered a book that lacks a spine, and three one-hour lectures, bound together, is at best little more than a pamphlet.

The three lectures that I delivered under the title *The Revolt Against Beauty* at what turned out to be the 100th Anniversary of the American Philosophical Association on December 26–28, 2001, in Atlanta, Georgia, correspond to Chapters 1, 2, and 4 of this book, though much expanded, and in the case of Chapter 4 radically altered. Chapter 3, "Beauty and Beautification," is a greatly modified version of a contribution to Peg Brand's anthology, *Beauty Matters* (Bloomington: Indiana University Press, 1998), refitted to the context of the Carus Lectures. Chapter 2 borrows from my review of an exhibition of Paul McCarthy, which appeared in *The Nation*, 23 April, 2001, as well as from a response to an argument by Jean Clair, "Marcel Duchamp and the End of Taste: A Defense of Contemporary Art," which appears in English in *Tout-fait: The Marcel Duchamp Studies On-line Journal* 1, 3, www.tout-fait.com, but otherwise only in Dutch translation as "Marcel Duchamp en her einde van de smaak: een apologie van de moderne kunst." *Nexus* 27: 199–217. I am grateful to the Nexus Institute for inviting my response to Jean Clair, which opened up the concept of disgust for me in valuable ways.

Chapter 5, "Beauty and Politics" draws some of its language from "Beauty and Morality," which was delivered as a keynote address at the conference, "Whatever Happened to Beauty?" held at the University of Texas at Austin, and published in my *Embodied Meanings: Critical Essays and Asesthetic Meditations* (New York: Farrar, Straus, Giroux, 1994). Chapter 6 is almost unrecognizably different from "The Museum as Will-to-Power," presented at a conference on the museum at Skidmore College and published in *Salmagundi*. An adaptation of Chapter 7 was presented as "The American Sublime," in a conference organized by the University of Ghent under the title "Shadows of the the Sublime," in October 2002. My preface draws on an Afterword, written especially for a collection of my writings that appeared in Dutch translation, under the title *De Komedie van de Overeen-komsten,* edited by Frank Ankersmit and Wessel Krul (Groningen: Historische Uitgeverij, 2002). And the Introduction was inspired by a preface especially written for the Spanish translation of *Beyond the Brillo Box.*

I am grateful in the first instance to the American Philosophical Association, which selected me as the Carus Lecturer for 2001; and to Open Court Publishing Company for sponsoring the lectures and for publishing the book which grew out of them. It meant a great deal to me that Richard Rorty, Peg Brand, and Noel Carroll agreed to introduce the three sessions at which the lectures were delivered, but to Peg Brand I owe a particular debt for having encouraged me to write on the topic of beauty in the first instance. David Ramsay Steele, editor at Open Court, subtly encouraged me to ready the book rather earlier than I might have, which was all to the good. My marvelous wife and companion, the artist Barbara Westman, blesses my life. Her unfailing cheerfulness, humor, love, and high spirits are the elixir that explains my happiness and productivity.

David Carrier, and then Richard and Margaret Kuhns read the lectures before they were delivered, and I am obliged to them for their comments, and grateful for their friendship and love. After the lectures were presented, I sent copies to a number of friends, artists and others, eager to have their responses, which greatly encouraged me to go on to the larger project of this book. I particularly thank David Reed, Robert Mangold, Sean Scully, Robert Zakanitch, George and Betty Woodman, Frank Ankersmit, Michael Kelly, Karlheinz Lüdeking, Jonathan Gilmore, Fred Rush Jr., Lydia Goehr, Mary Mothersill, Bill Berkson, James Ackerman, Amelie Rorty, and John Perrault for their thoughts. Martha Nussbaum's enthusiasm for the lectures and for this project meant an immense amount.

Various stages of my thought on this topic were worked out during my residences at the Acadia Summer Program in the Arts, on Mt. Desert Island in Maine, which exists through the generosity and imagination of the remarkable Kippy Stroud. In dedicating an earlier essay to Kippy, I wrote that The Acadian Summer Program in the Arts is the closest to Duino Castle the United States affords. She is the Princess of Thurn und Taxis: it is not her fault that her guests from the art world are not all Rilkes! Barbara and I cherish her as a person and as a friend, and the present book is but one of the many things she has helped make possible.

Acknowledgments for Illustrations

Illustrations in this book appear by permission. Cover image: *L.H.O.O.Q* (Replica of, from Boite-en-Valise) by Marcel Duchamp (1950-134-934). Philadelphia Museum of Art: The Louise and Walter Arensberg Collection. Reproduced by permission; Frontispiece: *Vir Heroicus Sublimis* by Barnett Newman, © Estate of Barnett Newman, Digital image © The Museum of Modern Art/Licensed by SCALA / Art Resource, NY.

Valoche: A Flux Travel Aid by George Brecht, Collection Walker Art Center, Minneapolis, Walker Special Purchase Fund, 1989; ARS (Artists Rights Society) for *Woman with Hat* and *Blue Nude* by Henri Matisse, © 2003 Succession H. Matisse, Paris / Artists Rights Society (ARS), New York; The Baltimore Museum of Art: The Cone Collection, formed by Dr. Claribel Cone and Miss Etta Cone of Baltimore, Maryland, BMA 1950.228, for *Blue Nude (Souvenir de Biskra)* by Henri Matisse; Damien Hirst / Science Ltd for *A Thousand Years* by Damien Hirst; the photograph of *Expanded Expansion* by Eva Hesse is reproduced with the permission of the Estate of Eva Hesse, Galerie Hauser & Wirth, Zurich; SFMOMA (San Francisco Museum of Modern Art) for *Femme au chapeau (Woman with Hat)* by Henri Matisse; Daniel Joseph Martinez for *Museum Tags: Second Movement (Overture)* or *Overture con Claque—Overture with Hired Audience Members* by Daniel Joseph Martinez, courtesy The Project Gallery, New York; VAGA (Visual Artists and Galleries Association, Inc.) for *Elegy for the Spanish Republic #172* by Robert Motherwell; David McKee for *The Studio* by Philip Guston, © Estate of Philip Guston; Museum of Art, Rhode Island School of Design, Mary B. Jackson Fund, for *The Wedding of Peleus and Thetis* by Joachim Wtewael; *Onement I* and *Vir Heroicus Sublimis*, © Estate of Barnett Newman, Digital images © The Museum of Modern Art / Licensed by SCALA / Art Resource, NY.

INTRODUCTION

The Aesthetics of
Brillo Boxes

> Art is for aesthetics what the birds are for ornithology.
>
> TESTADURA

I was required, as a graduate student of philosophy in Columbia University at the beginning of the 1950s, to become sufficiently conversant with the literature of aesthetics to pass an examination, qualifying me to teach the subject in the unlikely event of finding an academic position. I found the readings interesting but largely irrelevant, since I was never able to see what they had to do with the art that had brought me to New York in the first place. It was not that aesthetic considerations, in a larger sense, were irrelevant to the culture of Abstract Expressionism: they were, rather, central in the endless discussions that took place about the exciting painting that one went to see in the galleries that showed this work, or wrangled over at artists' parties. It was just that nothing I had learned about in the canonical aesthetic texts seemed remotely connected with what was happening in the art. The questions that exercised the painters I knew seemed so distant from the philosophy that claimed to touch upon art that one who knew both sides of the matter had to wonder what the point of the philosophy was. It was long after the occasion on which he first said it that I heard a version of the celebrated putdown of aesthetics by the witty and truculent artist, Barnett Newman— "Aesthetics is for art what ornithology is for the birds."—but it seemed to put into a nutshell the frustrating disconnection between the two sides of my life.

It rather pained me to learn that Newman's particular target was my teacher, and later my friend, Susanne K. Langer, in a panel convened to discuss "Aesthetics and the Artist" at Woodstock, New York, in August, 1952, the year I was appointed to an instructorship at Columbia. The form of the putdown reflected a certain *esprit d'escalier*. What Newman had actually said was that he had never encountered an ornithologist who thought what he was doing was "for the birds," which was a wicked *double entendre,* given the vernacular use of that expression. But perhaps Newman sensed that the theme of the panel really did imply a somewhat patronizing picture of the artists learning from some aesthetician what they were really doing—as if the birds were to take notes from the ornithologists on what it meant to be a bird. If that was the intention of the panel, what aesthetic knowledge it could have been from which the artists might have learned something about being artists, remains to this day closed to me.

Meanwhile, the overall attitude among analytical philosophers, with whom I aligned myself, was that aesthetics itself was for the birds. It was just not something "real" philosophers did. So for some years aesthetics languished in a kind of no-man's-land between philosophy and art, which meant that I was able to live the two parts of my life as if they had nothing much to do with one another, writing analytical philosophy with one hand, as it were, and painting with the other. When I came to write my first piece in the philosophy of art in 1964, I modeled it on the kind of thinking that characterized the philosophy of science and the theory of language that defined "respectable" philosophy at the time. Abstract Expressionism was giving way, in the early 1960s, to a movement—really to a set of movements—so entirely at odds with its attitudes and spirit that one felt one had entered a new and even a revolutionary moment in the history of art. But it was a moment in which it at last seemed to me that it was possible to think philosophically about art, and even that it was now necessary to do so. Unlike Abstract Expressionism, in which aesthetics as a form of lived experience—as distinct from aesthetics as a philosophical discipline—was so central to its being as art, the brash and irreverent art of the early 1960s seemed to have no room for aesthetics at all. It was as if it and analytical philosophy were made for one another.

Both were indifferent to edification and exaltation, both appealed to a kind of hard-edge thinking. It was for me a particularly exhilarating moment. I would have had no interest in being an artist in the new period. But I found it intoxicating to be a philosopher of art when art had shuffled off all the heavy metaphysical draperies the Abstract Expressionists were happy to wear as their intellectual garments, and were content to produce works that looked for all the world like commonplace objects of daily life.

Pop art was among other things an effort to overcome the division between fine and vernacular art—between the exalted and the coarse, the high and the low—where the latter was exemplified by the imagery of comic strips or the logos of commercial art. I had in particular been overwhelmed by a 1964 exhibition I have since written about extensively—and perhaps obsessively—in which Andy Warhol displayed a large number of wooden boxes painted to resemble the cartons in which Brillo pads were packed and shipped from their place of manufacture to the stores in which they were sold. I was struck by the question of how it was possible for Warhol's boxes to be works of art while their counterparts in everyday life were but utilitarian containers with no artistic pretensions whatever. Aesthetics seemed to bear on this issue not at all, since the two sets of boxes, which seemed to have distinct philosophical identities, so resembled one another that it seemed scarcely credible that one of them should have aesthetic qualities the other lacked. So aesthetics simply dropped out of the equation, and never particularly figured in the extensive philosophical literature my 1964 essay, titled "The Art World," engendered.

I have, however, recently come to think that aesthetics did have a certain role to play in the fact that it was with specific reference to the Brillo Boxes that I framed my question. For those were not the only boxes that Warhol showed on that occasion. As I remember the exhibition, Warhol simulated five or six different cartons: Kellogg's Corn Flakes, Delmonte Peach Halves, Heinz Ketchup, Campbell's Tomato Juice, in addition to Brillo. All these boxes were made of plywood, with their commonplace logos stenciled onto their surfaces. And like *Brillo Box*, these boxes looked very like their counterparts in commercial life, though the latter were customarily made of corrugated cardboard. They were like enough, in any case, to raise for me the question that came to occupy my philosophical passion for some time—why were

Warhol's boxes works of art, to be recorded in the *catalogue raisonné* of his work and displayed as sculptures in countless exhibitions, while the boxes in the supermarket were just paper containers, to be used for endless utilitarian purposes—for storage or as second-hand mailing containers, or bundled up to be recycled as waste-paper? There were of course differences between the commercial cartons and Warhol's "sculptures"—but the differences seemed too trivial for the philosophical purpose of distinguishing art from reality.

Now these questions could have been raised with *any* of the boxes in the show. Why was *Brillo Box* somehow the fulcrum I used for lifting the issue that was to form the foundation of my philosophy of art? I think it had to have been because it was somehow visually outstanding, which is what one would expect from a piece of successful commercial art, as the original Brillo carton was. But this was not something Warhol was responsible for. It was, I subsequently was to discover, a part-time package designer named James Harvey who came up with the wonderful design. Harvey was a somewhat tragic figure—an exceptionally promising Abstract Expressionist painter, who had to earn his living as a commercial artist, just as Warhol himself had had to do, but who died too early to fulfill his promise. I have seen a photograph of Harvey, holding his Brillo box while kneeling in front of one of the large and energetic paintings that had already earned him a certain reputation as an artist with great expectations. As it is, he is quite forgotten today. But I owe him a great deal, for he is the one who conceived that brilliant design, so urgent and contemporary, that caught my eye nearly forty years ago. Of course, Warhol had the genius to make art out of what looked like the most banal of everyday objects in consumer culture. But would the question that obsessed me ever have been raised had it not been for Harvey's achievement as a prodigy of commercial design? I think Warhol himself owes something to James Harvey as well. It is difficult to know what the impact on art world consciousness would have been, had his show of boxes consisted only of *Brillo Box*'s relatively drab peers—the Kellogg's Corn Flake box, for example, or the buff brown container for tomato ketchup. *Brillo Box* made the show an instant success. It, rather than any of the other boxes, were featured in a famous photograph by Fred McDarrah, which shows the artist, standing like a

FIGURE 2   James Harvey holding his Brillo carton, 1964
A prodigy of commercial design

stockroom clerk, pale and pasty-faced, surrounded by what, though works of art, could have been simple packing cases full of Brillo. The Brillo Boxes were, thanks to James Harvey, the star of the show and have gone on since to become stars of art history. And it is aesthetics that explains their glamour, even if Warhol himself had nothing to do with that.

My singling out *Brillo Box* for philosophical attention was one of the countless decisions all of us make at every moment of our lives, based on differences in aesthetic appeal. It is a good example of how design compels choice—makes us reach for one product rather than for one of its competitors instead, whether we are picking out a soap pad or a necktie or, for the matter, an oil painting. Part of the success of Pop Art as a world movement was that its practitioners appropriated the achievements of often nameless designers, initially made in order to lend products a certain edge in the ruthless struggle for market advantage. The dissident artists, Vitaly Komar and Alexandre Malamud told me that they discovered Pop Art from seeing it in half-tone illustrations in various art magazines that had a clandestine circulation in the Soviet Union, and appropriated its strategies for their own subversive purposes in a movement they called "Zotz Art." One result of *Glasnost* was the ceremonial exchange of art exhibitions, which is one of the ways in which nations symbolically express friendship for one another; and the Zotz artists could scarcely contain their excitement when a show of American Pop Art in Moscow was announced. What they were unprepared for, Alex Malamud remembers, was how *beautiful* Pop Art was! But that was to be credited entirely to commercial artists, with their use of intense colors and simple forms and smooth outlines—all those aesthetic strategies that, as Warhol once said, the Abstract Expressionists would not look at twice. The extent to which America's victory in the Cold War can be credited to the aesthetics of American commercial art can hardly be exaggerated. The image of all those gay packages densely arrayed on supermarket shelves made the sparse dreary shelves of government dispensaries insupportable.

The Disappearance of Beauty

It is a matter of some irony in my own case that while the aesthetics of Pop Art opened art up for me to philosophical analysis, aesthetics itself has until now had little to contribute to my philosophy of art. That in part is because my interests have largely been in the philosophical definition of art. The issue of defining art became urgent in the twentieth century when art works began to appear which looked like ordinary objects, as in the notorious case of Marcel Duchamp's readymades. As with the Brillo boxes of

Andy Warhol and James Harvey, aesthetics could not explain why one was a work of fine art and the other not, since for all practical purposes they were aesthetically indiscernible: if one was beautiful, the other one had to be beautiful, since they looked just alike. So aesthetics simply disappeared from what Continental philosophers call the "problematic" of defining art. I must admit this may have been an artifact of the way I set about addressing the problem. Still, aesthetics had been too closely associated with art since it first became a topic for philosophy in ancient times to be entirely disregarded in a definition. And as my experience with the *Brillo Box* demonstrates, the aesthetics of artworks has a place in an account of why they please us, even if it is not much different from the way aesthetics functions in everyday choices—in selecting garments or choosing sexual partners or picking a dog out of a litter or an apple out of a display of apples. There is doubtless a psychology of everyday aesthetics to be worked out, and if there are what one might call laws of aesthetic preference, it would be greatly to our advantage to learn what they are. Intuitively, apple merchants polish pieces of fruit, and give prominence to especially well-formed items. And everyone knows the way cosmetics are employed to make ourselves look more desirable—to make the eyes look larger and the hair shinier and fuller and the lips redder and more moist. But is that the way it is with the aesthetics of works of art? To make them look more attractive to collectors? Or has it some deeper role to play in the meaning of art?

The philosophical conception of aesthetics was almost entirely dominated by the idea of beauty, and this was particularly the case in the eighteenth century—the great age of aesthetics—when apart from the sublime, the beautiful was the only aesthetic quality actively considered by artists and thinkers. And yet beauty had almost entirely disappeared from artistic reality in the twentieth century, as if attractiveness was somehow a stigma, with its crass commercial implications. Aesthetics, as I said at the beginning of this introduction, was the very substance of artistic experience in Abstract Expressionist culture. But what made paintings "work" seemed poorly captured by the way beauty had been classically formulated, with reference to balance and proportion and order. "Beautiful!" itself just became an expression of generalized approbation, with as little descriptive content as a whistle someone might emit in the presence of something that especially wowed them. So it was no great loss to the discourse of art when the early Logical Positivists came to think of beauty as bereft of cognitive meaning altogether. To speak of something as beautiful, on their view, is not to describe it, but to express one's overall admiration. And this could be done by just saying "Wow"—or rolling one's eyes and pointing to it. Beyond what was dismissed as its "emotive meaning," the idea of beauty appeared to be cognitively void—and that in part accounted for the vacuity of aesthetics as a discipline, which had banked so heavily on beauty as its central concept. In any case it seemed to have so little to do with what art had become in the latter part of the century that what philosophical interest art held could be addressed without needing to worry overmuch about it—or without needing to worry about it at all.

Another Look at Beauty

Things began to change somewhat in the 1990s. Beauty was provocatively declared to be the defining problem of the decade by the widely admired art-writer Dave Hickey, and this was hailed as an exciting thought. My sense is that it was exciting less because of beauty itself, than because beauty was proxy for something that had almost disappeared from most of one's encounters with art, namely enjoyment and pleasure. In 1993 when Hickey's essay was published, art had gone through a period of intense politicization, the high point of which was the 1993 Whitney Biennial, in which nearly every work was a shrill effort to change American society. Hickey's prediction did not precisely pan out. What happened was less the pursuit of beauty as such by artists than the pursuit of the idea of beauty, through a number of exhibitions and conferences, by critics and curators who, perhaps inspired by Hickey, thought it time to have another look at beauty.

A good example to consider is an exhibition that took place at the Hirschhorn Museum in Washington, in October 1999. In celebration of the museum's fiftieth anniversary, two curators—Neil Ben Ezra and Olga Viso—organized an exhibition called *Regarding Beauty: Perspectives on Art since 1950.* In 1996 the same two curators had mounted an apparently antithetical exhibition titled *Distemper: Dissonant Themes in the Art of the 1990s.* Only three years separate the two shows, but the contrast is sharp enough to have raised a question of whether there had not been some artistic turning point in this narrow interval—a hairpin turn in the *Kunstwollen*—and even a reappraisal of the social function of art. Dissonance had been the favored ambition for art for most of the preceding century. The shift from dissonance to beauty could hardly appear more extreme.

Olga Viso told me that it was the fact that many who saw the first show remarked to her on how beautiful many of the "dissonant" works struck them, that inspired her to put together a show just of art that was expressly made with beauty in mind. But if in fact the dissonance in contemporary art turned out to have been compatible with the works' being beautiful, dissonance could not have been quite so anti-aesthetic as the term and the spirit it expresses suggested. If, that is to say, the works from *Distemper* were found beautiful, they were probably not that different from the works in *Regarding Beauty* after all, and in fact that turned out to be the case. My own view, which will emerge more sharply as this book evolves, is that the beauty of the works in the earlier show would have been incidental rather than integral to their meaning, as was supposed to be the case in the second show. But still it would be there. By "integral" I will mean that the beauty is internal to the meaning of the work.

Consider, for illustrative purposes, the notorious example of Marcel Duchamp's perhaps too obsessively discussed *Fountain*, which, as by now everybody knows, largely consisted of an ordinary industrially produced urinal. Duchamp's supporters insisted that the urinal he anonymously submitted to the Society of Independent Artists in 1917 was meant to reveal how *lovely* this form really was—that abstracting from its function, the urinal looked enough like the exemplarily beautiful sculpture of Brancusi to suggest that Duchamp might have been interested in underscoring the affinities. It was Duchamp's patron, Walter Arensberg, who thought—or pretended to think—that disclosing the beauty was the point of *Fountain*—and Arensberg was a main patron of Brancusi as well.

Now Duchamp's urinal may indeed have been beautiful in point of form and surface and whiteness. But in my view, the beauty, if indeed there, was incidental to the work, which had other intentions altogether. Duchamp, particularly in his readymades of 1915–1917, intended to exemplify the most radical dissociation of aesthetics from art. "A point which I very much want

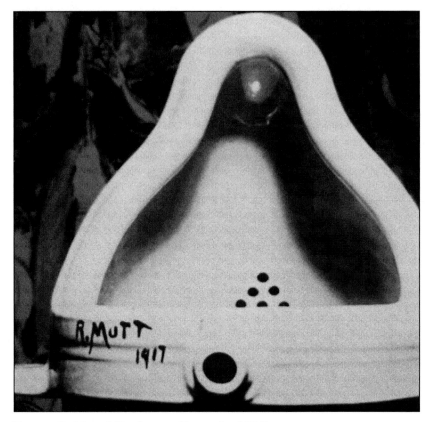

FIGURE 3 Marcel Duchamp, *Fountain*, 1917
The loveliness is incidental.

to establish is that the choice of these 'readymades' was never dic-
tated by aesthetic delectation," he declared retrospectively in
1961. "The choice was based on a reaction of visual indifference
with at the same time a total absence of good or bad taste . . . in
fact a complete anesthesia." Still, Duchamp's supporters were aesthetically sensitive persons, and though they may have gotten his
intentions wrong, they were not really mistaken about the fact,
incidental or not, that the urinal really could be seen as beautiful.
And Duchamp himself had said that modern plumbing was
America's great contribution to civilization.

Let's say the supporters believed the beauty internal to the
work, while I and many others think it incidental. But there can be
no question that the work was, for many reasons, *dissonant*. So it

could appear in an exhibition meant to thematize dissonance—or it could appear just as easily in a show called *Regarding Beauty*. And this might be quite generally the case, so that we can imagine two distinct exhibitions, but containing all and only the same works, the one show illustrating dissonance and the other illustrating beauty. The objects in both shows would in fact be beautiful, and in fact be dissonant. It might be unduly costly to put on two distinct shows, requiring two sets of largely indiscernible objects. One could instead simply have one show called *Distemper,* and then another called *Regarding Beauty,* and have them run one after the other by changing the banners outside the museum. Or we could have two entrances to the same show, those with a taste for dissonance entering through one and those with a thirst for beauty through the other. Mostly, I think, the two bodies of visitors would be satisfied with what they saw—though there would always be the danger of two people meeting inside, having split up since she has a taste for dissonance and he for beauty—and each then wondering if they had made a mistake, walking through the wrong entrance. All sorts of Shakespearean fun can be dreamed up. We could train the docents to say, to one set of visitors, that the beauty (or dissonance) was incidental in the one show and inherent in the other—but this is carrying things too far, since there are cases where beauty is internally related to the dissonance—where the work would not be dissonant if it were not beautiful. This would be the case with the two artists most closely associated with conservative attacks against the National Endowment of the Arts—Robert Mapplethorpe and Andres Serrano.

Readers will object that I am simply indulging my imagination, and letting it run wild. We all know that there are plenty of dissonant works that are not even incidentally beautiful, and plenty of beautiful works without any dissonant aspect at all. Can we not just work with clear-cut cases? The answer perhaps is No, and explaining why will be one of the merits of this book, if the explanation is sound. Meanwhile, it will be of some value to recognize that the connection between *Fountain* and the particular urinal that Duchamp appropriated is pretty close to that between Warhol's *Brillo Box* and the Brillo carton designed by James Harvey. It was the aesthetics of the latter that got me so interested in the former, which had no aesthetics to speak of, other than what it appropriated from Harvey's boxes. But then Harvey's boxes had none of the philosophical depth of Warhol's, for much the same reason that the urinal manufactured by Mott Iron Works had none of the philosophical—and artistic!—power of *Fountain*, which after all helped transform the history of art. But it would be questionable whether the aesthetic power of the urinals—which were designed to be attractive, the way the Brillo cartons were—belongs to *Fountain* as a work of art at all. For that matter, the dissonance of *Fountain* is not a property of urinals as such, which are perfectly straightforward fittings for bathrooms. In any case, there is a metaphysical question in distinguishing between *Fountain,* and the urinal it consisted of, not altogether different from distinguishing between a person and his or her body.

Born of the Spirit and Born Again

Since I am a philosopher with a known involvement with the artworld, I found myself invited to several of the conferences convened to discuss beauty, and I wrote a number of essays as well. The first time I had to confront the question of "Whatever Happened to Beauty?"—a conference sponsored by the Art History Department at the University of Texas in Austin in 1993—I found myself looking into Hegel's great work on aesthetics. Ever since I had begun to write on the subject of the End of Art, I found myself consulting Hegel, who of course had written on that same subject in the 1820s. His book became a kind of treasury of philosophical wisdom for me, in fact, and whenever I embarked on a subject new to me, I found it valuable to see if Hegel might not have had something to say about it. There were two thoughts, on the very first page of his work, which became deeply stimulating to me when I began to ponder the philosophy of beauty. One was the rather radical distinction he drew between natural and artistic beauty, in the very first lines of his text. And the other was his gloss on why artistic beauty seemed "superior" to natural beauty. It was because it was "born of the Spirit and born again." That was a grand ringing phrase: *Aus den Geistens geborene und wiedergeborene.* It meant, as I saw it, that artistic beauty was in some sense an intellectual rather than a natural product. That did not entail that the two kinds of beauty were, other than through their explanations, necessarily different. If someone painted a field of daffodils, to use a Romantic example, it might have been beautiful in just the same way a field of daffodils itself is beautiful. Still, the fact that the painting was "born of the spirit" meant that for Hegel it would have an importance that the natural phenomenon would lack. As always, I found profoundly stimulating the idea that two things might look quite alike but have very different meanings and identities—like *Brillo Box* and the Brillo boxes.

It was with this in my mind that I found a way of drawing a distinction that began to seem quite fruitful. I began to think that the beauty of an artwork could be internal to it, in the sense that it was part of the artwork's *meaning.* This idea dawned on me in thinking about Robert Motherwell's *Elegies for the Spanish Republic,* which I discuss at length in a later chapter of this book. Motherwell's paintings were, in some sense, political—after all they were occasioned by an event in the political history of Spain. Their patent beauty followed naturally from being elegies, since elegies are in their nature meant to be beautiful. Somehow the beauty of the elegy is intended to transform pain into something endurable. So the beauty would be internal to the meaning of the works. By contrast, the beauty of the urinal, if indeed urinals are beautiful, seemed to me quite external to *Fountain,* just as the aesthetics of the Brillo boxes were external to Warhol's *Brillo Box.* They were not part of the meaning. In truth I do not know what the aesthetics of Warhol's *Brillo Box,* if indeed it has any aesthetics, are. It, like *Fountain,* is essentially a conceptual work.

Motherwell, who was a close friend, had recently died, and though I am not a superstitious person, I could not help but feel that the distinction between internal and external beauty, and the connection of the two with meaning, was a sort of gift. I thought that what was distinctive of a work of art as against a natural phenomenon, was that it had some kind of meaning, which would go some distance toward rendering into somewhat contemporary terms Hegel's idea of something being born of the spirit and born again. The meaning of a work of art is an intellectual product, which is grasped through interpretation by someone other than the artist, and the beauty of the work, if indeed it is beautiful, is seen as entailed by that meaning. It was not difficult to find other examples. I thought, for example, of Maya Lin's *Vietnam Veterans' Memorial,* where the beauty is internally generated by the work's meaning. And many other examples were ready to hand. It was, in any case, the first time that I had found a piece of structure in the concept of beauty that might lend itself to philosophical analysis. It was perhaps not a lot of a structure—but it was something to begin to build a piece of philosophy with.

When I was invited to deliver the Carus Lectures before the American Philosophical Association at the annual meeting of its Eastern Division in 2001, I decided to devote them to the subject of beauty. It took a certain amount of nerve to stand up before that organization and talk about beauty—hardly any more a cutting-edge subject in philosophy than in art. But by that time I had found a way of connecting the history of modern art together with my own philosophical interest in the definition of art, and to put both together with the idea of internal as against external beauty. The present book develops the three Carus Lectures in a somewhat systematic way. It might be considered the third volume of a contemporary philosophy of art, the first being my 1981 *The Transfiguration of the Commonplace,* which works out what one might call the ontology of the artwork; and the second the 1997 *After the End of Art,* in which I develop what I think of as a philosophical history of art.

Initially, I felt somewhat sheepish about writing on beauty. This was a lingering consequence of the attitude toward aesthetics that prevailed in my early years in analytical philosophy—that the really serious work to be done by philosophy was in language and logic and the philosophy of science. I sometimes wondered if I ought not to be devoting the immense opportunity of the Carus Lectures to address some more mainstream philosophical topic—something closer to the collective heart of my profession. I had certain ideas, for example, on the concept of mental representation, which I would yet like to work out while I have the mind for it. But what had happened in art in the 1960s and afterward was a revolution, to the understanding of which my writings had somewhat contributed, and I felt that the passing from artistic consciousness of the idea of beauty was itself a crisis of sorts. But even if beauty proved far less central to the visual arts than had been taken for granted in the philosophical tradition, that did not entail that it was not central to human life. The spontaneous appearance of those moving improvised shrines everywhere in New York after the terrorist attack of September 11th, 2001, was evidence for me that the need for beauty in the extreme moments of life is deeply ingrained in the human framework. In any case I came to the view that in writing about beauty as a philosopher, I was addressing the deepest kind of issue there is. Beauty is but one of an immense range of aesthetic qualities, and philosophical aesthetics has been paralyzed by focusing as narrowly on beauty as it has. But beauty is the only one of the aesthetic qualities that is also a value, like truth and goodness. It is not simply among the values we live by, but one of the values that defines what a fully human life means.

Beauty and the Philosophical Definition of Art

It is self-evident that nothing concerning art is self-evident any more, not its inner life, not its relation to the world, not even its right to exist.

THEODOR ADORNO, *Aesthetic Theory,* 1969

It is the mark of the present period in the history of art that the concept of art implies no internal constraint on what works of art are, so that one no longer can tell if something is a work of art or not. Worse, something can be a work of art but something quite like it not be one, since nothing that meets the eye reveals the difference. This does not mean that it is arbitrary whether something is a work of art, but only that traditional criteria no longer apply. The Whitney Biennial of 2002 included a performance piece by the collaborative *Praxis,* which offered visitors to its storefront space in New York's East Village choices from a menu of services, which included hugs, footbaths, dollar bills, and affixing band-aids accompanied by a kiss. One of Biennial 2002's most popular and moving works was a sound piece by Steven Vitiello, consisting of a 1999 recording of the sounds made by Hurricane Floyd outside the ninety-first floor of Tower One in the World Trade Center. Everything is now possible for visual artists, though one consequence of this radical openness is that being a work of art no longer exempts it from the sanctions it would be exposed to if it were just part of life. The would-be assassin of Andy Warhol,

Valerie Solanis, might convincingly have argued that she intended shooting him as a performance piece—but her First Amendment rights were uninfringed when she faced the legal consequences of attempted homicide. The composer Karlheinz Stockhausen pro-claimed as "the greatest work of art ever" the terrorist attack on the World Trade Center in New York on September 11, 2001. As his language conveyed extreme admiration, he was instantly dis-graced, but the fact that such a claim could be made at all under-scores the total openness of the domain, however monstrous it would be to crash airliners into heavily occupied buildings in order to make a work of art.

"Anything" seems a thin and disillusioning answer to the ques-tion "What is art?" But that is because it was long assumed that works of art constituted a restricted and somewhat exalted set of objects that everyone would be able to identify as such, the ques-tion only being what accounted for their status. The mark of the contemporary condition in the *philosophy* of art is that a philo-sophical definition of art must be consistent with the radical open-ness that has overtaken the domain. It is still true that works of art constitute a restricted set of objects. What has changed is that these cannot easily be identified as such, since anything one can think of might be a work of art, and what accounts for this status cannot be a matter of simple recognition. It is by now well understood that something can resemble a work of art entirely and yet itself not be a work of art at all. This would hardly have seemed credible much before 1917, when Marcel Duchamp had already established an oeuvre of perhaps fourteen readymades. The set of readymades— a bicycle wheel, a snow-shovel, a plumbing fixture, a typewriter cover, a grooming comb for dogs, and the like—might far more resemble what might be found in a neighborhood garage sale than anything on display in the Louvre's *Salon Carré*. Duchamp, as we shall note, had somewhat severe criteria for which commonplace objects were in candidacy for the status of readymades, so even he might have wanted to draw a line that the subsequent evolution of the art world has more or less erased. And of course he left unad-dressed the question of what entitled readymades to the status of artworks, while leaving unredeemed the objects in the garage sale. Or the latter from those in an as yet uncreated work of art— *Garage Sale*—which duplicates them exactly: a snow shovel, a typewriter cover, a plumbing fixture, and so forth.

In previous writings I have spoken of the present state of things as The End of Art—a characterization I imagine Adorno would have accepted, with the difference that he would do so as an expression of cultural despair, whereas I mean only that one can now begin seeking a philosophical definition of art without waiting to see what further, by way of objects, the future history of art will bring forth. Since anything can be a work of art, there may in the future be surprises, but they won't be philosophical surprises. A tenable philosophical definition of art will have to be compatible with whatever art there is. A critic once tried to remind me that a definition has to exclude something. But of course a philosophical definition of art covers all and only works of art. It excludes everything else. It excludes for example the hugs and kisses that the members of Praxis give when they are simply being affectionate, and not engaging in a piece of performance art. I salute Adorno for his astute recognition that, contrary to what philosophers traditionally believed about art, nothing, absolutely nothing, is any longer self-evident.

The posthumous publication of Adorno's book in 1969 coincided with the end of a decade of remarkably intense inquiry, conducted by artists as well as by philosophers, though largely in independence of one another. Or rather, the inquiry was entirely philosophical, though much of the philosophy and most of the best of it was produced by artists exploring the limits of art from within. A parallel between modernist art and a certain form of philosophical practice was remarked upon in an essay with which the decade properly began—Clement Greenberg's 1960 "Modernist Painting"—in which he compared modernism in art with a form of self-criticism exemplified in the philosophy of Kant, whom he complimented in consequence as the first modernist. Self-critique in the arts, as understood by Greenberg, consisted in purifying the medium unique to any art of whatever was extrinsic to it. In an example with which Greenberg's thought has been identified, *flatness* is what is unique to the medium of painting, which must accordingly be purged of illusionism of any kind, and depth given over by right to sculpture. Modernism had inherited much the same array of media that was available to artists at the time of Vasari, with the important if controverted exception of photography. In rendering itself "pure," Greenberg predicted, each art would "find the guarantee of its standards of quality as

well as of its independence." But "respect for the medium" as a
critical criterion too has vanished from contemporary discourse.
Today anything goes with anything, in any way at all. Modernism,
as Greenberg presented it, was a kind of conceptual cleansing, to
borrow a scary political metaphor. In our post-modernist era,
purity is an option, and pretty much out of fashion at that.

These issues notwithstanding, Greenberg's agenda was one of
art defining itself from within, and there can be no question that
this quasi-Kantian endeavor was pursued, often with a certain puritanical fervor, by a number of artists bent on making art in its conceptually purified condition. This was particularly the case with the
so-called "Minimalists," and it is not difficult to see their program
as parallel in many respect to philosophy as practiced by such figures as Nelson Goodman or indeed any philosophy based on a program of radical elimination or of reduction to some favored
base—observation, behavior, or whatever. Whether there was an
influence between such philosophies and artistic practice is difficult
to say, but certain of the Minimalists studied at universities like
Princeton and Columbia, where such philosophy was taught, and
the minimalist slogan voiced by the painter, Frank Stella— "What
you see is what you see"—expresses a not unfamiliar philosophical
attitude of the time.

In truth, philosophy and avant-garde art in the 1960s shared a
great many attitudes. One aim of Pop, for example, was to ironize
the distinction between high and vernacular art—between the
heroized painting of the previous generation of artists, the
Abstract Expressionists, and the popular imagery of the comic strip
and commercial advertisement—the "High and Low" of a controversial exhibition at the Museum of Modern Art in 1992. But
comparably, it was an effort of analytical philosophy to overcome
the pretensions of what we might call "high" philosophy—the
cosmo-tragical visions of the Existentialists, or of the metaphysical
titans who loomed behind them—by criticizing their language
against either the standards of ordinary discourse, where we know
whereof we speak, or of a scientific discourse governed by strict
considerations of verifiability and confirmability. It is difficult to
resist the impulse to see a cultural equivalence between canoniza-
tion of ordinary language, cultivated by the Oxford School of
Linguistic phenomenology, and the studied aesthetic of everyday
objects in Warhol's Factory or Claes Oldenberg's 1962 Store on

East Second Street in Manhattan, where one could buy painted effigies of gym shoes, automobile tires, and women's underpants or tights. Philosophy was marked by a willed down-to-earthness in its examples. Wanting a sip of beer served as the paradigm of desire, turning the lights on or off by flipping a switch was (is) the standard example of human action.

Switching the lights on and off was tendered as a minimal work of art by the composer George Brecht, a member of Fluxus, a movement in which I have a particular interest, since my own philosophical ideas on art were first worked out in the early 1960s, when I knew nothing of Fluxus's thought or practice, though I now wish I had. It is perhaps one sign of a true movement of thought when individuals begin to do or think the same kinds of things while unaware of one another's existence, although there is a rather natural historical explanation for such parallels as may have existed between philosophical and artistic attitudes in the early sixties. The members of Fluxus were alumni of John Cage's seminar in experimental composition at the New School, and subscribed to certain ideas emanating from Dr. Suzuki's seminars in Zen Buddhism at Columbia, both of which took place in the late 1950s. Zen ideas, as framed by Suzuki, had a vast transformative influence on the intellectual life of New York in those years. My own thought, set out in the already mentioned 1964 article, "The Art World," is seasoned with imagery I acquired from sitting in on Suzuki's class, as well as from his books. Cage is widely known for his endeavor to overcome the distinction between music and mere noise—a program generalized by Fluxus as "closing the gap between art and life." In those crucial years, especially in and around New York, the commonplace world of everyday experience had begun to undergo a kind of transfiguration in artistic consciousness. And this is a direct consequence of Suzuki's teaching. I found it philosophically thrilling to realize that nothing outward need distinguish a work of art from the most ordinary of objects or events—that a dance can consist in nothing more remarkable than sitting still, that whatever one hears can be music—even silence. The plainest of wooden boxes, a coil of clothesline, a roll of chicken wire, a row of bricks, could be a sculpture. A simple shape painted white could be a painting. The institutions of high culture were not well suited to this moment. It was unreasonable to pay admission to watch a woman not move, or to listen to oneself breathe as someone else, sitting before a piano, did not touch the keys. So much the worse for the institutions of the art world! At any time the weather allowed, a group could assemble to perform Dick Higgins's 1959 *Winter Carol*, listening to the snow fall for an agreed upon period of time. What could be more magical? Anyone could perform Yoko Ono's early "instruction work," *Match Piece*, in which one strikes a match and watches it until the flame goes out. The dying of the light— what could be more poetic?

How much of any of this fell within the horizons of official aesthetics is historically problematic, but somehow the avant-garde, such as it was within that philosophical specialty, appeared to have understood that the definition of art had to be undertaken as if something like it were true. Richard Wollheim's "Minimal Art" appeared in 1965, initially in an art periodical, and Wollheim is credited with coining the term Minimalism, though he admits having known nothing of the works that finally became so designated. His concern, rather, was whether there are minimal criteria for something being art, and his paradigms were monochrome paintings, which existed only as philosophical jokes until perhaps 1915, and the ready-mades, which appeared in the history of art at more or less the same time. In this, Wollheim followed the official philosophical model according to which having a concept meant possessing criteria for picking out its instances. It was a Wittgensteinian commonplace that instances can be culled out successfully without benefit of definitions, as in the example that he made famous, of games. In fact there can be no criteria for distinguishing a ready-made metal grooming comb from an indiscernible metal grooming comb that was not a readymade, nor a monochrome white painting from a panel all over which white paint had been slathered—so the question of definition became urgent after all. The tried and true method of "picking out instances" loses its appeal when dealing with the inventory of Fluxus: George Brecht's 1975 *Valoche (A Flux Travel Aid)* is a wooden box containing toys: a jump rope, some balls, a top (perhaps), a children's block with a snowman painted on it, a chess piece, a plastic egg or two, and what might or might not be prizes from boxes of Crackerjack. Wittgenstein's prestige notwithstanding, his was probably always the wrong approach to such matters. He would not be the first philosophical genius whose central ideas and proposals were deeply wrong.

FIGURE 4 George Brecht, *Valoche (A Flux Travel Aid)*, 1975
Wittgenstein's approach won't work here.

My article, "The Art World," presented at the annual meeting of the American Philosophical Association in 1964, was based on the central difficulty that pairs of objects were now available, entirely alike so far as appearances went—*Valoche* or a mere box of toys—but such that one was a work of art and the other not. I first encountered this possibility earlier that year at an exhibition of Andy Warhol's cartons at the Stable Gallery in East 74th Street in Manhattan. His *Brillo Box* looked enough like the commercial cartons in which Brillo pads were packed that a photograph of one would look entirely like a photograph of the other. So what accounted for the difference? My sense at the time was that they would have different historical explanations—that Warhol's *Brillo Box*, for example, had been made by someone who had internalized the recent history of art and commanded a body of theory, for the benefit of those who also knew that history and those theories, by contrast with the actual Brillo carton of the supermarket, conceived of by a free-lance package designer, for those who had to decide how their product was to be shipped to supermarkets. Warhol's, by contrast, was made for an art world that was in position to appreciate it, which was George Dickie's formulation in his Institutional Theory of Art, according to which something is a work of art (a) if it is an artifact (b) upon which some person or persons acting on behalf of the art world has conferred the wary status of a "candidate for appreciation." In art-historical fact, there was no *the* Art World in the 1960s, but a number of overlapping groups of artists and critics, many of whom were prepared to say that what others were doing was not really art at all. In 1963, Richard Artschwager sent a dozen identical kits to various institutions and individuals he thought might be interested in his work. The Guggenheim Museum responded that it was craft, not art. The director of the Castelli Gallery invited him to come round. What gives any art world its authority can hardly be answered without a more cognitivist definition than Dickie's, but I'll not pursue the matter here.

Philosophers like to appeal to "our" concept of this or that. Wollheim worried that a certain artistic practice would result in "the disintegration of our concept of 'art' as we have it." But in truth very little of "our" concept actually survived the avant-garde experiments of the sixties. What was revolutionary about Fluxus was that it removed from the received conception of art almost everything that had been thought to ground the distinction, as in the following partial catalog I excerpt from George Maciunas's 1966 *Fluxus Manifesto*: "Exclusiveness, Individuality, Ambition . . . Significance, Rarity, Inspiration, Skill, Complexity, Profundity, Greatness, Institutional and Commodity Value." Here in the same spirit is an agenda articulated by Yvonne Rainer in an agenda for the Judson Dance Group: "NO to spectacle no to virtuosity no to transformations and magic and make believe no to the glamour and transcendency of the star image." With the advent of Conceptual art at the end of the decade, it was no longer required that there be a material object (an "artifact"?), nor was it necessary that, if there were in fact an object, it had to be made by the artist. One could make the art without being an artist, or be an artist without making the art for which one claimed credit. "I've stopped making objects," the artist Douglas Huebner said in a 1969 interview. "And I'm not trying to take anything away from the world. Nor am I trying to restructure the world. I'm not trying to tell the world anything, really. I'm not trying to tell the world that it could be better by being this or that. I'm just, you know, touching the world by doing these things, and leaving it pretty much the way it is." Leaving the world as we found it, we had been told by Wittgenstein, this time profoundly, is the way it is with philosophy. Artists need not follow in the footsteps of Huebner, but at least they can and still be artists. The definition of art would have to be built on the ruins of what had been thought to be the concept of art in previous discourses.

Beauty Dethroned

What follows from this history of conceptual erasure is not that art is indefinable, but that the conditions necessary for something to be art will have to be fairly general and abstract to fit all imaginable cases, and in particular that very little remains of "our concept of art" that the framer of a real definition can rely on. In *The Transfiguration of the Commonplace* I advanced two conditions, condensed as "*x* is an art work if it embodies a meaning," the chief merit of which lay in its weakness. Missing from my proto-definition, as from all the definitions of the sixties known to me, was any reference to beauty, which would surely have been among the first conditions to have been advanced by a conceptual analyst at the turn of the twentieth century. Beauty had disappeared not only from the advanced art of the 1960s, but from the advanced philosophy of art of that decade as well. Nor *could* it really be part of the definition of art if anything can be an artwork, when not everything is beautiful. Beauty might be listed as a disjunct in the vocabulary of appreciation, and hence covered by Dickie's main concept. But beauty rarely came up in art periodicals from the 1960s on without a deconstructionist snicker. Not long after the John Simon

Guggenheim Memorial Foundation was established in 1925, the founders saw as its immediate beneficiaries "Men and women devoted to pushing the forward the boundaries of knowledge and to the creation of beauty." Art was tacitly defined in terms of creating beauty, and creating beauty is put on equal footing with expanding the boundaries of knowledge. The logo of the Institute for Advanced Studies in Princeton in 1930 shows two allegorical females, one draped and the other nude, labeled Beauty and Truth in that order, the garment perhaps implying that Beauty is Truth with a dress on. But reference to the creation of beauty all but drops out of the enabling language for the National Endowment for the Arts, about forty years later, not just because beauty had largely disappeared from the artistic agenda in 1965, but because, we learn from Michael Brenson's recent study of the NEA, its sponsors saw artists as sources of ideas which might be of value in the national agenda of winning the Cold War.

In those years, nevertheless, modern art was dismissed as subversive and destructive, and essentially anti-American by such figures as Congressman George A. Dondero of Michigan, who wrote "Modern art is communistic because it is distorted and ugly, because it does not glorify our beautiful country, our cheerful and smiling people, and our material progress. Art which does not beautify our country in plain simple terms that everyone can understand breeds dissatisfaction. It is therefore opposed to our government and those who create and promote it are our enemies." The newspaper magnate William Randolph Hearst, Brenson states, "equated any form of artistic radicalism with communism, and assumed that of the work produced in a non-traditional manner was a disguised means of communist propaganda." This is but one instance, as we shall see, of the politicization of beauty.

In the early 1990s, the critic Dave Hickey was asked what he thought the central issue of the decade would be. "Snatched from my reverie, I said 'Beauty,' and then, more firmly, 'The issue of the nineties will be *beauty.*'" This was greeted, he recalls, with a "total uncomprehending silence . . . I had wandered into this *dead zone,* this silent abyss." Let me begin to put this the silence into one possible perspective by considering the photography of Robert Mapplethorpe, which had become notorious in 1989 when his exhibition, *The Perfect Moment,* was cancelled by the Corcoran

Museum of Art in an ill-advised pre-emptive move against the danger that funding for the National Endowment of the Arts might be voted down if our legislators saw what the fund was supporting. The fear was based on the charged sexual content of his signature images—though it was central to Mapplethorpe's achievement that his work was self-consciously beautiful as well. It was its beauty, rather than its often gamy content, that alienated the photographic avant-garde from him as an artist. When I was writing my book on Mapplethorpe, *Playing with the Edge,* I asked a photographer who was at the time experimenting with pinhole cameras what he thought of him. He dismissed Mapplethorpe as a *pompier*—an artist so concerned with elegance as to have lost touch with the limits of his medium. The imperatives of Modernism tended to make the simple grainy snapshot the paradigm of photographic purity, which applies to photography Greenberg's purgative view of the quest for what is inherent in the medium. The charge against Mapplethorpe was that his work was too beautiful to qualify for critical endorsement. "One writer claimed that if I painted sex and violence, it would have been okay, but one isn't allowed to paint anything beautiful," Gerhard Richter recalls. "The changed fashion of the time," if I may appropriate Kant's mournful language regarding the fate of Metaphysics, "brings beauty only scorn; a matron outcast and forsaken."

There is more to the dethronement of beauty, however, than the discovery that it has no place in the definition of a given art, or, in the light of post-modernist pluralism, in the definition of art in general. There is the widespread sense that in some way beauty trivializes that which possesses it. The casual philosophy of beauty has rested content with the thought, often ascribed to David Hume, that it is merely in the eye of the beholder. Hume indeed held, in the essay *Of Civil Liberty,* "that beauty in things exists in the mind"—but this in no sense distinguished it, for Hume, from anything else, inasmuch as "tastes and colours, and all other sensible qualities, lie not in bodies but in the senses,"as he writes in "The Skeptic."

> The case is the same with beauty and deformity, virtue and vice. This doctrine, however takes off no more from the reality of the latter qualities than from that of the former . . . Though colours were allowed to lie only in the eye, would dyers or painters ever be less regarded or esteemed? There is a sufficient uniformity in the senses

and feelings of mankind to make all these qualities the objects of art
and reasoning, and to have the greatest influence on life and manners.

But even a philosophical argument that beauty might claim the
same ontological weight as virtue and vice would not entirely erase
the felt sense that there is something almost derelict or even inde-
cent in the pursuit of beauty—an attitude that does not arise with
the other aesthetic categories we were advised by Oxford analysts
to canvas if we were interested in making some progress in aesthetics—"the dainty and the dumpy," to cite J.L. Austin's examples. But none of them carries the moral weight of beauty in the
aesthetic tradition. The real conceptual revolution, in truth, is not
purging the concept of art of aesthetic qualities so much as purging the concept of beauty of the moral authority one feels it must
have possessed in order that possessing beauty should have come
to be taken as morally questionable. At the height of the Vietnam
War, the painter Philip Guston bade farewell to the beautiful paintings on which his reputation was based, and instead began to paint
allegories of evil that could not consistently with their intended
moral message possess the stigma of beauty.

In a letter to Thomas Monro in 1927, George Santayana wrote
of his generation "We were not very much later than Ruskin, Pater,
Swinburne, and Matthew Arnold. Our atmosphere was that of
poets and persons touched with religious enthusiasm or religious
sadness. Beauty (which mustn't be mentioned now) was then a living presence, or an aching absence, day and night." It was precisely
its beauty that justified the esteem in which art was held in
Santayana's time. Here, for example, are some thoughts from the
early writing of Santayana's contemporary, G.E. Moore, that are
almost unintelligible today: "I cannot see but what that which is
meant by beautiful is simply and solely that which is an end in
itself. The object of art would then be that to which the objects of
Morals are means, and the only thing to which they are means.
The only reason for having virtues would be to produce works of
art." In his early text, *Art, Morals, and Religion,* Moore wrote:
"Religion is merely a subdivision of art," which he explicated this
way: "Every valuable purpose which religion serves is also served
by Art; and Art perhaps serves more if we are to say that its range
of good objects and emotions is wider." There can be no doubt
that Moore believed that art can take religion's purposes over

because of the beauty it essentially possesses. Proust was greatly moved by the 1897 work by Robert de Sizeranne titled *Ruskin et la religion de la beauté.*

Now I would like to offer an historical speculation. It is that the immense esteem in which art continues to be held today is an inheritance of this exalted view of beauty. It is widely and sometimes cynically said that art has replaced religion in contemporary consciousness. My speculation is that these Victorian or Edwardian attitudes have survived the abjuration of beauty itself. I will go even further and suggest that if there is a place for beauty in art today, it is connected with these survivals, which are deeply embedded in human consciousness. Beauty's place is not in the definition or, to use the somewhat discredited idiom, the essence of art, from which the avant-garde has rightly removed it. That removal, however, was not merely the result of a conceptual but, as I shall argue, a political determination. And it is the residue of aesthetic politics that lingers on in the negativity we find in attitudes toward beauty in art today. The idea of beauty, the poet Bill Berkson wrote me recently, is a "mangled sodden thing." But the *fact* of beauty is quite another matter. In a passage near the beginning of *Within a Budding Grove,* Marcel (the Narrator), traveling by train to Balbec, sees a peasant girl approaching the station in the early morning, offering coffee and milk. "I felt on seeing her that desire to live which is reborn in us whenever we become conscious anew of beauty and of happiness." I believe Proust's psychology profound in connecting the consciousness of beauty with the feeling of happiness—which has also been trivialized in modernist times—providing we are not conflicted because of a negativity that had not inflected the idea of beauty in the generation of Proust, Moore, and Santayana. I would like to press this further. It was the moral weight that was assigned to beauty that helps us understand why the first generation of the avant-garde found it so urgent to dislodge beauty from its mistaken place in the philosophy of art. It occupied that place in virtue of a conceptual error. Once we are in position to perceive that mistake, we should be able to redeem beauty for artistic use once again. Conceptual analysis, without the reinforcement of a kind of Foucauldian archeology, is insufficiently powerful to help us in this task. Had it not, for example, been for the artistic avant-garde in the twentieth century, philosophers almost certainly would continue to teach that the connection between art and beauty is conceptually tight. It took the energy of the artistic avant-garde to open a rift between art and beauty that would previously have been unthinkable—that, as we shall see, remained unthinkable long after it was opened, largely because the connection between art and beauty was taken to have the power of an a priori necessity.

Moore's Revelation

In the latter sections of *Principia Ethica,* Moore wrote "By far the most valuable things we know or can imagine, are certain states of consciousness, which may roughly be described as the pleasures of human intercourse and the enjoyment of beautiful objects." He thought the point "so obvious that it risks seeming to be a platitude." No one, Moore claims, "has ever doubted that personal affection and the appreciation of what is beautiful in Art or Nature, are good in themselves." Nor, he continues, "does it appear probable that any one will think that anything else has *nearly* so great a value as the things which are included under these two heads." Moore's confident appeals seem today almost shockingly parochial, but I'll suppose they were commonplace in his world. What would not have been commonplace, however, is what he next goes on to claim, namely that "this is the ultimate and fundamental truth of Moral Philosophy" and that these two values "form the rational ultimate end of human action and the sole criterion of social progress." People might come to accept these as truths, but they appear, Moore said, to be "truths which have been generally overlooked."

I think Moore must have been correct that if these were truths, they were generally overlooked, since they were received as having the force of revelation by the Bloomsbury circle, whose entire philosophy of art and of life derived from Moore's teaching and his example. In *My Early Beliefs,* John Maynard Keynes characterized Moore's ideas as "Exciting, exhilarating, the beginning of a renaissance, the opening of a new heaven on a new earth, we were the forerunners of a new dispensation, we were not afraid of anything . . . one's prime objects in life were love, the creation and enjoyment of aesthetic experience and the pursuit of knowledge. "A great new freedom seemed about to come," according to Vanessa Bell. When Lady Ottoline Morrell died in 1938, she was memorialized with a surprisingly uninspired epitaph, considering the literary stature of its authors—T.S. Eliot and Virginia Woolf: "a brave spirit, unbroken,/Delighting in beauty and goodness/And the love of her friends." Any member of the Bloomsbury circle, to which Woolf and Lady Ottoline centrally and Eliot marginally belonged, would wish to have been memorialized in precisely these terms. Puccini's librettist for *Tosca* put what in effect were Bloombury ideals in the heroine's aria: *Vissi d'arte, vissi d'amore*— I lived for art, I lived for love." The opera was staged in 1900— *Principia Ethica* was published in 1903—though set in the year 1800, when it seems to me a person like Tosca would have said that she had lived for *pleasure*, which was the central concept in Enlightenment moral psychology, as we can see even in Kant, when he addresses the topic of beauty. I find it hard to believe anyone lived for art in 1800, though this would have been the romanticist's philosophy of life. But love and art—and art because of its beauty—were precisely the defining values of Bloomsbury, whose scheme of values derived from *Principia Ethica*. Love and friendship, on the one hand, and what Moore speaks of "as the proper appreciation of a beautiful object" were to suffice, without the need for religion, the main moral needs of modern human beings.

Beauty Is Universal

With the exceptions of Hume and Hegel, the classical aestheticians drew no crucial distinction between "Art or Nature" in regard to the appreciation of beauty, and it must be borne in mind that that indifference was but rarely contested in philosophical aesthetics or in artistic practice itself when Moore composed *Principia Ethica*. If anything, I think, Moore supposed the appreciation of natural beauty superior to the appreciation of artistic beauty, largely because "We do think that the emotional contemplation of a natural scene, supposing its qualities equally beautiful, is in some way a better state of things than that of a painted landscape; we would think that the world would be improved if we could substitute for the best works of representative art *real* objects equally beautiful."

This merits an aside. At one point Moore invites us to consider two worlds. "Imagine the first "as beautiful as you can; put into it whatever on this earth you most admire—mountains, rivers, the sea; trees and sunsets, stars and moon." Imagine the other as "simply one heap of filth, containing everything that is most disgusting to us . . . and the whole, as far as may be, without one redeeming feature." Now "the only thing we are not entitled to imagine is that any human being ever has or ever, by any possibility, *can* ever see and enjoy the beauty of the one or hate the foulness of the other." Moore's argument now takes on logical energy on which the Ontological Argument turns, and we may paraphrase him in its terms. These two worlds now have, since we have imagined them, what earlier philosophers would have designated "objective reality." That is, they have the reality of something we have succeeded in thinking about—they are "objects of thought." Would it not be intrinsically better that they have—using again the earlier philosophical idiom—*formal* reality as well? Would it not be better, that is, that the beautiful rather than the ugly world actually exist, though no one can enjoy it? "The instance is extreme," Moore concedes. And he concedes as well "that our beautiful world would be better still, if there were human beings in it to contemplate and enjoy its beauty." This of course is what Moore is really interested in, though it remains important to him that "the beautiful world *in itself* is better than the ugly."

I happen to believe that Moore's characteristically ingenious argument has a great deal of psychological truth. I mean that there are descriptions of states of affairs that would be accepted as beautiful and as ugly pretty much by anyone, especially in contrast to one another. As an example of the first, here is an observation by the art critic and moralist, John Berger:

> In Istanbul, the domestic interior, in both the shantytowns and elsewhere, is a place of repose, in profound opposition to what lies outside the door. Cramped, badly roofed, crooked, cherished, these interiors are spaces like prayers, both because they oppose the traffic of the world as it is, and because they are a metaphor for the garden of Eden or Paradise.
>
> Interiors symbolically offer the same things as Paradise: repose, flowers, fruit, quiet, soft materials, sweetmeats, cleanliness, femininity. The offer can be as imposing (and vulgar) as one of the Sultan's rooms in the harem, or it can be as modest as the printed pattern on a square of cheap cotton, draped over a cushion on the floor of a shack.

With variations in taste and circumstance, such symbolic Edens—interiors or gardens—would incorporate more or less the kinds of things and qualities Berger enumerates. I have encountered a contrastingly stark description by a Central American guerilla, of how to treat prisoners whose will and spirit one wants to break: shut them up in cold damp spaces without light of any sort, with vermin and bad food, surrounded by their own excrement. It is what one might term aesthetic torture. Choosing which of these conditions is preferable is not a matter of *taste*! Offered the choice, everyone would choose Paradise over jungle hell. Beauty may indeed be subjective, but it is universal, as Kant insisted. And this must be the intuition that underlies Moore's thought that connects beauty with goodness and connects beauty and happiness for Proust. It connects with something inherent in human nature, which would explain why aesthetic reality is as important as it is, and why aesthetic deprivation—depriving individuals of beauty—should have taken on the importance it did in the artistic agendas of the avant-garde.

Good Art May Not Be Beautiful

In any case, Moore believed that so far as the pictorial arts are concerned, a beautiful painting is a painting of a beautiful subject. And this I think gave a certain importance to the museum of fine arts which began to be seen as a site in which to experience beauty in those years. In Henry James's novel, *The Golden Bowl* (1905), his character, Adam Verver, a man of immense wealth living abroad, has conceived the idea of building a "museum of museums" for "American City," which gave him his wealth. He is doing this to "release the people of his native state from the bondage of ugliness." There would be no way—or no easy way—to transform Detroit or Pittsburgh into the Catskills or the Grand Canyon. But artistic beauty was portable, and if the aesthetically deprived citizenry of American City could be put in the presence of "treasures sifted to positive sanctity," this would be an immense benefit if Moore were right that contemplation of beautiful objects is of the highest moral good. It helps explain why museum architectures should have taken the form of the temple in James's time.

The problem was that Modernist painting at just that moment was beginning to veer, somewhat starkly, away from the mimetic model. Roger Fry, Moore's disciple, was a modernist painter and critic. He organized two notorious "Post Impressionist" exhibitions at the Grafton Gallery in London, in 1910 and in 1912, in which artistic representations so deviated from the motifs they transcribed, that even professional art critics saw no way of dealing with them. Fry wrote: "The generality of critics have given vent to their dislike and contempt in unequivocal terms. One gentleman is so put to it to account for his own inability to understand these pictures that he is driven to the conclusion that it is a colossal hoax on the part of the organizers of the exhibition and myself in particular." Here is Fry's attempt to explain their incapacity to see what the Bloomsbury Moderns and, for that matter, Moore himself, who came to think of the 1910 exhibition as the most important event of that year, regarded as the objective beauty in these unprecedented works:

> Almost without exception, they tacitly assume that the aim of art is imitative representation, yet none of them has tried to show any reason for such a curious proposition. A great deal has been said about these artists searching for the ugly instead of consoling us with beauty. They forget that *every new work of creative design is ugly until it becomes beautiful*; that we usually apply the word beautiful to those works of art in which familiarity has enabled us to grasp the unity easily, and that we find ugly those works in which we still perceive only by an effort. (Italics mine)

The perception of them as ugly is in effect, on Fry's view, the projection onto them of a mental confusion, which a course of aesthetic education will remove, enabling their beauty to be seen. Post-Impressionist painters, Fry goes on to say, affirm "the paramount importance of design, which necessarily places the imitative side of art in a secondary place." This is the basis of Fry's formalism.

But Fry himself made a mistake even more profound than thinking it the aim of painting to imitate nature. The mistake is that it is the aim of paintings to be beautiful. I give Fry great credit for thinking that something needed to be explained in order that those who scoffed might perceive the excellence of Post-Impressionist painting, just as Bloomsbury did, but I draw special attention to the a priori view that the painting in question really *was* beautiful, if only viewers knew how to look at it. It is a commonplace that the history of modernism is the history of acceptance. This story is told over and over by docents and lecturers in art appreciation. The history of art always has a happy ending.

Manet's *Olympia,* vilified in 1865, was a world treasure a century later, and that supports a little homily on critical restraint. In *The Guermantes Way,* Proust writes of the way "the unbridgeable gulf between what they considered a masterpiece by Ingres and what they supposed must for ever remain a 'horror' (Manet's *Olympia,* for example) shrink until the two canvases seemed like twins." How does this happen? Fry believed that it happens through critical explanation. People have to be brought to understand the work, and then they will see the way in which it is excellent. That, more than the actual explanations Fry gave, is his great achievement. For it makes clear that artistic goodness often requires explanation if it is to be appreciated, something that Hume understood completely. "In many orders of beauty, particularly those of the finer arts," Hume writes in Section One of his *Enquiry Concerning the Principles of Morals,* "it is requisite to employ much reasoning in order to feel the proper sentiment; and a false relish may frequently be corrected by argument and reflection." Hume is eager to point out that "moral beauty partakes much of this latter species."

With qualification, I accept Fry's point, as well as the spirit of Hume's marvelous observation. What I want to deny, however, is that the history of appreciation always culminates in the appreciation of *beauty.* It may indeed culminate in the appreciation of artistic goodness, which is what Hume really wanted to argue for in his great essay on how critically—and objectively—to arbitrate differences in taste. The mistake was to believe that artistic goodness is identical with beauty and that the perception of artistic goodness is the aesthetic perception of beauty. But that, as I see it, was the assumption of Edwardian Aesthetics, which the kind of art selected for the Grafton Gallery exhibitions ought to have called into question. The Edwardians, for example, were entirely right to begin to appreciate African art. They were even right in thinking that, on formal grounds, it could be seen as beautiful. The Victorians had thought that "primitive peoples" were, in making art, trying to make beautiful objects, only they did not know exactly how— hence their "primitivity." The Edwardians thought themselves advanced because formalism enabled them to see what Fry called "Negro sculpture" as beautiful. But they were wrong in thinking that they had learned through formalism to see the beauty that was the point of African art. That was never its point, nor was beauty

the point of most of the world's great art. It is very rarely the point
of art today.

Having lived through the *Sensation* exhibition at the Brooklyn
Museum in 1999, we can sympathize with Fry. The critics pretty
much to a person condemned the art, and were certain they were
being put upon. But they were ready to see it as a First
Amendment rather than an aesthetic matter, and in this they were
perhaps more right than someone would have been who hoped
that through argument one would at last see the beauty. It is not
and it never was the destiny of all art ultimately to be seen as beautiful. There would have been no way for David Hume to have
known about this, And it was perhaps historically too early for
Roger Fry to have known about it as well, not least of all because
the art that was so difficult for his contemporaries to accept often
turned out to be artistically good in just the way he anticipated and
Hume explained—through patient critical analysis. A lot of what
prevented people from seeing the excellence of early modern
paintings were inapplicable theories of what art should be. But that
did not mean that even when one came around to see that the art
that had so alarmed and enraged Fry's critics was after all good,
one was going to see it as beautiful! Matisse's *Blue Nude* is a good,

FIGURE 5   Henri Matisse, *Blue Nude,* 1907
Possibly great, definitely unbeautiful

even a great painting—but someone who claims it is beautiful is talking through his or her hat. In order to find in what way beauty can have a role to play in the art of our time, we shall have to free ourselves from the Edwardian axiom that good art is categorically beautiful, if only we recognized how. It is an achievement of the conceptual history of art in the twentieth century that we have a very much more complex idea of artistic appreciation than was available to the early Modernists—or to Modernism in general, down to its formulation in the writing of Clement Greenberg as late as the 1960s. I'll take this up in the next chapter, which addresses what I designate as the Intractable Avant-Garde.

The Intractable Avant-Garde

I have a mad and starry desire to assassinate beauty . . .

TRISTAN TZARA

Near the opening of *A Season in Hell*—allegedly an allegorical account of his tumultuous relationship with the poet Paul Verlaine—Rimbaud writes: "One evening, I sat Beauty on my knees; and I found her bitter, and I abused her." The "bitterness of beauty" became epidemic among the avant-garde artists of the following century, but it was a rare thought in 1873 when Rimbaud published this poem. In Fantin-Latour's group portrait of the previous year, *Un Coin de Table,* Rimbaud is shown seated with Verlaine and a number of other bohemians in a group called *Les villains bonhommes—The Bad Eggs*—of whom Verlaine and Rimbaud were one might say the "baddest." The portrait of Rimbaud—the only true likeness of him we possess—is of a singularly beautiful, almost angelic-looking youth with golden curls, shown in a pensive state. He was eighteen and a rakehell; and the disparity between his character and his appearance, as in Oscar Wilde's character, Dorian Gray, is a familiar failure of fit that has helped give beauty a bad name. His badness extends even to his aesthetic preferences, which he catalogs in the *Délires* section of his poem: "Idiotic pictures, shop signs, stage sets, backcloths for street-entertainers, billboards, vernacular images, old fashioned stories, church Latin, badly spelt pornography, romance novels for elderly ladies, fairy tales, little books for children, old operas, silly refrains, naïve rhythms." What Rimbaud would not have known was that his inventory was to fit the canon of an alternative aesthetic a century later, under the name of "camp."

Though I have no wish to lose myself in interpreting Rimbaud's poem, it can, perhaps must be read as a tribute to the power of beauty, the disparities notwithstanding. Until he abused Beauty in the third line, his life had been a celebration, "in which every heart was opened and wine flowed freely." But now it is as if the poet were sentenced to madness—a season in hell—in penalty. He explicitly titles the section of the poem in which he declares his anti-aesthetic preferences as *Ravings*. That section ends with what feels like Rimbaud coming to his senses, though it can be read as heavy irony: "All that's behind me now. Today I know how to bow down before beauty." It is as if Rimbaud intuited a thought I can hardly suppose he could have read in Kant's *Critique of Judgment,* that "the beautiful is the symbol of the morally good."

Kant's text is not entirely easy to follow, but he clearly wants to say that finding something beautiful is more than simply taking pleasure in experiencing it. The beautiful "gives pleasure with a claim for the agreement of everyone else." For this reason, "the mind is made conscious of a certain ennoblement and elevation above the mere sensibility of pleasure received through sense, and the worth of others is estimated in accordance with a like maxim of their judgment." In enunciating recently the principles of décor that had been followed in creating a home for former prison inmates, the director said "We tried to do this beautiful because beautiful matters. Beautiful tells people they matter." Kant goes on to claim "the subjective principle in judging the beautiful is represented as *universal,* i.e., valid for every man." The abuse of beauty, on this view, is the symbolic enactment of an offense against morality and hence in effect against humanity. "I had armed myself against justice," Rimbaud says just after confessing his crime, the poem describing the price he paid.

Anthropology of Beauty

It is not clear, even if it would have been possible for him to have imagined it, that the abuse of beauty would be regarded by Kant as *ipso facto* a moral evil, since beauty only *symbolizes* morality, and between moral and aesthetic judgments there is only the kind of analogy, to use his example, that may hold between a commonwealth and a living body. So aesthetic imperatives are moral imperatives only symbolically. Kant recognizes that not everyone will agree, case by case, on questions of beauty, but the analogy requires the belief that they ought to, whatever may be the force of the ought. There was an Enlightenment tendency to believe that the same moral principles—the Golden Rule for example— were to be found in every society, so universality must have seemed co-extensive with humanity. Would there have been a parallel view in regard to beauty? Kant interestingly handled moral and aesthetic differences in systematically parallel ways. He learned about the South Seas from reading Captain Cook's voyages, and clearly he was struck by the otherness of the societies Cook describes. The question comes up for him whether those other lives are ones *we* would morally be able to live. In the schedule of cases in which he attempts to illustrate the working of the categorical imperative, he considers a talented individual in comfortable circumstances who "prefers indulgence in pleasure to troubling himself with broadening and improving his fortunate natural gifts." It would be entirely consistent with the laws of nature that everyone should live like "the inhabitants of the South Seas," so by one formulation of the categorical imperative, it would be permissible that a man "should let his talents rust and resolve to dedicate his life only to idleness, indulgence, and propagation" (Kant cannot bring himself to think of sex, even in the South Seas, in terms other than those of generation!) But *we* "cannot possibly will that this should become a universal law of nature, for "as a rational being, one necessarily wills that all one's faculties should be developed inasmuch as they are given to one for all sorts of possible purposes." The implication is that the South Sea islanders are not quite rational, but even so ought to live in conformity with the Protestant ethic, and that is what we must teach them as moral missionaries. Kant was in no sense a moral relativist. What relativists regard as differences in culture Kant will regard as but differences in development on the model of the differences between children and adults. The South Sea islanders are primitive Europeans, as a child is a primitive adult.

But Kant similarly contests South Sea aesthetics, as he understands them. Presumably based on anthropological illustrations he must have seen, Kant was aware that there are parts of the world in which men are covered with a kind of spiral tattoo: "We could adorn a figure with all kinds of spirals and light but regular lines, as the New Zealanders do with their tattooing, if only it were not the figure of a human being," he writes in the *Critique of Judgment*; and in the same section of that book he says "We could add much to a building, which would immediately please the eye if only it were not to be a church." These are imperatives of taste, and it is striking that Kant considers the tattoo as merely a form of ornamentation, say like gilded statuary on a church, rather than a set of marks which may, in anthropological truth, have nothing to

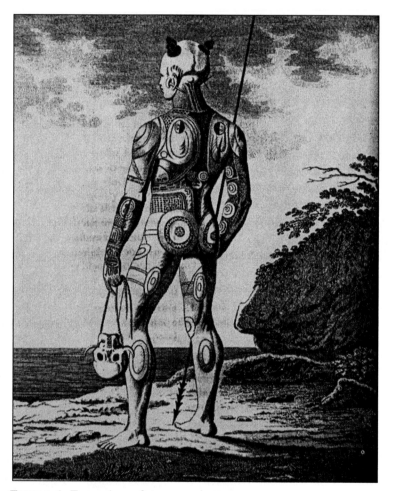

FIGURE 6   Engraving of a tattooed man
Something other than ornamentation

do with beautification, but serve rather to connect the tattooed person with some larger scheme of the world. The tattoo may conduce to admiration of its bearer—but not for aesthetic reasons so much as for whatever it is in a person the tattoo signified—military prowess, say, or cosmic rank, or as evidence of having come through some ordeal. Similarly with the brass neck coils affected by the Paduang women of Burma. The number and height of the coils may imply that the wearer is a figure of substance without this implying that it is an attribute of beauty. And something of the same sort may be true of ornament in, say, the German baroque church Kant evidently finds offensive to taste—as if the passions of Northern European Iconoclasm were merely expressions of aesthetic revulsion. It is, then, with reference to cognitive rather than aesthetic judgments that both ought to be assessed. I would hesitate to say that all cases of so-called beautification can be deflected in this way, but the possibility suggests that a universal beauty may be entirely consistent with cultural differences, our mistake consisting in regarding certain things as aesthetic when they have some quite different and more cognitive function. The aesthetic diversity of the world's art is consistent with beauty as such being everywhere more or less the same, if one cared to defend that thesis, and that wherever it were found it would evoke the same sense of ennoblement in its beholders.

If, on the other hand, tattooing in the South Seas really is beautiful "in the eye of the South Sea Islander," Kant must feel himself entitled to the view that they are just wrong. They just don't know what beauty is, which he would have defined in terms of what we may as well term the Protestant Aesthetic. Even Hegel, the first major philosopher I know of who actually went out of his way to look at paintings and listen to music, and was as we shall see an extraordinary art critic, had a difficult time with other traditions. "The Chinese," he states in his *Lectures on the Philosophy of History*, "have as a general characteristic, a remarkable skill in imitation, which is exercised not merely in daily life but in art. They have not yet succeeded in representing the beautiful as beautiful; for in their painting, perspective and shadow are wanting." Parenthetically, Clement Greenberg noted at one point that Manet pushed shadows to the edges of his forms—the way, Greenberg surmises, that he saw them in photographs—and this inevitably flattened his figures, which accounts in some measure for the outcry against his work, and at the same time explains how Greenberg should have regarded Manet as the first modernist painter, having stumbled onto the flatness that Greenberg declared the defining attribute of painting. Hegel's implication in any case is that the Chinese have either no idea of beauty or a wrong one. Unlike the artists of Oceania or Africa, they really do draw in ways that imply mimetic competence. The Chinese "observes accurately how many scales a carp has; how many indentations there are in the leaves of a tree, etc. [but] the Exalted, the Ideal and beautiful is not the domain of his art and skill." It would obviously sound crazy to characterize a great civilization like China's as primitive. In fact it was somewhat crazy to think of the Oceanic or African artists as primitive, with the assumption that they were trying to achieve beauty through accurate mimesis, but were, like children, not up to the task, and simply needed a robust *beaux arts* education. Hegel notes, sourly, that the Chinese are "too proud to learn anything from Europeans, although they must often recognize their [our] superiority." In historical fact, the Chinese did recognize the objective correctness of western perspective when they were shown it by missionaries in the seventeenth century. Their attitude was in effect "So what?"—not that there is no such thing as correct and incorrect, but that optical correctness had no bearing on painting as they practiced it in their culture. Chinese art in any case was beautiful enough to have been appropriated for decorative purposes in Europe from the seventeenth century on. But the Chinese culture had a very different idea of the aims of representation and of the relevance of visual truth. Yet no one could count their art as ugly, which is the operative thought in Roger Fry's dictum that things will be perceived as ugly until they are perceived as beautiful. It was Hegel who required aesthetic education, fixated as he was on the renaissance paradigm of mimesis as the ideal. But like everyone, as he says in his Preface to *The Philosophy of Right*, he was a child of his times.

Roger Fry understood, as a modernist, that the ligature between beauty and mimetic representation had been irreversibly loosened in his time. He knew that one could not argue the hostile reviewers of his exhibition into agreeing that Cézanne or Picasso show the world as we really see it—though there were certainly theorists prepared to argue that they had. Fry had instead to argue that this is not relevant, and that the emphasis must be not on vision but on design—to use the terms of his famous title, *Vision and Design*. *Then* we can see the beauty of African and Chinese art, having surrendered the misleading mimetic criteria so compelling to Hegel. Loosening the beauty-mimesis ligature made it possible for Fry to become a great formalist art critic, but because he continued to see the ligature between art and *beauty* as that of a necessary connection, so that of necessity art is always beautiful, it failed to occur to him, as a theorist, that whole artistic traditions have existed in which beauty was never the point at all. Beauty was not the rainbow that awaited us as the reward of sustained looking. It was never the case that the only proper way to address art was that of aesthetic contemplation at all. To put it another way, it never occurred to Fry, any more than it had occurred to Ruskin, that the beauty that was incontestably present in, for example, the great cathedrals, may have been a means rather than an end. The point was not to stand in front of the church and gape at the ornamentation, but to enter the church, the beauty being the bait, as it so often is in entering into sexual relationships.

Fry's one contemporary who appears to have understood this was Marcel Duchamp. In conversations that took place in 1967, Duchamp said: "Since Courbet, It's been believed that painting is addressed to the retina. That was everyone's error. The retinal shudder!" His argument is quite historical: "Before, painting had other functions, it could be philosophical, religious, moral. Our whole century is completely retinal, except for the Surrealists, who tried to go outside it somewhat." Duchamp, to whom I'll return, expressed this to Pierre Cabanne, but he had been almost unique in recognizing the deep conceptual disconnection between art and aesthetics in his readymades of 1913–1915 which, art-historically speaking, was just the right time for this to have reached consciousness as a philosophical possibility, when what we might call "The Age of Aesthetics" was drawing to a close, and our present age, which artistically owes so much to Duchamp, beginning, faintly, to dawn.

In 1905, ruminating on the somewhat farcical trial between Whistler and Ruskin that had entertained London audiences in 1879, Proust wrote that while Whistler had been right that there is a distinction between art and morality, on another plane Ruskin was right that all great art is morality." In 1903, as we saw, Moore seriously argued that the consciousness of beauty was among the supreme moral goods. We are safe, I think, in speaking of an atmosphere at the beginning of the twentieth century in which Rimbaud's image of abusing beauty could still have been seen as an abuse of morality. I can think of no more vivid a gesture of abusing beauty by abusing great art than Duchamp's 1919 work in which he drew a moustache on a postcard of Mona Lisa, and lettered a mild obscenity beneath that paradigm of art at its greatest. Like everything by Duchamp, this work is a field of fiercely competing interpretations, but I want to use it as an historical signpost of a deep change in attitude that calls for an historical explanation. I want to focus on an art-historical episode in the course of which, greatly to the benefit of the philosophical understanding of art, a logical space was definitively opened between art and beauty. It was a space that remained invisible to the members of Bloomsbury who, for all their modernist ideals, were essentially late Edwardians. It was invisible to them because they had the idea, expressed in Fry's dictum, that works of art, perceived as ugly, will ultimately be perceived as beautiful. In fairness, that was a dictum that continued to define what we might consider the a priori of artistic perception down to the threshold of our time. "All deeply original art," Clement Greenberg declared, "is initially perceived as ugly." "The highest responsibility of the artist is to hide beauty," John Cage said in his so-called Julliard Lecture in 1952, quoting W.H. Blythe's *Haiku*. It was a gap that remained invisible until the great conceptual efforts of the 1960s to define art. The opening of the gap is the contribution in my view of what I shall term the Intractable Avant-garde.

A Revolt Against Beauty

I want, in setting the scene for of my historical explanation, briefly to return to Moore's philosophy, and in particular to the connection between the two supreme goods he holds up for examination. Moore sees a clear connection between goodness and beauty. "It appears probable that the beautiful should be *defined* as that of which the admiring contemplation is good in itself." The two values, Moore claims, are so related to one another "that whatever is beautiful is also good." He goes further: "To say that a thing is beautiful is to say, not indeed that it is itself good, but that it is a necessary element in something which is: to prove that something is truly beautiful is to prove that a whole, to which it bears a particular relation as a part, is truly good." So Moore sees some near-entailments between art and beauty, and between beauty and goodness. "With regard to the question what *are* the mental qualities of which the cognition is essential to the value of human intercourse, it is plain that they include, in the first place, all those varieties of aesthetic appreciation which formed our first class of goods." With this, I think, Moore is seeking a connection between the cognition of beauty and the kind of human intercourse in which those for whom beauty is a value endeavor to participate. They will seek human intercourse with those who are exactly like them in highly prizing aesthetic experience. They will seek to form relations with those as much like themselves as possible—those whose "mental states," to use Moore's expression, are themselves good. And this indeed was the principle on which Bloomsbury friendship was based: It consisted almost entirely of those who assigned to beauty the highest moral priority. The Bloomsburys saw themselves as the true vessels of civilization.

And they perhaps supposed it the mark of a civilization that it create individuals of the sort they exemplified. In this, I think, they were not so far from Kant, in the light of his concluding proposition that beauty is the symbol of morality, even if connected, in his view, by way of a kind of analogy. Beauty, Kant writes, introducing an unlovely term from rhetoric, is an *hypotyposis* of morality, presenting moral concepts with a certain vividness and poetry. Kant observes that, "we often describe beautiful objects of nature or art by names that seem to put a moral appreciation at their basis. We call buildings or trees majestic and magnificent, landscapes laughing and gay, even colors are called innocent, modest, tender, because they excite sensations which have something analogous to the consciousness of the state of mind brought about by moral judgments." There is in aesthetic judgment, moreover, an entailed disinterestedness as well as a universality, which in Kant's philosophy was *sine qua non* for moral conduct. The person who values aesthetic experience has a moral fineness in that she or he is *enobled* through the disinterestedness. Remember, further, that Kant defined Enlightenment as mankind's coming of age—a cultural stage he would have believed the South Sea Islanders have not and perhaps for a long time will not have attained. And now the question was: how is it that just those nations defined by civilized high-mindedness should have made the most savage and protracted war that history up to that point had known?

It was with this question that the concept of beauty became abruptly politicized by avant-garde artists around 1915, which falls midway in the period of the readymades in Duchamp's career. It became that in part as an attack on the position, under which art and beauty were internally linked, as were beauty and goodness. And the "abuse of beauty" became a device for dissociating the artists from the society they held in contempt. Rimbaud became an artistic and moral hero—the poet everyone wanted to be. "I believe in the genius of Rimbaud," the young André Breton wrote Tristan Tzara, the author of the Dada Manifesto of 1918. It is Dada to which I primarily refer in the project of disconnecting beauty from art as an expression of moral revulsion against a society for whom beauty was a cherished value, and which cherished art itself because of beauty. Here is a recollective account by Max Ernst:

> To us, Dada was above all a moral reaction. Our rage aimed at total subversion. A horrible futile war had robbed us of five years of our existence. We had experienced the collapse into ridicule and shame of everything represented to us as just, true, and beautiful. My works of that period were not meant to attract, but to make people scream.

Ernst knew the war—he had been an artilleryman—and his art was aggressive, as his perception of the war-makers as hateful required it to be. In some measure this was true of German Dada in general. The First International Dada exhibition in Berlin had signs declaring that art was dead—"*Die Kunst ist Tot*"—adding "Long life to the *maschinen Kunst Tatlins*". Its members were not out to vilify German values—they were bent on destroying them by forcing upon German consciousness an art it could not swallow. Its means were a kind of aggressive foolishness. The original spirit of Dada was a kind of exaggerated play in the shadow of the war, a way of demonstrating by infantile actions its contempt for the clashing patriotisms: the term itself was baby-talk for "rocking horse," and the Zurich Dadaists registered their protests though buffoonery against what Hans Arp called "the puerile mania for authoritarianism which could use art itself for the stultification of mankind:"

While the thunder of guns sounded in the distance, we pasted, we recited, we versified, we sang with all our soul. We searched for an elementary art that would, we thought, save mankind from the furious folly of these times. We aspired to a new order.

And here is Tristan Tzara in the Dadaist Manifesto of July, 1918:

There is a great negative work of destruction to be accomplished. We must sweep and clean. Affirm the cleanliness of the individual after the state of madness, aggressive complete madness of a world abandoned to the hands of bandits, who rend one another and destroy the centuries.

Hence Tzara's dream to assassinate beauty.

Dada art was vehemently ephemeral—posters, book jackets, calligrams, pamphlets, recitations, as we would expect from a movement made of poets as well as artists. These ephemera, in their very ephemerality, were what Tzara celebrated as "means of combat." An exhibition of Dada art would consist of scraps of paper, yellowing snapshots, and a few sketches from the Café Voltaire in Zurich, where it all took place. Dada refuses to be found beautiful—and that is its great philosophical significance when we consider the consoling narrative that with the passage of time, what was rejected as art because not beautiful becomes enfranchised as beautiful and vindicated as art. This perhaps did happen with the avant-garde art of the nineteenth and early twentieth centuries. Matisse, for example, became for many a paradigm of beauty, as did the Impressionists so reviled in their time. I see Dada by contrast as the paradigm of what I am terming The Intractable Avant-Garde, the products of which are misperceived if perceived as beautiful. That is not its point or ambition.

From Taste to Disgust

The narrative of aesthetic redemption assures us that sooner or later we will see all art as beautiful, however ugly it appeared at first. *Try to see this as beautiful!* becomes a sort of imperative for those who look at art that does not initially appear beautiful at all. Someone told me that she found beauty in the maggots infesting the severed and seemingly putrescent head of a cow, set in a glass

FIGURE 7 Damien Hirst, *A Thousand Years*, 1990
Try to see this as beautiful?

display case by the young British artist Damien Hirst. It gives me a certain wicked pleasure to imagine Hirst's frustration if hers were the received view. He intended that it be found disgusting, which was the one aesthetically unredeemable quality acknowledged by Kant in the *Critique of Aesthetic Judgment*. Disgust was noticed by him as a mode of ugliness resistant to the kind of pleasure which even the most displeasing things—"the Furies, diseases, the devastations of war"—are capable of causing when represented as beautiful by works of art. "That which excites *disgust* [*Ekel*]," Kant writes, "cannot be represented in accordance with nature without destroying all aesthetic satisfaction." The representation of a disgusting thing or substance has on us the same effect that the presentation of a disgusting thing or substance would itself have. Since the purpose of art is taken to be the production of pleasure, only the most perverse of artists would undertake to represent the disgusting, which cannot "in accordance with nature," produce pleasure in normal viewers.

I don't know what works of art, if any, Kant could have had in mind as disgusting, and he may have counted the very idea of disgusting art as incoherent: if a piece of mimesis was of something disgusting, it would itself be disgusting, contravening its status as art, which in its nature is meant to please. I have seen a sculpture

FIGURE 8 *The Prince of the World*, St. Sebald, Nürnberg, 1310
A high moral purpose, in poor taste

from Nuremberg from the late Gothic era, where a figure, known as "The Prince of the World," which looks comely and strong from the front, is displayed in a state of wormy decay when seen from behind: the body is shown the way it would look decomposing in

the grave. Such sights explain why we actually bury the dead. It is
intended thus to be seen as revolting by normal viewers, and there
can be no question of what is the intended function of showing
bodily decay with the skill of a Nuremberg stone carver. It is not
to give the viewer pleasure. It is, rather, to disgust the viewer, and
in so doing, to act as a *vanitas,* reminding us through presentation
that the flesh is corrupt, and its pleasures a distraction from our
higher aspirations, namely to achieve everlasting blessedness and
avoid eternal punishment. To show the human body as disgusting
is certainly to violate good taste, but Christian artists were prepared to pay this price for what Christianity regards as our highest
moral purpose. One has, I suppose, a choice between denying that
it is art since it contravenes taste, as I surmise that Kant would have
done; or to dismiss taste as he and his contemporaries understood
it as too narrow a criterion for defining art.

That we have no difficulty in acknowledging as art *The Prince
of the World*—or even Damien Hirst's maggoty *tête de vache*—
shows how far we now are from eighteenth-century aesthetics, and
how complete a victory the Intractable Avant-Garde has achieved.
Indeed, it has recently been argued by Jean Clair, a conservative
French critic, that what Kant notices as a marginal case has become
in contemporary art a "new aesthetic category" made up of
"repulsion, abjection, horror, and disgust." Disgust, Jean Clair
explains, is a "common trait, a family resemblance" of the art produced today "not only in America and Europe, but even in the
countries of central Europe thrown open to western modernity."
The French language permits a play on words between *goût* (taste)
and *dégoût* (disgust) unavailable in English, which finds no such
clear morphemic nexus between *taste* and *disgust*. It allows us to
paraphrase Jean Clair's view of *la fin de l'art* as *the end of taste*—a
state of affairs in which disgust now occupies the position
antecedently occupied by taste. And this indeed, as Jean Clair sees
it, expresses the sad decline of art over the past few centuries:
"From taste . . . we have passed on to disgust."

My sense is that Jean Clair grossly overstates the case. There
are, to be sure, those who derive a perverted pleasure in experiencing what the normal viewer finds disgusting: who have, one
might say, "special tastes." James Joyce's hero, Leopold Bloom,
who relished the faint taste of urine in his breakfast kidney, fur-
nishes a mild example of what I have in mind. Andres Serrano,

whose photograph, *Piss Christ,* became a talisman in the culture wars of the 1990s, made a less notorious photograph in a series he called *The History of Sexuality.* It shows a man lying down, his mouth opened to receive a stream of urine from a pretty woman standing over him. The act is associated with degradation, as indeed the use of urine is in *Piss Christ.* It belongs to the story of Christ's suffering—his passion—that he was subjected to the indignities Serrano's subject willingly pursues. But the affect of urine must remain associated with disgust or the pursuit of it loses any point. Artists interested in representing the disgusting would not have this special audience in view. Their aim is precisely to cause through their art sensations that, in Kant's phrase, "we strive against with all our might." Kant would have had no recourse but to regard this as the perversion of art. It would be of no value to such artists if a taste for the disgusting were to be normalized. It is essential to their aims that the disgusting remain disgusting, not that audiences learn to take pleasure in it, or find it somehow beautiful, which sounds like what Jean Clair claims has happened. Critics may applaud the use of disgust in contemporary art, not because they have a new aesthetic but because they applaud the use of it the artists make. But in view of the vehemence of Jean Clair's polemic, it is worth dwelling for a moment on the phenomenon of disgust in contemporary art.

"Disgusting" has a fairly broad use as an all-round pejorative, but it also and I think primarily, refers to a specific feeling, noticed by Darwin in his masterpiece, *The Expression of the Emotions in Man and Animals,* as "excited by anything unusual in the appearance, odor, or nature of our food." Evidence for the centrality of food "includes the facial expression, which focuses on oral expulsion and closing of the nares, and the physiological concomitants of nausea and gagging." It has little to do with literal taste. Most of us find the idea of eating cockroaches disgusting, but for just that reason few of us really knows how cockroaches taste. "A smear of soup in a man's beard looks disgusting, though there is of course nothing disgusting in the soup itself" is one of Darwin's examples. There is nothing disgusting in the sight of a baby with food all over its face, though, depending on circumstances, we may find it disgusting that a grown man's face should be smeared with *marinara* sauce. Like beautification, which I shall discuss later, disgust is one of the mechanisms of acculturation, and there is remarkably little variation in our schedules of what disgusts. So disgust is an objective component in the forms of life people actually live. The baby is very quickly taught to wipe its face lest others find it disgusting, and we hardly can forebear reaching across the table to remove a spot of chocolate from someone's face—not for their sake but for ours. What he speaks of as "core disgust" has become a field of investigation for Jonathan Haight, a psychologist at the University of Virginia. He and his associates set out to determine "the kinds or domains of experience in which Americans experience disgust." Foods, body products, and sex, not unexpectedly, got high scores when people were queried on their most disgusting experiences. Subjects also registered disgust in situations in which "the normal exterior envelope of the body is breached or altered." I was philosophically illuminated to learn that of the seventeen or so authenticated feral children, *none* evinced disgust at all. But I am also instructed by the fact that my cultural peers are disgusted by what disgusts me, more or less.

This overall consensus encourages me to speculate that most of us would unhesitatingly find disgusting the work of the widely admired artist, Paul McCarthy, which characteristically uses food in ways that would elicit disgust were we to see someone doing that in life, confirming Kant's observation. Consider what may be his masterpiece—the video of a performance titled *Bossy Burger*, which transpires in a hamburger stand, the interior of which is utterly nauseating, with dried splotches and piles of food pretty much everywhere. McCarthy, togged out in an initially immaculate chef's uniform and toque, wears the Alfred E. Newman mask that connotes imbecility, and his character grins his way through fifty-five minutes of clownishly inept food preparation. Thus he pours far more ketchup into a sort of tortilla than it can possibly hold, folds it over with the ketchup squishing out, and moves on to the next demonstrations. These involve milk and some pretty ripe turkey parts. The character is undaunted as his face, garments, and hands quickly get covered with what we know is ketchup but looks like blood, so he quickly takes on the look of a mad butcher. He piles the seat of a chair with food. He makes cheerful noises as he bumbles about the kitchen or moves to other parts of the set, singing, "I love my work, I love my work." I can hardly write about this piece without feeling queasy, and there can be little doubt that it is McCarthy's purpose to elicit disgust. He may, like the sculptor of *The Prince of the World*, have a larger purpose. He may, for example, intend to "debunk the false idealism [he] regards as rampant in Hollywood films, advertising, and folklore," as one commentator writes. His work may "relentlessly and rigorously probe the air-brushed innocence of family entertainment to reveal its seamy psychic underpinnings," to cite another critic. So it may, by virtue of what Kant calls hypotyposis in connection with beauty, show what really underlies it all, as the worm-riddled backside of *The Prince of the World* was intended to underscore our common mortality. But that does not erase the fact that maggots count as disgusting. So possibly McCarthy is a kind of moralist, and his works are really meant to awaken us to awful truths and their disgustingness is a means to edificatory ends. That leaves intact the revulsion their contemplation evokes. It does not erase the disgust.

A critic might, without redundancy, say that McCarthy's work is disgusting because it is disgusting. Its being disgusting, descriptively speaking, might give a reason, might even entail, that it is disgusting aesthetically, and as a matter of critical assessment. Once we open up the distinction between the use of the same term to appraise and to describe, McCarthy's enthusiasts would be entitled to say that it is beautiful because it is disgusting. The position of Dada, after all, could have been expressed as follows: It is disgusting because it is beautiful. That would be a way of saying that artists have no business making beautiful things for an immoral society! Max Ernst told Robert Motherwell that he and his fellow Dadaists once staged an exhibition of their art in a toilet.

It is a protraction of Bloombury imperatives, however, that moves McCarthy's commentators not so much to praise it for being disgusting, but to say instead that it must be descriptively beautiful after all. "I wanted to think about the question of beauty in your work," an interviewer murmured, "to move from the manifest to the latent." The *Times* speaks of the "unlikely beauty of the work," adding that it is "Not standard beauty, obviously, but a beauty of commitment and absorption." I have to believe that McCarthy's perceptions can be very little different from the rest of us. He has indeed almost perfect pitch for "disgust elicitors," and accordingly making the art he does must be something of an ordeal. That may have the moral beauty that undergoing ordeals possesses, especially when undertaken for the larger welfare. But if it is this sort of ordeal, it has by default to be disgusting, even if we find it "beautiful" that it is so. I find it inconceivable that he is aiming at beauty after all!

Abject Art

"Nothing is so much set against the beautiful as disgust," Kant wrote in his 1764 essay, *Observations on the Feeling of the Beautiful and the Sublime*. The sublime is too large a topic to address at this point in my inquiry, but it is worth noting that in that pre-critical text, Kant deliciously observes that the antonym of the sublime is the *silly*, which suggests that the effect of Dada was less the abuse of beauty than the rejection of the sublime. But just possibly the disgusting, as logically connected to beauty through opposition, can also have the connection with morality that beauty does. In the early 1990s, curators recognized a genre of contemporary art they designated "Abject Art," which may be what Jean Clair has primarily in mind. "The abject," writes the art historian Joseph Koerner, "is a novelty neither in the history of art nor in the attempts to write that history." Koerner cites, among other sources, a characteristically profound insight of Hegel: "The novelty of Christian and Romantic art consisted of taking the abject as its privileged object. Specifically, the tortured and crucified Christ, that ugliest of creatures in whom divine beauty became, through human evil, basest abjection." Rudolph Wittkower begins his great text on art and architecture in Italy after the Council of Trent by recording the decision of that council to display the wounds and agonies of the martyred, in order, through this display of affect, to elicit the sympathy of viewers and through that to strengthen threatened faith. "Even Christ must be shown 'afflicted, bleeding, spat upon, with his skin torn, wounded, deformed, pale and unsightly' if the subject calls for it." Hegel cites the art historian, Count von Rumohr on an earlier Byzantine tradition:

> Accustomed to the sight of gruesome physical punishments, [they] pictured the Saviour on the Cross hanging down with the whole weight of his body, the lower part swollen, knees slackened and bent to the left, the bowed head struggling with the agony of a gruesome death. Thus what they had in view as their subject was physical suffering as such. [By contrast] the Italians were accustomed to give a

comforting appearance to the face of the Saviour on the Cross, and so, as it seems, followed the idea of the victory of the spirit and not, as the Byzantines did, the succumbing of the body.

The tendency in the Renaissance to beautify the crucified Christ was in effect a move to classicize Christianity by returning the tortured body to a kind of athletic grace, denying the basic message of Christian teaching that salvation is attained through abject suffering. The aestheticism of the eighteenth century was a corollary of the rationalism of natural religion. It was Kant's stunning achievement to situate aesthetics in the critical architectonic as a form of judgment two small steps away from pure reason. Romanticism, as in the philosophy of Hegel, was a re-affirmation of the Baroque values of the Counter-Reformation. The problem with art, as Hegel saw it, lay in its ineradicable dependence upon sensuous presentation. As with the blood, the torn flesh, the shattered bones, the flayed skin, the broken bodies, the reduction of consciousness to pain and agony in Baroque representation. What Abject art has done is to seize upon the emblems of degradation as a way of crying out in the name of humanity. "For many in contemporary culture," the critic Hal Foster writes, "truth resides in the traumatic or abject subject, in the diseased or damaged body. Thus body is the evidentiary basis of important witnessings to truth, of necessary witnessings against power."

Down with the Alps!

In view of the history of human suffering which beyond question was the chief cultural product of the twentieth century, it is astonishing how dispassionate, how rational, how distancing, how abstract so much of twentieth-century art really was. How innocent Dada itself was, in its artistic refusal to gratify the aesthetic sensibilities of those responsible for the First World War—to give them babbling in place of beauty, silliness instead of sublimity, injuring beauty through a kind of punitive clownishness. The Intractable Avant-Garde's spirit of play—or even, if one wants to be censorious, of silliness—remains alive in art today.

Consider, for illustrative purposes, a marvelous exhibition that was installed in 1998 at the Kunsthaus in Zurich—a stone's throw from the old Café Voltaire where Dada originated—named after one of the whimsical "non-negotiable demands" of a student uprising there in the early 1980s: "Down with the Alps! *Ein frei Sicht zum Mittelmeer*—An uninterrupted View of the Mediterranean!" Initially a protest against rebuilding the municipal opera house, the riots escalated into an action militant enough to call for plastic bullets and tear gas, but imaginative enough to produce some crazy ideas, like demolishing the Alps to open up a free view of the Mediterranean: Razing the Alps was a metaphor for changing national identity ("Switzerland must be re-invented!") The demand is also pure Dada, as so many of the works in the show were. The exhibition's political subtext was to demonstrate through its art that Switzerland belonged to the same artistic culture as, say, Germany or the United States. That means that official artistic culture today is Dada through and through—which means in turn that virtually everything on view belonged to the Intractable Avant-Garde.

Neo-Dada no longer has the hope that it will reform the modern nation by abusing beauty. But perhaps by weakening if not destroying the supposedly internal relationship between art and beauty, it has made it possible for art more directly to address the inhumanities that so revolted the generation of artists after World War I. And this may explain the emergence of Abject Art as well as the sort of aesthetic that Jean Clair finds so distressing. The Intractable Avant-Garde did not really address the human body as the site of suffering and the object of political outrage.

Beauty and Other Aesthetic Qualities

I regard the discovery that something can be good art without being beautiful as one of the great conceptual clarifications of twentieth-century philosophy of art, though it was made exclusively by artists—but it would have been seen as commonplace before the Enlightenment gave beauty the primacy it continued to enjoy until relatively recent times. That clarification managed to push reference to aesthetics out of any proposed definition of art, even if the new situation dawned very slowly even in artistic consciousness. When contemporary philosophers of art, beginning with Nelson Goodman, set aesthetics aside in order to talk about representation and meaning, this was not done with the expectation that we will return to aesthetics with an enhanced understanding. It was done, rather, with the awareness that beauty belongs neither to the essence nor the definition of art.

But that does not mean that *aesthetics* belongs neither to the essence nor the definition of art. What had happened was that aesthetics had become narrowly identified with beauty, so that in ridding art of beauty, the natural inference was that we are in position to segregate the philosophical analysis of art from any concern whatever with aesthetics, all the more so since aesthetics was as much taken up with natural as with artistic beauty. The more reason, then, to put aesthetics to one side and concentrate on the philosophical questions of art, which had such deep affinities with the kinds of issues that appealed to philosophers, in the analysis of language and of science.

What the disgusting and the abject—and for the matter the silly—help us understand is what a heavy shadow the concept of beauty cast over the philosophy of art. And because beauty became, in the eighteenth century especially, so bound up with the concept of taste, it obscured how wide and diverse the range of aesthetic qualities is. Disgust, for example, provokes the viewer to feel revolted by what the work of art that possesses it is about. It does so in just the same way that eroticism arouses the viewer to be sexually attracted to the subject of the work. These observations are slightly simple-minded, of course. It may take considerable interpretation to see what the fact that it is disgusting *means* in a work of art. The purposes of eroticism in a work of art may be to get the viewer to think about his or her inhibited personality or emotionally impoverished life.

Cuteness in a work of art, exactly as in life, is a way of getting us to feel warm and protective toward what is seen to possess it. Given these kinds of examples, aesthetics may itself explain why we have art in the first place. We have it in order that our feelings be enlisted toward what the art is about.

What the Intractable Avant-Garde achieved, it seems to me, in addition to removing beauty from the definition of art by proving that something can be art without having beauty, was that art has had far too many aesthetic possibilities that it was distorting to think of it as though it had only one. I do not believe, with Jean Clair, that we have, with disgust, a new aesthetic, in which distaste replaces taste. We have, rather, a new appreciation of aesthetic possibilities, including a fresh way of thinking about beauty itself. Or at least of beauty as an aesthetic quality of art when it is beautiful. The difference between beauty and the countless other aesthetic qualities is that beauty is the only one that has a claim to be a value, like truth and goodness. The annihilation of beauty would leave us with an unbearable world, as the annihilation of good would leave us with a world in which a fully human life would be unlivable. But we may not lose a lot if artistic beauty were annihilated, whatever that means, because art has a number of other compensatory values, and artistic beauty is an incidental attribute in most of the world's artistic cultures. The pressing philosophical question then is what is the appropriate connection between art and beauty. And we might find some guidance in the rather clearer case of disgust. Disgust is clearer because what we are disgusted with in art is pretty much what we are disgusted with in reality. This is, if I may be excused, what is so beautiful in Kant's discovery that disgust cannot be disguised, so that when the disgusting is represented, its representation is as disgusting as what is represented. There is no temptation, then, to distinguish between the naturally and the artistically disgusting, as there is between natural and artistic beauty. To be sure, we may be disgusted with art because it happens to show disgusting things. The Flemish artist, Wim Deloye, made some bathroom tiles in which he pictured some very realistic turds. If we are disgusted with the art, it will be because we are disgusted by what the art is of. The photographer Ariane Lopez-Cuici made some photographs of what is medically designated a morbidly obese woman. People were not only disgusted with the photographs because they have been taught to be disgusted with fat, they were disgusted with Lopez-Cuici because she chose such models when there is no end of "beautiful," that's to say slender, models to chose from. But what is the relationship between natural and artistic beauty? I want to examine and even widen this question before addressing the place of beauty in the beautiful work of art.

Beauty and Beautification

The history of aesthetic reflection since the eighteenth century moves from a discourse in which it is not especially perceived as relevant to distinguish natural from artistic beauty, through the recognition that there is some kind of a boundary between them, to the perception that they are separated by a more or less vast and largely unmapped territory, sharing boundaries with natural beauty on the one side and artistic beauty on the other. Beauty of what we may speak of as the Third Realm plays a far greater role in human conduct and attitude than either of the (philosophically) more familiar kinds, since most persons have little occasion to think about the fine arts, or to gaze upon natural wonders, though what Kant speaks of as the starry heavens above may occasion awe and a sense of vastness in even the simplest of persons. By natural beauty it is perhaps best to think of beauty the existence of which is independent of human will, like the night sky or the sunset, mighty seas or majestic peaks. So the beauty of a garden would not be natural beauty, leaving it a question of whether it belongs to art or to the Third Realm. No one can be unaware of Third Realm Beauty in daily life, but the history of aesthetics, which has drawn examples from it, has often, perhaps typically, failed to note how different these are from either natural or artistic beauty.

Kant exemplifies the first moment of this history, as his choice of examples implies: he discusses green meadows just after discussing fine palaces, dissociating aesthetic judgment from whatever interest one may have in either. "A coat, a house, or a flower is beautiful," presumably in the same way; and Kant seems anxious that from the perspective of aesthetic analysis, no distinction is to

be drawn between flowers and floral decorations—"free delineations, outlines intertwined with one another." So "Nature is
beautiful because it looks like art," while "beautiful art must look
like nature," hence, from the perspective of beauty, in his scheme
at least, the distinction between art and nature does not greatly
signify. In this Kant was very much a man of the Enlightenment, a
period of cultivated taste, in which even the moderately affluent
were liberated from the urgencies of immediate interest to the possibility of a disinterested contemplation of natural beauties and
beautiful products of artistic genius. And the world was beginning
to feel safe enough for people to travel about, to see the Alps or
the artistic wonders of Italy.

Hegel defines the history's second moment, in that from the
outset he finds it crucial to distinguish sharply between artistic
beauty, on the one side, and "a beautiful color, a beautiful sky, a
beautiful river; likewise beautiful flowers, beautiful animals, and
even more of beautiful people." Artistic beauty is "higher" than
natural beauty, and "born of the spirit." Like natural beauty, artistic beauty "presents itself to *sense*, feeling, intuition, imagination."
But it does more than gratify the senses: when "fine art is truly art"
it "place[s] itself in the same sphere as religion and philosophy,"
bringing to our awareness "the deepest interests of mankind, and
the most comprehensive truths of the spirit . . . displaying even the
highest [reality] sensuously." At a minimum, art has a content that
must be grasped; it is, by contrast with skies and flowers, about
something. Of course, the distinction would be obliterated if one
thought of Nature as a Divine Visual Language, following Bishop
Berkeley or the painters of the Hudson River School, who saw
God addressing us through the medium of waterfalls or Catskill
cliffs. Moreover, the idea of content arises late in our understanding of art, at that point—which Hegel identifies as the end of art—
where art becomes a topic for intellectual judgment, rather than a
sensuous presentation of what is taken to be a reality. Art becomes
a topic for intellectual judgment when it enters the museum. In
the years in which Hegel was lecturing on aesthetics in Berlin,
Schinkel's *Altes Museum* (as it came to be called) was undergoing
construction nearby. Hegel was excited by the prospect of visiting
the collections, and seeing the development of the various schools
of painting historically. But he had a vivid sense of the difference
between a set of statues placed in a museum, and hence segregated

from life and treated as an object of study; and that same set of statues as part of a form of life in which they represent a pantheon of gods. In the latter role, they embody, for those who believe in them, the spirit of the gods themselves. They are the gods, so to speak, in the midst of those who worship them. When transferred to the museum, by contrast, they become objects of scholarly attention or connoisseurship, and their content a matter for art historical investigation.

There is in Hegel a kind of art which he mentions mainly to dismiss, as it does not qualify as a subject for "Science"—a term which in his usage has little to do with natural science, which is negligibly treated in his system. It designates, rather, "The Science of the *true* in its *true shape*," which is, after all, the way Hegel thinks of the processes through which Spirit arrives at an essential knowledge of its own nature. "Art can be used in fleeting play," he writes, "affording recreation and entertainment, decorating our surroundings, giving pleasantness to the externals of our life, and making other objects stand out by artistic adornment." Art so considered is not free but "ancillary"—it is *applied* to ends external to itself, whereas art *as* art is "free alike in its end and its means." It is only as such that it pertains, as with philosophy, to what he terms Absolute Spirit. Hegel is concerned to characterize art, which relies upon sensuous presentation, from thought. But there is a distinction to be made in regard to thought itself, which parallels entirely the distinction between fine and applied art: "Science may indeed be used as an intellectual servant for finite ends and accidental means" he concedes, and not for the high purposes of Science (with a capital S). This would have been expected from the consideration that art and thought are one, with the difference that art uses sensuous vehicles for conveying its content. In any case, Hegel has identified what I have pre-emptively designated as a third aesthetic realm, one greatly connected with human life and happiness. It is, in fact, coextensive with most forms of human life:

> Beauty and art does indeed pervade all the business of life like a friendly genius and brightly adorns all our surroundings whether inner or outer, mitigating the seriousness of our circumstances and the complexities of the actual world, extinguishing idleness in an entertaining way. . . . Art belongs rather to the indulgence and relaxation of the spirit, whereas substantial interests require its exertion.

. . . Yet even though art intersperses with its pleasing forms everything from the war paint of the savages to the splendor of temples with all the richness of adornment, these forms themselves nevertheless seem to fall outside the true ends and aims of life.

Someone who thinks of art in these terms might consider it "inappropriate and pedantic to propose to treat with scientific seriousness what is not itself of a serious nature," as Hegel has set out to do in his *Lectures on Aesthetics*. I am not certain Hegel disagrees with this, despite his remarkably cosmopolitan personality. For it will not be as applied that he is to discuss art in the great work he has devoted to the subject. Like philosophical thought, art is a modality of free spirit. So there can be no question of "the *worthiness* of art" to be treated as philosophically as philosophy itself. Art is *worthy* of philosophical address only under the perspective of its highest vocation, which it shares with philosophy. So Hegel spends little time in exploring the territory he has uncovered, in which art is applied to the enhancement of life, even if it may, in certain periods, like the Renaissance, have been difficult to distinguish it from Art-capital-A. When Alberti was commissioned to give a new facade to Santa Maria Novella in Florence, was this upscale decoration or was it high art? We have such a problem today with the distinction between craft and art proper.

But the other border of the Third Realm is equally non-exclusionary, especially when we consider what Hegel singles out, under the head of beautiful people, the kind of beauty possessed by Helen of Troy, say, which we must suppose a wonder of nature. But Helen's choice of hairstyles, make up, or garment, would have belonged to the Third Realm, since it would have been chosen for enhancement, like the setting of a jewel. A great many of Kant's examples fall in this Third Realm—such as coats and gardens. These could not have been examples of free art in Hegel's thought, and this somewhat helps distinguish our own situation from that of our great predecessors.

In my own work, for example, I was from the first anxious to find a way of distinguishing real things from art works when there was no obvious way of doing so by examination, as in the case (my favorite!) of Brillo boxes and Andy Warhol's *Brillo Box*—a problem that did not and perhaps could not have arisen in Hegel's time. There was no way for a coat, for example, to be a work of art in

FIGURE 9

Marie-Ange
Guilleminot, *Le
Mariage de Saint-Maur
à Saint-Gall*, 1994
Meaning embodied

1828, as there is today, and subject to misuse if in fact used for the purposes of coats. In seeking to distinguish art works from what I termed "mere real things," I used *aboutness* as a principle of differentiation. It is a necessary condition for something to be an artwork that it be about something. Since something can possess aboutness without being art, more than content is accordingly needed to distinguish the artworks from mere real things. Aboutness, on the other hand, will not especially serve to distinguish art from applied art. Consider a wedding dress that was shown in the exhibition, discussed in Chapter 2, at the *Kunsthaus* in Zurich. It was by the French artist, Marie-Ange Guilleminot. It was not a work of art in the sense in which we praise wedding dresses generally as works of art—as marvelously designed, skillfully sewn and fitted, with appropriate rich fabrics and tasteful decorations. It was white, but rather plain and severe, and somewhat shroud-like. It could have been worn as a wedding dress, and was indeed so worn by the artist herself in a somewhat disturbatory performance work. We have reached a point in the history of art where there is no reason why a wedding dress—or a house dress, for that matter—cannot be a work of art, even if not a "work of art" in the commendatory vernacular sense in which we speak of the adorned bride herself as "looking like a work of art." What we are required to see is that Guilleminot's dress demands an interpretation, an ascription of meaning which explains its manifest properties. (It helps to know that she had sewn several kilos of lead under the skirt, perhaps to remind us of the weight, or burden, of marriage.) The dress was, and this idea is hardly un-Hegelian, what I have termed an *embodied meaning*. As a garment, the meaning of a wedding dress is its use: it is worn to be married in, and proclaims the purity of the wearer as well as the wealth of the bride's parents. That complex of symbolic uses is part of the meaning of the wedding dress as work of art, which is not itself intended to be used for anything but art. If someone actually wore Guillminot's dress *to be married in*, this would be close to what Duchamp termed a "reverse readymade," a little closer in this case to the art work reversed than his own example of using a Rembrandt for the purpose of an ironing board.

Part of what makes Kant's aesthetics so inadequate to the art of our time is that a work like this falls under neither of the kinds of beauty he distinguishes. It is neither free nor dependent. A (real) wedding dress has dependent beauty, in virtue of its connection with ritual and use. But as art it falls outside the domain of application entirely. Beauty is "free," according to Kant, when it "presupposes no concept of what the object ought to be." Kant uses as examples of free beauty that of flowers, birds, sea shells, but also of "delineations *à la grecque*, foliage for borders or wall papers." Interestingly, Kant classes "all music without words" as exemplifying free beauty. The beauty of a wedding dress, on the other hand, is quite clearly connected with a concept. The concept governs who wears it when and for how long a time and what it means that it be white and its wearer veiled. But a wedding dress as art is not covered by that same concept. Rather, *it* covers the concept, in that it absorbs it as part of its meaning. It is plain from this that Kant has no independent concept of beautiful art, since art possesses neither kind of beauty. What Kant lacks is the concept of meaning. Hegel requires art to have content if the parallels between it and philosophical thought hold, but his emphasis upon adornment, ornamentation, the refreshment of the spirit through objects of applied art overlooks the role that meanings play in the Third Realm: think, once more, of *Brillo Box* and the Brillo boxes. They have entirely different kinds of meaning, as I have demonstrated elsewhere. The concept of art is part of the meaning of the former, but it is not part of the meaning of the Brillo carton as applied, or as commercial art. It is somewhat interesting to observe that Hegel thinks aesthetically of the objects of the Third Realm from Kant's perspective of free beauty. They *please*, like sea shells and wallpaper borders, free from any concept and in themselves.

Nothing more sharply distinguishes the philosophy of art in Kant and in Hegel than the fact that *taste* is a central concept for Kant whereas it is discussed only to be dismissed by Hegel: "Taste is directed only to the external surface on which feelings play," he wrote. "So-called 'good taste' takes fright at all the deeper effects of art and is silent when externalities and incidentals vanish." As I have suggested, taste was, as much as reason, the defining attribute of the Enlightenment. In the *Analysis of Beauty*, Hogarth draws attention to the serpentine line, whether it characterizes a dancing master's leg or the leg of a chair, a woman's figure or the shape of a tea pot. Hogarth argues that anybody, and not just "painters and connoisseurs," know what good taste is—much as his contemporary, Bishop Berkeley, argued that "The illiterate bulk of mankind complain not of any want of evidence in their senses, and are out of all danger of becoming skeptics." Hogarth could argue this because English life embodied styles of dress, of decoration, and of craft to such a degree that an appropriately placed Englishman or Englishwoman would acquire taste as naturally as they would acquire their language. Or they could if they were situated in a fortunate social class, like their counterparts in Heian Japan, also a period of all but impeccable taste. All of this is absent from Hegel's analysis, and I consider this to be progress toward taking art seriously. The shift takes us from the sphere of the refinement of the senses to the sphere of meaning. The problem with Hegel's introduction of the Third Realm is that he tends to treat it from the eighteenth-century perspective rather than from that of the nineteenth century, where art is taken so seriously as to be coupled in solemnity with philosophy.

The Third Realm of Beauty

It is now time to address the Third Realm of beauty, which, though it embraces the domains of *Vanity Fair* and *Human, All Too Human*, has been the deer park of moralists and satirists down the ages, and only been taken *au serieux* by what in the past decade or so is labeled Cultural Studies. It has certainly received relatively little in terms of direct philosophical attention. *Relatively* little, since pride (in Aristotle, Hume, and Davidson) and shame (in Sartre and perhaps Kierkegaard) have generated a logical as well as a moralistic literature. It is as if philosophers, by shunning it, pay tacit homage to Hegel's thought that, since not entirely free, Third Realm beauty can have no claim to philosophical attention. It can certainly not be regarded as a displaced form of philosophy, as art in its "highest vocation" is claimed by Hegel to be. Third Realm beauty is the kind of beauty something possesses only because it was *caused* to possess it through actions whose purpose it is to *beautify*. It is the domain, in brief, of *beautification*. In this realm, things are beautiful only because they were beautified—and beautification has perhaps seemed, to a puritanical philosophical consciousness, to be—the term is Hegel's—*unworthy* of philosophical attention. Morality has always been of central philosophical concern, but discussions of manners, which Hobbes sneers at as "small morals," has barely been noticed. And this somewhat parallels the distinction between considerations of beauty as against beautification. The explanation of this perhaps goes back to the most ancient of philosophical distinctions—that between reality and appearances—in that almost invariably Third Realm practitioners are bent on changing the appearances of things in order to beautify or prettify them, without these changes penetrating what it really is: "Beauty is only skin-deep." Skills at inducing such changes are learned and applied by what in many languages are called *aestheticians* (or in English *beauticians*), and perhaps because beautification seems an exercise of frivolity, touching nothing fundamental or essential in those who pursue it, it is not difficult for philosophers to assimilate philosophical aesthetics as such to the study of beautification—to *aesthetics* as the practice of (for example) cosmetology—and hence to write the discipline off as having at best a marginal relationship to the True and the Good.

This would be, however, a piece of moral taxonomy, inasmuch as it expresses an unconscious disapproval of activities held to be unworthy of human beings. One gets a whiff of the grounds of such disapproval from Kant's remark on the use of a golden frame, "to merely recommend the painting by its *charm*." It is, Kant pronounces, "then called *finery* and injures genuine beauty." We can see exactly what Kant means when we consider the way modern curators often hold picture frames in contempt, and order their removal from around the paintings in their care. It is as if, instead of putting paintings in gold frames, we were to sew lace flounces around their edges, which would be—appealing to Webster on finery—"dressy or showy," and hence an insult to the art. Finery is intended to produce a certain effect, hence it really is akin to rhetoric, the skills of which are bent on making the case look worse or better than it is. "Finery," "dressiness," "show"—these are expressions of moralistic disapproval, and in a way they imply an underlying imperative, that people should not appear other than the way God made them. Hence Kant's contempt for tattoo-covered bodies, when the body—after all the image of God—is already as beautiful as it can be. The imperative is expressed in sumptuary codes, the purpose of which is not merely to regulate conduct since all codes have that purpose, but to control any propensity to extravagance or luxury. And of course to mislead viewers, who believe one's presented beauty to be one's own rather than due to artifice.

Beautification as a modality of moral self-consciousness presupposes a fairly complex epistemology and a metaphysics of the self, which may be made explicit by referring to the role the mirror image plays in its transactions. We look into the mirror not merely to see how we look, but how we expect others to see us, and, unless amazingly self-confident, we attempt to modulate our appearances in order that others shall see us as we hope to be seen. Happiness and unhappiness in this world are indexed to our appearances—which is perhaps why we have a concept of Heaven as a world in which happiness is not so indexed, since God sees us as we are without reference to how we appear. Sees us "for ourselves alone and not [our] golden hair," as Yeats puts it in a wry poem.

If we assimilate our concept of art to the concept of beautification, then, Hegel writes, "it is not itself of a serious nature," though it can have serious consequences.

> On this view, art appears as a superfluity, even if the softening of the heart which preoccupation with beauty can produce does not altogether become deleterious as downright effeminacy. From this point of view, granted the fine arts are a luxury, it has frequently been necessary to defend them in their relationship to practical necessities in general and in particular to morality and piety, and since it is impossible to prove their harmlessness, at least to give grounds for believing this luxury of the spirit may afford a greater sum of advantages than disadvantages.

I expect that the decision to establish a National Endowment for the Arts might have been justified by appeal to such considerations—that even if taxpayers ought not be asked to support luxury, an argument is available according to which art conduces to a certain softening of the human material. The ground disappeared from under this justification when the Endowment supported art which seemed to have the opposite moral effect, and the question, "Why should we support art perceived as *harmful* to the fabric of political society?" could not be avoided.

What is evident through this entire discussion, then, is that the very existence of a third aesthetic realm is internally related to moral considerations in a way in which art in its "highest vocation" is not, nor nature in its aspect as beautiful. Both of these, of course, can entail imperatives, especially when it becomes evident that preservation is in order when beauty is threatened. We cannot take it for granted that the beauties of nature or of art will be joys forever. But beautificatory practices themselves intersect every step of the way with various particular moral imperatives, which specify what we might call the bounds of taste (whose realm this is), viz, that something is too plain, or too ornate, or whatever. These aesthetic complaints can be, and typically are, over-ridden by moral considerations. When Kant wrote disapprovingly of ornamenting a church, it was perhaps his view that ornament was inconsistent with the momentousness of something being the house of God— as if the architects were bent on flattery by adding carving, let alone images. Consistently, it would similarly be prohibited to wear fine clothes to religious service, as if the church were, like a ball, the scene of flirtations or seduction. (There is a passage in *The Pillow Book* of Lady Sei Shonogun where she complains that a Buddhist monk is too good looking for the exercise of piety, through his looks drawing her to the world from which his preaching is to liberate her. So beware handsome priests and beautiful nuns!)

God, it might be said, was not quite so austere in his tastes. There is a famous candelabrum in the Bible, one which a curiously finicky God orders Moses to construct. It is a very ornate candelabrum for what after all was a desert people, but it was to be placed in a sanctuary fit for God, and to represent an offering and a sacrifice on the part of the children of Israel "that I might dwell among them." The candelabrum was to be made of pure gold, and God specifies its structure in a brief sufficiently detailed that it might be in a contract with a goldsmith:

> Of beaten work shall the candlestick be made: his shaft and his branches, his bowls, his knops, his flowers, shall be of the same.
>
> And six branches shall come out of the sides of it: three branches of the candlestick out of the one side, and three branches of the candlestick out of the other side:
>
> Three bowls made like unto almonds, with a knop and a flower in one branch; and three bowls made like almonds in the other branch, with a knop and a flower: so in the six branches that come out of the candlestick.
>
> And in the candlestick shall be four bowls made like unto almonds, with their knops and flowers.
>
> And there shall be a knop under two branches of the same, and a knop under two branches of the same, according to the six branches that proceed out of the candlestick.
>
> Their knops and branches shall be of the same: all it shall be one beaten work of pure gold.
>
> And thou shalt make the seven lamps thereof: and they shall light the lamps thereof, that they may give light against it.

The specification goes on, and it is clear that God means for the sanctuary, in which the candelabrum is to be placed, to be a simulacrum of God's own dwelling.

By the testimony of *Exodus,* God was not an aesthetic minimalist. A candelabrum of the sort he demands placed a serious burden on his subjects, which meant that it was perceived as a sacrifice. And we see, in religious custom, practices entirely opposite to the puritanism of Prussia. It is not uncommon to create highly ornamental frames for certain holy pictures, not, as Kant says about golden frames, to recommend the painting, which needs no recommendation, but to pay homage, in the only way one knows how to, to the being of whom it is the picture—a *bambino sacro,* the merciful Madonna, or the *nothilfige* saints to whom thanks are due for benign interventions. Appreciation is expressed through sometimes massive ornamentation, well beyond the boundaries of good taste and across into the boundaries of what we might consider bad taste, like lace on the wedding dress when it crosses a border into *froufrou.* The ornamental frame of the Pentecostal church has no business being tasteful because it has no business being bounded by the limits of good taste. If it is not too much then it is too little. The decorative programs of Flamboyant Gothic are quite clearly at odds with the anti-decorative program of Modernism, as in the writing of Adolf Loos—and in the architectural practice of Ludwig Wittgenstein—both of whom would have endorsed Kant's association of austerity with piety. The philosophical point, however, is that the exercise of taste is associated with how people believe they ought to live. Taste is not the mere application of discernment and fine discrimination. It belongs to ritual. If one thinks about it, church architecture belongs to applied religion, and differs from it as applied art differs from art "in its highest vocation," or as (continuing to follow Hegel) to applied in contrast with pure thought. Each of the three moments of Absolute Spirit in fact has a practicum in the Third Realm where human life is actually lived. And every practice is connected with some vision of what a human life ought to be.

Let us consider from this perspective Kant's example of a figure "adorned" with spirals "as the New Zealanders do with their tattooing." Hegel mentions body painting, as we saw, but has, so far as I can tell, no special attitude toward it other than as a primitive form of beautification, a misguided form of gilding the lily. For

Kant, by contrast, the human form is like the form of a church. As the handiwork of God, it cannot be improved upon. It needs no finery, though his discussion of coats suggests that he was thinking of good tailoring and gold buttons. For both philosophers, anthropological knowledge exceeds anthropological understanding. Neither, for example, understands what it means painstakingly to cover the surface of the body with regular circular lines by tattooing—or to paint the body in ways Hegel must have seen in engravings of Africans or Native Americans. This cannot, I think, strictly be considered beautification. It cannot because the paint or pattern serve important functions of a symbolic or magical kind. They involve ordeals for the sake of the power they confer. They connect the person who bears them to the greater forces of the universe: to spirits and deities. Taste has no application, though obviously ornamentation can be overdone. A heavily ornamental *mazuzzah* can in principle confer no higher power than the plainest of *mazuzzahs*. If it did, then all *mazuzzahs* should possess it. So it has to be gratuitous, which is what moralism holds in regard to beautification generally. It is mere luxury, toward which we can, with Kant, be negative or with Hegel be indifferent, or with Philip Johnson (when he fitted a pediment to the AT&T Building) be positive. These are competing philosophies of taste which, in a cosmopolitan culture such as our own, exist side by side. Theories of taste, however, are not matters of taste: they bring with them entire philosophies of conduct and of life. The ornamentation of a Hindu statue or of a miraculous icon can be painful to a disapproving minimalist, just as the latter's austerity can be criticized as lack of gratitude for favors conferred. So the absence or presence of ornament always transcends questions of aesthetics alone. And this will be true of the enhancement of human beings, where the no-make-up look proclaims, or can proclaim, commitment to the view that 'tis a gift to be simple. Beautification may accordingly also carry symbolic weight, which can be perverted if something is used for looks alone. Were the long locks of the Chasidim to be accepted merely as coiffeur, as in "The Chasidic Look," they would for those who take them up as fashion not have any symbolic weight at all, and certainly would not express the commitment to an entire form of life which the Chasidim are presumed to have made. There would be a difference between circumcision "because it looks better" and circumcision as a condition for entering the covenant with God. Perhaps nothing cosmetic is without symbolic meaning.

In discussing human beauty, Kant does not suppose that there is a single model for it, since he has become aware of racial differences, and recognizes that the different races will have non-congruent conceptions of human beauty. For any given race, the idea of a beautiful person, physiognomically considered, is the product of a kind of unconscious averaging, a statistical composite of the productive imagination which specifies a norm which "is at the basis of the normal idea of the beauty of the [human figure.]" as Kant writes in Section 17 of his *Critique*. There are now computer programs which are capable of extracting the norm from as many images as one cares to scan into one's machine. The resultant morph is unlikely to match any individual we may encounter, and it is similarly unlikely that an individual human being will perfectly exemplify the prevailing idea of beauty. In fact, it has recently been demonstrated that a consolidated image of perhaps sixty people will be voted more attractive than the images of most of those who participated in the consolidation. But as a morph it will coincide with the idea of beauty at which everyone with a comparable degree of experience will have arrived. It is, within certain limits to be discussed shortly, universal, without corresponding to reality. To the degree that we appreciate symmetry and regularity as the co-ordinates of beauty, they really do define a norm which actual persons fall away from by various degrees, to the point where genuine ugliness attaches to asymmetry or irregularity. (One of the problems of living in a world where human beings are represented who are closely conforming to the norm, as in television, is that the rest of us feel inadequate or even villainous!) The limits on universality are set by the circumstance that the norm of beauty will vary from society to society, especially insofar as each society consists of members of a distinct racial type: "Thus," Kant writes, "necessarily under these empirical conditions a Negro must have a different normal idea of the beauty of the [human figure] from a white man, a Chinaman a different normal idea from a European, etc. . . . It is the image for the whole race."

There were probably very few "Chinamen" or "Negroes" in most European centers in Kant's time, but Koenigsberg, where he spent his entire life, was a Hanseatic port, and he had ample opportunity to practice comparative physiognomy. I would surmise that if the averaging crossed racial lines—if the morphing operation were extended to cover the Caucasian, the Negro, and the Oriental racial types—there would be a kind of hypermorph which members of various races might pick out as beautiful, invariantly as to questions of racial identity. This is an entirely empirical matter: recently some computer-enhanced images of racially undifferentiated female heads were deemed most beautiful by both Western and Japanese males. And by now, perhaps, through television and cinema, everyone has seen everything.

One supposes, if beautification is the aim, that everyone would want to approach the hypermorph in looks. Kant cites a work of Polycleitus, the *Doryphorus* or *Spear-carrier*, which came to be known as the *Canon*, inasmuch as it so perfectly embodied the correct proportions of the ideal male form as to serve as an atlas for sculptors. But normic beauty is curiously bland: an authority writes that "balance, rhythm and the minute perfection of bodily form . . . do not appeal to us as they did to the Greeks of the Fifth Century." Kant himself is anxious to press the point that we must "distinguish the *normal idea* of the beautiful from the *ideal*," which—uniquely in the case of human beings—lies in the expression of *moral* qualities. "This shows that a judgment in accordance with *such a standard can never be purely aesthetical and that a judgment in accordance with an ideal is not a mere judgment of taste.*" So ideal beauty may involve a trade-off between normic beauty and the expression of what Kant enumerates as "goodness of heart, purity, strength, peace, etc.—visible as it were in bodily manifestations (as the effect of that which is internal)." Hegel characterizes Romantic Art as responsive to the demand for making inwardness visible, of showing what a person is so far as that person is coincident with his or her feelings. And that would explain why *The Spear-carrier* is bland: classical art, if Hegel is right, had no concept of inwardness. It explains as well why a contemporary artist, Orlan, who submits herself to plastic surgery in order to make herself conform to aesthetic prototypes, in fact looks, well, creepy. She shows no inwardness. And it explains why the life-likeness induced by mortuary intervention underscores the death of the body—even if the face is given a happy smile. It also explains, I think, why the case presented to Socrates by Adeimanthus in the *Republic* is less readily imagined than one might believe: a perfectly unjust man who appears to be perfectly just. We can, within limits, feign looks, but not consistently. The kind of person we are shows through the kind of person we appear to be, there is a limit to the possibilities of expressional cosmetics, of making ourselves look kind or thoughtful or sensitive. Someone may feel that the reason they are unloved is because they appear too fat, which may be true or false—true under the criterion of normic beauty, false under that of inner beauty, which may alert others to the fact that someone is cruel or vacuous, or their opposites. Kant is entirely right in his suggestion that inner beauty is not a matter of taste alone, as that is exhibited in adolescents, who fall in love with football heros and prom queens, or by tycoons who marry models, whom they display as trophies. Inwardness sets a limit to how far hair transplants, nose jobs, liposuction, breast implants and the like will carry one. But the literature of moralists and cynics, back to ancient times, is replete with applicable wisdom, whether or not it shows up in classical art.

There is a certain set of political considerations involved in beautification, which would not, I think, have shown up in this literature, inasmuch as they only began to enter consciousness in relatively recent times. They arise when members of a certain group begin to think that they have sought to conform to a norm of beauty which in fact was imposed upon them by a politically dominant class—by men in the case of women, or by whites in the case of blacks, or, a—somewhat weaker case—by Gentiles in the case of Jews. As a corollary of contemporary feminism, it occurred to women that they aspired to an ideal of beauty which had been imposed upon them by men; or to blacks that they aspired to conform to a standard of beauty which in fact belonged to whites. When the possibility of imposition became a matter of a raised consciousness, beautificatory practices changed abruptly. In the case of African-Americans, even as militant a figure as Malcolm X went through a period in which he underwent a hair-straightening procedure, at considerable cost in pain, but felt to be worth it if in the end he would be perceived as not possessing the tight curls identified with negritude. So he would consider himself in terms of hair non-Negro (soft curls would be consistent with that). Hair is a very charged bodily part in black culture, mainly because kinked hair is part of the Negro stereotype—or would turn up in the averaging which defines the norm for the race, on Kant's view. But with the recognition that they had been applying a norm to themselves that was not their own, kinked hair became something to be proud of (and a black born with straight hair might have recourse to negrification of this feature.) The Afro hairstyle became a weapon in the aesthetico-racial wars: it flaunted what under prevailing norms would have been held to be disfiguring, by others and by oneself, so long as one subscribed to the racial status quo. "Black is beautiful" is a political refusal not to be oppressed aesthetically. That is a return to Kant's distinctions; it entails accepting a norm of beauty specific to the race. Black culture radiated out from cosmetic changes: the choice of African names, the wearing of African costumes, changing ones religion from Christianity to Islam. The moral quandary of a black person who looks white is the perduring theme of Adrian Piper's art.

The case of feminism is different in certain ways, in that there was not a time in which women sought to define feminine beauty in terms of male beauty—though flattened breasts in the 1920s served to reduce to invisibility a traditionally feminine attribute. Women sought—and by the evidence of the literature they still seek—to define female beauty as men are perceived to define it, and hence become what men want them to be. Co-eval with the Afro was the ritual bra-burnings, in which a garment identified with femininity, and which served to construct a female figure along certain lines, was cast out and women's natural contours were flaunted. Breasts were allowed to swing freely, nipples to show through tee-shirts. And, collaterally with the emergence of a politicized black culture, a politicized female culture appeared through which women sought to live in conformity with their own sexual reality as they perceived it, in which beauty as previously specified was now perceived as a trap.

None of this will be unfamiliar to anyone who lived through the later decades of the twentieth century, nor is it unfamiliar in the forms it assumes today. It is certainly subject to satire and caricature, but there can be little doubt that the struggle over whose canon of beauty we are to apply to ourselves goes well beyond what Kant described as taste, and well beyond the expression of moral states he felt must be adjoined to it. In a way which I shall leave until a later occasion to examine, not allowing one's self-definition to be imposed from without is close enough to what Kant thought of as autonomy to suggest that there is a deep connection between the aesthetics of the Third Realm and the realm of ethics.

It is to reject a categorical imperative in regard to how we shall appear, and to endorse one restricted to who we are in terms of race and gender—and such other facticities as may in the course of time emerge politically. This has its dangers, and, especially in the case of women, it has some far from well understood limits. The differences between races, while accounted for through evolution, is not required for human evolution. It is a difference more connected with variation than with speciation. With sexual difference, on the other hand, there has thus far been a bimorphic basis for generation. And this shows up in the role of sexual attraction. The human male is so constituted that he must be aroused, or there will be no erection, hence no pregnancies, hence no survival of the species. Feminine beauty is thus connected with the power to arouse and excite—and reproduce—and the now legendary "male gaze" is an agency of evolution.

This, of course, can change if the replenishment of the species can be detached from the psycho-chemistry of arousal. Viagra still requires sexual stimulation, but almost certainly there will be erectile prosthetics which dispense with this atavism, allowing the erection to be a matter of will, thus reproducing what Saint Augustine proposes was the condition of Adam before the Fall, able to plant his seed without the storms of passion. No longer under the imperatives of attractiveness, the human female will be free to appear as she cares to, indifferent to what turns men on. It is far from plain, moreover, that post-Adamic methods of impregnation are written into the genome. With cloning and the like, we can imagine and perhaps even foresee a time when men are sexually required only for sexual pleasure—or might even be cloned out because of social disorders blamed on testosterone. We are entering a brave new world, and Third Realm aesthetics gets less and less frivolous every day.

The Paradigm of Beautification

Part of Dada's heritage has been a distrust of beauty, at least in art. If beauty was not actively hated, there was at least a corollary attitude: Better the art be disgusting than beautiful. The pursuit of beauty in terms of personal looks, by contrast, is the aim of a major industry. In an interview conducted shortly before her untimely death, the innovative sculptor Eva Hesse grew almost shrill in declaring her distaste for beauty—for "prettiness"—in art. But as

FIGURE 10   Eva Hesse, with her *Expanded Expansion*, 1969
Shunning beauty as distasteful

we know from her diaries, she was preoccupied with her own beauty as a woman. When Kant opposed beauty with disgust in his early text "Observations on the Feeling of the Beautiful and the Sublime," he was thinking that the last thing a woman—Kant inevitably shared his era's attitudes toward gender—who aspires to be thought beautiful would want is to be found disgusting. This may seem a long way from the philosophy of art, but the term "aesthetics" is used in many cultures for the kind of ministrations on offer in what in American English we call "beauty shops." A young instructor in a Canadian university once told me that whenever she sees a position in aesthetics advertised by a philosophy department, she cannot suppress the thought that they are looking for someone able to do nails. And the question is whether we are dealing with different concepts of beauty, as the idea of three realms implies, or if there is not a greater unity here than at first appears.

In eighteenth-century philosophy, all three realms were obviously enough connected, which is why Kant was able to treat the three domains as one. Since painting was understood as mimetic, beautiful paintings were understood as paintings of beautiful scenes and beautiful persons. Persons of taste were eager to be surrounded with beautiful objects as a matter of course, which meant that if they collected paintings, they would be beautiful paintings, which in consequence meant specifically paintings of beautiful things—of things that looked beautiful in the same sense of "looking beautiful" that we have been canvassing here. However marginal beautification has been in philosophical aesthetics, it was the central concept in Kant's philosophy, which saw no special reason to provide a different analysis for natural and artistic beauty. Third Realm aesthetics was aesthetics as such—but beautification was the paradigm. So the discussion of this chapter was less an interlude than a preparation for addressing the question of what importance beauty can have in art, after its abuse at the hands of the Intractable Avant-Garde. This will be the topic in the next chapter.

Internal and
External Beauty

On Renaissance principles, paintings were windows on the world, pure transparent openings through which one saw what one would have seen standing outside, looking at what the picture instead showed. So a picture drew its beauty from the world, ideally having none of its own to contribute to what one saw, as it were, through it. This of course overlooks the contribution of the frame, as shaping the way the world presents itself through pictures to the eye. The stereotypical painter crooks the index finger against the thumb, framing the world until it resolves itself into a picture—until it looks the way she wants her picture to look—like Lily Briscoe in *To the Lighthouse,* or, we imagine, any of the Bloomsbury painters—Roger Fry and Vanessa Bell among others—scouting the south of France for what the traditional art schools designated *motifs.* Kant was famously a stay-at-home, but he lived in an era of aesthetic tourism. The well-to-do went abroad to see the sights: the Alps, the Bay of Naples, as well, of course, as the Piazza San Marco, the Pantheon, the Leaning Tower, the Acropolis. A pictorial industry grew up to provide souvenirs—objective memories—of what one had seen. This I take to be the background of Kant's somewhat surprising remark, cited but not discussed above, at §45 of the *Critique of Judgment:* "Nature is beautiful because it looks like art," when one would have expected the opposite instead. Kant seems to be saying that the world is beautiful when it looks the way painters represent it, when one thought they represented it because it was beautiful in the first place, if we understood rightly the Renaissance idea that the beauty we see pictured on the canvas or the panel is, since the picture is a pure transparency with nothing of its own to contribute, the sum-total of the picture's beauty.

One encounters this concept of pictorial transparency in discussions of the aesthetics of photography today. Roger Scruton writes: "If one finds a photograph beautiful, it is because one finds something beautiful in the subject." It is difficult to see how this account will survive the admittedly overdetermined case of Robert Mapplethorpe's photographs. As we saw earlier, Mapplethorpe's photographs were artistically faulted, by his modernist contemporaries, through the fact that they were hopelessly beautiful, though in the view of the general public they were objectionable, or even disgusting, because of their explicit sexual content. In *Civilization and Its Discontents,* Freud wrote that beauty's "derivation from the realms of sexual sensation is all that seems certain; the love of beauty is a perfect example of a feeling with an inhibited aim." On the other hand, Freud continues, "the genitals themselves, the sight of which is always exciting, are hardly ever regarded as beautiful." If Freud is right, we only get beauty if we do not depict the site of sexual pleasure directly. Mapplethorpe can be seen as endeavoring to overcome this by beautifying the way genitals are shown, to achieve images that are beautiful and exciting at once: pornography and art in the same striking photographs. "There are two distinct roads in photography," according to an early writer, Charles Caffin: "The utilitarian and the aesthetic: the goal of one being a record of facts, and of the other an expression of beauty." Caffin thought that photography as a fine art (the title of his book) "will record facts but not as facts," and he doubtless had in mind the model of Pictorialism—taking pictures which looked as much as possible like tonalist paintings such as those of Inness and perhaps Whistler. Mapplethorpe's X Portfolio images are fusions of the pornographic picture and the kind of photographic elegance he found in Steichen and Photo Secessionist camera work, which he admired in the exhibition *The Painterly Photograph,* organized by his friend John McKendrie, at the Metropolitan Museum in 1973. Before that, he could not see how photography could be an art, perhaps thinking that photography was essentially documentary, to use Caffin's term. His new aim, as he put it, was to "play with the edge" between art and pornography. It takes a certain suspension of moralist attitude to see a Polaroid, which Mapplethorpe devoted to his own engorged penis, held erect like a blunt club by means of a leather loop around his testicles, in the same aesthetic terms as the Photo-Secessionist masterpieces in *The Painterly Photograph*, say Steichen's exquisite *Flatiron Building*. But that was the paradox of his achievement—to show what one can sometimes barely stand to look at in photographs so beautiful one can hardly takes one's eyes off them. He was as obsessed with beauty as he was with his special approach to sex, and his aim throughout was to fuse these disparate obsessions.

The age of photography was not to begin for half a century after Kant wrote his text on aesthetics. Its inventor, Fox Talbot, because of his acknowledged deficiencies as a draftsman, sought a way in which Nature would transcribe *itself*, without the mediation of an artist: the photographic camera was, in his words, "Nature's pencil." The camera was built on Renaissance principles, which is why, until the invention of digitalization, photographs performed forensic roles. The camera was like an eye-witness. So if one aimed at beautification, one was obliged to beautify the object of the photograph, and then record that, which Mapplethorpe did in part with lights and shadows. Thus the theory of pictorial transparency survives.

This cannot, however, have been the whole story, not even for Kant, who recognized that art was capable of representing as beautiful the most paradigmatically ugly things. So the picture must somehow contribute to its beauty, since such motifs have none. It is here that Kant makes his parenthetical observation on disgust, as the "one kind of ugliness which cannot be represented in accordance with nature without destroying all aesthetic satisfaction, and consequently *artificial beauty*." I emphasize "artificial beauty." It is what I have been calling "beautification"—aesthetic sophism, making the worse appear better, which involves cosmetics, fashion, interior decoration, and the like, where we are not dealing with natural but with enhanced beauty. In the eighteenth century, in France especially, a close parallel was drawn between painting pictures and painting faces, so that, in his portrait of *Madame Pompadour at Her Vanity*, which shows the great lady with her rouge-brush before a mirror, François Boucher is virtually saluting a fellow artist. With the made-up face, Kant's follow-up thought would be exact—"we are conscious of it as art while yet it looks like nature." It looks like nature in nature's most aesthetically striking instances. So it is a kind of visual falsification—a trap for the unwary.

FIGURE 11   François Boucher, *Madame Pompadour at Her Vanity*, 1758
Applying is lying.

The French term for "to make up" is "farder" or "to color"
which explains in part why there was a traditional mistrust of colors—why Descartes went so far as to say we really did not need our
eyes to know what the world was like, since the blind can feel the
outlines and know the shapes of things. Ruskin appears to have had
beautification—or artifice—in mind when, in support of the
British Pre-Raphaelites, he condemns pretty much the entire his-

tory of painting from the time of Raphael down. In the first of two letters to *The Times* in 1851, Ruskin wrote that his young protégés

> desire to represent, irrespective of any conventional rules of picture making; and they have chosen their unfortunate though not inaccurate name because all artists did this before Raphael's time, and after Raphael's time did *not* do this, but sought to paint fair pictures rather than represent stern facts, of which the consequence has been that from Raphael's time to this day historical art has been in acknowledged decadence.

It did not incidentally matter that the reality was only imagined—"made up" by the artist in the other sense of the expression—that it was "false" in the sense that it did not exist, so long as if it did exist, it was not falsified in the interests of beautification.

Inevitably, the camera served as model for Ruskin's disciples. With the American Pre-Raphaelites, committed to Ruskin's agenda of visual truth, the highest accolade a painting could be paid was that it looked as if it were done with a camera. My sense is that appeal to photography was the arbiter even with the British Pre-Raphaelites—that like their American counterparts, their paintings were to be praised as transparent, as if they had been done by a camera, in the spirit of documentation. They were not "fair" but truthful pictures.

Deliberately "aesthetic" photography entered the discourse with Pictorialism, where Stieglitz and his peers tried to make photographs look beautiful (and by Ruskin's criterion, false) by making them look like paintings. But painting itself had changed. It has become, so to say, *Post-Raphaelite*. It had abandoned transparency—it was something to see in its own right, rather than something to see through. It was not abstract—it had recognizable subjects. But it created an atmosphere for them by absorbing them, one might say, into the paint. A movement had begun which would culminate in Abstract Expressionism where it was possible for paint to be its own subject. When Mapplethorpe complained that photography was not an art, he was not using painting as his model, much as he admired the Pictorialists who did. His teachers at Pratt were inculcated with Abstract Expressionist ideas, but *his* idea of the model artist was Duchamp. Abstract Expressionism did not and would not have allowed him to "play with the edge." But this takes me ahead of my story.

The Modernist paintings that Roger Fry featured in his two exhibitions at the Grafton Gallery were done midway in the trajectory from Manet to, let us say, Jackson Pollock and Franz Kline. Transparency could hardly be attributed to them. If they were beautiful, that could neither be attributed to the beauty of their subjects—since there was no way of telling what the subjects really looked like from the pictures—nor to beautification. We could take Picasso's word that the woman depicted in *Ma Jolie* was indeed *jolie*—but the painting itself showed no evidence that she was. So if the works were beautiful, it would have to be in some way other than through showing a beautiful subject, or by beautifying through artistic intervention a subject that was less than beautiful. Art criticism needed to find these new ways. Fry more or less delayed the search by insisting that they were really beautiful, but difficult. In this chapter my aim will be to show how to use the concept of beauty with a clearer sense of art-critical responsibility than has thus far been the case. And at the same time I shall blur the boundaries between the three realms of beauty addressed in Chapter 3.

Seeing Beauty that Isn't There

When Matisse exhibited his startling *Woman with Hat* to wide derision in 1905, he was approached by a German artist who asked what was the actual color of Madame Matisse's dress when she sat for this portrait. Matisse impatiently replied "Obviously black." What could he have meant by "obviously"? Perhaps only that women in Madame Matisse's class wore black as a matter of course. That would not be obvious from the painting, but the question then would be what had the color of Madame Matisse's dress to do with how the artist painted it? Mallarmé's wonderful directive—*Peindre non la chose mais l'effet qu'elle produit*—might have come to Matisse's lips at that point, but *then* the question would be: What is meant by "the effect"? We know that Amalie Matisse was a strong and determined woman, who supported her family as a milliner at a time when Matisse was selling almost nothing. The spectacular hat is the chief element in the painting, and I like to believe Matisse showed her wearing that hat for reasons like those that moved Pope Julius to ask Michelangelo to depict him with a sword—that hat was her sword, the emblem of her victory, her

FIGURE 12   Henri Matisse, *Woman with Hat*, 1905
A moral advertisement

dignity, and her force. It was a moral advertisement: in 1905, a woman wearing a hat like that could face the world and take on all comers. *Of course* she would be wearing black! And Matisse himself had to make his portrait as brave and powerful as his wife by taking great risks with form and with color. Roger Fry misses this entirely by saying that Matisse was interested in design and that the design is what we should be looking at and would in time find beautiful—that the artist distorts is in the interests of design. No: in my view at least it is a strong painting of a strong woman. But it is not a beautiful painting of a beautiful woman. And in truth there is no way, without doing violence to the concept, to see the painting as beautiful. One's initial impression of it as ugly is closer to the artistic truth it expresses. But of course to grasp the truth one does have to stop seeing it as ugly because of the way it was drawn. The "bad" drawing was part of "the effect."

When one executes a piece of art criticism such as this, it is inevitable that someone will say that she or he really sees *Woman with a Hat* as beautiful. When, in a conference on beauty some years ago, I mentioned Matisse's *Blue Nude* as a painting that could not be seen as beautiful, a fellow art critic disagreed by saying that *he* saw it as beautiful. *Blue Nude* was one of the scandals of the 1913 Armory Show, the other being Duchamp's *Nude Descending a Staircase*. The scandal of the latter was that no one could find the nude. It seemed that viewers were told one thing and shown another—that they could not trust their eyes. Even Duchamp's fellow cubists had problems with his painting, and asked that he withdraw it from an exhibition in Paris. Perhaps it was because he sought to depict movement, in violation of some convention regarding stasis in cubist art. The case of *Blue Nude* was somewhat different: if someone were to have asked Matisse what was the color of his model's skin, he might have replied impatiently "Obviously pink." The blue was in the painting, which violated the principle of transparency. What could Matisse have been getting at? Why paint as blue what in reality is pink? And why paint as hideous what might in reality have been beautiful—or at least pretty? When one says that *Blue Nude* is beautiful, one is merely expressing admiration for its strength and power, for Matisse's decision to present us with a powerful painting rather than a pleasing one, to draw our attention to the painting rather than to the person—or to express, by hypotyposis, the power of female beauty through the power of a painting that is not beautiful at all. Most of the world's art is not beautiful, nor was the production of beauty part of its purpose. *Blue Nude* is morally rather than visually true. Beauty is really as obvious as blue: one does not have to work at seeing it when it is there. One has rather to work at seeing a painting as good despite its not being beautiful, when one had been supposing that beauty was the way artistic goodness was to be understood.

I want one further example, which comes from Hegel, a great art critic, writing about a masterpiece by the artist the Pre-Raphaelites were to despise. "It is a familiar and frequently repeated critical reproach against Raphael's *Transfiguration* that it falls apart into two actions entirely devoid of any connection with one another," Hegel writes. "And in fact this is true if this picture is considered externally: above on the hill we see the transfiguration, below is the scene with the child possessed of an unclean spirit.

> But if we look at the *spirit* of the composition, a supreme connection is not to be missed. For, on the one hand, Christ's visible transfiguration is precisely his elevation above the earth, and his departure from his disciples, and this must be made visible too as a separation and a departure; on the other hand, the sublimity of Christ is here especially transfigured in an actual simple case, namely in the fact that the Disciples could not help the child without the help of the Lord. Thus here the double action is motivated throughout and the connection is displayed within and without in the fact that one disciple expressly points to Christ who has departed from them and thereby he hints at the true destiny of the Son of God to be at the same time on earth, so that the saying will be true: Where two or three are gathered in my name, there am I in the midst of them.

"Design" is as weak as "beauty" is inappropriate in responding to this tremendous work. The design is entailed by the meaning Raphael means to convey—*l'effet* of the event he has undertaken to depict by visual means when the meaning of transfiguration is not entirely visual. Ruskin would be right about Raphael: "externally" *The Transfiguration* lacks visual truth, but internally it conveys truth of a profounder kind. What we see in the painting could not have been seen by anyone there: they would either have been dazzled by Christ's transfiguration, or caught up with concern for the possessed child. Raphael brought these disparate perceptions together in a single astonishing vision.

One sees from this passage the remarkable difference between a thinker like Hegel, who was deeply engaged by great art, and

FIGURE 13   Raphael, *The Transfiguration*, 1518–1520
Disconnected by design

Kant, who was not, and for whom experiencing art was of a piece with experiencing natural beauty, like that of flowers or sunsets or lovely women. And this is finally what is missing in Moore's way of thinking of art as well. He thought of artistic beauty on the model of natural beauty, as we can see from his thought of how much better it would be for something beautiful to exist in reality than merely in pictures. He was not wrong in thinking that, when a painting was beautiful, it was beautiful in the way in which nature is beautiful. He was wrong in thinking that if a painting was good, it was because of its beauty, and that if he could not see the beauty, he would have to look harder, as his disciple Roger Fry insisted is required when we are dealing with difficult art.

David Hume, for all his astuteness, makes the same mistake, by thinking that there are two species of beauty. He takes this up almost as an aside, in order to point up an analogy between two views of moral truths, namely "whether they be derived from Reason or Sentiment." Sentimentalists claim that "To virtue it belongs to be *amiable*, and vice *odious*." The latter term evokes a distant echo to disgust: a moral revulsion that verges on physical recoil. By symmetry, the former evokes a kind of natural attraction: we are drawn to what we perceive as good in others. Hume allows that there is a kind of beauty of which the latter may be true: "Some species of beauty, especially the natural kinds, on their first appearance command our affection and approbation; and where they fail of this effect, it is impossible for any reasoning to redress their influence, or adapt them better to our taste and sentiment." It is in regard to this sort of beauty that one might say there is no disputing taste. But Hume, as a man of letters, had a vivid sense of the transformative power of critical reasoning. And here I repeat a great passage from his writing: "In many orders of beauty, particularly those of the finer arts, it is requisite to employ much reasoning in order to feel the proper sentiment; and a false relish may frequently be corrected by argument and reflection. There are just grounds to conclude that moral beauty partakes much of this latter species, and demands the assistance of our intellectual faculties in order to give it a suitable influence on the human mind."

The kind of reasoning Hume appeals to, I think, is illustrated in Hegel on Raphael's *Transfiguration*, or in that I sought to employ in discussing *Woman with a Hat* or *Blue Nude*. Hume was a man of letters, and his writing on literature gives evidence of the way in which we bring one another round to the point of seeing that one piece of writing is artistically better than another, and why it is so. His mistake lies in supposing that we are brought round by reasoning to apprehend its *beauty,* when what he really means is literary excellence, superiority, and depth. The term "aesthetic" was not in wide use in Hume's time, or at least not in English usage. It would have helped immensely had Hume been able to distinguish between *aesthetic* beauty and what we might call artistic beauty. It is aesthetic beauty that is discerned through the senses. Artistic beauty requires discernment and critical intelligence. *But why use the word beauty at all in this latter case?* Some people are beautiful, some are not, some are downright ugly. These are differences we register through the senses. We are attracted to people because of their beauty, and even fall in love with them because they are beautiful. But human beings have qualities of intellect and character that attract us to them despite their lack of beauty. When Alcibiades praises Socrates in the *Symposium,* he means to say that there are qualities in Socrates that engage him, and which override his conspicuous and legendary ugliness. Simone de Beauvoir loved Sartre not because he was beautiful but because of that unlikely constellation of intellectual and sexual qualities that made him Sartre. To be sure, we often commend these qualities by speaking of them as "beautiful"—but this has nothing to do with aesthetic considerations at all, and it seems to me that it muddles the concept of beauty irreparably if we say that these qualities are another species or order of beauty. It muddles it the way Paul McCarthy's enthusiasts do when they seek to find beauty in his overtly and undeniably disgusting work—"Not standard beauty, but the beauty of commitment and absorption." Comparably, we may come to admire Matisse's *Blue Nude,* despite its ugliness, above Chabanel's *Birth of Venus,* despite its transparent presentation of the goddess's pink beauty. I propose we restrict the concept of beauty to its aesthetic identity, which refers to the senses, and recognize in art something that in its highest instances belongs to thought. Where Fry, for all his artistic aventurousness went wrong was to insist that the Grafton paintings were beautiful when everyone who entered the gallery could see with their own eyes that they were not. Instead of that he developed his idea of the deferred beauty that rewards "hard looking." As though we would ultimately be rewarded by the kind of sensuous thrill that beauty in aesthetic sense causes in us without benefit of argument or analysis.

Hegel and the End of Art

Hegel is greatly to be admired because he is the first philosopher who attempts systematically to distinguish, perhaps too sharply, between aesthetics and the philosophy of art. Aesthetics, he observes, is "the science of sensation or feeling," and concerns art "when works of art are treated with regard to the feelings they were supposed to produce, as, for instance, the feeling of pleasure, admiration, fear, pity, and so on." This is a great advance over Kant, who more or less confines the relevant repertoire of affects to pleasure and pain, making an important exception for sublimity. Artistic beauty, Hegel insists is "higher" than the beauty of nature, and he wrote with a marvelous thunder that "The beauty of art is beauty *born of the spirit and born again.* What Hegel wanted to stress is that art is an *intellectual* product, and that its beauty too must express the thought the art embodies. But then why does he not argue that fear and pity, to take two examples that he assigns to aesthetics, are also intellectual products? They were deeply related to tragedy, according to Aristotle in the *Poetics,* and are components in catharsis, which is enlisted as part of the reason we relate to tragic presentations. He does not, evidently, because these are feelings, as the sense of beauty is as well when art is considered aesthetically. But what exactly then is *artistic* beauty when it is not aesthetic?

It is here, I think, that Hegel becomes confused and probably inconsistent, for he writes that "the beauty of art presents itself to *sense,* feeling, intuition, imagination; it has a different sphere than thought, and the apprehension of its activity and its products demands an organ other than scientific thinking." That is why in large part art has come to an end, to invoke his celebrated thesis. We have risen above the sphere of sense in the respect that *philosophy*—or *Wissenschaft*—is an exercise of pure understanding and analysis. What he prizes art for is that in its various golden ages, it did what philosophy can do, but in a limited way because of the constraint of sensuous media: "The beautiful days of Greek art, like the golden age of the later Middle Ages are gone." By contrast with the experience of art "The development of reflection in our life today has made it a need of ours . . . to cling to general considerations and to regulate the particular by them, with the result that the universal forms, laws, duties, rights, maxims, prevail as determining reasons and are the chief regulator." With art "we demand . . . a quality of life in which the universal is not present in the form of law and maxim, but which gives the impression of being one with the senses and the feelings." So "the conditions of our present time are not favorable to art." The end of art in Hegel thus has nothing to do with the decline of art but with the fact that we no longer require that ideas be communicated in sensuous form. So art could be glorious and it would still be over, as far as Hegel is concerned. In a way, his object to art is something like Kant's objection to the use of examples. Examples are, as Kant puts it, "the go-cart of the understanding." For Hegel, art was the go-cart of spirit. We enter the highest stage of what he calls Absolute Spirit when we no longer require art to satisfy our "highest needs."

But this leaves us with the question of how beauty, understood in sensuous terms, can really be "born of the spirit and born again." Hegel does not give us good examples of artistic beauty. He gives us good examples of art, the excellence of which can be brought out through astute art criticism, as in his magnificent account of the *Transfiguration,* or in his unmatched analysis of Dutch paintings, which really are, or often are, beautiful—but beautiful in a sensuous way. No one admires Hegel's philosophy of art more than I. What we must do in order to accept it is to recognize the way art can, indeed must, be rational and sensuous at once. And then determine how its sensuous properties are related to its rational content, which will be my task for the remainder of this book.

Duchamp and Art Without Aesthetics

Consider once again Marcel Duchamp, whose art neither Hegel nor any of his contemporaries could have considered as such. It was Duchamp above all others whose work was intended to exemplify the most radical dissociation of aesthetics from art, particularly in his readymades of 1915–1917. In 1924, Duchamp made it clear that finding an object with no aesthetic qualities was far from simple, but we can get a sense for his intention if we consider his

Comb (1916), which Calvin Tompkins characterizes "the most serenely anaesthetic of all Duchamp's readymades." No one can be said to have either good or bad taste in metal grooming combs! They embody the principle of the readymade through the fact that there is "no beauty, no ugliness, nothing particularly aesthetic about it," and from this perspective one of them is as good as any other. But he certainly never liberated his art from what we might term objecthood, nor hence from sensation. At a symposium held at the Museum of Modern Art in 1961, Duchamp spoke on the relationship between the readymades and "Art"—understood to mean the aesthetically pleasing. He said that he did not see the readymades as "coming to nothingness or zero" but that he was doing something "without having to invoke aestheticism or feeling or taste or any of these elements." And he concluded "I don't want to destroy art for anybody else but myself." What then if an artist means to reintroduce beauty, that being after all an option, if not for Duchamp then for others?

Duchamp gave a kind of answer to this in connection with his most notorious readymade, the urinal he attempted to get accepted under the title *Fountain* in the 1917 Society of Independent Artists' exhibition. As is well known, the work was signed R. Mutt—not known at the time to be one of Duchamp's myriad aliases. After the fiasco, he wrote "The Richard Mutt Case" in the short-lived magazine, *The Blind Man,* saying that "Mr. Mutt . . . took an ordinary article of life, placed it so that its useful significance disappeared under the new title and point of view—created a new thought for that object." Identifying this "new thought" has obsessed his interpreters since 1917. Duchamp's patron, Walter Arensburg, supposed that the thought was "A lovely form has been revealed." That, I think, is inconsistent with the philosophy of the readymade, but I have no wish to press the matter here. The point is that the work is the thought plus the object, it being in part a function of the thought to determine which properties of the *object* belong to the *work*. The urinal may be beautiful—and an argument could be made that as a piece of domestic furnishing it was intended to be attractive and express the very substance of sanitary purity in its glazed whiteness. But was beauty relevant to Mr. Mutt's thought? The object may be beautiful, but not necessarily the *work*. We have to identify the meaning of the work as given by the thought, in order to see whether the work is beautiful. And this would be the way Hume would enjoin us to see the matter. It is "our intellectual faculties" that identify the thought through which the object is to be interpreted. And our intellectual faculties direct us to those of its sensuous qualities which bear upon its interpretation. Was the beauty of the urinal relevant to the goodness of *Fountain?* Or is it merely relevant to the goodness of urinals relative to the principles that govern the interior decoration of bathrooms, without having anything to do with the "thought" of *Fountain* itself? Or better, does the beauty, if indeed there is beauty, contribute or not to the *meaning* of the work?

These are matters that cannot be determined without reference to an interpretation of *Fountain.* Jean Clair writes that the symbolic role of the urinal "is not to raise the status of a manufactured object to that of a work of art [but] to underwrite the archaic sacralization of human refuse and the infantile worship on one's own dung." It is for this reason that he explains the aesthetics of disgust above all through the influence of Duchamp. I by contrast see Duchamp as the artist who above all has sought to produce an art without aesthetics, and to replace the sensuous with the intellectual, as Hegel insisted has been achieved as a matter of course by the historical evolution of the "spirit." As I see it, the aesthetics of the urinal, as a plumbing fixture, has no role in its meaning. Neither has it any meaning in Jean's Clair interpretation, since it is its association with disgust that inflects its historical importance. It is too controversial a case to use to show how beauty and meaning are internally connected when the beauty of a work *is* part of its identity.

The Apple Trees at Balbec

I want now to present a pair of examples, one of natural, one of artistic beauty, in both of which beauty plays a pivotal role in experience. The beauty in both cases is aesthetic. And it is, moreover, simple and striking, in the sense that it would present itself to anyone as such, without benefit of much by way of education. In the artistic case, however, there may be *resistance* to the beauty because of certain prejudices regarding art. In order to accept the beauty, these resistances have to be overcome by a kind of education in what art is. This education does not lead to some higher order of beauty, because there is no higher order. What it leads to is an understanding of how aesthetic beauty plays a role in the meaning of the work to which it belongs. One can say that in such a case, the beauty is born of the spirit because the meaning of the work is internally related to its aesthetic qualities. The beauty is part of the experience of the art. But the experience is richer by far than the "retinal shudder" Duchamp impugned, not because it is something to be ashamed of, but because there is more to art than optical thrills.

I have selected the examples because they raise some striking psychological issues which bear on the moral grounds evoked in treating beauty as shallow and false to the reality of the world. I intend the examples, in brief, to help remove the stigma from beauty, to restore to beauty some of what gave it the moral weight it had in Edwardian aesthetics. Needless to say, it is not my purpose to plead for beauty's restoration to the definition or essence of art!

The first, somewhat overdetermined example comes from Proust. In a section called "The Intermitancies of the Heart," in the fourth volume of *In Search of Lost Time,* the Narrator has returned to the seaside resort of Balbec. On his first stay there, he had been accompanied by his beloved grandmother, who has since died. The section of the book in which he describes his grandmother's death is curiously clinical and detached, which is somewhat inconsistent with what we would expect, given their earlier bond: we feel we have learned something through this about the character of Marcel, who seems a much colder person than we would have believed him to be. This proves to be false: the moment he sits in his room at the Grand Hotel, he is overwhelmed with a sense of loss and bereavement, and descends into an acute depression in which his grandmother's irrevocable absence floods his consciousness completely. Marcel now sits gazing at his grandmother's photograph, which tortures him. He realizes how self-centered he had been when he had been the object of his grandmother's totally dedicated love—how he had failed, for example, to notice how ill she had been on that first sojourn to Balbec. This mood lasts until he goes for a walk one day in the direction of a high road, along which he and his grandmother used to be driven in the carriage of Mme. de Villeparisis. The road was muddy, which made him think of his grandmother and how she used to return covered with mud when she went walking, whatever the weather. The sun is out, and he sees a "dazzling spectacle" which consists of a stand of apple trees in blossom.

> The disposition of the apple trees, as far as the eye could reach, . . . in full bloom, unbelievably luxuriant, their feet in the mire beneath their ball-dresses, heedless of spoiling the most marvelous pink satin that was ever seen, which glittered in the sunlight; the distant horizon of the sea gave the trees the background of a Japanese print; If I raised my head to gaze at the sky through the flowers, which made its serene blue appear almost violent, they seemed to draw apart to reveal the immensity of their paradise. Beneath that azure a faint but cold breeze set the blushing bouquets. [It was] as though it had been an amateur of exotic art and colors that had artificially created this living beauty. But it moved one to tears because, to whatever lengths it went in its effects of refined artifice, one felt that it was natural, that these apple trees were there in the heart of the country.

The example is overdetermined because only someone like Marcel would have seen this glorious sight as he did. He is like his counterpart, Swann, in seeing everything through the metaphors of art. Someone who had never seen prints by Hiroshige or an Ascension of the Virgin, or in whose life there were no ball-gowns, or pink satin, could hardly have experienced the apple trees quite as he did. Still, it was a piece of natural beauty, which might have taken the breath away from anyone fortunate enough to have seen it. Marcel tells us that from this moment, his grief for his grandmother began to diminish: metaphorically, one might say, she had entered paradise.

The apple trees at Balbec might be on anyone's short list for G.E. Moore's world of beauty. A world with such sights in it would be better, Moore is confident in arguing, than a world of ashes. That would be as obvious as the fact that his two hands exist, to invoke one of Moore's most famous arguments. You cannot argue anyone into accepting that if they are uncertain of it—for what could be more certain than it, on which a proof could be based? If they doubt that, their doubt is irremediable. This I think is Hume's point about natural beauty. You can't argue anyone into feeling it. The natural beauty was at the core of Marcel's experience, even if there was an aura of metaphors drawn from his experience of art, which enters into his descriptions. One could be uplifted by the beauty of the apple-trees without bringing to the experience the needs that they helped Marcel resolve. But the example involves beauty as an ingredient in healing a sickness of the heart. The Prophet Isaiah writes:

Give unto them beauty for ashes,
the oil of joy for mourning, the
garment of praise for the spirit of heaviness.

Marcel had been given beauty for ashes.

The Vietnam Memorial

My second example is of a relatively contemporary work, Maya Lin's *Vietnam Veterans' Memorial* of 1982, which I select because it is widely regarded as possessing great beauty, both by those in the art world and by quite ordinary persons for whom it has become one of the most widely admired sights in Washington, D.C. The Memorial is simplicity itself. It consists of two symmetrical triangular wings, sharing a vertical base, and bent away from one another at a mild angle—125 degrees—like arms, one might say, which gently enfold those who approach it. It is a very reduced form of the structure in front of St. Peter's in Rome, but performing the same role. Maya Lin was an undergraduate at Yale when she presented the idea, and was told by her instructor that the angle between the two wings "had to mean something." The two walls are in polished black granite, and inscribed with the names of every American soldier killed in the Vietnam War, about 58,000 in all, listed in chronological order rather than, as somewhere along the line had been suggested, in alphabetical order. Lin's fellow students criticized the work as "visual poetry"—it is, after all, a kind of book—but were uncertain of its architectural merit. It took her all of six weeks to complete the winning model, selected unanimously from 1,421 entries in blind review. It has the quality of a fairy tale: Maya Ying Lin was twenty-one years old, of Oriental descent, and had lost no one she loved in the conflict. She failed all the tacit tests the designer of such a memorial was supposed to meet. The jurors naturally supposed it was by a man.

When the organizer of the competition, a rifleman in the Vietnam struggle, Jan Scruggs, first saw the work he was profoundly disillusioned. "A big bat. A weird-looking thing that could have been from Mars. Maybe a third-grader had entered the competition. All the fund's work had gone into making a huge bat for veterans. Maybe it symbolized a boomerang." Scruggs thought, "It's weird and I wish I knew what the hell it is." It is amazing that it was not voted down. Everyone wondered how the general public would react, but one person told Scruggs that "You would be surprised how sophisticated the general public really is." That of course turned out to be true. But the structure of controversy was at first governed by the fact that people held views to the effect that a memorial should not be "abstract." That explains why, to placate them, the sculpture of a trio of highly realistic soldiers was erected in front of the memorial. By 1982, however, the general public had benefited by having traveled and visited museums, and having studied art history in school, or simply from having seen programs about art on television. It was prepared to accept beauty that moved it. In 1982, Tony Silvers and Henry Chalfont made a film, *Style Wars,* about the graffiti then being painted on the sides of subway cars in New York. The "writers," as they called themselves, were from the poor sectors of society—from housing projects and often from broken families. But they had a remarkable sophistication and artistic literacy, as one can tell from the iconography of their works.

The beauty of the *Memorial* is almost instantly felt, and then perhaps analyzed and explained by reference to the way the visitors, many of whom come to see the name of someone they knew or loved, and to do a rubbing of it to carry home, see themselves reflected in the same wall that carries the name of the dead, as if there were a community of the living and the dead, though death itself is forever. It is possible to see the three soldiers reflected in the wall, and one can even read them as seeing themselves reflected there, as well as in having their names inscribed in the Book of the Dead. If one is sympathetic, one can even see the memorial as a vision that appears to them, explaining their rapt expressions. Possibly there is an analogy to a natural phenomenon, the surface of a very still body of water in which the sky is reflected, as in Monet's immense paintings of water-lilies, which is my model for thinking about the Wall, since those paintings make visible the way clouds and flowers seem to occupy the same space. Whatever the explanation of the felt beauty of the Wall, it is understood with reference to the "thought." It is part of the meaning of the work. In Proust's orchard, the thought is his. In the *Vietnam Veteran's Memorial*, the thought belongs to the work and explains the beauty. In natural beauty, the beauty is external to the thought, in art the beauty is internal to the work.

Jan Scruggs's account of how the memorial came into being is titled *To Heal a Nation*. It was his idea that the terrible political wounds caused by the war could only be healed by a memorial erected in the Mall in Washington, D.C., which is in effect sacred soil. To the extent that a work of art is capable of healing a nation, the *Vietnam Veterans' Memorial* is in candidacy for such an achievement. But I predict that it will be seen as beautiful, and its beauty seen as internal to its meaning, well after the conflict that gave rise to it fades in the national memory—the way the War of 1812 has, for example. Like the apple trees of Balbec, it may lift the spirits without necessarily healing the soul.

Internal Beauty

I certainly have no wish to build the idea of healing into the analysis of beauty as such, since we are not always ailing when we are struck by the beauty of something. Sometimes beauty simply stops us in our tracks. "My heart leaps up when I behold a rainbow in the sky" expresses a core perception of beauty, the poetry coming after the beholding takes place. "Earth has not anything to show more fair" was avowedly written from the roof of a coach bound for France: "This city now doth like a garment wear/The beauty of the morning" We have all had those aesthetic surprises. And we have them even in museums.

I remember first seeing one of Robert Motherwell's *Elegies for the Spanish Republic* while walking through an exhibition of abstract painting at the Metropolitan Museum, knowing nothing about it or about him at the time, but knowing, immediately and intuitively, that it was something I had to stop for. At the time, I made no effort to analyze the work critically, but, I shall show in Chapter 5 how Motherwell's *Elegies* were to become a paradigm for me in thinking about the place of beauty in the philosophy of art.

What interests me at this point is, however, the idea of "internal beauty," where the beauty of the object is internal to the meaning of the work. It is connected to the "thought" of the Vietnam Memorial that it be experienced as beautiful. By contrast, on at least my reading of *Fountain,* the beauty of the urinal is external to Mr. Mutt's thought, which we must attempt to recover in order to experience the work as we ought. Natural beauty is perhaps always external, unless we see the world itself as a work of art, and its meaning the symbol of its goodness. Something like this would have been Kant's view, which ascribed far greater importance to natural than to artistic beauty, so far as there were grounds for distinguishing them. He saw in natural beauty the assurance of a deep intended harmony between the world and us.

Internal beauty requires no such metaphysical assumptions. It serves to illustrate one mode in which feeling is connected with the thoughts that animate works of art. There are modes other than beauty, of course, that connect feeling and thought in works of art: disgust, eroticism, sublimity, as well as pity and fear and the other cases Hegel mentions as having to do with aesthetics. And these modes help explain why art is important in human life, despite Hegel's brash claim that we have reached a stage in the history of spirit when philosophy alone can satisfy "the deepest interests of mankind and the most comprehensive truths of the spirit." Because these interests are connected with the way we are made, they might help us begin the detoxification of beauty in contemporary art and philosophy, always recognizing that both have shown that it is not part of the definition of art. Beauty may be a mode among the many modes through which thoughts are presented to human sensibility, and explain the relevance of art to human existence, and why room for them must be found in an adequate definition of art.

5

Beauty and Politics

When Dave Hickey floated the idea, in 1993, that beauty would be the defining problem of the decade, it would have been difficult to find much by way of corroboration for such a forecast in the art being made at that time. The work presented in the 1993 Whitney Biennial, for example, was for the most part accusatory, and angrily political in character. Visitors were polarized at the admissions desk, where they were issued flat metal badges, designed by Daniel Martinez and themselves one of the artworks included in the show, which bore all or part of the provocative slogan "I can't imagine ever wanting to be white." Also part of the show was the famous videotape, played continuously, showing over and over the beating of Rodney King by members of the LAPD. The person who had made the tape was not an artist, but

FIGURE 14   Daniel Martinez, *Admission Badges*, 1993
Polarizing slogans

103

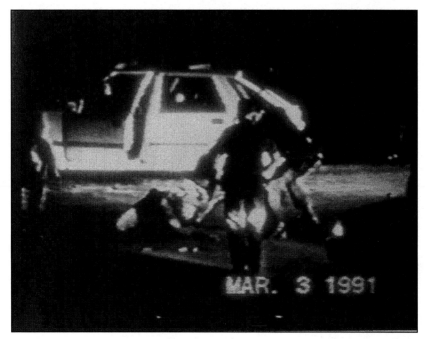

FIGURE 14   George Holliday's videotape of the Rodney King beating,
            1991
            Not the work of an artist

simply someone who happened to be there with a camcorder, and
there were questions raised as to whether it ought to have been
included at all, since its status as a work of art was uncertain. It had
not been submitted, in the manner of Duchamp's *Fountain* in
1917, but had, rather, been selected by the curators of the show,
who decided what was to be exhibited and what was not, and its
presence reflected the changing status of curators, who were
increasingly becoming the defining figures of the art world. More
and more members of the 1990s curatoriat had come of age in the
1960s, and saw art as a means of advancing political and social
agendas. But at the moment the distinction between art and visual
culture was under pressure, and the tape certainly reflected what
had happened to the definition of art in the sixties, when so much
that had long been thought to form part of the concept of art had
been eliminated. Who said that to be a work of art something had
to be made by an artist? It was in any case clear that nothing made
by an artist, least of all by a video artist, had anything like the

impact on society that the King tape had had. Aired nationally and internationally on television, it became an emblem of the strained relationships between minorities and the police in American cities. It became an agency of change. Whether it was art mattered less to the curators than the kind of reality it showed. In that respect it stood as a model for a politically committed art. It had helped transform society.

The 1993 Biennial was deeply resented. It was resented in large measure because in attempting to transform society, its immediate effect was to transform the museum as an institution that was still thought of in terms that Henry James would have understood, as an institution dedicated to knowledge, if not indeed as a sanctuary for beauty. James's great character in his late novel, *The Golden Bowl*, the art collector Adam Verver, had himself been transformed by beauty, and was dedicating himself to a life of aesthetic philanthropy. His vision was to bestow on American City a museum filled with objects of beauty for the benefit of its aesthetically deprived citizenry. His aim was to make accessible to them a kind of knowledge ordinarily available only to persons of cultivated leisure, with time and money enough to experience works of artistic beauty in the conviction that this was one of life's supreme goods. This exalted view of art had undergone a great many changes since the abuse of beauty by the Intractable Avant-Garde, which began only a decade after the novel's publication, but the museum was still thought of as a place of knowledge. Art retained a certain aura of sanctity, though the knowledge that museums purveyed was increasingly the knowledge of art itself. It would, I think, be extremely ill-advised for a museum in quest of funds today to justify its solicitations on grounds that Verver took for granted. If they are not aesthetic skeptics, funding agents are disposed to think of beauty as a luxury rather than a spiritual necessity. Public funding is predicated on education, but what have museums to put in place of poor battered Beauty today?

Two educational models have evolved in museums in recent decades—the art-appreciation model, and the cultural insight model. In the latter the art is a means to knowledge of a culture; in the former art is an object of knowledge in its own right. It is knowledge of art as art, and this often means arriving at an understanding of works through noting their formal features. This may or may not be accompanied by historical explanations—what work influenced the artist, and perhaps what work the artist herself influenced. Still, the object of knowledge is the artwork, and funding agencies might wonder what is the value of such knowledge, and they might, again, raise the issue of elitism. Is it justified to spend the taxpayer's money on something so unconnected with the lives of those who tramp through the museums, let alone the lives of those who don't? If one responds by saying that knowing about art does something the taxpayers *should* think is valuable, well, it would be valuable to say what it is. And it is here that the other model is brought forward. Art helps us understand the cultures to which it belongs, and in the particular case of American art, it helps Americans understand their own culture and hence themselves. Much of the Whitney's advertising promises that its shows will help viewers "make sense" of America. Works of art are so many windows into the inner life of the culture—and of ourselves as members of the culture.

And this would have been seen as the function of the Whitney Biennials. They are intended to provide knowledge of what American artists have been doing in the preceding two years. Those who attended Biennial 1993 expected to gain knowledge. And in a sense this *is* what they gained: they learned that American artists were deeply engaged in opposing the injustices of race, of class, of gender in America. But the artists were not simply concerned that the viewers should know what they were doing. Those viewers were themselves part of the society the artists were concerned to change. The problems were their problems too. The implication is that you are not just to look at what we, the artists, have done: you have to help us change the world. The show itself was like the admissions badges: you were somehow engaged in issues of race in the act of attaching them to your jacket lapel. The visitors were put on the spot. And this is not what they had come for; this is not what they expected to happen to them in the museum, this is not what they wanted the museum to be or art to be.

Good Art Can Be Ugly

It can be seen in hindsight that the 1993 Biennial was a high-water mark of the politically tumultuous 1980s. And perhaps Hickey saw more deeply than those who were caught up in the ideological conflicts being enacted in the art world of those years that a period—or at least a phase of art history—was nearing an end. In that case Hickey's conjecture might have been that artistic activism had run its course, and that a return to beauty might be a natural reflex. In that same extraordinary year, 1993, the art history department of the University of Texas in Austin sponsored a conference devoted to the question "Whatever Happened to Beauty?" Its organizer, the distinguished art historian Richard Schiff, posed the question in terms of whether the pursuit of what he called "artistic excellence" was compatible with "socio-economic discourse."

I find it interesting that he should have used the expression "artistic excellence" as more or less synonymous with "beauty." But it is extremely important to distinguish between *aesthetic* beauty and a wider sense of artistic excellence where aesthetic beauty may not be relevant at all. Let us once again consider Roger Fry's crucial discussion of the Post-Impressionist painting he showed early in the last century in London, which critics found so appalling. Fry was unquestionably right to defend the works as artistically excellent, but wrong to say that they would be seen as beautiful when one came to understand the principles on which they were made. His critics entered his exhibitions with a certain fixed idea of what a painting should look like, and what they saw was so dissonant with that that they could hardly regard it as art. Modernism had changed what paintings were going to look like. But Fry made it sound as if they were going to look aesthetically beautiful once they were understood. And my thought has been that it is important to recognize that the works might still be perceived as ugly even when we have come to see their "artistic excellence." The recognition of excellence need not entail a transformation in aesthetic perception. They don't change before ones eyes, like frogs into princes. That is my argument regarding such modernist works as Matisse's *Woman with a Hat* and *Blue Nude.* The ugly does not become beautiful just because the ugly art is good. My sense is that artistic excellence is connected with what the art is supposed to do, what effect it is intended to have. The work in Biennial 1993 was intended to change the way we think and act on matters of injustice. A feminist work is not intended to secure our admiration for itself, but to compel a change in the way women are thought about and treated in our society. If it has that effect, if it makes viewers see injustices where before they were blind or indifferent to them, it is artistically excellent. One may study the work from the perspective of how it achieved its intended effect. But that is not the primary way in which we are meant to relate to it. The work is meant to change the way those who view it view the world. To see the world as a scene of injustice is *ipso facto* to be moved to change it.

In any case, most of those who spoke at "Whatever Happened to Beauty?" took the term "artistic excellence" to mean aesthetic beauty—work that was artistically excellent *because* it was aesthetically beautiful—and their response, especially so with the artists, was that beauty was alive and well in *their* work. And so it was—but that left unaddressed the question of whether there is a conflict between beauty and "socio-economic discourse." I would now like to rephrase Schiff's question: Can art be aesthetically beautiful when its content concerns social issues? In the 1993 Biennial, for example, Sue Williams presented an installation that concerns the victimization of women. It included a fairly realistic pool of (plastic) vomit, an obvious enough elicitor of disgust. And it almost certainly expressed the artist's revulsion toward men as sexual oppressors. Would it be a valid criticism of the work that it lacked aesthetic beauty? Or, conversely, would it have been a valid criticism of a work that addressed the same subject and expressed the same attitude, that it was beautiful? Is there or is there not an internal conflict between beauty and certain contents? Or better: is not disgust the more appropriate aesthetic for an art that deals with the kind of content advanced in Sue Williams's piece? Was it a mark of "artistic excellence" that her piece should have aroused disgust in her viewers—not so much with the work but with what the work was about? So that beauty in connection with that content would not be irrelevant but artistically wrong?

Motherwell's *Elegies*

Let's consider a case where aesthetic beauty is artistically right— Robert Motherwell's *Elegies for the Spanish Republic*. I have already mentioned how beautiful I found one of these paintings to be when I first saw it, without knowing anything more about it than that. The critic Clement Greenberg used to cover his eyes while someone put a painting in place, and then abruptly opened them, acting on the thesis that what strikes the eye without refer-

FIGURE 16   Robert Motherwell, *Elegy for the Spanish Republic No. 172 (with Blood)*, 1989 © Dedalus Foundation, Inc./Licensed by VAGA, New York, NY
The beauty belongs to the meaning.

ence to previous thought is the test of a painting's excellence. In a way, Greenberg's methodology connects with a thought on beauty by Kant. Kant writes that "The beautiful is that which apart from concepts is represented as the object of universal satisfaction." I want to stress "apart from concepts." It suggests that beauty is a non-conceptual content of certain experiences, which of course can contribute to a larger experience of an artwork, when it is taken up as part of the latter's meaning, as we saw in the previous chapter. Greenberg, if I am right, sought to get an impression of the object before a concept could come into play, and rest his judgment of the work on this conceptually uncontaminated "first glimpse." In my own view, we have no clear idea of how much extra-aesthetic information comes with the first glimpse. But I must admit that when I first saw Motherwell's painting, I knew that it was beautiful by this test—I had been stopped in my tracks by its beauty. At the time I did not much reflect on what it meant. But when I did, I came to the view that the *Elegies*—Motherwell painted over 170 of them by the time of his death—

were artistically excellent not simply because they were beautiful but because their being beautiful was artistically right. By that I mean that when I grasped their *thought*, I understood that their aesthetic beauty was internal to their meaning.

The *Elegies* are characteristically large black-and-white compositions, with occasionally a spot of red or ochre. There are usually two or three black ovals interspersed with wide vertical bars. They are freely and rather urgently painted—the black paint feels as if it is splashed on, with some residual spatters and drips. *Elegy for the Spanish Republic 172 (with Blood)* also has a *tache* of blood-red paint. Viewers have read the forms in different ways. Some have seen the ovals as the testicles, the uprights as the penis of a bull, but this loses plausibility when there are more than two ovals and more than one vertical. Some see ovals and uprights with reference to the traditional egg-and-dart decorative motif, but that makes the title of the paintings obscure. I saw the ovals as figures in black shawls, and the verticals as broken uprights, as if remnants of shattered buildings. The beauty of the paintings does not translate into thinking that what these forms represent are themselves beautiful. "How beautiful those mourning women are beside the shattered posts of their burned and bombed houses, standing against the pale morning sky" is not a morally permissible vision. If, that is, one were to see a sight like that in reality and find it beautiful, one would wonder what sort of monster one had turned into, and quickly think instead of what could be done to help. Motherwell's stark black forms nevertheless do feel like shapeless figures set in a broken landscape, which has to be a scene of suffering. But the works are unquestionably beautiful as befits the mood announced by their titles as elegies. They are visual meditations on the death of a form of life. Elegies are part music and part poetry, whose language and cadence are constrained by the subject of death and loss and which express grief, whether the artist shares it or not. The *Spanish Elegies*, as they are called, express, in the most haunting forms and colors, rhythms and proportions, the death of a political ideal, whatever the awful realities that may historically have been part of it.

Elegy fits one of the great human moods; it is a way of responding artistically to what cannot be endured or what can only be endured. Motherwell was honored by the Spanish government, after the death of Franco, for having sustained the only mood morally acceptable through the years of dictatorship, a kind of abiding moral memory unmatched, I think, by anything else in twentieth-century art. Picasso's *Guernica,* for example, is not elegiac. It expresses shock and outrage. It too is black and white, but it would be false to call it beautiful. It was widely exhibited to raise money for anti-fascist causes. In its way, *Guernica* was painted in the spirit that inflected the work in Whitney Biennial 1993.

Elegies are artistic responses to events the natural *emotional* response to which is sorrow, which Webster's defines as "deep distress and regret (as over the loss of something loved)." I feel we understand too little about the psychology of loss to understand why the creation of beauty is so fitting as a way of marking it—why we bring flowers to the graveside, or to the funeral, or why music of a certain sort defines the mood of mourners. It is as though beauty works as a catalyst, transforming raw grief into a tranquil sadness, helping the tears to flow and, at the same time, one might say, putting the loss into a certain philosophical perspective. Recourse to beauty seems to emerge spontaneously on occasions where sorrow is felt. In the 1980s, when so many young men were beginning to die of AIDS, the gay funeral became a kind of art form. The victims would plan their funerals with care and originality, and fill them with what had given beauty to their lives. The beauty embodied the values they had lived by. Again, in the immediate aftermath of the terrorist attack on the World Trade Center, impromptu shrines appeared all over New York City. They were all more or less the same, and very moving: votive candles, flowers, flags, balloons, sometimes scraps of paper with poems. They were the immediate vernacular responses to the immense sadness that overcame everyone in New York. The mood was elegiac rather than angry, and the shrines were the outward expression of hearts broken by what was perceived as the end of a form of life. "Nothing will ever be the same" was the common remark in those first days after 9/11.

The conjunction of beauty with the occasion of moral pain somehow transforms the pain from grief into sorrow, and with that into a form of release. And since the occasion of the elegy is public, the sorrow is shared. It is no longer one's own. We are taken up into a community of mourners. The effect of the elegy is philosophical and artistic at once: it gives a kind of meaning to the loss by putting it at a distance, and by closing the distance between those who feel it—who are in it, as we say, together. I think this is what the Spanish government must have felt that Motherwell's paintings had done. They kept the feeling alive. Because these are elegies, they universalize through philosophization. But there is another kind of response, precisely the response of anger—the response evoked by *Guernica* in the case of art and "the war against terrorism" in the case of politics. It is one thing when distant empires have collapsed, and all that remain are the ruins, the trunkless legs of Ozymandias, King of Kings, and the boastful legend is rendered instantly pathetic by the surrounding wastes and the thin desert winds. We do sentimentalize ruins, which is why they were so stirring to the temperament of the Romantics, who could stand beneath or within them, and reflect on the transitoriness of glory. But we hardly can do this before raw wreckage, where the blackness is not so much the patination of age and nature, but the charred effect of fire and dried blood. Is the elegiac mood ever appropriate to so close a political catastrophe? Doesn't beauty distance it too abruptly? Have we a moral right to wax elegiac over something that was not all that inevitable or universal or necessary? Think, to bring it back to the individual death, to which beauty itself is the human response, when one feels that death was not inevitable (though death abstractly considered is): suppose one's lover has died of AIDS, and one feels that something should or could have been done, one feels anger that it has not been done, one blames and accuses: then beauty to which one is spontaneously moved also seems wrong, wrong because one is called upon to act (to "act up") and not to philosophize. Then elegy conflicts with the impulse to counteraction and the prolongation of struggle.

This might be a criticism to which Motherwell's paintings are subject. The *vita contemplative* and the *vita activa* point to different paths, in art no less than in moral conduct. My immediate concern is philosophical. It is to stress that the beauty of Motherwell's paintings is internal. The paintings are not to be admired because they are beautiful, but because their being so is internally connected with their reference and their mood. The beauty is ingredient in the content of the work, just as it is, in my view, with the cadences of sung or declaimed elegies. But it is also true that it is wrong at times to present as beautiful what calls, if not for action, then at least for indignation. Beauty is not always right. Sabastao

Salgado's photographs of suffering humanity are beautiful, as his work invariably is. But have we a right to show suffering of that order in beautiful ways? Doesn't the beauty of the representation imply that its content is somehow inevitable, like death? Are the photographs not unedifyingly dissonant, their beauty jarring with the painfulness of their content? If beauty is internally connected to the content of a work, it can be a criticism of a work that it is beautiful when it is inappropriate for it to be so.

Beauty As Consolation and As Relish

In a review of John Richardson's life of Picasso, the London critic, Richard Dorment, writes:

> It now seems odd that for one moment Picasso thought that Puvis de Chavannes's decorative classicism might be an adequate conduit for the tragic emotions he sought to express in the series of paintings inspired by the syphilitic prostitutes in the Saint-Lazare prison, but he did. Many of his gorgeously maudlin paintings of these lonely figures shuffling across empty landscapes or huddled in the white moonlight are fundamentally phony because their seductive beauty is at odds with the genuine misery on which they are based.

I am uncertain of this assessment, simply because I am uncertain of its implications for Motherwell's *Elegies*. What artistic address *is* appropriate to the depiction of jailed prostitutes? A clear documentary style conveys one message, a depiction embodying rhetorical anger another. Picasso need not have painted the whores at all, but it seemed a natural subject for someone who shared the late nineteenth century's sentimentalizing attitude toward such women, a kind of Baudelairean legacy. There can be little question that the sentimentalization of suffering gave a kind of market to such works—think of how moved audiences still are by cold, hunger, poverty, sickness, and death in *La Bohème*. John Richardson writes, "there is a hint of eroticism, even of sadism, to their portrayal." In a way, Picasso beautified the women because he relished the idea of a beautiful woman being caused to suffer. An ugly woman, or a woman rendered ugly by the harshness of her circumstances, blocks off the possibility of this perverted pleasure. Think, after all, of the history of depicting female victims, naked and chained to rocks, awaiting their rescuers. No one, presumably, would be erotically interested in rescuing a hag, or a woman shown starved and emaciated. But this means that by and large beauty in the depiction of such victims comes in for a moral criticism connected not so much with "the gaze" as with the fact that the gazer takes pleasure in the agonies of a beautiful female. So Picasso's works from this period are not altogether phony: they belong to a certain tradition, in which the use of beauty is perverse. Perhaps the right way to depict such victims, from a moral point of view, is to exclude any such pleasure and hence to exclude beauty in favor of documentation or indignation. In any case, it is important to recognize that, if this is true, it is incorrect, on Dorment's part, to speak of Picasso learning "to do without the consolation of visual beauty." Beauty in such cases is not a consolation but a relish, a device for enhancing the appetite, for taking pleasure in the spectacle of suffering. Indeed, Richardson says, "Picasso would describe women with some relish as 'suffering machines'." But that then raises the question of whether Picasso's subjects were not always victims of his style, of his imposing his will by rearranging their bodies to suit his appetite.

Against these considerations it is somewhat difficult to accept Dorment's assessment that Picasso's general eschewal of beauty "is what makes him an infinitely greater artist than Matisse," as if Matisse could not live without the "consolation." In truth, as I have argued, it would be very difficult to accept the claim that Matisse's *Blue Nude* is at all beautiful: she is fierce and powerful and sufficiently ugly that voyeurism seems ruled out, let alone arousal—almost as if the ugliness were a sort of veil of modesty with which Matisse covered her nakedness. Still, it is something of a critical commonplace that the work of Matisse's Nice period is inferior to his work from the period of *Blue Nude,* on just the grounds that it is almost floridly beautiful. I am not of that view at all. The beauty of these works is internal to their meaning. The world Matisse's works depict is a world of beauty, and the works themselves belong to the world they show. Matisse is absolutely coherent in this way, a hedonist and voluptuary rather than a sadist: he has sought to create a world which excludes suffering and hence the pleasure that might be taken in it. His characteristic corpus has the aesthetic quality of a medieval garden—a garden of love—from whose precincts everything inconsistent with the atmosphere of beauty has been walled off. To be in the presence of a Matisse is to look into that garden and to be in the presence of— the embodiment of—the spirit of the garden: a fragment of the earthly paradise. But what precisely is wrong with creating a place of beauty in a bad world? Matisse knew what the world is like. He created a sanctuary of beauty in his hotel room in Nice, with flowers and draperies and lovely women (and his own paintings on the easel or on the wall!) in much the same spirit, I would say, as those rooms in Istanbul that John Berger describes. They put the harshness of the world at a distance, and in that regard belong to the same space as the *Elegies*. This is what Matisse meant for his work to do.

I am extremely hesitant, on the basis of these considerations— or these considerations alone—to see Matisse as inferior to Picasso, let alone "infinitely" inferior, but Dorment's claim that he is so seems clearly based on some disapproval of beauty as an aesthetic quality to be at all sought after or used. As I see it, in his view beauty is a consolation, and consolation means mitigating the bitter truth, which it is morally more admirable to admit and to face than to deny. And to the degree that this represents the current attitude, it is not difficult to see what has happened to beauty in contemporary art. It is not art's business to console. Dorment's attitude is clearly in the spirit of the Intractable Avant-Garde. The relationship between art and society is that of irreconcilable antagonism, in which artistic beauty is bedding down with the enemy. But that is tantamount to an acknowledgment that beauty has the effect I have ascribed to it of consolation and mitigation, as in the paintings from Matisse's Nice period, the *Spanish Elegies,* the *Vietnam Veterans' Memorial*—or the post-9/11 shrines. It serves to put suffering in a kind of philosophical perspective.

Does the World Deserve Beauty?

I think it was in just such terms that Adam Verver must have viewed his museum for American City, as an island of light in the bleak world of an industrial city. It was in its way like a church. The church is a place of light and music and praise. Traditionally people bathed on Saturday night to make themselves clean for the Sabbath; and they changed into special clothing on Sunday morning when they entered its space, in symbolic acknowledgement of the moral difference between inside and outside, which metaphorically enacts the difference between the vale of tears in which human life is spent and the glorious kingdom that awaits them. But the contrast implied a certain acceptance of the way things are outside the church. Verver shows no sense of responsibility for changing the world that had made him a rich man, and for making daily life better for those whose labor enabled him to buy Damascene tiles and Siennese altarpieces for their aesthetic edification, let alone marrying a great beauty for his own aesthetic welfare. Why not instead put his money into hospitals and schools? Why not make the world outside the museum beautiful enough that the need for the compensatory beauty inside it disappears? With religion, it was possible to argue that the reason women bring children forth in pain and men earn their bread in the sweat of their brow is the original disobedience that drove our first parents out of paradise and into the harsh world they deserved. Life is a punishment. Beauty is for the life to come if we do our duty here. Who dares question the way of the Lord? But Verver lived on the cusp of the twentieth century. Why do we need to endure the world as it is, or mitigate it by building islands of beauty for intervals of relief, when we can mitigate it directly?

An argument can certainly be made that it would be a breach of morality to be philosophical about the things that seem instead to call for action and change. To say, in connection with sexual aggression against women, that well, men will be men, as if that were an eternal truth, is clearly wrong. Or, to take another case, there is clearly something wrong in using Christ's saying that the poor we shall always have with us as an excuse for doing nothing about the homeless. If beauty is linked with being philosophical, there are clear arguments against the moral appropriateness of beauty. And if art is internally linked with beauty, there is a moral argument against art. The artists of the 1993 Whitney Biennial could be grateful to the Intractable Avant-Garde for breaking that link. Why should they make beauty for a bad world?

The American painter Phillip Guston made lyrical abstractions in the 1950s and early 1960s, and then asked himself what right he had to be making beauty when the world was a scene of horrors, after which he painted allegorical political cartoons, with detached limbs and hooded figures smoking cigars. The question for Guston was how one could go on painting beautiful pictures when the

FIGURE 17 Philip Guston, *The Studio*, 1969
Completion without collaboration

world was falling apart. The pursuit of aesthetic purity was not an acceptable option. He needed to find an art that was consistent with his moral disquiet. "The Vietnam War was what was happening in America, the brutality of the world." And here his language really does take on a lyrical intonation:

> What kind of man am I, sitting at home, reading magazines, going into a frustrated fury about everything—and then going into my

studio to *adjust a red to a blue*. I thought there must be some way I could do something about it. I knew ahead of me a road way laying. A very crude inchoate road. I wanted to be complete again, as I was when I was a kid.

Guston began to see his earlier style of painting as somehow no longer morally acceptable, given the way the world had gone. If there is to be art, it should not be beautiful, since the world as it is does not deserve beauty. Artistic truth must accordingly be as harsh and raw as human life itself is, and art leached of beauty serves in its own way as a mirror of what human beings have done. Art, subtracted of the stigma of beauty, serves as what the world has coming to it. Beautifiers are, so to speak, collaborationists.

Optional Beauty

But is there not a question of the appropriateness of art itself? For even if the art is not beautiful, art itself is already internally enough connected to philosophy that simply making art at all rather than acting directly where it is possible to act directly raises questions of moral priority. That is rather a dangerous question for philosophy, and hence precisely for just such a piece of writing as this. The *Spanish Elegies* put political loss in a philosophical perspective—but if that is wrong, how right can philosophy itself be, which puts *everything* in philosophical perspective?

I think the answer to this lies in what made Hegel think of art and philosophy as deflected forms of the same thing. Both were moments of what he termed Absolute Spirit, by which he means that in both of them—and in religion as the third such moment—spirit becomes its own subject, putting itself in perspective. The term "spirit" is sadly unavailable to us, but what Hegel is talking about is accessible enough. He is talking about self-knowledge—of the self's knowledge of its own deep reality. He felt that art was inferior to philosophy only in that it was dependent upon having to put its content into some sensory medium or other. But that need not concern us here. The important consideration is that art is one of the ways in which we represent ourselves for ourselves, which is why, after all, Hamlet spoke of art as a mirror. Philosophy is a struggle to put into words what we as human beings are in the most general terms we can find. We are *res cogitans*. We are machines. We are *Dasein*. We are *will-to-power*. We are *Geist*. It is very difficult, as we know, to visualize what the authors of these ideas mean. There really is no way of finding a picture that entirely captures these ideas, and Descartes was quite explicit that any picture was a falsification of what we really are. But Hamlet found a way of putting into a dramatic representation what he knew his uncle was—a poisoner, a fratricide—and to do it in such a way that the uncle not only recognized himself but knew that Hamlet knew a truth that the uncle had believed was hidden.

That is what the artists in the 1993 Biennial were attempting to do. They were presenting their fellow-Americans as victims and as victimizers. There was very little beauty in the show, but how, critically, could there have been if beauty would be incompatible with such contents? How could they be content to "adjust a red to a blue" when society seemed to them a scene of injustice and oppression? The difficulty was not with the individual items so much as with the sense that the entire show was like a market-place for grievances. It was like a congress of street-corner moralizers, each attempting to make the viewers conscious of their moral short-falls. But this was the fault, really, of the curators. Their show was certainly different from the Biennials of distant memory, with still-lifes, landscapes, nudes, interiors, and portraits—contents in connection with which beauty could be internally related. These were the traditional contents that the early modernists, whom Roger Fry had gathered together in the years just before the Great War, had presented in ways that were *not* beautiful. But the contents the artists of 1993 were addressing were not the traditional contents at all. Theirs were contents it would have been wrong to beautify. Their aim was to change people's moral attitudes. And beauty would have gotten in the way. It would have been artistically wrong.

The great consequence of beauty having been removed from the concept of art was that whether to use beauty or not became an option for artists. But that made it clear, or ought to have made it clear, that when and how to use beauty were matters governed by certain rules and conventions. That made a prediction that beauty was going to be the defining problem of the 1990s fairly chancy. More than beauty would be at issue. The 1993 Biennial may have been the high-water mark I have claimed it was. Or the Whitney learned a lesson about curating. Artists have always created for patrons—for princes and cardinals in one period, for businessmen in another. Ours is increasingly the age of the curator. The curator herself has been transformed from someone whose role, by etymological implication, was that of taking care of art, to someone whose imagination had in its own right a claim to art—an entrepreneurial spirit, creative in the discourse of exhibitions, put together for the benefit of the larger cultural consciousness, mirrors for the modern self. Some historian will want some time to track the causal route whereby curators replaced the kings and cardinals who had once been their patrons, and came to define the way our society would see art as well as what art it should see. To predict the way art will be is for the immediate future to predict what the interests of curators will be.

But there is a philosophical point to raise, having to do with the definition of art. It has been clear from the onset of modernism that something can be art without being beautiful. So beauty is not and cannot be part of the essence of art. Content, on the other hand, is a necessary condition for art, or at least I have so argued since *The Transfiguration of the Commonplace*. We have seen in this chapter that it is right or wrong to present certain contents as beautiful. This is so much the case that a cultural decision, if one were made, to have art that was beautiful would *ipso facto* be a decision as to what content art would have. In the twentieth century, disgust seemed the feeling appropriate to certain contents that might traditionally have been shunned when beauty seemed almost the default condition for art. As a default condition, it inevitably restricted what the content of art should be. The beauty of art reconciled viewers to a world seen in terms appropriate to it being viewed as beautiful. But there is a very wide range of feelings that artists have been called upon to arouse. When the revolutionary leaders urged David to paint the death of Marat—with which the art historian T.J. Clark has proposed that modernism begins—the aim was to arouse anger and indignation, and to increase revolutionary fervor and hatred against the enemies of revolution. The painters of the Counter-Reformation depicted the saints as suffering, in order to evoke pity. Sometimes beauty is compatible with these, sometimes it is not. If the aim of a painting is to arouse desire, it is appropriate that it be beautiful. If it is to arouse loathing, it is perhaps more appropriate that it be disgusting.

We have no specific term for these qualities. In the early theory of signs, the distinction was drawn between syntax, semantics, and pragmatics, the latter having to do with the relationship between signs and their interpreters. The latter term, clearly borrowed from "pragmatism," carried too heavy a burden of associations to simply call these qualities "pragmatic," though used in contrast with "semantic," it helps to note that pictures have typically been thought of in semantic terms, with reference to what they are pictures of, where pragmatics would instead draw attention to what the picture is intended to get viewers to *feel* toward the latter. "Beautification" is clearly pragmatic: it is intended to cause viewers to be more attracted to something than they would be without benefit of beautifiers. And that of course explains why beautification is regarded as tantamount to falsification. Charles K. Morris, to whom the theory of signs is due, observed that "rhetoric may be regarded as an early and restricted form of pragmatics."

It would be possible to designate the range of qualities to which beauty belongs as rhetorical, in that they dispose the viewer to take certain attitudes toward a given content. But "rhetorical" also carries too many associations for my purposes. The logician Frege uses the term "color"—"Farbung"—to designate the way terms are inflected by poets—and this comes close to characterizing the way beauty, for example, is used to cause viewers to have a certain attitude to what is shown. Perhaps it would be suitable to introduce "inflectors" as a term for this purpose.

In any case, the question that I merely raise at this point is whether it belongs to the definition of art that something is an artwork if it is inflected to cause an attitude to its content. Beauty has by far been the most important of the inflectors, but disgust would be another, and outrageousness a third. The readymades are not simply industrially produced found objects, but objects so inflected as to cause an attitude of aesthetic indifference. I won't say that the number of inflectors is boundless. But it is too great by far to suppose that even beauty, for all its credentials, will be the defining inflector for the art of the immediate future.

Nevertheless, if beauty is viewed as an inflector in art, then Hegel's marvelous thought—"Artistic beauty is born of the spirit and born again."—makes perfect sense. It goes from the artist's mind to the viewer's mind through the senses. Natural beauty is not born of the spirit, but it need not follow that natural and artistic beauty differ phenomenologically. The phenomenology of beauty is less important in the present study, however, than the recognition that the point of creating artistic beauty is not to abandon the viewer to its contemplation, but to grasp it as internal to the thought of the work. As, in my example, the use of beauty in the *Spanish Elegies* is to cause the viewer to feel an appropriate emotion about a form of political life that was vanquished many years ago now, that many hoped would have been beautiful had it survived and prevailed.

Whether we must widen the definition of art to make inflection a necessary condition need not be argued here. But at least inflection helps explain why we have art in the first place. We do so because, as human beings, we are driven by our feelings. Morris's thought that pragmatics is what had once been the discipline of rhetoric validates this thought, because the rhetoricians studied how to manipulate the feelings of their auditors, especially in law courts, to render the decisions they favored—or at least to be favorably disposed toward their client. So artists traditionally portrayed their subjects in such a way as to engage suitable feelings toward them on the part of the viewers—that they were powerful, kind, just, wise, fearful, or whatever. Or that they were holy persons, or pure souls, or deserved our compassion. When Hegel proclaimed the end of art, he supposed that we might now be more driven by reason than by feelings—but that would have meant, really, the end of a certain sort of humanity. What a suitably inflected work of art does is seduce the feelings of viewers and auditors, or to show that the subject as possessed of attributes that would on their own seduce those feelings. After all, people really are majestic or charismatic. If artists paint them that way, they are being true to the appearances. If not, than what they do is of a piece with beautification, a kind of falsification.

But these considerations explain why beauty itself is not the defining inflector it once was. When portraiture was a central genre of art, the primary media were painting and sculpture, both of which lend themselves in a natural way to mimetic practice, and hence the re-presentation of individual persons. And beauty itself is an attribute of individual persons, and hence of portraits, considered transparently. Where the person is insufficiently beautiful for rhetorical purposes, beautification is the natural recourse. But this can be generalized. There is a natural appetite for beauty, which meant that the subjects of the artist were expanded to include landscapes and still lifes, where natural and artistic beauty again coincide. Indeed, wherever this was true, there was subject matter for the artist. With religious paintings, especially in the Christian narrative, there were problems connected with martyrdom and crucifixions, imposing on artists a choice of transparency, in which case there would be blood and torn flesh, or beautification, as happened in the Renaissance. Beautification was a natural move when painting became taken up with narrative in general, since the scenes that were depicted would not in historical fact have been beautiful. Still, one was showing human beings in relationship to one another and in natural settings, so there was room for beautification. It may have been this that attracted Ruskin to the Pre-Raphaelites, because he so believed in visual truth. Beautification carries, as was argued earlier, an insinuation of falsification. But Ruskin was also a Victorian, which meant that he would find depictions of sex disgusting. That is what explains his giving the order that Turner's erotic studies should be burned. Indeed, he argued that they were symptoms of insanity. Members of the United States Congress in connection with Mapplethorpe's art used that kind of language—it was "sick."

Most of the work in the 1993 Biennial was made up of installations, and these would not naturally be objects of beauty, especially given their rhetorical intentions, namely to outrage visitors to the museum not at the art but at what the art represented. There has been less and less painting in the recent Biennials, and less and less of what would even in modernist times have been regarded as sculpture. These traditional genres play a decreasingly central role in the contemporary system of the arts, if there *is* a system of the arts today at all, when, as I began this book by observing, anything can be a work of art. But as the system has changed in recent times, beauty itself has less and less enjoyed the primacy that was taken for granted in the tradition of aesthetics we inherited. When aesthetics was changed, in the 1960s, beauty was scarcely mentioned.

It was premature, to say the least, to have proclaimed beauty the central issue of the 1990s—to declare, as one writer did—that "Beauty is back." Beauty is too humanly significant an attribute to vanish from life—or so one hopes. It can only become what it was once in art, however, if there is a revolution not just in taste, but also in life itself. That will have to begin with politics. When women are equal, when the races live in harmony and peace, when injustice has fled the world, then the kind of art the Whitney Biennial presents to a resentful world—this writer included!—will stop being made. Or when artists stop caring about these things, and just go back to painting for its own sake. Or if the world goes through so terrible a time that all that artists can do is comfort through elegy. Whatever the case, aesthetic attributes do not stand alone. They are part of much, much larger frameworks, for just the reason that art itself is inseparable from the rest of life. When one puts beauty in art in the context of life, then to predict that the beauty will be the issue of the future is implicitly to say that the whole of life, in which beauty plays its roles, will be the issue of the future. It is too vast a claim by far to be a matter merely of what art will be in the future.

Three Ways to Think
about Art

I once agreed to participate in a symposium organized as part of the inaugural celebrations for an art school's new president. I did so because a real exchange of views seemed an auspicious departure for an occasion otherwise merely ceremonial, with edifying orations, the glee club, and a prim reception afterward—and because the president is someone I quite admire and like. So I was somewhat daunted to learn, some weeks after accepting the invitation, that the subject was to be edifying after all—"The Transformative Power of Art"—a title that, like "The Joy of Creativity" or "Art and Human Freedom"—emitted the stale, sour whiff of a commencement address. My initial impulse, like Herr Goebbels upon hearing the word "culture," was to reach for my revolver. But this was followed, almost immediately, with the recognition that we—we at least in the artworld if not in the public relations or development offices of institutions of art education—almost never any longer talk about art in such terms at all. Really, it occurred to me, we almost always talk about works of art as objects—objects of a certain complexity to be sure, but objects nonetheless. All at once, it struck me that the idea of transformative power connects with an aspect of art largely lost sight of in the way art has become the subject of a professionalized body of discourses.

The way we think of museums today is largely connected with these discourses, particularly since the abuse of beauty, together with the subsequent disconnection of aesthetics from the discussion of art, left the role of the museum somewhat up in the air. It is now viewed as a place for acquiring knowledge, and the knowledge, as I previously noted, is of two kinds. One kind is the knowledge of art as such, which in effect treats works of art as objects with an internal organization not unlike that of complex molecules. The other is the knowledge of art as a cultural product, where we visit the museum in order to see how the art of different cultures relate to the lives of those whose form of life they defined. This in effect is to see art in the way it is shown in anthropological museums—in dioramas, say, in which figures are shown in their native costumes, in settings which includes the gear by means of which they lived and the horizons that bounded their beliefs. One could in principle, I suppose, see the great museums of the western world—the Louvre, the Metropolitan, the Prado, the Uffizi—as anthropological museums, in which the culture happens to be our own.

In general, I think, the chief operative theory of art as knowledge of the first kind is one or another version of formalism. Formalism is no longer quite the favored posture for addressing works of art in museum and academic precincts that it had been in the 1960s, when we were invited, by critics and docents, mainly to consider diagonals and rhythms and internal references, similarities, repetitions, and the like. It offered, in the period of its ascendancy, ways of looking at art as objects internally composed under principles of design. Indeed, it was precisely to their design—their *disegno* to revert to a term used by Vasari—that Roger Fry appealed as the basis for judging the excellence of Post-Impressionist paintings. As such, formalism yielded a universal mode of understanding any work whatever, irrespective of its historical or cultural origin, and it, more than anything, dissolved the progressive model of artistic development, which had lasted from the Renaissance through the end of the nineteenth century. It liberated museums from the format of organizing art into national schools, which so inspired Hegel, and within schools into succeeding historical periods. Under formalist analysis, objects could be compared with one another in point of visual organization, as in the standard two-projector lecture, where one is directed to note affinities and discontinuities, and to exercise ones discriminatory powers. Art-objects could be juxtaposed irrespective of provenance, and one could trace their points of resemblance in the air as one's audience scanned the paired images on the screen. One could group objects together to "communicate with one another" in exhibitions which might contain Persian pots, Baule masks,

Renaissance bronzes, a piece of fiber art by Ann Hamilton, and some Navajo weavings—works which have no connection with one another except as art objects perceived to have this or that affinity. I would go out of my way to see a show with some such contemporary title as *Beauty Matters*, composed of just such a heterogeneous array of artworks. It could be a demonstration, perhaps, that beauty is much the same everywhere, irrespective of culture and history—though whether the beauty were internal or external could hardly be raised, let alone resolved, on formalist principles alone.

"Formalism permitted me," one of our rightly most celebrated critics and scholars of modern art once declared, "to separate myself from the type of subjective, romantic and poetic criticism practiced, among others, by Harold Rosenberg." That means, it seems to me, that the focus of her interest was on a kind of syntactic inquiry into works of art considered objectively—that is, as objects with certain resident structures it was the task of the critic to identify and clarify, independent of any external reference—of semantics, so to speak—and in particular of any pragmatic reference to those who experience them. She was speaking of criticism as a kind of autonomous *Kunstswissenschafft*—almost in the spirit of positivism—practiced by experts. Artistic Formalism, so considered could have been the subject of a monograph in that canonical work of Logical Positivism, *The Encyclopedia of Unified Science*—in which Charles Morris's influential *Foundations of A Theory of Signs,* cited at the end of the previous chapter, was first published.

I think it is very valuable for students to learn how to look at works of art as formal exercises, to "look under the hood" as the scholar I have just quoted—it is of course Rosalind Krauss—puts it in a study of the work of Cindy Sherman. That was not my way of thinking of Sherman's work—I happen to have a taste for "subjective, romantic, and poetic" responses—and feel I learn a lot about art from reading that kind of criticism, as well, of course, as the writings of Krauss herself, or her disavowed mentor, Clement Greenberg, on individual works of art. Consider, for example, the profound response to an archaic torso of Apollo by the poet Rilke. Rilke describes a downward curve in the figure's torso, but hardly in the spirit of a formalist observation. The curve leads down to the limbless figure's genital area, and it really does not matter that the genitals themselves might have been broken off long ago, in the spirit of iconoclasm or perhaps to secure a sexual talisman. Actual stone genitals are no more important to Rilke's experience than the statue's head, which is also missing. We do not see the figure's eyes, but somehow we feel ourselves seen by the entire body—"there is no spot that does not look at you." And for the same reason, there is no spot that is *not* genital: the whole torso expresses a sexual energy so powerful that that the poet sees himself as a very weak, very wanting sort of being. In the ferocity of the god's thrusting strength, the poet cannot help but ask what kind of a man he himself is. If it were a woman, I should think, there would be a sense that her lover must be replaced, or that something in her has been awakened that only a god could satisfy. "You have to change your life," with which the poem ends, is the crushing thought induced by seeing oneself in the perspective of the god's body.

Disturbing as it is, it is an experience one would want to have if one could. Put in general terms, it is what, having read Rilke's poem, would send one to the gallery of antiquities, not to learn about the evolution of "the Apollo figure" but to be addressed and challenged from across the millennia. Yet there are limits to what we can turn ourselves into. What after all did Rilke himself do? He wrote the poem. It is a poem at the very least about how a work of art can get us to ask what we are, and what we must in the end settle for, given our human dimensions. "You are what you understand," the tremendous *Erdgeist* tells Faust, who cringed before her. This may itself be a "subjective, romantic, poetic" response to Rilke's poem. One can look under the poem's hood, and acknowledge its sonnet-like structure. But if the poem does not have something like the effect on the reader that the sculpture had on the poet, something has failed.

Let us turn to the other kind of knowledge, which has become increasingly important to the art profession since, and partly as the cause of the weakening of the formalist model. We see art as referring to and expressing the inner life of a culture. Tramping through the Rijksmuseum in Amsterdam once, I made my way among clumps of cognitive pilgrims, addressed in various languages, and it became clear to me that the purpose of their being there had less to do with disinterested contemplation than with acquiring information and experience, much like our eighteenth-century predecessors on the grand tour. What was the knowledge for? Well, these twentieth-century tourists learned a lot about seventeenth-century Dutch culture. And listening to their docents, I learned a lot as well. One docent unpacked a marriage portrait, from which I learned something about how married love was portrayed in those days. But in the end I felt that the Dutch were being treated as a tribe like the Trobriand Islanders. And I then thought about the American tribe, to which I belong. But no painting tells more about what it is to live American culture than the movies, the sit-com, the popular music, the dances, the clothing, the hair-styles, the automobiles, the plumbing, the guides to sex and stock investment—all those semiotic systems which define our form of life. In a newspaper interview in 1915, Duchamp said

> The capitals of the Old World have labored for hundreds of years to find that which constitutes good taste and one may say that they have found the zenith thereof. But why do people not understand what a bore this is? . . . If only America would realize that the art of Europe is finished—dead—and that America is the country of the art of the future . . . Look at the skyscrapers! Has Europe anything to show more beautiful than these? New York itself is a work of art, a complete work of art . . .

And of course he famously said that America's great contribution to civilization was modern plumbing.

There was an exhibition recently titled *Kitchen and Bathroom/The Aesthetics of Waste*. It showed the evolution of these two rooms so central to modern domesticity, once appliances became available in the nick of time to replace servants. Advertisement after advertisement from the 1930s and 1940s showed perky wives in pretty aprons, loading washing machines, brewing coffee, using the toastmaster, serving their husbands. The bathroom was filled with hard shiny surfaces, easy to clean. If one opened the cupboards or refrigerator, one would behold prepared foods, which took the drudgery out of cooking—all one needed to do was add water and heat. Feminism casts a backward illumination under which women were domestic slaves, which perhaps connects the kitchen with the paintings of Hopper, showing a lonelier America. But they show it in no way better than the advertisements in womens' magazines themselves show it—or than bathroom fixtures and kitchen appliances do.

For the matter, then, one could make American culture available without putting into a show any works of art at all—as with the famous 1969 exhibition, *Harlem on my Mind,* at the Metropolitan Museum of Art, in which all that was on view were enlarged photographs of Harlem, with Cotton Club music piped into the galleries. That show was exceedingly controversial. Harlem artists were outraged. The Jewish Defense League was outraged by the anti-Semitic implications of the catalogue. The critics were outraged that a great art museum had been turned into an annex of the museum of natural history. But that is what the second model does. It anthropologizes art. However, art is no better for these purposes than cook books, Polaroids, the Sears Roebuck catalog. So what is the point of an *art* museum, filled with expensive fragile objects collected by various rich persons for their private taste, and turned over to the public in exchange for tax benefits?

Art's Transformative Power

There is a characteristically hectoring and in the context unsettling image by Barbara Kruger, installed in the lower lobby of the Wexner Center for the Arts in Ohio State University. A woman is shown holding her hands to her head, like the screaming figure in Munch's celebrated painting. White letters on a red banner ask: Why are you here? Kruger's questions always throw us off balance, especially when she follows them up.

Here she asks: To kill time? To get cultured? To widen your world? To improve your social life? These are not contemptible motives. When I first moved to New York, one could almost always count on meeting someone nice in front of Picasso's *Guernica*, at the time in the Museum of Modern Art. That was before the bar scenes, or the personals ads in the New York Review of Books. Did the art do more than confer on the site a certain elevating tone, guaranteeing that those we meet are likely to be our sorts of person? Or give us something we can break the ice with by talking about it in its presence? A story by Don de Lillo about a pick up, admittedly a not very satisfying one, involves a man and a woman who talk to one another—who cannot help talking to one another—in a gallery in which Gerhard Richter's *17 October, 1978* is displayed, which depicts the prison deaths of members of the

FIGURE 18   Barbara Kruger, *Untitled (Why Are You Here?)*, 1991
To be transformed?

Baader-Meinhof Gang. If it means the same thing to you as it does to me, the characters seem to think, then perhaps, just perhaps, there is hope of some deeper bond.

It would be wonderful if we could in honesty respond to Kruger's questions by saying: We are here to be transformed. We have come here to become different persons. And this brings me back to the topic of The Transformative Power of Art. Having said all this, it is undeniable that transformation or something like transformation is occasionally an effect that art has on those who encounter it, and I was too good a guest, finally, not to register this truth, and to try to connect it with the teaching of art. I had been thinking, as it happened, about Maya Lin's *Vietnam Veterans' Memorial*, Though the work has a complexity connected with its site, its occasion, and with tragedy and memory—there is no question in my mind that its beauty, as I proposed in Chapter 4, is internally related to the profound effect it has on those who come to mourn, but also on those who merely come to experience it as a profound work of art. Maya Lin has recently described how the idea of the memorial formed in her mind, and I thought it particularly suitable to observe that it came out of an undergraduate seminar in funerary architecture at Yale, and a class expedition to the Mall in Washington, D.C. That connected it with the art school as an institution, and it gave the concept of transformation legitimacy as a theme for the occasion we were celebrating.

How many of the students were likely to become transformative is difficult to say. Mostly the school will turn out the artworkers the society needs—designers and teachers, photographers and filmmakers, craftspersons and draughtspersons. But how many of my own students in philosophy are destined to be Platos or Kants or Wittgensteins? When one talks about philosophy in an educational context, one does so in terms of what Hegel calls, in talking about art, its "highest vocation." Still, the *Vietnam Veterans' Memorial* stands as a challenge to the entire complex of attitudes toward artworks as objects, with which I began. More than this, I think, the *Memorial* emblematizes the role that art plays in most of our lives, even if we happen to be members of the cognitive art establishment. In his remarkable book, *Painting as an Art,* Richard Wollheim has this to say: "Many art historians make do with a psychology that, if they tried to live their lives by it, would leave them at the end of an ordinary day without lovers, friends, or any insight into how this had come about." We need only think of quite ordinary works and what they mean to us to realize how inadequate most of what is written and taught about art is for explaining how this happens. My own life has been transformed by reading Proust or Henry James, both of whose works have made me a quite different person from what I would have been had I not read at all, or had never encountered them. Proust's novel teems with characters who see their lives in terms of paintings, stories, melodies, bits of architecture, gardens, essays. I have the view that they are transfigured by seeing themselves in the framework of these works. But everyone can talk about how his or her life was changed by a movie or a play or even simple piece of visual art. I remember how the very modern heroine of one of Margaret Atwood's novels was moved to tears by a simple print of happy peasants harvesting vegetables in China at the time of Mao.

Do these considerations help in any way in meeting Kruger's confrontational question? Or is her question addressed more to the museum as a cognitive establishment, not all that different, when one thinks about it, from the university itself, especially in connection with its humanistic wing, which does not have especially good answers to the question of why students should pay high tuitions to study works of art as objects? What, really, without taking refuge in the edifying discourse to which the very issue of "The Transformative Power of Art " belongs, are presidents of institutions of higher learning to say? Kruger, we appreciate, is by her own example concerned that there be an art that, to use an expression of Claes Oldenberg, does something more than sits on its ass in some museum or other. Her images enter the stream of life, they raise hell, which is part of what makes the image she did for the Wexner Center somehow disconcerting and ungrateful, and even subversive. She does not want us to study her works as objects. She wants us to change our lives for the better through their agency— to lead better lives, to treat one another with greater dignity. But what then is the museum to do? *Her* objects enter life through the gift shop, as coffee mugs and tote bags, bearing their political messages into the streets and on to kitchen counters. But is this really what we want from art, or for the matter from the museum?

What Do Art Museums Want?

In a widely discussed article in the *New York Times,* the critic Roberta Smith raised a question not unlike Kruger's, but addressed not to museum visitors, but to museums themselves: Why are you here? Smith asks "What do art museums want?" It cannot be a coincidence that her question paraphrases Freud's infamous "What do women want?" Her question, she feels, has a particular urgency at a moment when museums seem to "want to be anything but art museums?" What I believe bothers her—and the tenor of her text expresses this—is that art museums want as institutions to be what Barbara Kruger wants art to be. They want the way they show art to change the lives of those who use them. This, I think, is what Smith means by saying that they want to be "anything but art museums." My sense is that Smith's concern reflects the transition from the first model of the museum as an institution of knowledge to the second model—from seeing the museum as a place where we learn to understand art to one where we use art to learn about the cultures art is part of—from art as an end to art as a means. I belong to a generation that went to the museum as a kind of sanctuary, where one simply took great satisfaction in looking at what one saw there, without reference to learning anything much at all. The museum where I grew up was a quiet empty place with fascinating pictures in gold frames. I never much looked under the hood, and I knew too little of history to connect what I saw with distant events. In a way, looking at art was like reading books. I never asked why the museum was there, or who paid for it. If someone were to have asked me, in the spirit of Barbara Kruger, Why are you here?, I am not sure I could have given much of an answer. It would be like having to answer why I walked along the beach. It was just one of life's pleasures. But you could not get very far with city councils, let alone national endowments, without some better justification than that.

Smith picked out for particular notice an instructively controversial exhibition, *Made in California: Art, Image, and Identity, 1900–2000*, installed at the Los Angeles County Museum to mark the end of the century. It sought "to place art and artists within a particular historical, political, social, and economic context," according to the Foreword to the exhibition's catalog, written by the LACMA's director, Andrea Rich. What the exhibition in effect did was to strip works of art from their privileged position in society by treating them as simply part of visual culture, expressing the society they were part of, but no differently than an other part of California's visual culture—the clothes, the houses, the cars, the roads—California the way the museum of Natural History treats Borneo or New Guinea, using the art as cultural indices. Visitors from New Guinea or Borneo—or from distant planets—could use the exhibition as a way of finding out about how the Californians lived in their exotic culture. Critics could and obviously did say, in effect, that artworks are not just artifacts, and that to treat them as such is to put those who view them in just the wrong relationship to what they see. I shall return to this in a moment, but I want also to point to the Kruger-like questions the curators put: "Which California?" "Whose California?" Like Kruger's, these questions are intended to put us, at least if we are Californians, off balance. The exhibition set out to show that the California presented in the art was not necessarily the California that everyone living in California actually lived. It implicitly criticized the art because of that. The show gave Californians a mirror in which to see themselves. It was a cracked mirror—or a cracked society. The museum in a way turned itself into an agency for transforming its viewers into critics of the society that supported the museum. Trustees may ask: Is this what our taxes are paying for? Is this what art should be used for? At the very least the curators were asking if the taxes should all go to support an art that represented but part of the population of the state. Ought not all parts of it be represented? Not just the art of the white middle class, but of Chicanos and Blacks and the Chinese and Japanese that are also California?

Made in California had a point, but it depressed me to think about it. It did so because it put a lot of the art I loved in a perspective that had nothing to do with why I loved it. It made it into social-science specimens, products of a certain class and race. That was not the way I had thought and written about Richard Diebenkorn's paintings, or those of Joan Brown or Elmer Bischof or Richard Arneson or Robert Irwin or Ed Kienholz. As a New Yorker, I take a definite pride in the art of the New York School. But I don't think of it as "our" art. I think it belongs to the world. Probably, *Made in California* was a tacit plea for artistic multiculturalism, a way of saying that there are a lot of Californias, not just the California of the Bay area and Los Angeles art-worlds.

I once aired these issues in a talk for an organization of museum directors by using some ideas of the Hegel that I have always found valuable. Hegel's central concept is that of *Geist,* which literally translates as "spirit," though the latter term is too associated with communications from a world beyond to capture what he meant. Let's just translate *Geist* as "mind." Hegel distinguished "subjective mind"—the mind that connects with the body in some deeply un-understood and possibly, as the philosopher Colin McGinn has argued, un-understandable way—from what he called *objective* mind. This consists in all the objects, practices, and institutions which together define a form of life actually lived. These are products of mind and not of nature, and are internalized by those educated in the conduct of life. A form of life that is complex enough that human beings can live it will always have something in it we can think of as art, whatever meaning may be assigned it by those in whose life it figures. Objective spirit lends itself as a concept to the "art as cultural index model," as it does to multiculturalism. It is an idea taken up as iconology by Professor Panofsky, who uses the example, as I recall it, of tipping a hat as a way into our system of meanings, which exposes him to the question of what the purpose of art can be for the iconologist other than as further elements in the language of the culture. Even perspective, for Panofsky, was a symbolic form. It represents a certain cultural decision, to represent the objective world spatially in terms the orderly recession of objects in space. That does not make perspective a convention. For we in fact do perceive the world perspectively—we really do see railway tracks converging at the horizon. That is the way our optical system is made. Perspective was *discovered* in the sense that Brunelleschi *learned* how to show things the way they are actually seen. Still, it was a cultural decision to show them that way. When perspective was explained to the Chinese, they saw right away that that is the way we see. But they had no interest in using it for their own artistic ends. It had nothing to do with the way art fit into their culture. Their eyes were like our eyes. But the "objective spirit" of China was different from that of *quattrocento* Florence.

Hegel had another concept of mind—what he termed *Absolute Spirit*. There were, he thought, three "moments" of Absolute Spirit: art, religion, and philosophy. Art made palpable the highest values of the human spirit, and in a sense showed human beings what it meant for them to be bearers of these values. It translated religious beliefs into sensuous images. The temple and the cathedral thus expressed their cultures, but they did something more than this: they expressed the vision of the world under which the people of those cultures lived. But in this way, art performed a philosophical function. It *was* philosophy in a displaced form. Hegel famously felt that this was no longer a possibility for art, that it had been superseded by philosophy for persons who no longer needed illustrative images to understand its propositions. This was his notorious "End of Art" thesis, which I have frequently alluded to in these pages, and a variant of which I have discussed in my own writings.

Now my own version of the end of art is not like Hegel's in the sense that I do not think that art has been superseded by philosophy. Philosophy is simply hopeless in dealing with the large human issues. When I think of those Dutch marriage portraits—or of Van Eyck's portrait of the Arnolfini couple—against what philosophers have said on the topic of marriage, I am almost ashamed of my discipline. Kant, who knew nothing of marriage as a lived state, defined it in *The Metaphysics of Morals* as "the union of two persons of different sexes for the purpose of lifelong mutual possession *of one another's sexual organs,"* which is more a coarse joke for a peasant wedding than a considered proposition in the metaphysics of matrimony. Kant does add, to this reductive characterization, that procreation cannot be the entire story "for otherwise the marriage would dissolve of its own accord when procreation ceases"—but he never offers a positive account to guide persons in an age like our own when procreation and what he characterizes (in Latin, of course) as *usus membrorum et facultatum sexualium alterius* are, while not exactly neither here nor there, not entirely at the heart of the matter either, since both are available to couples who still ponder the option of marriage. A dear friend who once contemplated suicide asked whether I could direct him to some philosophical text that could help him decide whether to go on living, and I could not. What philosophy does is try to put the whole of everything in some kind of metaphysical nutshell. But it really aspires to universality.

I told the museum directors about an exhibition I had discussed with a young curator, which seemed to me to exemplify what it might mean to think of art as doing what philosophy tries, or ought to try to do, but in a concrete way, with what Hegel would dismiss as sensuous objects. The curator originally titled his show *The Vanitas Theme in Contemporary Art,* but had begun to think of calling it *Meditations on Beauty and Death.* There is, as I have sought to show, a connection between beauty and death in that it is through beauty that we vest death with meaning, as in funeral ceremonies, with flowers and music and fine ceremonial words. Kant writes that death is appropriately expressed by means of a "beautiful genius." Perhaps beauty confers meaning on life in much the same way, as though its existence validates life. I once wrote about a Tibetan *tanka* which shows the death of Buddha. The Buddha dies in a garden, in a beautiful pavilion, surrounded by plantings, on a beautiful day. He says farewell to the world at its most beautiful, which is when a Buddha would choose to die: the beauty of the world that holds lesser persons back from fulfilling their higher purposes. That is what the *vanitas* form is all about. It often is a still life in which a skull is surrounded by beautiful objects which the painting means to tell us are vain, are distractions, are ephemeral. The term *vanitas* means "nothing." And of course under Christianity one is urged not to be distracted, whatever the temptations, and to fix ones mind on the next world. Thus the connection between beauty and death. That connection is extended by this exhibition into works very different from the Dutch *vanitas* of the seventeenth century. There is, for example, a work by Felix Gonzales-Torres, consisting of two identical clocks, which keep time synchronously. They are very modern clocks, of the kind that would hang in a kitchen or a schoolroom, though hardly as a pair. Who needs two clocks? One could always check one against the other, but which one would one trust? The fact that there is a pair of them means that Gonzales-Torres is not presenting them as a "readymade." In fact Torres was saying something about love and marriage. One of the clocks will stop running before the other. Time will stop for it before it stops for its mate.

FIGURE 19   Felix Gonzales-Torres, *Untitled (Perfect Lovers)*, 1991
One will die before the other.

It would be a beautiful thing if they both stopped running on the same tick, as it were, like a couple dying in unison. Gonzales-Torres's lover had died of AIDS, as he himself was to do not much later. It is a memorial and a monument at once to the idea of "till death do us part" which is built into our concept of the meaning of marriage. It is a very tender, and very moving piece of art. It is a meditation. But as a "meditation," a genre of philosophizing, it connects with the great mysteries of human life and meaning. It is interesting to see the two clocks as a *vanitas*. It helps us understand why we need contemporary art to address these questions for contemporary men and women. The forms are different from culture to culture, but the questions transcend difference in culture. No culture is without a way of dealing with death, or a strategy for handling suffering. And that I feel is what the concept of Absolute Spirit is about. It connects the art of a given culture with humanity in the largest sense of the term.

Artworks As Embodied Meanings

I have a different model than either of the two with which I began this chapter. It is the model of *embodied meanings*. It is a model I use as an art critic all the time, trying to say what a given work means, and how that meaning is embodied in the material object which carries it. What I have in mind is what the thought is that the work expresses in non-verbal ways. We must endeavor to grasp the thought of the work, based on the way the work is organized. Let me give an example of how I like to proceed.

The Museum of the Rhode Island School of Design in Providence decided to celebrate its 125th birthday by inviting a number of individuals to write a short statement about one of the works in its collection that they particularly admire. The idea was to put the statements up next to the work described, so that visitors can read how someone thinks about the piece that they are looking at. I selected a painting by one of my favorite artists, the Dutch Mannerist, Joachim Wtewael. There is something crazy about Wtewael's work, and beyond question it represents an eccentric taste on my part that I go out of my way to see his paintings whenever I can. The RISD Museum has a great Wtewael, which represents the wedding of Peleus and Thetis, for most Americans a fairly obscure motif.

FIGURE 20   Joachim Wtewael, *The Wedding of Peleus and Thetis,* 1610
A mortal among immortals

The painting is not in great condition, being somewhat the worse for having been restored. One can see that it is beautifully painted, but I defer for the moment any aesthetic opinion, other than to say that it is exuberantly—or perhaps exquisitely—mannerist.

Whenever I spend time with one of Wtewael's oblique and arcane works, I try to feel myself addressed as part of the rare and refined audience for whom he must have painted. It was an audience that expected the meaning of art to be concealed but accessible, so Wtewael's pictures are elegant mazes, tissues of delicate references and implications that challenged the learning and flattered the sophistication of his patrons. He expected them to know the stories—to know, in the *The Wedding of Peleus and Thetis,* what brought bride and groom together and who the guests were, and why the subject was worth painting. I like to imagine a group of worldly Dutch men and women, members, historically speaking, of the Dutch aristocracy, seated at a table, dressed in garments as stylish as the painting itself, challenging one another's interpretations the way we do when we talk about an artful film or novel. Their table is a still life of crusts and fruit peels, and partly empty goblets. Wtewael's painting hangs in the room, and it is luminous under candle flame and firelight reflected from mirrors and polished cupboards, pearls and satin skirts, and it hangs in their midst like a vision of peace and pleasure. As in the painting, there is a sleeping dog, indifferent to the witty toasts, the manneristic compliments to host and hostess, and to the merriment the topic of marriage always arouses. The men and women know that the wily Thetis metamorphosed herself through a sequence of scary forms before yielding to Peleus, and that the chief gods allowed Peleus— a mortal—to marry the beautiful sea nymph only because her son was fated to be stronger than his father. Their son in fact was to be the great hero Achilles, mostly a god, marginally but decisively mortal. But why is Peleus shown so much older than his delicious bride? Plenty of room there for ribald speculation and whispered innuendos! And there is another joke: it would be a pretty puny son that would find difficulty in besting this senior citizen with the receded hairline. Actually, Peleus looks something like me, and someone might tease me by saying that what I like about the painting is the fact that it shows a man of my age and looks, with his arm around the waist of a very pretty young woman, both of us as naked as pagans.

The bridal pair is seated in the place of honor at a festive table with fruits and goblets and flowers, and all the other guests are gods and goddesses. That gives a deep reason why Peleus looks as old as he does. He is the only one in the picture who will age, and the only one who will die. The rest are immortal. So the picture in a strange way is something of a *vanitas*. The poet Sappho said that we know from the gods that death is a bad thing—for if it were a good thing, the gods themselves would die. The gods have youthful beautiful bodies and live without fear of what we fear every day of our brief lives.

The Dutch, knowing their Ovid, are aware that terrible times lie ahead. All the gods save one have been invited to the celebration. The uninvited guest—Eris, goddess of disorder—is about to throw a golden apple onto the table. On it was written "To the most beautiful"—but which of the goddesses was that? Juno, the goddess of power, Minerva the goddess of wisdom, or Venus the goddess of erotic love? Everyone knew what happened after that— a world torn apart, the golden age, in which gods and mortals married one another and sat down to share a meal, was irremediably shattered. It was in fact the last occasion on which gods and mortals sat down with one another to table. If only someone could stop Eris! It is a characteristic of Mannerist compositions that the central figure is difficult to identify. In Bruegel's *Landscape with the Fall of Icarus*, Icarus is a tiny pair of legs that could belong to a diver, an incidental detail. The Ploughman is the foreground figure, but the painting is not about him except in the sense that he is going on about his business, entirely unaware of the tremendous failure of a boy falling out of the sky. He tried to emulate a god—Apollo—and drowned in the attempt. Which one is Eris? Where is the apple of discord? And what does the story of this last supper mean for us, sitting here in our castle, on top of the world, enjoying the good things of life—art, wine, tasty things to eat, and one another's company?

Is the painting beautiful? Well, of course it is beautiful in the way Mannerism defined beauty—elegant and ornamental, like the gods and goddesses Wtewael shows. Its beauty is internal; in the way I earlier argued Matisse's paintings from his Nice period are beautiful. They themselves belong in the reality Matisse painted. If the svelte and slender immortals had paintings, they would look the way Wtewael's paintings look. Is it a transformative work of art? I don't truly know. But I know that if it is to transform its viewers, they need to see it as something more than an example of what the Dutch aristocratic class around Utrecht in the late sixteenth century wanted to be surrounded with. And I cannot imagine what it would be to look under the hood of the painting without knowing its meaning. The meaning, if I have it right, is philosophical, and internally related to its viewers. It put their lives in perspective. It tells them what, really, they already know.

Beauty and Sublimity

In 1948, *The Tiger's Eye*—an influential magazine devoted to literature and the arts—published a symposium titled "Six Opinions on What is Sublime in Art?" There had been little of note written on this topic since Hegel's lectures on aesthetics in the 1820s, but it must have seemed to the editors of the magazine, who were very close to the Abstract Expressionist movement, that something was beginning to happen in painting that put it in candidacy for sublimity. Two of the movement's more intellectual figures—Robert Motherwell and Barnett Newman—were among the symposiasts, but it was Newman who wrote with an excitement and conviction that the title of his contribution perfectly conveys: "The Sublime is Now." Early that year, allegedly on his forty-third birthday—January 29th, 1948—Newman had made what he regarded as a major breakthrough, not only in his own painting, but in painting as such, with a work he was to call *Onement I.* There can be little question, I think, that Newman connected this work with the tremendousness conveyed by the idea of the sublime. It was somehow too momentous an achievement, in his mind at least, to think of as merely beautiful, or beautiful, really, at all. Some decades later, the post-modernist thinker, Jean-François Lyotard, was to write that in the "aesthetic of the sublime . . . the logic of the avant-garde finds its axioms." And it is clear from the way in which Newman polarizes the two concepts, that he saw no possibility of finding the axioms of his art in the aesthetic of the beautiful. If there was to be an aesthetic for *Onement I,* nothing less than the sublime would suffice. There are, as I have pointed out, a great many aesthetic qualities other than beauty. But none of them poses

FIGURE 21
Barnett Newman,
Onement I, 1948
**Beyond mere
beauty**

quite the challenge to beauty that sublimity does, and I shall close my discussion of the abuse of beauty with this last chapter in its history.

Avant-garde intellectuals, in mid-twentieth-century America, and especially in New York, inevitably saw the world in terms of polar opposition. This was doubtless a consequence of having been brought up on the *Communist Manifesto*, in which society is dramatically portrayed as now split into "two great hostile classes facing each other: Bourgeoisie and Proletariat." The subtext of

Greenberg's "Avant-Garde and Kitsch," for example, was the struggle between two incompatible philosophies of culture which he respectively identified with Fascism (= Kitsch) and Socialism (= Avant-Garde). Philip Rahv, an editor of the influential *Partisan Review*, in which Greenberg's essay had been published, spoke of American writers as grouped into two polar types: "Paleface and Redskin," exemplified respectively by Henry James and Walt Whitman. Newman could not resist placing the sublime with the beautiful in polar contrast with one another:

> The invention of beauty by the Greeks, that is, their postulate of beauty as an ideal, has been the bugbear of European art and European aesthetic philosophies. Man's natural desire in the arts to express his relation to the Absolute became confused and identified with the absolutisms of perfect creations—with the fetish of quality—so that the European artist has been continually involved in the moral struggle between notions of beauty and the desire for sublimity.

With equal inevitability, Newman sees the history of art as an aesthetic struggle, between "the exaltation to be found in perfect form" on the one side, and, on the other, "the desire to destroy form, where form can be formless." It is, he argues, "The impulse of modern art to destroy beauty," which has precisely been the argument of this book.

American Sublime

Newman framed the polarity between beauty and sublimity within another polarity, that between Europe and America. "The failure of European art to achieve the sublime is due to this blind desire . . . to build an art within a framework of the Greek ideal of beauty." This is because European art was "unable to move away from the Renaissance imagery of figures and objects except by distortion or by denying it completely for an empty world of geometrical formalisms." But—"I believe that here in America, some of us, free from the weight of European culture, are finding the answer, by completely denying that art has any concern with the problem of beauty and where to find it." This opposition between Europe and America is echoed by Robert Motherwell, the only American in the movement in fact to have visited Europe, and whose sensibility among masters of the New York School owed most to a kind of European culture. It was Motherwell who invented the term "The New York School" to distinguish what he and his peers were doing from "The School of Paris." And in an important interview of 1968, Motherwell said: "I think that one of the major American contributions to modern art is sheer size. There are lots of arguments as to whether it should be credited to Pollock, Still, Rothko, even Newman . . . The surrealist tone and literary qualities were dropped, and [it was] transformed into something plastic, mysterious, and sublime. No Parisian is a sublime painter, nor a monumental one."

Let me round off my little catalog of polarities by reverting to Rahv. "While the redskin glories in his Americanism, to the paleface it is a source of endless ambiguities." James may have been a paleface, but he tirelessly pursued the moral allegory of the culturally and morally innocent American among the sophisticated (and corrupt) Europeans. He could not resist giving the hero of his 1877 novel, *The American,* the allegorical name "Newman." The New Man has come to the Old World on a cultural pilgrimage in 1868, having made his fortune manufacturing wash tubs; and James has a bit of fun at his hero's expense by inflicting him with an "aesthetic headache" in the Louvre, where his story begins. "I know very little about pictures or how they are painted," Newman concedes; and as evidence, James has him ordering, as if buying shirts, half a dozen copies of assorted old masters from a pretty young copyist who thinks he is crazy, since, as she puts it, "I paint like a cat."

By a delicious historical coincidence, Barnett Newman—another New Man—visits the Louvre for the first time in 1968, exactly a century later. By contrast with James's hero, this Newman has had the benefit of having read Clement Greenberg and had himself gone through a Surrealist phase. So he is able to tell his somewhat patronizing guide—the French critic Pierre Schneider—to see Uccello's *The Battle of San Romano* as "a modern painting, a flat painting," and to explain why Mantegna's Saint Sebastian bleeds no more than a piece of wood despite being pierced with arrows. He sees Géricault's *Raft of the Medusa* as 'tipped up' like one of Cézanne's tables—"It has the kind of modern space you wouldn't expect with that kind of rhetoric." And in general the new New Man is able to show European aesthetes a thing or two about how to talk about the Old Masters—and incidentally how to look at his own work, which so many even of his New York School contemporaries found intractable. In Rembrandt, for example, Newman sees "All that brown, with a streak of light coming down the middle of them—as in my own painting." His guide, the critic Pierre Schneider, European to the core, pretends to see Newman as a redskin—"a noble savage with a protective disguise, just as the Huron, to be left in peace, pretends to be an oilman."

Surpassing Every Standard of Sense

Beauty had been put on the defensive as early as the eighteenth century, when the concept of the sublime first entered Enlightenment consciousness through the translation by Boileau of a text on the subject by a somewhat obscure rhetorician, traditionally known as Longinus; and *A Philosophical Enquiry into the Origin of the Sublime and the Beautiful,* by the Irish statesman, Edmund Burke. Beauty, in the Enlightenment had become inextricably connected with taste, and refined taste was the defining mark of aesthetic cultivation. Aesthetic education implies that there are rules that one can learn, as in moral education, though it would be expected that in both, the pupil will in time be on his or her own, and know when something is beautiful or right respectively through having acquired good taste in each. It was entirely correct of Newman to connect the idea of beauty with perfection. The mark of the sublime by contrast was ecstasy or *enthusiasmos.* These terms or, better, their equivalents, continue to play a role in the vocabulary of aesthetic appraisal. We speak of ourselves as "blown away" or as "knocked out" or "bowled over" or "shattered" by a work of art, and this goes well beyond finding ourselves enough pleased to judge it perfect. Reading Longinus caused the cultivated audiences of the eighteenth century to wonder why their art never lifted them out of themselves, which is what "ecstasy" means, and thus the idea of the sublime collided with the sphere of the tasteful as a disruptive force, much in the way the god Dionysus invaded Thebes in Euripides's unsettling play, *The Bacchae.* Grace and beauty all at once seemed paltry and insufficient. A recent commentator compared the impact of *On the Sublime* to that of Freud's writings on our own times. In proposing sex as the main drive in human conduct, Freud made everyone restless and emotionally uncertain, and feeling that in terms of orgasmic promise, something was missing from our civilized little lives. Think of Thomas Mann's character in *Death in Venice*. Beauty was a source of pleasure—but sublimity, in art and especially in nature, produced what Burke spoke of as "the strongest emotion which the mind is capable of feeling."

But what exactly was that feeling? In a review devoted to some pictures by the German Romantic painter, Caspar David Friedrich, in which one or more personages is shown from behind and gazing at the Moon, the *New Yorker* art critic, Peter Schjeldahl, expressed reservations on the critical usefulness of the term. The sublime, he writes, is a "hopelessly jumbled philosophical notion that has had more than two centuries to start meaning something cogent and hasn't succeeded yet." And he goes on, affecting a sublime historical cluelessness: "As an adjective in common use, the word is correctly employed not by Immanuel Kant but by Frank Loesser: 'The compartment is air-conditioned, and the mood sublime.'" Nothing that rocked an entire and largely self-congratulatory culture like the Enlightenment could have meant something so innocuously gushy. Here is a good example of how the term was actually employed in common eighteenth-century usage. Abigail Adams, in 1775, describes in a letter to her husband, the noise of cannons, which she observed from the top of Penn's Hill in Boston. "The sound I think is one of the Grandest in Nature and is of the true Species of the Sublime. 'Tis now an incessant roar. But O the fatal ideas that are connected with the sound. How many of our dear country men must fall?" The Sublime was in fact associated with fear in Burke's writing, and in some degree in Kant's, but mostly Kant treated it with reference to such feelings as wonderment and awe—words he uses in the Conclusion of his *Critique of Practical Reason*, in one of his most famous passages:

> Two things flood the mind with ever increasing wonder and awe [*Bewunderung und Ehrfurcht*], the more often and the more intensely it concerns itself with them: the starry heavens above me and the moral law within me.

So a piece of art would be sublime that elicits in a subject this complex mixture of wonder and awe. The German word is compounded of two morphemes, connoting deference and fear, though the latter is scarcely implied by its English equivalent. More than a feeling for beauty, the responsiveness to sublimity, Kant realized, is a product of culture. But it "has its root in human nature." It is part of what we are. Longinus too says something to this effect:

> We are (heaven knows) somehow driven by nature to wonder not at small streams, even if they are clear and useful, but at the Nile and the Danube and the Rhine, and still more at the Ocean; nor, of course, are we more astonished by that little flame which we kindle . . . than by the gleam of the heavenly bodies, though they are often gloomed over, nor do we generally consider it [i.e., the little flame] more worthy of wonder than the craters of Aetna, whose eruptions carry up rocks and whole mounds from the abyss and sometimes pour forth rivers . . .

Kant cites such examples in his discussion of the Sublime:

> Bold overhanging, and as it were threatening rocks; clouds piled up in the sky, moving with lightning flashes and thunder peals; volcanoes in all the violence of destructive hurricanes with their track of devastation; the boundless ocean in the state of tumult; the lofty waterfall of a mighty river, and such like.

My "native informant" from the eighteenth century, Abigail Adams again, used a precisely Kantian vocabulary when she embarked on her first ocean voyage to join her husband in Europe. Finally able to go up on deck after suffering sea-sickness, she noted in her diary, that she "beheld the vast and boundless ocean before us with astonishment, and wonder."

What is fascinating in Kant is that we are in the same way "driven by nature" to have a comparable attitude toward morality, which he explicitly characterizes in terms of the power or might "which it exercises in us," whatever our personal interests. Abigail Adams, in whom duty almost always trumped personal interest and inclination, would have accepted this totally. But where would we find a comparable power in art? Here Kant's experience was severely limited by what Newman speaks of as "the Renaissance imagery of individuals and objects." The art Kant knew was entirely representational, and though sublime things can be represented, they cannot be represented as sublime. This is one major difference between the beautiful and the sublime: the beautiful *can* be represented as beautiful. "The sublime of art is always limited by the conditions of agreement with nature," he writes, which restates the mimetic theory of art Kant takes as given. The mimetic theory rests on a congruity of boundaries, which is the condition of drawing. Kant specifies that "the beautiful in nature is connected with the form of the object, which consists in having definite boundaries." The sublime, by contrast, "is to be found in a formless [what Adams speaks of as "boundless"] object, so far as in it or by occasion of it boundlessness is represented, and yet its totality is also present to thought."

Consider the paintings of the artist, Vija Celmans, who does pictures of the starry heavens or of the ocean. These are paradigms of the sublime, since we know that what they depict are "boundless totalities." Yet we could not easily think of her paintings themselves as sublime, mainly because they do not elicit in us any special feeling of wonder on the scale that sublimity seems to require. And that in part is because of the scale of the pictures themselves, which one could hold in one's hands, as at a picture-dealer's. Somewhat closer might be the seascapes or landscapes exhibited recently at the Pennsylvania Academy as examples of "The American Sublime"—the paintings whose makers subscribed to the theory that God expresses himself in nature and does so with particular vehemence in those aspects of nature which have a certain grandeur. I refer to the so-called Hudson River School, which flourished in the mid-nineteenth century, and whose archetypically large-scale paintings featured nature itself at its largest—the Andes, or Niagara Falls, or the Grand Canyon. Such paintings perfectly illustrate Longinus's descriptions of the natural sublime, though I am uncertain whether there would have been paintings in his age which could have done so. There can be little question that the Hudson River artists reverted to large size in order to instill the awe and wonderment their depicted scenes aroused.

Kant, who of course never visited Rome, does speak of

The bewilderment or, as it were, perplexity which it is said seizes the spectator on his first entrance into St. Peter in Rome. For there is here a feeling of the inadequacy of his imagination for presenting the ideas of a whole, wherein the imagination reaches its maximum and, in striving to surpass it, sinks back into itself, by which, however, a kind of emotional satisfaction is produced.

I have often been struck by the fact that the original decorative program for the Sistine Chapel had the vault painted as the starry heavens above—which would in anticipation of Kant have had what went on in the chapel itself as "the moral law within," inner and outer reference giving an architectural embodiment to the two sublimities. Julius II wanted something more "modern" when he commissioned Michelangelo to decorate the vault—and the Sistine ceiling itself, I believe, is a good example of at least part of how the sublime works in art. It is so if we consider that the sublime belongs, if we may borrow Wittgenstein's expression, to "the world as we find it," without any prior or special knowledge. Let me explain by returning to the starry heavens for just a moment.

Neither of the great wonder-eliciting things that Kant writes about in the *Second Critique*'s Conclusion is "shrouded in obscurity beyond my own horizon." Rather, Kant says, "I see them before me and connect them immediately with my own existence." I stress the fact of immediacy in connection with the starry heavens, because Kant wants to say that if we are to speak of it as sublime, "we must regard it, just as we see it, as a distant, all embracing vault." *Just as we see it* means that we would see it as sublime no matter in what relationship we stand to the history of astronomical science. That is part of the reason that it belongs to aesthetics. In respect to its sublimity, we are on the same footing as what Kant would refer to as savages. So we must see the starry heaven the way anyone anywhere would see it, whatever their cultural condition. Kant of course had written on the nebular hypothesis, and even seems to have entertained a thesis about life on other planets. Thus he writes that if we regard the starry heavens as sublime, "We must not place at the basis of our judgments concepts of worlds inhabited by rational beings and regard the bright points, with which we see the space above us as filled, as their suns moving in circles, purposively fixed with reference to them." But sublimity has nothing to do with scientific thought.

To round the point off, this is what he says about the ocean as well:

If we are to call the sight of the ocean sublime, we must not *think* of it as we ordinarily do, as implying all sorts of knowledge (that are not contained in immediate intuition). For example, we sometimes think of the ocean as a vast kingdom of aquatic creatures, or as the great source of those vapours that fill the air with clouds for the benefit of the land . . . To call the ocean sublime we must regard it as the poets do, merely by what strikes the eye.

Whatever, then, Kant may have meant by "the oftener and more steadily we reflect on *Der bestirnte Himmel*," he cannot have meant: "The more astronomical knowledge we acquire." The wonderment remains that of the poet and not of the scientist. The scientist, if anything, destroys the sublimity, the way Newton, to Keats's despair, unraveled the rainbow. "Science murders to dissect" was Wordsworth's putdown. The more we know, one might say, the less we feel. The mark of being in the presence of sublimity is, as with Stendhal, the swoon. If I remember rightly, there were female swooners at Gauguin's exhibition in 1888 in Paris. One gets a whiff of what the sublime must have meant in the eighteenth century when one reads Gauguin on the academic painters of his own time, who lived by the rules. "How safe they are on dry land, those academic painters, with their *trompe l'oeil* of nature. We alone are sailing free on our ghost-ship, with all our fantastical imperfections."

This is just how we feel when we first visit the Chapel to see the great work. Who understands what is happening up there? More important, one might say, who needs to understand it as far as the *sublimity* of the experience is concerned? The ceiling's restorer prided himself on getting as close as possible to "Michelangelo as artist and as man" by proceeding brushstroke by brushstroke across the vast expanse. But that is like the nightbird winging beneath the starry heavens. It gives it no sense of the circumambient sublimity. Neither, in fairness, does an image-by-image analysis of the ceiling, from the Creation to the Drunkenness of Noah. One does not need to know that program, tremendous as it is, to feel the sublimity of the painting. That feeling is importantly at odds with that kind of art historical knowledge which is on the same level as the theory of infinite worlds alluded to in the *Critique of Judgment*. So I take it then that this is what Kant has in mind with reference to "connecting [it] immediately with my own existence." And this in turn refers to his point about sublimity having to do with human nature and not merely with culture. The sublimity of things has nothing to do with special knowledge. Interestingly enough, this is analogous with something Kant says about the experience of beauty having nothing to do with bringing what we experience as beautiful under a concept. We find it beautiful before we know anything about it, as happened, in my own case, when I first saw one of Motherwell's *Spanish Elegies.*

In any case, Kant would not have known any example of sublimity in Koenigsberg, nor, given the Renaissance model with which he worked, could he have, though this requires a distinction. There is a sense in which he ought to have been able to imagine something that at least would be in candidacy for the sublime, and a sense in which he could not. He could not have imagined as art the kind of paintings Newman and Motherwell did. His position in the history of art limited his imagination severely. But he ought to have been able to think about artistic wonders, since the idea of wonders was certainly part of his culture. Let me discuss this briefly.

It is told of Michelangelo that he was seized with a remarkable vision in the course of several trying months spent in the marble quarries of Carrara, where he had gone in 1503 to select stones for the tomb of Pope Julius II. One day, his biographer Condivi tells us,

> He saw a crag that overlooked the sea, which made him wish to carve a colossus that would be a landmark for sailors from a long way off, incited thereto principally by the suitable shape of the rock from which it could have been conveniently carved, and by emulation of the ancients . . . and of a surety he would have done it if he had had time enough.

Michelangelo's inspiration was presumably the Colossus of Rhodes, one of the Seven Wonders of the ancient world—an immense sculpture, estimated to have stood more than 110 feet high, that according to legend straddled the mouth of a busy harbor. It was a wonder even when seen lying on the ground. "Few people can make their arms meet round the thumb," according to Pliny.

One tends to think of grace and balance, beauty and *disegno* as the paramount aesthetic virtues of Renaissance art, and indeed as marks of good taste in the fine arts well into modern times. But the idea of the colossus seems to belong to another aesthetic altogether, in which wonder and astonishment play the defining role. This other aesthetic was certainly embodied in the Seven Wonders themselves, and it inflected the great artistic figures of the sixteenth century, Leonardo and Michelangelo pre-eminently, who radiated, like some figure of ancient mythology, the aura of wizards. The colossus somehow emblematizes Michelangelo's visionary imagination, embodied in many of his signature works—the gigantic *David*, the immense decorative program enacted singlehandedly over the course of fifteen years across the Sistine ceiling, the tremendous vision of the Julian tomb itself, which, as perhaps the greatest sculptural commission of modern times, was to have incorporated more than forty large-scale figures. Leonardo's projected equestrian monument to Francesco Sforza was described by a contemporary as "the most gigantic, stupendous, and glorious work ever made by the hands of man." Leonardo worked on it over the course of fifteen years, and it stood twelve *braccia* high.

I have selected these colossi as paradigms only in part for the immensity of their scale, but mainly because, like the Seven Wonders—had the Julian Tomb been realized it would have been an eighth—they were meant to elicit feelings of wonder and awe, to which their scale contributes. Something is a colossus, for example, only because it underscores the limitations of those who experience it. It is perhaps in order to make visible the difference between themselves and their subjects that rulers have themselves represented as colossal, as in a seated portrait of Constantine the Great, thirty-odd feet tall, remnants of which still astonish when we see them in Rome.

But the idea of sublimity must entail something more than great size: "I attach little importance to physical size," the logician Frank Ramsey once wrote. "I take no credit for weighing nearly seventeen stone." So it is easy to understand why Kant—or Burke—felt that he had to add the sense of terror as the further condition. But Longinus's literary paradigms were the *Iliad* and a great poem of Sappho's, neither of which are terrifying. What they may do is remind us of our own limitations if we have artistic ambitions, and I think the feeling of wonder is connected with limitations in this way. "And still they gazed, and still their wonder grew, that one small head could carry all he knew," Edward Arlington Robinson wrote about a village prodigy. Kant brings these considerations into play in one of his formulations: "The sublime is that, the mere ability to think which shows a faculty of mind surpassing every standard of sense." I think the beauty of Helen of Troy was sublime in this sense. There is a very moving passage in Book III, where Helen leaves her weaving behind, and walks to the gates of Troy, to watch the warriors, who have paused for a moment before Menaleos, her husband, and Alexandros, her lover, fight over her. The elders of Troy were just then sitting in council—"And these, as they saw Helen along the tower approaching, murmuring softly to each other uttered their winged words: 'Surely there is no blame upon Trojans and strong-greaved Achaians if for long time they suffer hardship for a woman like this one. Terrible is the likeness of her face to immortal goddesses'."

We can imagine that someone was as beautiful as Helen, but we cannot imagine her beauty. That is one of the deep differences between words and pictures. In a related way, we can possess pictures of the Colossus of Rhodes, but no picture can show us its size. It can at best show us its scale, by showing a lot of tiny humans at its base, the way Piranesi did when he wanted to show the monuments of Rome as wondrous. But this brings us back to the limits of art as Kant understood it. Since sublimity is internally related to size, indeed to vastness, it cannot be pictured. That is one of the problems with Newman. The reproductions in a catalog of his characteristic paintings are incapable of showing their size, nor hence their sublimity. You have to be in front of and in fact rather close to them, in order to experience it. But again, terror is no part of the experience. My own sense, for what it is worth, is that the sort of vicarious terror Kant, and especially Burke had in mind, does play a role in human enjoyment—in ghost stories, horror movies, scary rides in amusement parks, in "cheap thrills," as it were. There may be cases where the experience of the sublime has terror as a component feeling, but it is not integral to the concept, in the way wonder itself is. After all, neither the starry heavens above nor the moral law within induce terror when we contemplate them. Parenthetically, fear continues to play its role in, of all things, the postmodern theory of the sublime developed by Lyotard, who speaks of the feeling in question as "an admixture of fear and exaltation." One cannot but wonder—I at least cannot—how often Lyotard can have had this feeling in front of works of art. If it is like ecstasy, it cannot be something we can be overcome by several times in a single visit to a gallery of art. My sense is that Lyotard was overcome by the literature on the subject rather than by actual aesthetic experiences he had had on the rue de Seine in Paris.

It is difficult not to wonder, on the other hand, whether Kant would have written the lyrical and romantic conclusion to the 1788 *Critique of Practical Reason*, in which he has recourse to an aesthetic vocabulary and a set of relationships for which there is really no place in the critical system as he had so far developed it, had it not been for the concept of the sublime. The starry heavens above and the moral law within can in effect be consigned to the domains respectively covered by Kant's first two critiques—the realm of nature, one might say, and the realm of freedom. And these in turn are referred to the two great powers of the human mind—to represent the world as a rational system, as covered by universal laws; and to prescribe the laws which universally define moral conduct. The philosophical portrait drawn by the first two critiques is of a being at once cognitive and legislative. But it is not an entirely adequate portrait if the concluding passage represents part of our reality as human. Wonder and awe are feelings that do not seem to belong to the somewhat austere, even severe person-age the first two critiques would lead us to believe ourselves to be. So we learn something fundamental about ourselves in contem-plating our portrait that the portrait itself does not show. We learn that we are not "pure intelligences" but creatures of feelings, and not simply of feelings, but of powerful feelings, such as astonish-ment and awe. Small wonder, as we say, that a third critique had to be written to connect us to the other two aspects of our being. And since the capacity for wonder is disclosed to us in this striking passage, the sublime—which is wonder's content—can hardly be an afterthought in the *Critique of Judgment*. And the world as an aesthetic presence is inseparable from what we are.

The Rediscovery of Man

Let us now return to Newman. There is a remarkable passage in Kant that does bear on Abstract Expressionist aesthetics:

Perhaps the most sublime passage in Jewish Law is the commandment "Thou shalt not make unto thee any graven image, or any likeness of anything that is in heaven or on earth, or under the earth," etc. This commandment alone can explain the enthusiasm that the Jewish people in its civilized era felt for its religion when it compared itself with other peoples, or can explain the pride that Islam inspires.

This in effect prohibited Jews or Muslims from being artists since, though of course, like all the Commandments, it was and is violated in both religions. But until Modernism, there was no way of being a painter without making pictures. One could at best engage in decoration, which is the only alternative to picturing that Kant acknowledges. Paintings that are not pictures would have been a contradiction in terms. This in effect ruled out the possibility of making paintings that were *sublime*. But modernism opened up the possibility of aniconic painting, and this somehow brought with it the possibility of sublimity as an attainable aesthetic. As Newman said, "The Sublime is now."

Newman regarded his breakthrough work, *Onement I*, as a painting and not a picture. The catalog text to a major exhibition of Newman's work says that *Onement I* "represents nothing but itself"—that it is about itself as a painting. I can't believe that. I can't believe that what Newman regarded in terms momentous enough to merit the title, was simply a painting about painting. It is about something that can be said but cannot be shown, at least not pictorially. In general, the suffix "-ment" is attached to a verb—like "atone" or "endow" or "command "—where it designates a state—the state of atoning, for example—or a product. So what does "Onement" mean? My own sense is that it means the condition of being one, as in the incantation "God is one." It refers, one might say, to the oneness of God. And this might help us better understand the difference between a picture and a painting. Consider again the Sistine Ceiling, where Michelangelo produces a number of pictures of God. Great as these are, they are constrained by the limitation that pictures can only show what is visible, and decisions have to be made regarding what God looks like. How would one *picture* the fact that God is one? Since *Onement I* is not a picture, it does not inherit the limitations inherent in picturing. Abstract painting is not without content. Rather, it enables the presentation of content without pictorial limits. That is why, from the beginning, abstraction was believed by its inventors to be invested with a spiritual reality. It was as though Newman had hit upon a way of being a painter without violating the Second Commandment, which only prohibits images. Lyotard, incidentally, attempts to build the unpresentability of its content into his analysis of the sublime—but I think he had to mean that the sublime was *unpicturable*. Boldly post-modern as Lyotard took his aesthetic to be, it was curiously limited to painting.

Newman himself gave to one of his paintings the title *Vir Heroicus Sublimis,* which meant, as he explained to David Sylvester, "that man can be or is sublime in his relation to his sense of being aware." And it was his view, so far as I understand it, that he used scale to awaken this sense of self-awareness in relationship to his paintings: they imply, one might say, the scale of the viewer:

> One thing that I am involved in about painting is that the painting should give a man a sense of place: that he knows he's there, so he's aware of himself. In that sense he related to me when I made the painting because in that sense I was there. . . . Standing in front of my paintings you had a sense of your own scale. The onlooker in front of my painting knows that he's there. To me, the sense of place not only has a mystery but has that sense of metaphysical fact.

It is this "mystery," this "metaphysical fact," that scale and wonder evoke when we speak of the sublime. Scholars speak of the Renaissance discovery of man. We can, I think, accordingly speak of the rediscovery of man in Abstract Expressionism. But it is important that we recognize that we whose existence is implied by such paintings are not diminished, as we are by the starry heavens above. The scale of the painting is intended to induce a certain self-awareness, and this is what brings the status of sublimity with it. It implies the body of the viewer, without making us small because the painting is large. What Newman aspired to instill through such paintings as *Vir Heroicus Sublimis* is wonder and awe at ourselves as here. I cannot help but think that the concept Newman required was that of Heidegger's central notion, namely that of *Dasein*—of being-there and aware of being there.

But there is another way of thinking about this that I find magnificently expressed in an answer given by the great Russian novelist, Vladimir Nabokov, when an interviewer asked him if he was surprised by anything in life. Nabokov responded:

FIGURE 22   Barnett Newman, *Vir Heroicus Sublimis*, 1950–1951
A sense of your own scale

The marvel of consciousness—that sudden window swinging open on a sunlit landscape amid the night of non-being.

I find this passage sublime, and it is a matter of chagrin to me that until fairly recent times, no philosopher has spoken of consciousness with this kind of wonder and awe. Certainly Kant did not. He finds the starry heavens and the moral law within as matters of wonder and awe without noticing that they pale in comparison with the fact that he is aware of them, that the universe, inner and outer, is open to something that is in itself unpicturable and perhaps even unintelligible, given the internal limits of human understanding. Small wonder philosophers took it for it granted—it never became an object that had to be reckoned with in drawing up the inventory of wonders.

Meanwhile, I note that Nabokov cannot forebear speaking of something beautiful as the object of consciousness—a landscape, sunny, and seen through a window frame. If consciousness disclosed only unrelieved disgustingness, we would wonder why we had such an endowment. But this brings us back to the two worlds of G.E. Moore that we considered early in our study. The world of sheer disgustingness would not be one we would wish to be conscious of for very long, nor for the matter live a life that would lose its point without sunlight. If I point to a painting of a sunlit landscape and pronounce it sublime, someone might correct me and say I am confusing the beautiful and the sublime. I would cite

Nabokov and reply that the beautiful *is* the sublime "amid the night of non-being." Kant brings these considerations into play in the formulation we noted above: "The sublime is that, the mere ability to think which shows a faculty of mind surpassing every standard of sense." I might even, if feeling impish, add: It is sublime because it is in the mind of the beholder. Beauty is an option for art and not a necessary condition. But it is not an option for life. It is a necessary condition for life as we would want to live it. That is why beauty, unlike the other aesthetic qualities, the sublime included, is a value.

Index

Abject Art, 56, 57

Absolute Spirit, 136

Abstract Expressionism, 2–3, 20, 84, 85, 156; and aesthetics, 1,7

Achilles, 141

Adams, Abigail, 148, 149, 150

Adeimanthus, 75

Adorno, Theodor, 19

Aeschylus, xviii

aesthetics, 1–2; and beauty, 7–8, 59–60, 91; and black culture, 76–77; and ethics, 77; and feminism, 77; of photography, 82

aesthetic tourism, 81

Alberti, Leone Battista, 64

Alcibiades, 91

Alexandros, 155

Apollo, 142

Arensberg, Walter, 9, 94

Aristotle, 68; *Poetics*, 92

Arneson, Richard, 135

Arnold, Matthew, 28

Arp, Hans, 48

art: aboutness of, 65–66; and aesthetics, xxiii, 2, 7, 10, 58–59; as distinct, 94; as anthropology, 130; and beauty, xviii–xix, xxiii, 25–26, 29–30, 83, 95, 100, 110, 121, 122, 123–24; —as distinct, xix, 8, 14, 33–37, 45, 46, 58–59, 60, 88, 101, 107, 108, 119, 120, 145, 160; —inappropriate,

112–13; —internal, 112–13; to change society, 105–08, 119; concept of, xviii–xix, xx, xxi; —in ancient Greece, xvii–xviii; defining, xxiii, 6, 22, 25; defining itself, 20; and disgust, 50–52, 53, 59, 60; as embodied meanings, 139–142; end of, xxii–xxiii, 19, 136–37; history of, xxii; identity of, xxiii; and indiscernible pairs, 23–24; inflection in, 121, 123; as inner life, of culture, 128–29; institutional theory of, 24; and inwardness, 75–76; as knowledge, types of, 126–29; meaning in, 13; mid-sixties, xx; modern, 19–20, 120, 145, 146; —and Cold War, 26; and the museum, 62–63; 1960s, xx, 2–3, 14, 19, 20; philosophical definition of, xx; philosophical history of, xxii; and philosophy, connection between, 118, 137; philosophy of, xxii; pluralism of, xxiv; political, 103–04, 107–08, 119; and politics, 123; pragmatic properties, xix, xxiii; question of appropriateness, 118; radical openness in, 17–18; as rational and sensuous, 93; and real things, distinguishing, 64–65; semantic property of, xxiii; self-critique in, 19; and socio-